OSF DCE

J. Ranade Workstation Series

OSF DCE

Guide to Developing Distributed Applications

Harold W. Lockhart, Jr.

McGraw-Hill, Inc.

New York   San Francisco   Washington, D.C.   Auckland   Bogotá
Caracas   Lisbon   London   Madrid   Mexico City   Milan
Montreal   New Delhi   San Juan   Singapore
Sydney   Tokyo   Toronto

Library of Congress Cataloging-in-Publication Data

Lockhart, Harold W.
    OSF DCE : guide to developing distributed applications / Harold W.
Lockhart, Jr.
        p.   cm. — (J. Ranade workstation series)
    Includes index.
    ISBN 0-07-911481-4
    1. Electronic data processing—Distributed processing.
2. Application software.   I. Title.   II. Series.
QA76.9.D5L62   1994
005.7′12—dc20   93-44557
                                                                CIP

        4 5 6 7 8 9 0   DOC/DOC   9 0 9 8 7 6

P/N 0-07-038273-5
PART OF
ISBN 0-07-911481-4

*The sponsoring editor for this book was Jerry Papke and the production
supervisor was Donald F. Schmidt. This book was set in Century Schoolbook by
North Market Street Graphics.*

Printed and bound by R. R. Donnelley & Sons Company.

To Leslie
"You were always on my mind"

Contents

Part 3   Distributed System Design Solutions   225

Preface

The early 1990s mark a turning point in the computer industry. Several independently developing trends have suddenly intersected to produce a startling discontinuity with the immediate past. Already the effects in the marketplace have been dramatic. Household names in the computer business have stumbled and are scrambling to recover, or in some cases, filing for bankruptcy. Even some that rose to prominence in the 1980s riding one of the great waves of that decade are casting about frantically to understand the implications of the sudden shift in the wind.

The first great change was the PC revolution, which IBM joined belatedly and to which it added the imprimatur of respectability and sufficient marketing weight to achieve critical mass, only to discover, to their puzzlement, that they could no longer control their creation as they had always controlled markets in the past. Even today, very few people, even in the industry, really understand the PC phenomenon. What the PC revolution showed us was the enormous power of a mass market. Power to create unprecedented innovation, variety, and price/performance.

What made this market possible, initially, was lowering the absolute unit cost of a computer to the point where millions of new users could afford or authorize its purchase. Once this occurred, the existence of standardized, de facto hardware and software interfaces reduced the barriers of entry for both software and hardware suppliers to the point where a huge, self-sustaining market destroyed the advantage of the traditional vertically integrated systems makers. The lesson was that standardized interfaces that are widely accepted, whether de jure or de facto, can unleash unprecedented opportunities for buyer and supplier alike.

The second wave of change in the 1980s came with the development of RISC and the closely related open systems movement. What RISC taught us, contrary to what many (including me) believed in the 1970s, was that tying software architectures closely to machine hardware architectures not only could lead to an unhealthy dependence on a single vendor, but, much more significantly, could be an insurmountable barrier to taking advantage of hardware designs with startlingly new price/performance points. The lesson was that software systems that are not built around standardized, high-level interfaces run the very real risk of suddenly being doomed by their dependence on an obsolete hardware platform.

The third wave was the networking movement, which actually began much earlier, but which entered a new phase with the development of LAN technology and a recognition of its benefits in interconnecting PCs and workstations. Here the lesson was the same, but delivered in negative form. The lack of standards for interoperability greatly retarded the growth of distributed applications.

The greater complexity of distributed systems precluded rapid acceptance of de facto standards to address a large pool of perceived requirements, as had been the case in the PC market. Some proprietary standards which solved limited problems became popular, as did the networking technology derived from the government-funded ARPANET (now the Internet). Still, the lack of universally accepted high-level network standards resulted in very limited development of distributed software applications by either end users or software vendors.

The conjunction of these trends, like some rare alignment of the planets, has brought us to the present paradoxical moment in history. The paradox, widely recognized, is that everyone in this industry is dependent on their competitors. To be a pioneer in areas of software infrastructure risks double failure. If no one follows your lead, your investment is wasted and you have lost ground to the competition. On the other hand, if everyone follows you, your engineering effort benefits your competitors without providing any sustainable advantage.

The founders and later members of the Open Software Foundation (OSF) understood this very well. OSF was and is chartered to bring to market, as rapidly as possible, vital core technologies which provide capabilities not previously available but which are sufficiently basic to create enormous new opportunities for innovation by opening previously untapped markets.

The OSF Distributed Computing Environment (DCE) is just such an offering. It provides a well-integrated combination of components that provide high-level interfaces for developing distributed applications. Working individually, OSF members would have spent years competing with each other with functionally equivalent but incompatible products. Instead, the OSF Request for Technology (RFT) process (which some observers consider OSF's most significant contribution) resulted in a melding of "best of breed" offerings which, although it represents a significant advancement of the state of the art, will have the overall effect of greatly increasing, rather than reducing, the competitive opportunities in the distributed systems market.

This book grew out of my experiences designing and implementing distributed systems for many purposes over many years. I was frankly impressed by the initial descriptions that I read of DCE, for I realized that it would do more to solve some of the thorniest difficulties presented by distributed applications than anything available then or anything else available now. As I considered the matter further, I realized that DCE was only the beginning of the story. Many obstacles still exist; and further, the possibilities created by DCE would attract a whole new flood of developers who had little experience with the problems posed by distributed systems.

Therefore, this book is an attempt to share the lessons that I have been taught by the many people I have worked with and have learned by bitter experience. I have tried to show not just what DCE is and how it works, but how it can best be used and what problems it cannot solve. If this book encourages the development of better-designed and more-reliable distributed systems, I will have accomplished what I set out to do.

Harold W. Lockhart, Jr.

Acknowledgments

It would not have been possible to write this book without the help of many other people. First of all I am grateful to my wife Leslie, whose life was most directly affected by the project, and to my daughters Lily and Julie who, while it was going on, made do with considerably less of my time. I thank my editor, Sheila Osmundsen, who untangled my most inscrutable prose and worked tirelessly to bring clarity to the presentation and consistency to the book's use of terminology. Fred Oldfield coauthored the example programs, provided many helpful suggestions for the manuscript, and created the IDL and ACF syntax summaries that appear as appendices. Andy Gaus not only carefully reviewed all of the content, but also brought his considerable editorial and proofreading skills to bear.

I am very grateful to Gradient Technologies, Inc., especially their president, Lynn Halio, for providing me with access to their product, SysV-DCE. Without this support, the book would never have been written. I also benefited from invaluable help of Chung Yen and Bill Blackwell at Gradient. I am also extremely grateful to my employer, Onsett International Corporation, especially our founder, Nina Tsao, for the encouragement and material support given to me.

I especially thank Sidnie Feit, not only for a number of helpful comments about the manuscript, but especially for her kind words of encouragement, which had a huge impact at a crucial point in the project. Bill Leddy and Ward Rosenberry also provided helpful comments, as did my colleague, Paul Cashman, with whom I actually developed some of the ideas in the book, particularly those in Chapter 23.

I received many kinds of help and encouragement from people at the Open Software Foundation—Greg Lebovitz, who cleared the obstacles to my using the Gradient product; Ram Kumar, who put me in touch with McGraw-Hill; Doug Hartman, who cut through the red tape to get me the ACL manager source code; Howard Melman, who provided technical answers; Bob Hathaway, David Chinn, and Weidong Wang, who all played a vital role in getting the last bug out of the program examples.

Many others provided ideas, encouragement or help in other forms, including: from IBM—Clay Boyd, Brad Freese, David Spencer, and Sidney Gottesman;

from Citicorp—Larry Poleshuck, Richard Goldstein, Chii-Ren Tsaii, Marianna Chou, Miky Lo, Eric Maiwald, and John Dale; and also Sumner Blount, Scott Dietzen, Mark Heroux, John Rose, Chris Horricks, Mike Burati, and Ted Baker.

I am especially grateful to Jay Ranade and Gerald Papke of McGraw-Hill for their faith and patience. I thank my brother, Sam Lockhart, who made various legal arrangements. And last but not least, thanks to Bob Sharby, who drew the clever sketches that appear in Chapter 16.

Trademarks

Apple, AppleTalk, and Macintosh are registered trademarks of Apple Computer, Inc.

Banyan and VINES are registered trademarks of Banyan Systems Incorporated.

DEC, DECnet, Digital, and VMS are registered trademarks of Digital Equipment Corporation.

Gradient is a trademark of Gradient Technologies, Inc.

HP and Network Computing System are registered trademarks and Apollo and Hewlett-Packard are trademarks of Hewlett-Packard Company.

IBM is a registered trademark of International Business Machines Corporation.

Intel is a registered trademark of Intel Corporation.

ISO is a registered trademark of the International Organization for Standardization.

Microsoft, MS-DOS, and Visual Basic are registered trademarks of Microsoft Corporation.

MIT is a registered trademark and Kerberos is a trademark of the Massachusetts Institute of Technology.

NetWare and Novell are registered trademarks of Novell, Inc.

Sun and Sun Microsystems are registered tradmarks and NFS, Network File System, and ONC are trademarks of Sun Microsystems, Inc.

OSF is a registered trademark and Open Software Foundation and DCE are trademarks of the Open Software Foundation, Inc.

PostScript is a registered trademark of Adobe Systems Incorporated.

UNIX and UNIX System Laboratories are registered trademarks of UNIX System Laboratories, Inc.

Xerox is a registered trademark of Xerox Corporation.

X Window System and its derivations are trademarks of the Massachusetts Institute of Technology.

X/Open is a trademark of the X/Open Company Limited.

Introduction

Purpose

The purpose of this book is to provide practical, usable advice about how to build distributed software applications with the Open Software Foundation's Distributed Computing Environment (DCE). The book suggests how to think about the design of distributed systems, with particular emphasis on the things that make distributed applications different from monolithic ones.

This book is intended to enable the building of "industrial strength" distributed systems—systems that can be depended upon to perform necessary tasks day in and day out. It excludes systems that work erratically, can easily be subverted by unauthorized individuals, or require continual human intervention.

Audience

The intended audience for this book is people who have previously implemented software applications on a single system. This is not a first book on programming. On the other hand, the reader is not assumed to be familiar with the use of software in any kind of network environment, nor is any particular knowledge of UNIX required.

The primary audience of the book is people who actually intend to implement a distributed application using DCE. The book will also be useful, however, to anyone, such as a manager or executive, who wishes to acquire an understanding of the problems and techniques associated with distributed systems.

The book also will be of value to people who have previously implemented distributed applications by other means and wish to become familiar with the use of DCE. Much of the book is relevant to anyone who is implementing a distributed application, regardless of the tools being used.

The reader is assumed to have a reading knowledge of the C language, since that is the language generally required to implement DCE applications. Still, a great deal of the book can be understood without knowing C.

Readers who are actually implementing applications using DCE are assumed to have access to the DCE reference manual. This might be in the form of MAN pages or other online reference, or in the printed form of the *DCE Application Reference Manual*.

Scope

Many different software implementation methodologies are currently in use. The use of DCE is consistent with any of them. The scope of DCE is limited to just a few of the phases of a software life cycle, however. Similarly, this book, although broader in scope than DCE, addresses only a few of the phases.

The following is a representative list of phases in the software life cycle.

- Requirements
- Feasibility
- Functional specification
- System architecture
- Detailed design
- Coding
- Testing
- Integration
- Installation
- Maintenance

This book mostly addresses the system architecture, detailed design, and coding phases. There is also some discussion of the feasibility and testing phases.

Overview

The book consists of four parts. The first part is introductory in nature. Important concepts relating to distributed systems are introduced and described briefly. Next, the major benefits and advantages provided by distributed systems are characterized. Finally, a number of problems associated with developing distributed systems that are not present in nondistributed systems are described.

Part 2 of the book describes the Distributed Computing Environment itself. An overview of DCE is given and certain DCE components that are not directly related to application development are described briefly. Because DCE itself has a specialized terminology, a section is devoted to introducing the most important concepts used by the DCE services.

Then the five components of major interest to software developers—RPC, Threads, the Security Service, Directory Service, and Distributed Time Service—are discussed in detail. The emphasis is on information not readily available in the DCE manuals, such as appropriate uses for the various capabilities of DCE, what combinations of features are most useful, and why certain things work the way they do.

Part 3 of the book is devoted to the practical aspects of building distributed applications. Drawing on the list of problems associated with distributed systems development from Part 1, this part discusses those problems that DCE helps to solve and how it does so. Next, problems that DCE does not address are discussed and methods for dealing with them are described.

Finally, a number of issues unique to distributed applications, rarely appearing in nondistributed systems, are presented. A number of suggestions of ways to best deal with these issues during the design, development, and testing of distributed applications are presented.

Part 4 of the book presents a number of specific models for the structure of client/server applications. Four processing flow models are presented, followed by four server state models. Then, for each of the processing flow models, a working C language example program using DCE is presented.

The example programs are provided with the book on floppy disk and can be used as the starting point for writing real applications. Select the model most appropriate for the application and add additional code as required. These models will satisfy the needs of a large percentage of distributed applications.

Distributed Computing

Part 1 of this book introduces the reader to the field of distributed systems. The first chapter explains the most important concepts in the field of distributed systems, which are referenced throughout the rest of the book. The field of distributed systems is relatively new and some of the terminology is used differently by different authorities. This book uses the longest-established and clearest terms whenever there is a choice. The terminology introduced in this chapter is used consistently throughout the rest of the book.

The second chapter discusses the many advantages and benefits that may be derived from the use of distributed systems. It seems important to establish these at the outset, for otherwise why should we bother to go to all of the trouble to implement them?

Chapter 3 describes 12 general problems that are present in distributed systems, but absent or less important in nondistributed systems. Each problem represents a significant obstacle to the developer of a distributed system. These 12 problems form the cornerstone of this book. After DCE has been discussed in Part 2, we will return to these 12 problems to examine which ones have been addressed by DCE and which have not.

Part 1 has several purposes. First, it is necessary to ensure that every reader has at least a minimum understanding of the concepts and terminology used throughout the rest of the book. Second, because DCE is a complex software system, it is easy to become bewildered by its many features and capabilities. The best way to understand how its features work is to appreciate the problems that it is trying to solve and the benefits of its use.

Third, since this book takes the stance that the reader's objective is to develop distributed systems and that DCE is a means toward that end, it is not sufficient merely to cover the features of DCE. It is necessary to give the reader a sense of the field as a whole, to keep in mind as he or she grapples with the difficulties and experiences the benefits of distributed systems, whether DCE is used or not.

Distributed Processing Concepts

Distributed computing carries with it a number of terms and concepts that may be unfamiliar to some readers. Many of the terms have not yet become standardized and are used to mean different things by different people. Vendors, for example, frequently extend the meaning of a term to include their product in a competitive market, or invent a new term to exclude a competitor product.

This chapter explains some of the basic concepts of distributed processing and introduces a set of terms that will be used throughout the book. Those familiar with distributed processing may wish to skip over some or all of the chapter. Other terms that relate to a specific subject will be introduced later as they apply.

1.1 Distributed System, Distributed Processing, Distributed Application

A *distributed system* is a combination of hardware, software, and network components in which the software components execute on two or more processors and communicate via a network. Figure 1.1 represents the hardware configuration of a minimal distributed system consisting of just two computers connected by a network.

This definition is very broad and could be construed as including software execution on, for example, a multiprocessor, in which a number of processors share a common bus. While it is true that a multiprocessor shares many of the same problems as, say, a group of workstations on a LAN, it is desirable to further restrict the definition. For the purpose of this book, it is assumed that the network in a distributed system has a throughput capacity of at least an order

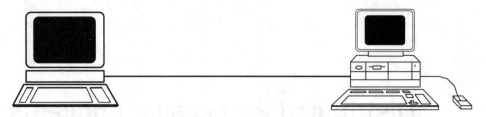

Figure 1.1 A minimal distributed system.

of magnitude less than that of the bus that connects any of the CPUs in the distributed system to its main memory.

Furthermore, the networks referred to in this book will connect several rooms at a minimum. More typically, the network will run throughout a building or campus and most likely encompass locations that are geographically separate. Networks that cross time zones and national boundaries are not uncommon, and many features of DCE are designed with this in mind.

The use of such a distributed system is called *distributed processing* or, as in DCE, *distributed computing*. Since, from the application designer's point of view, the details of the hardware often are irrelevant to the design of a distributed system, we also may refer to the distributed system as a *distributed software application,* or simply a *distributed application*.

The term *monolithic system* is used in this book as a less awkward synonym for nondistributed system.

1.2   Computers and Nodes

Distributed systems consist of software executing on computers connected by a network. In this context, *computer* means any kind of system in which the developer can modify the software. This includes mainframes, minicomputers, workstations, servers, supercomputers, PCs, etc. It does not include devices such as X-windows terminals or PostScript printers, because, although they contain computers, their software cannot be modified. (Of course a manufacturer of PostScript printers might consider them to be part of a distributed system.)

A computer in a network is often referred to as a *node*. This term is borrowed from the mathematical discipline of graph theory, nodes being the intersection points of the lines, or arcs, in graphs. Many computer network problems, such as how to route messages across a network, have been analyzed using graph theory. For some reason, graph theory's term "arc" was not similarly adopted into network terminology. Instead, the network connections between computers are most often called *links*.

In TCP/IP networks, the term *host* is used instead of node. This book avoids this use of the term host because it has quite different connotations in other computer contexts—as in "host computer," frequently denoting a computer different from other computers in some way; for example, bigger and more powerful or sitting at the hub of the network or containing the master database.

1.3 Networks

The term *network* encompasses a wide range of technologies. Over the years, many different methods have been invented for transmitting data over short and long distances. Many books have been written on the subject, some of which are listed in the Recommended Reading section at the back of the book. The following short introduction is intended to emphasize those aspects of networks most relevant to distributed applications.

1.3.1 Types of networks

First of all, the links connecting network nodes generally fall into one of two categories: local and wide area. As a result, networks are usually classified as *local-area networks* (LANs) and *wide-area networks* (WANs). Increasingly, WANs consist of two or more LANs connected by wide-area links. Such a network is sometimes called an *internet,* and the local networks may be called *subnetworks.*

LANs and WANs differ in a number of characteristics. The most obvious is geographic scope. A LAN is usually restricted to a single building or a few adjacent buildings within one organization's facilities. The maximum distance between any two nodes on a LAN is typically less than a mile. (This distance is known as the *network diameter.*) In contrast, a WAN usually crosses public rights-of-way and is unlimited in scope.

Compared to WANs, LANs are also characterized by high data capacity* and low error rates. LANs generally operate at 1 million bits per second or more, whereas the most commonly used types of wide-area links operate at 64,000 bits per second or lower. Wide-area links experience errors on the order of one bit in error out of 100,000 (10^5) bits transmitted. For LANs the error rate is in the range of one in 1 million (10^9) bits. These are the raw error rates of the transmission medium under normal operating conditions. A variety of mechanisms is used to see to it that distributed applications see only error-free data.

LANs are usually owned by the organization that uses them; wide-area links are most often provided by someone else, such as a telephone company. Wide-area links generally use equipment originally designed to transmit voice,

---

* Capacity should be distinguished from speed. *Capacity* is the amount of data that can be transferred per unit of time, for example 64,000 bits per second. *Speed* is the rate at which data is moved from one point to another, for example 100,000 miles per second. Think of a truck versus a racing car. Because speed is important only in certain special situations, such as when satellite links are used, everyone (including this author) tends to use speed as a synonym for capacity.

adapted to carry data. LANs, on the other hand, have been designed from the start for data.

By far the two most widely used LAN types are Ethernet and Token Ring, also referred to by the IEEE standards for these protocols, 802.3 and 802.5, respectively. (There are some small differences between the original Ethernet—often called DIX for originators Digital Equipment Corporation, Intel Corporation, and Xerox Corporation—and the IEEE 802.3 standard, but generally they can be ignored.)

A distinction between LANs and WANs of particular importance to distributed applications is that LANs are multiaccess. This means that any node on a LAN can send a message directly to any other node without involving a third node. This is illustrated in Fig. 1.2. In contrast, wide-area links usually connect just two nodes. In a WAN, data must be passed from node to node until it reaches its destination.

Another consequence of this difference is that LANs provide the ability to send multicast messages. A *multicast message* is one that is sent to more than one destination. Since all the computers on a LAN can receive all the traffic, no special effort is required to send a multicast message. The sender simply uses an address in the message that is designated as a *multicast address,* also known as a *group address.* Multicasting is illustrated in Fig. 1.3. Although a WAN, in theory, could provide multicast by making copies of the message, there are practical difficulties in doing this, so it is rarely done.

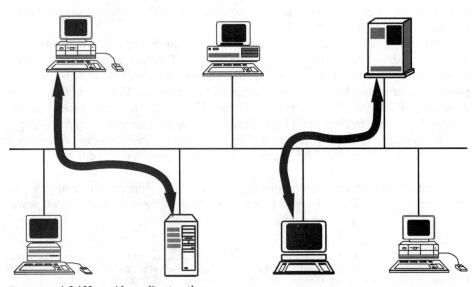

Figure 1.2 A LAN provides a direct path.

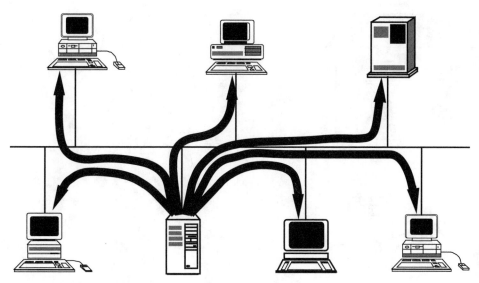

Figure 1.3 Multicasting on a LAN.

A *broadcast message* is a special case of multicast, addressed to every node on the LAN. People often loosely use the term broadcast when they mean multicast. A *unicast* message* is simply the usual type sent to a single node.

A third type of network is the *metropolitan area network* (MAN). Currently, there are very few MANs in existence, but they are expected to become very common within the decade. As the name suggests, MANs cover a geographic area intermediate between the area covered by LANs and WANs. MANs are generally provided by a telephone company or other common carrier and cover an area up to 50 to 100 miles. MANs generally interconnect LANs and provide transmission capacities higher than that of LANs, currently in the range of 50 to 150 million bits per second.

Two terms often used (and confused) to describe networks are *network topology* and *network geography*. Network topology refers to the configuration of links and nodes within a network. By extension, it is often used to refer to the type of physical links involved, for example, Ethernet or point-to-point leased line. A network's geography is the location of the network components on earth. As an example, topology ignores the difference between a LAN running around a single room and one stretching across a factory complex. Figure 1.4 shows two networks with the same topology, but different geography.

---

* The term *unicast* is an example of a retronym. A retronym is a new name for something old, invented to distinguish it from something new. Probably the best known retronym is "analog clock."

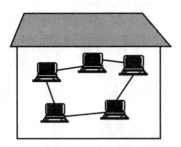

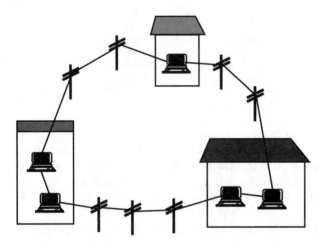

Figure 1.4 Two networks with the same topology but different geography.

Typically, the geography of a network is given as a requirement and the network topology is designed based on the needs for connectivity, engineering constraints, and cost tradeoffs. Geography also dictates various practical aspects of the distributed system. The alarm display on a network operator's screen may be different for equipment located in the same room and for equipment located elsewhere. Two users more easily share a printer if they are in adjacent offices than if they are on different floors.

These considerations, however, are the exceptions. One of the virtues of modern network protocols is that when designing a distributed application we can usually ignore the network geography. In contrast, network topology does not generally affect functionality, but may affect performance. Since this is mostly caused by throughput limits on WAN links, we may eventually reach a day when this can be ignored as well. When the geographical and topological characteristics of the network are unimportant, the network will be pictured as a cloud, as in Fig. 1.5.

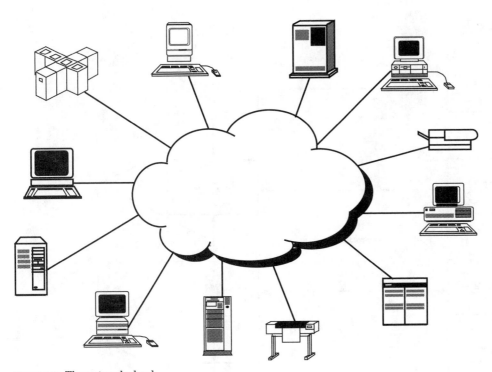

Figure 1.5 The network cloud.

1.3.2 Communications protocols

Computer networks do not consist of hardware alone. Communications software sends and receives messages in agreed-upon formats called *communications protocols*. Strictly speaking, a communications protocol consists of the message formats and the rules for when they should be sent. However, the term *protocol* is commonly used to refer to the software that implements a certain protocol. The context usually makes it clear which meaning is intended.

Communications protocols provide many useful services to applications communicating across a network. Some examples are detecting and correcting errors, ensuring that messages reach the correct destination, allowing multiple applications to share the same network, detecting and taking various actions when network components fail, buffering data until a program is ready to receive it, and translating data from one format to another. Modern communications protocols are designed in layers, collectively called a *protocol stack*. This is an application of the principles of structured programming and is consistent with the object-oriented idea of encapsulation. Each protocol layer deals with certain types of issues and is insulated from the actions of other layers. Figure 1.6 illustrates the operation of layered protocols. Conceptually, data

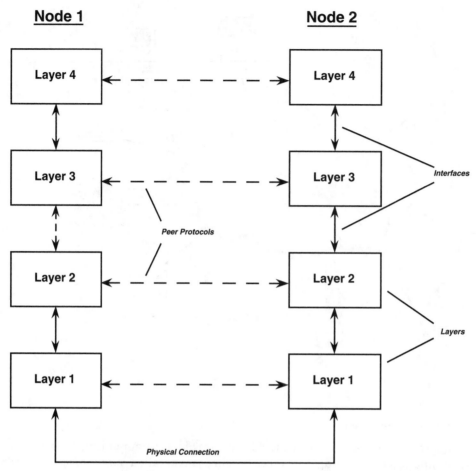

Figure 1.6 Protocol layering.

from an application flows down the layers in one node, across the physical network, and up the layers at another node. The boundaries between adjacent protocol layers are called *interfaces*.

The protocols actually consist of the interactions between corresponding layers within different nodes. As the data flows downward in a node that is transmitting a message, each layer adds, to the message, information that the layer needs to do its job. For example, different layers add checksums to detect errors, addresses to identify the source or destination of the message, and sequence numbers to keep the data in order. As the data flows upward at the receiving node, each corresponding layer inspects and removes the information that it is interested in. Layers can also generate their own messages to convey information about the state of the protocol to their counterparts at other nodes.

Sophisticated capabilities are built up by adding layer after layer on top of the basic ability to transmit and receive bits. Each layer views the data provided by the layer above it as a sealed package that must be passed along without being altered. Each layer views the layer below it as providing a number of well-defined but simpler services that it uses to do its job. Each layer has a limited set of responsibilities and doesn't have to worry about what the other layers are up to. Each layer can maintain its own internal tables which are not visible to any other layer.

The best-known model of layered protocols is the Open Systems Interconnection (OSI) model of the International Organization for Standardization (ISO). The OSI model has seven layers, shown in Fig. 1.7. Sets of related protocols are called *families* or *suites*. Other popular protocol suites, such as DECnet, SNA, SPX/IPX, TCP/IP, and XNS, use the layering principle as well, although their layers do not correspond exactly in number or purpose to those of the OSI model.

The concept of layers is very important to designing distributed applications, as will be explained in Chap. 16, but when developing distributed applications we can generally ignore the communications functions that take place below the session layer. All of the protocol suites mentioned provide comparable session-layer services. These are the ability to open connections, close connections, read data, and write data.

One distinction that is important to the application designer is between a datagram service and a virtual circuit service. A *datagram service* moves data across the network on a "best effort" basis. It ensures that no erroneous data will be delivered, but offers no other guarantees. Data may be lost or arrive out of order; the sender cannot find out (from the service) whether the data got there or not. Strictly speaking, there is no session: messages are simply sent and received with no relationship to any other message. For this reason, a datagram service is called *connectionless*.

A *virtual circuit service,* on the other hand, guarantees that all the data sent will be received correctly and in order. This is known as *delivery assurance*. Of course the network might experience a failure with the result that there is no longer any path between the sender and the receiver, but if this happens the sender will be able to find out that the data was not delivered. A virtual circuit service is called *connection-oriented*.

Both virtual circuit and datagram services have their uses. Datagrams require the protocols to do less work and therefore are typically faster. Datagram services often provide a multicast capability. But for most applications we do want the delivery assurance that a virtual circuit provides.

There are a few other cases in which the designer developing distributed applications may need to be aware of the characteristics of networks. First, some applications will make a distinction between nodes that are on the same LAN and nodes that are not. The DCE Distributed Time Service is an example of this. A second case is in the use of certain features—for example, the broadcast feature of the DCE RPC—which are limited because of their implementa-

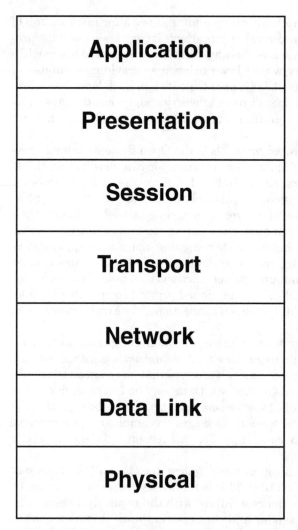

Figure 1.7   The OSI model.

tion to operate only across a single LAN. A third case arises when the designer must consider the delays introduced by WAN links, which may mean that a distributed application is simply not feasible.

1.4   Categories of Distributed Systems

Distributed systems can be categorized by various models. The best-known models are briefly described here. Later in the book we will take a more detailed look at certain of these models. Other models are possible, some of which no doubt will be recognized as important categories and given names in the future.*

1.4.1   The client/server model

The term *client/server* is commonly used in two different ways. The term *client/server computing* is used to describe the use of networks containing two types of processors. The first type is clients, usually PCs or workstations, which are used directly by a single human being. The other type is servers, which are only accessible over the network from clients and are typically shared by a number of clients (and hence a number of users). Used in this sense, client/server computing is commonly contrasted with mainframe-based computing or minicomputer-based computing or stand-alone PC-based computing. Some people further restrict the term client/server computing to refer specifically to the use of database servers and their clients.

A different use of the term client/server refers to the *client/server model*. This is the sense in which the term is used in this book. The client/server model is a processing flow model that is a subcategory of distributed system. In the client/server model each interaction is characterized by an asymmetrical relationship between two software processes. One, the client, makes requests for service and the other, the server, provides the service on request.

The processing flow is characteristically *synchronous* (blocking) in nature. That is to say, once the client makes a request, it does nothing further until the service has been performed. The communications discipline is therefore half-duplex: from client to server, then from server to client. Note that this definition allows clients and servers to change their roles from one interaction to the next.

This simple processing flow is the great advantage of the client/server model of a distributed system. Unlike some other processing flow models, in which the application must be prepared for messages to arrive at almost any point, the client, in particular, knows that the only time it will receive data is immediately after making a request. This corresponds exactly to the processing flow model of most classical computer programming languages. In spite of this simplicity, the client/server model is suitable for a wide range of computer applications.

1.4.2   Cooperative processing

Cooperative processing is a term used to refer to a particular type of client/server application. In this case, the client is almost exclusively concerned

---

* The entire history of software can be viewed as a search for useful abstractions. Third-generation languages, databases, spreadsheets and fourth-generation languages are all examples of abstractions that provided a more powerful way of performing a more limited set of tasks.

with implementing the human user interface and the server does almost everything else. Typically, the interface in question is a graphical user interface (GUI). It is not clear whether cooperative processing will turn out to be an important category of distributed system in the long run or whether it merely represents a transitional step from monolithic to distributed systems.

1.4.3 Peer-to-peer networking

Peer-to-peer networking is a term that has been in use for many years. During that time its meaning has changed considerably. In effect, its meaning has migrated up the protocol stack. In the 1970s, peer-to-peer networking referred to a symmetrical relationship between nodes at the lowest, or data-link, level of the protocol stack (i.e., to a point-to-point versus master-slave relationship). In the 1980s, it was used to refer to symmetry of nodes in respect to the middle protocol layers. For example, in TCP/IP any node can initiate a session, whereas in a traditional SNA network only a mainframe can send the bind message that initiates a session.

In the 1990s, peer-to-peer is a term mostly used in contrast to client/server to indicate that nodes do not have a fixed role as a client or server. This distinction commonly relates to a situation in which a piece of software is capable of acting as either a client or a server at different times. This sense of peer-to-peer actually falls under the definition of the client/server model given above. The peer-to-peer model is discussed in detail later in the book.

Peer-to-peer also describes a situation in which users access the files on other users' nodes, instead of on nodes dedicated to being servers. This is attractive for very small networks, but presents problems of management and administration in larger networks. In general, the peer-to-peer model has greater flexibility at the expense of greater complexity, as compared to the simple version of client/server.

1.4.4 Distributed messaging

Another distributed processing model is the *messaging model*. In this model, programs send messages to queues and receive messages from queues. Each queue operates in first-in–first-out (FIFO) order. There can be any number of programs reading and writing a given queue. Generally, writing to a queue always succeeds, whereas reading from an empty queue will cause a program to block until a message appears. A queue may be volatile, meaning the messages in it will be lost if the computer crashes, or nonvolatile.

Messaging has been around for some time as a local service. In a distributed messaging model, the communications software must keep track of the names and locations of the queues and transmit the messages from one node to another.

In a typical messaging application, each software process acts like a server, pulling work requests off a queue and putting completed work on other queues. The messaging model corresponds to the way human beings work in many factories and offices.

Like client/server, messaging avoids the problem of messages arriving at unpredictable times. Messaging, however, makes it difficult to correlate requests with responses and easier for something to get lost in the shuffle. Still, the messaging model is extremely useful for some types of distributed applications.

1.4.5 Distributed database

A *distributed database* is a database in which portions of the data reside on different nodes in the network; yet to an application program that accesses it, it appears just as if it were implemented entirely on a single node. All of the usual database features are provided, such as data integrity, multiple concurrent users, database transactions, and generalized queries. In addition, the distributed nature of the database may provide advantages in terms of performance and reliability. In principle, the application developer sees the same familiar database interface. In practice, to achieve adequate performance it may be necessary to pay attention to where in the network the data is located.

The distributed database should not be confused with the *database server,* which may house all the data on a single node, even though its clients are on other nodes. That makes the database considerably easier to implement than a distributed database.

1.5 Multiprocessors

The nodes of distributed systems actually fall within a category of multiprocessor system called *loosely coupled multiprocessors.* The complementary category, *closely coupled multiprocessors,* is characterized by high-speed channels to shared memory and peripheral devices and executes a shared operating system to perform a shared pool of tasks.

Asymmetrical or *master-slave multiprocessors* have one processor that has a special role. This usually means that it is both a performance bottleneck and a single point of failure. In contrast, in a *symmetrical multiprocessor* system, all of the processors can perform any task.

Advances in hardware and software technology are blurring the distinction between closely coupled and loosely coupled systems. In the future it may be possible to construct systems that are not clearly one or the other. Nonetheless, most systems will continue to fall squarely in one category or the other. Of course, it is perfectly possible for a closely coupled multiprocessor to act as a node within a distributed system.

1.6   Processes and Threads

An instance of a program that is active on a computer is called a *task,* or more commonly, a *process.** (On some systems the term *job* is used.) On a multiprocessor, all the processors can be executing distinct processes at the same time, and a multiprocessor is also called a *multiprocessing system.* On a single-processor system, the processor can only be executing one process at any given instant, but it is possible for the operating system to maintain a number of active processes and apply the processor to each of them in turn. This is referred to as *multitasking.* (The terms *timesharing* and *multiprogramming,* which roughly mean the same thing, are not heard much any more.)

Although the concept of processes is entirely local to a single computer, the design of distributed systems requires us to have a clear understanding of it, and particularly of the distinction between processes and threads.

The main reason for multitasking is that the processor of a computer is so much faster than the I/O devices that it can do a lot of work while waiting for the next keystroke or for a disk to rotate to the proper location. As a result, the system as a whole can perform a number of tasks in the same amount of time as just one of them would take without multitasking.

Originally, each process was identified with a distinct user. Later, it was realized that there were reasons why even a single user might want to have several processes. For example, imagine typing in a document while a different process performs a lengthy computation; then, as this is happening, an electronic mail message arrives from the network and is stored on disk.

1.6.1   Threads

More recently, single-user multitasking has come to be used in a different way. Sometimes it is useful for several processes to work cooperatively together, in effect acting as a single program. For example, some versions of UNIX did not provide any way of performing nonblocking or asynchronous I/O. When a program issued, say, a read call, the process would be stopped until the data had been delivered. In order to achieve an overlap between processing and I/O in this type of system, the program would be designed as several processes. The read call would be made from one process and other processing would occur in another. The read call still blocked, but the other process could proceed. Later, when the data arrived, it could be transferred from process to process by one of several mechanisms.

This solved the problem of overlapping processing and I/O, but it was not ideal. First of all, to provide multitasking, an operating system must retain information about all of the processes. On small systems, there could be a sig-

---

* In the Ada language, the term *task* is given a precise meaning, distinct from *process.*

nificant memory penalty in having a large number of processes active. Also, the work of switching the processor from running one process to another—*context switching*—requires the execution of a substantial number of machine instructions. If context switching is done very frequently, this overhead can consume a considerable amount of the computer's capacity.

Another problem with using processes in this way was the cost of transferring data from one process to another. All of the available methods involve extra processing overhead or programming complexity or both, as opposed to simply reading data from memory.

These considerations led to the development of *threads*, often referred to as *lightweight processes*. Like processes, threads are separately scheduled and can proceed independently of each other. Unlike processes, threads do not require the operating system to store much data or spend much time in context switching. Data can be shared between threads simply by their reading it from memory.

To understand exactly how threads work and how they differ from processes, consider how a C program is implemented on a typical computer.* A process has certain resources associated with it. They all boil down to places in which data is stored. They consist of processor registers and main memory. Main memory consists of several categories. There is executable code and read-only memory, or text. There is memory allocated for static variables and data structures. There is the *stack,* containing return addresses from subroutines, passed parameters, and automatic variables. There is also a pool of memory, the *heap,* from which memory is dynamically allocated by calls such as **malloc()**. In addition, the operating system must record the location in the program that is to be executed next; this value is loaded into the processor register called the *program counter,* or *instruction counter,* whenever the process begins execution.

All of these items are distinct between processes. The only exceptions possible are code and read-only data, but this is transparent to the process and is simply a way of reducing the amount of physical memory used.

Threads also have distinct program counters, machine registers, and stacks, but everything else is shared among all the threads in the same task. From a C-language point of view, automatic variables (which include routine parameters and registers) are local to threads, but static variables are shared by all threads. Dynamically allocated data structures are accessed by means of pointers. By selecting either static or automatic pointers, dynamic data can be

---

* In theory, a programming language implements a virtual machine that provides an abstract set of services. When thinking in a language like LISP, there is no choice but to visualize the virtual machine. However, C was designed to provide facilities that are so closely modeled on the operation of the real processor that I believe it is simpler and more useful to think about how the program is actually being executed. It is also my observation that this is how most expert C programmers think about it.

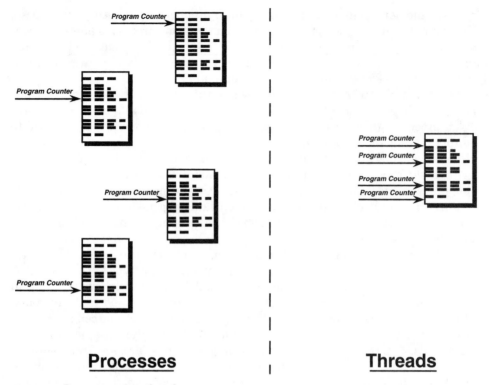

Figure 1.8 Processes versus threads.

shared between threads or not, at the programmer's option. Figure 1.8 illustrates this difference between threads and processes.

Some operating systems provide *nonpreemptive scheduling*. This means that a process will continue to execute until it voluntarily gives up the processor. This may be done by an explicit call to a scheduling routine, or implicitly upon calls such as I/O requests. Nonpreemptive scheduling is convenient from a programming point of view, since the designer can control exactly where the execution of the program can be interrupted. However, it allows a program to hog the processor and can lead to uneven performance by different processes.

True multitasking systems provide *preemptive scheduling*. This means that an executing process can be stopped at any point between two machine instructions. Since C statements usually correspond to several machine instructions, the program will typically be stopped in the middle of a C statement. It is the responsibility of the operating system to make this work. It is done by keeping track of all the process resources listed above and switching context between processes. Since, as we have seen, two processes never share any data (except code and text which cannot change), this works just fine.

Threads are a different story. Threads also are scheduled. (Remember that they have distinct program counters.) But all the threads in a process share the same static data. That means that one thread could be in the middle of updating some data structure and another thread could come along and try to access the same data with erroneous results. A number of methods of avoiding this type of problem will be discussed later in the book. The important point is that they must be explicitly provided by the program.

In summary, threads solve many problems. Thread context is minimal, context switching is fast, and data sharing is easy. On the other hand, multithreaded programs must be careful about bugs related to sharing data between threads. Also, languages like C do not have any built-in concept of a thread.

1.7 Concurrent versus Simultaneous Execution

This business of having several active threads or processes that can preempt each other is called *concurrent execution*. Thinking about the possible interactions requires a mental adjustment from the more common type of programming in which this cannot occur. Nevertheless, in a single-processor system, only one thing can actually be happening at any given time. In a distributed system or closely coupled multiprocessor, however, there can be as many processes and/or threads executing as there are processors in the system. This is known as *simultaneous execution*.

1.8 Standards Organizations

This book mentions a number of standards and standards organizations. The field of computer standards is enormous and even a superficial coverage of them is beyond the scope of this book. However, to give the reader some idea about what is being referred to, here is a brief explanation of standards and organizations mentioned.

The International Organization for Standardization (ISO) is an international body which produces standards in many fields. It has produced a large number of standards relevant to computers and communications, including the highly influential Open Systems Interconnect (OSI) Reference Model described earlier in this chapter.

The Consultative Committee for International Telegraph and Telephone (CCITT) develops international communications standards. CCITT standards include the X.25 standard for packet switching, the X.400 recommendation for exchanging electronic mail, and the X.500 recommendation for distributed directories.

The American National Standards Institute (ANSI) is the coordinating body for U.S. voluntary standards groups, and officially represents the United States to ISO. Like ISO, ANSI is involved with standards in many fields, not just computers. ANSI standards of interest to us include those for computer languages, such as ANSI FORTRAN, ANSI COBOL, and ANSI C.

The Institute of Electrical and Electronic Engineers (IEEE)* develops standards relating to electronics and computers, including LAN interface standards. The Ethernet and Token Ring LANs have been codified (with minor modifications) as IEEE 802.3 and 802.5, respectively.

Another area of IEEE activity of interest to readers of this book is the POSIX† standards. POSIX stands for Portable Operating System Interface for UNIX. The intent behind POSIX is to standardize human and computer interfaces to systems, while allowing vendors to implement the underlying systems in different ways. This enhances portability while allowing competition.

The POSIX standards are known as POSIX 1003.1, 1003.2, and so on. An approved shorter form is POSIX.1, POSIX.2, etc. Actually, only POSIX.1, which defines a basic set of services provided to a program by an operating system, has officially become a standard. The others are in various draft states. POSIX.2 defines a human, command-line interface, similar to that of the various UNIX shells. POSIX.4 deals with real-time extensions (including threads) and POSIX.6 with security enhancements (including ACLs).

The X/Open Company Ltd. is not a standards body, but a consortium that defines and promotes standards relating to the use of open systems. The X/Open Portability Guide is similar in concept to POSIX.1, but more comprehensive. Many X/Open standards consist of programming interfaces designed to allow access to ISO or CCITT-defined protocols. For example, the XDS interface provides a way of accessing an X.500 directory system.

There is an increasing trend for standards bodies to cooperate and coordinate their activities. They plan their work activities so that they do not duplicate the work done by each other. They make use of standards from each other where appropriate. For example, OSI higher-layer protocols ride over lower-layer protocols developed by CCITT and IEEE, and they also adopt each other's standards outright; for example, POSIX.1 is also recognized as ISO 9945.

1.9 Chapter Summary

This chapter defines a distributed system as a combination of hardware, software, and network components in which the software components execute on two or more processors and communicate via a network. The chapter explains a number of concepts relating to distributed systems including types of networks; communications protocols; the client/server model of distributed processing, multiprocessing, and threads; and concurrent and simultaneous processing.

---

* People usually say "eye triple e" for IEEE.

† Pronounced "pahz-icks."

Why Distributed Computing Is Good

Having come this far, we ought to consider why anyone would want a distributed system. Certainly there are many computer applications that work perfectly well as monolithic systems and there probably always will be.

But distributed systems possess certain unique advantages over monolithic ones. This chapter details these advantages of distributed computing because it is worthwhile bearing in mind that the purpose of embarking on a distributed system will be to achieve one or more of them, usually several of them. The need to preserve these advantages is reflected in many design problems associated with distributed systems and in their solutions as discussed in the rest of the book.

Generally speaking, the alternatives to a distributed system can be grouped into two general categories: computing with multiuser systems, typically mainframes and minicomputers; and computing with single-user systems, typically PCs and workstations. The advantages of distributed systems thus fall into three categories. (1) They provide the advantages of a multiuser system that are lacking in a single-user system. (2) They preserve the advantages of single-user systems that are lost in multiuser systems. (3) They inherently offer special advantages of their own. Each of these is considered in turn.

2.1 The Best of Timesharing

Small, stand-alone, single-user systems lack certain obvious capabilities that are available in multiuser systems. A few examples will show how distributed systems can fill this gap.

2.1.1 Multiuser applications

Many software applications revolve around the interaction of a number of individuals. Examples include electronic mail, group scheduling, work-flow automation, and computer-based publishing. Even traditionally solo activities are coming to be viewed as more effectively performed by collaboration between groups. A prime example is the concurrent engineering movement in the manufacturing industry.

Distributed computing makes such applications possible by interconnecting stand-alone systems.

2.1.2 Resource sharing

A stand-alone system must have dedicated access to all the resources it ever needs to use. Obviously, there are great drawbacks to this. No one is going to buy an expensive device, such as a color printer, if it is only used once or twice a month. If 100 users can all have access to the printer, however, it is worth the cost.

Similarly, by sharing a larger disk among a number of users, it is possible to buy a disk with faster performance at a lower cost per megabyte. In addition, suppose a user needs some extra storage temporarily, for example to sort some data. This is easy to accommodate on a shared disk, but on a single-user system it would be necessary to add equipment just for this one-time use.

It is easy to envision other scenarios of this sort. Distributed computing allows an organization to make the best possible use of all of its available physical resources.

2.1.3 Widespread access to data

Information used to be thought of as belonging to a person or a department. More and more organizations now realize the value of being able to access and combine information located throughout the enterprise.

A stand-alone system is very limited in the data it has access to. Even though the data is stored online on a computer, it is accessible only to users of that computer. Even multiuser systems can only access their own local data. Distributed computing is a necessary condition to gaining the benefits from recognizing information as an enterprisewide resource.

2.1.4 Centralized services

Operating a computer entails a variety of administrative and operational tasks. Some examples of these include: performing file backups, updating new software releases, and replenishing printer paper, ribbons, or toner. In a multiuser system environment there are usually individuals designated to perform these tasks on a regular basis.

In a stand-alone, single-user system environment, it is usually up to the end user to do them. This is undesirable for a number of reasons. The user may lack the knowledge to do the task. The user's time may be too valuable to be spent on these activities. Most importantly, the user may forget to do them. This is particularly true of backup. As organizations become more and more dependent on data stored on computers, the need for regular file backups and storage off site becomes more acute. There have already been cases of small businesses going bankrupt because the PC containing all of their accounts receivable files was stolen and they had no backups.

Even if an organization designates someone to do these tasks, it may be completely impractical to perform them in a stand-alone environment. For example, to back up the disk or update the software on 100 stand-alone PCs is a huge and error-prone job. If the same users are sharing a file server, the same tasks take a couple of hours or less. The centralized services possible with distributed computing make it practical to use single-user systems for mission-critical applications.

2.2   The Best of Single-User Systems

Obviously, there are very real benefits to the use of PCs and workstations. Distributed systems allow users to retain these advantages.

2.2.1   Price/performance

The PC revolution resulted in a dramatic transformation in the cost of computing. The creation of mass markets for hardware and software, combined with low barriers to entry for vendors, resulted in prices far lower than previous norms. The mass markets made it possible to invest far more in product engineering, particularly for software. As a result, the quality and functionality of products rose (especially in ease of use), even as prices were dropping.

As the open systems marketplace matures, the same kind of mass-market effects will be felt, particularly in software and peripheral devices. Reduced instruction set computing (RISC) is already recognized as providing price/performance substantially superior to that of the systems previously available.

Networking these types of computers into a distributed system allows users to retain their cost advantages.

2.2.2   Standard software packages

The use of PCs and, to a lesser extent, workstations permits the use of popular software packages. This has a number of advantages. The most obvious is cost. The software license price per user is much lower than for software on mainframes and minicomputers.

There are other advantages as well. Because these packages are so popular, many people know how to use them. This means that new employees and temporary employees will not have to be trained in their use. It means that users will be able to help each other in using the software and that any internal support people will be more familiar with it as well.

Another advantage is that when a program is popular, other software companies design their products to be compatible with it—for example, by providing the ability to create or read files in the same formats. This makes the software more convenient and powerful to use.

By incorporating PCs into a distributed system, users can continue to use popular software packages.

2.2.3   Ability to use current computing platforms

In many cases, the most likely potential users of a new application already have PCs or workstations on their desks. The advantages of making use of these existing computers are obvious. It not only avoids the expense of acquiring new hardware, but also the necessity for the users to learn a new system. It also eliminates the need to have several kinds of computer hardware on the user's desk.

This reason is so compelling that it is often considered a requirement, not merely an advantage, to incorporate these existing computers into a distributed system.

2.3   Inherent Advantages

Distributed systems also possess advantageous properties not normally present in either single-user or multiuser systems.

2.3.1   Flexibility

Distributed systems are very flexible. The hardware components of a distributed system can be located wherever they are needed. This could be driven by the needs of the enterprise—for example, to locate a workstation on the floor of a factory or a printer on the bridge of a ship. It could also be the result of operational requirements—for example, to locate a server in a locked room for security reasons.

As needs change over time, the components of a distributed system can be easily moved and reconfigured without impacting their ability to perform their function. In the future, many of the components of distributed systems may be mobile, connected to the network by wireless technology. Their ability to access the resources of the network from wherever they are will be the thing that makes them valuable.

2.3.2   Scalability

Because distributed systems are constructed out of multiple components, they are easily scaled to the requirements of the problem at hand. The system can be designed with as many or as few components as are required. As requirements change over time, the power of the distributed system can be increased by adding additional components, such as processors or network links, rather than replacing the old ones. Similarly, if less capacity is needed later on, components can be removed and used elsewhere.

In principle, distributed systems can be built to solve problems of any size, even ones much too large for any single computer system. For all these reasons, distributed systems are said to be inherently scalable.

2.3.3 Efficiency

Distributed systems are very efficient, because they can consist of heterogeneous components selected to be optimal for the task at hand. Instead of trying to do a variety of tasks with a single type of computer, it is possible to apply special-purpose machines, each of which has to solve only part of a problem.

The ability to locate their components flexibly and their scalability also contribute to the efficiency of distributed systems. Figure 2.1 illustrates a typical case: a high-speed computer-driven display. The processor that drives the display can be located close to it. Thus, the expensive high-speed channel can be quite short, while the link to the rest of the network can be a less expensive one.

Since distributed systems can be built using many smaller systems, rather than a single larger one, they can be more closely matched to the system capacity required. It is not necessary to allow a large margin of excess capac-

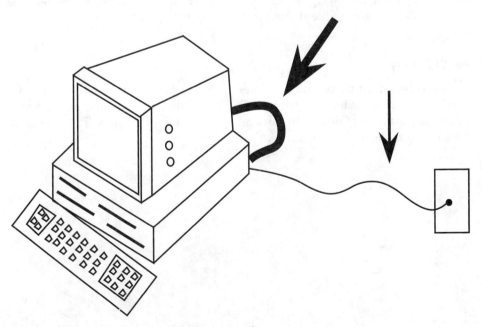

Figure 2.1 High-speed channel, lower-speed network.

ity for growth. Therefore, there is no need to pay for hardware that is not initially used.

2.3.4 Availability

Distributed systems can be made highly available. Because components can be duplicated, the system can be made immune to single points of failure. Furthermore, the flexibility of distributed systems means that they can be configured to survive any type of failure that can be imagined.

A fault-tolerant monolithic computer system may have no single point of failure, but it will not survive a tornado that destroys the building it is in. A redundant processor in a distributed system, on the other hand, could be located in another city or even on a different continent.

Distributed systems can also provide greater availability in the face of necessary, but planned, outages. Individual computers or links can be disconnected from the system for testing, repair, or modification, without impacting the availability of the system as a whole.

It is important to note that this benefit is neither automatic nor free. The design of the distributed system must provide the necessary level of redundancy. The majority of distributed systems in use today are not redundant, because it is judged that the expense entailed is not justified.

Also, as the next chapter discusses in detail, even in a distributed system that is highly available as a whole, the failure of individual components is, paradoxically, more frequent than in a monolithic system.

2.4 Chapter Summary

It can be seen that there are a number of very good reasons for the increasing deployment of distributed systems. The use of distributed systems, however, presents a number of difficulties not present in monolithic ones. The next chapter discusses these in detail.

3

Why Distributed Computing Is Hard

In the last chapter, we saw the many advantages provided by distributed systems, but in fact, it is generally agreed that a distributed system is harder to design, harder to implement, and harder to operate than a monolithic system. This chapter discusses a number of the most important reasons why this is so. Later in the book, after DCE has been described, we will revisit these difficulties and discuss how the use of the DCE components can and cannot help us overcome them.

3.1 Multiple Failure Modes

One thing distinguishing distributed systems from monolithic systems is that they can fail in so many different ways. Obviously this stems from the fact that distributed systems contain many more components.

But the difficulty is not simply that the large number of elements increases the statistical likelihood that one of them will fail. Rather, it is that an alarmingly large range of behavior can result from failure of various components; in classical engineering terms, the distributed system can produce a large variety of "failure modes."

Consider Fig. 3.1 of the most minimal possible configuration: two nodes connected by a network. Assuming the nodes have distinct roles in the network (for example, client and server), we can see that already there are three possible failure cases:

- Node A may fail.
- Node B may fail.
- The network may fail.

Further, each node has to be able to handle two of these possibilities. (In this example, we assume each node is either completely up or completely down.

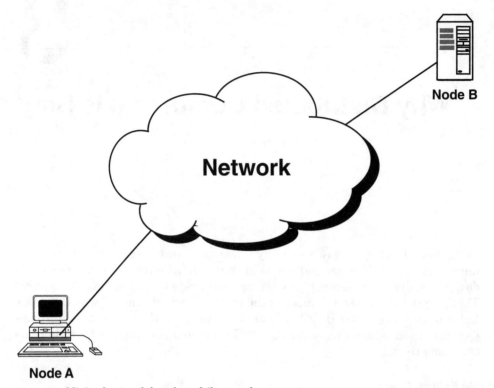

Figure 3.1 Minimal network has three failure modes.

There is no need for software to consider the case of the processor it is running on being down!) Therefore, from a design point of view, there are four cases to consider even in this simplified example.

Today, a typical corporate network contains hundreds of nodes. There are many networks in existence with thousands and even tens of thousands of nodes. Further, as more computers are being connected to networks and because existing networks are being connected to each other, these numbers are increasing rapidly.

Figure 3.2 shows a (slightly) more complex distributed system. Now there are four nodes connected to the network. Considering just the node failures, there are 14 possible cases.* Although in practice it is unlikely that each of these cases would require special handling, we can see that the number of cases increases dramatically as the number of nodes increases.

---

* There are four ways that one node can fail, six ways that two nodes can fail, and four ways that three nodes can fail. The case of all the nodes failing is not worth worrying about, because there is nowhere for any error-recovery software to execute.

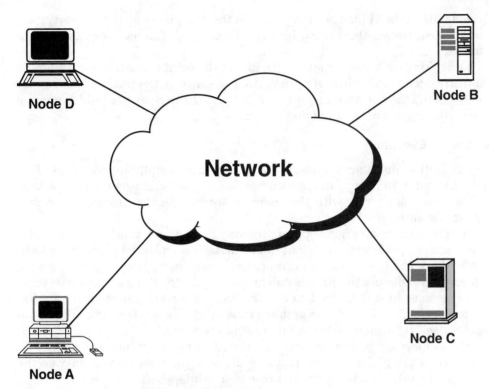

Figure 3.2 Four-node network has 14 failure modes.

This four-node system also contains the potential for a new type of failure. Imagine that the network fails in such a way that node A and node B can communicate with each other, but not with node C or node D and, at the same time, C and D can communicate with each other but not with A and B. This is known as a *partition* of the network. The problem is that from the point of view of A and B the "system" is up and they are the "system." Likewise, C and D believe that they are the "system." This can lead to all kinds of strange behavior, especially after the network has been repaired and everyone can communicate with everyone else again.

For example, suppose an important file has been duplicated on node A and node C so that it will still be accessible even if one of them fails. When the network is partitioned, both A and C will believe that they have the "official" version of the file. Each will continue to update the file in response to transactions performed on its part of the network. When the network partitions are rejoined, it will be quite difficult to figure out what should be in the file.

So far we have considered only cases in which a node fails completely. Many types of partial failures are possible, and can lead to unexpected consequences. Imagine, for example, a file server with two disk drives, and suppose one of them fails. It could turn out that users in the same room as the file server are unaffected, while other users, in a city thousands of miles away, experience errors.

Other kinds of failures could be listed, but the point is clear. When designing a distributed system, it is very important to consider the kinds of errors that may occur. It is not uncommon for error handling to comprise half or more of the software in a distributed application.

3.2 Simultaneous Execution

By definition, distributed systems involve the use of multiple processors. This means that a number of different processes will be occurring simultaneously. This contrasts sharply with the environment in which most application programs execute.

Most computer programs operate the way most people think. They consider alternatives, perform calculations, make decisions, and so forth, but they basically think about *one thing at a time*. Even real-time systems that deal with interrupts and multiple threads still are doing just one thing at any given time.

Languages such as COBOL and FORTRAN have no way to express simultaneous processing. In fact, the problem runs much deeper. The logic of the computer itself reflects the way we think about problems.*

Even interrupt processing can be related to ordinary human experience. You are reading. The phone rings. You mark your place. You answer the phone. You talk. You hang up. You resume reading where you left off.

Simultaneous processing, however, is alien to human experience. There may be those who claim to be able to think about two, or even ten things at once, but nobody claims to be able to think about a hundred things at once. Designing and implementing systems containing multiple processors requires practice in a different way of thinking.

It is true that this difficulty is not unique to distributed systems. It is shared by other systems that contain multiple processors, such as closely coupled multiprocessors and massively parallel systems. In fact, the many years it has taken for these systems to become practical is further evidence that the required thinking is unfamiliar.

3.3 Many Possible States

Distributed systems are complex to design because they have such a large number of potential states. What does that mean? The state of a system can be

---

* Alan Turing wrote a description of an abstract computing machine that John von Neumann later used as the basis for the design of a real computer. The machines we use today operate in fundamentally the same way and are in fact called "von Neumann machines." But Turing was not trying to design computers, he was trying to describe in very specific, step-by-step fashion, how he himself solved math problems!

defined as those properties of the system that vary over time. We can further limit the definition to include only those properties that affect some aspect of the system that we are interested in. The number of states that a system can assume is a good measure of its complexity.

A light switch is a simple system that has two states: on and off. The plastic it is made of is a property that does not vary over time. Its temperature is a property that probably does vary over time, but does not affect the system's behavior.

A computer is a very complex system with a large number of states. Technically, to describe the state of a computer or a piece of software it is necessary to specify the contents of memory, current point of execution, contents of registers, files open, etc. In practice, we can describe the state of a program informally, by stating what it is up to, just as we talk about a person's state of mind without specifying what all the neurons are doing. For example, a program might be waiting for a keystroke, or multiplying two numbers.

The reason that distributed systems have so many states is a simple matter of numbers. A distributed system consists of a number of components that can each independently assume different states. To calculate the total number of states a system can assume, we must multiply the number of states of each component together.

Imagine a simple, monolithic application that can assume three states—reading data, processing data, or writing data. Now imagine an equally simple-minded distributed application. The software on each node is either sending a message, processing the message, or receiving a message. Now even in the simplest possible configuration of two nodes, there are 3^2 or 9 possible states. With four nodes, there are 3^4 or 81 states, with ten nodes 3^{10} or 59049, and so on.

All those states make it very difficult to comprehend how the system will actually behave. The many possibilities make it very easy to overlook some of the cases. The best evidence of this comes from seeing how even experts can sometimes build distributed systems with holes in them.

The Internet, which used to be called the ARPANET, is a large, government-funded packet network connecting universities and businesses throughout the world. It was established for two complementary purposes. The first was to provide wide-area data communications to the academic and industrial research community. The second was to advance the technology of data networking through experience with operating a large-scale packet network.

Virtually every data network today contains technology derived from work on the ARPANET. Using measurements taken on the network, small-scale experiments, and theoretical studies, some of the smartest and most knowledgeable people in the networking field worked throughout the 1970s and 1980s to continually improve the reliability and increase the efficiency of the ARPANET.

Every software modification was the result of months of analysis, discussion, and consideration of alternatives. The software was carefully reviewed, checked, and tested very thoroughly before it was introduced into the network. Nevertheless, in a significant number of instances, the totally unexpected happened. Packets wandered around the network forever. In a famous case, a hardware failure (an admittedly unlikely one) not only took down most of the network, but effectively masked the cause for many hours.

These problems were not obvious ones. In one case, the network operated for 18 months before a problem was recognized. The point is, even people who have spent their careers designing distributed systems have a hard time anticipating the many possible scenarios that can occur.

3.4 Complex Processing Flow

Distributed applications are often characterized by a more complex processing flow than is typical of traditional programs. Even developers who have implemented numerous systems often find it difficult to adjust to this difference.

The logic of traditional programs can easily be represented using a flow chart such as the one shown in Fig. 3.3. If the path of execution is traced with a pencil, there is no need to lift the point from the paper. In contrast, many distributed system programs consist of a bunch of isolated pieces of code that can execute in many different sequences. The processing is coordinated by reading and writing variables in memory. The other set of flow charts, Fig. 3.4, is an attempt to represent such a design, but such a chart does not really convey any sense of how the program works.

Programs in distributed systems exhibit complex flow patterns principally because it is often impossible to know in advance when there is something to read from the network. A program that reads and writes a disk file can call the shots. The disk file just sits there.

But communication across a network always involves at least two programs. Any data that is read by one must have been written by another. Therefore, the writer is in control. The reader may not have to read the data until sometime after the writer has written it; usually a network service provides some buffering. But eventually the system will run out of buffers, so the reader cannot delay long. (Of course, there are other reasons not to take too long. The customer is waiting for his or her money from the ATM, the assembly line is waiting for the command to start operating, and so forth.)

In some cases, the reader can simply sit around doing nothing, waiting for data to arrive. If so, program logic will be greatly simplified. Unfortunately, quite often it is not possible just to wait for data to arrive. Other tasks, such as computation, sending data, and accessing I/O devices must be interspersed with attempts to read data. At the other end of the scale of complexity there may be many programs at many different nodes sending many different kinds of messages that in turn require different kinds of processing. There is no real limit to how complicated things can get.

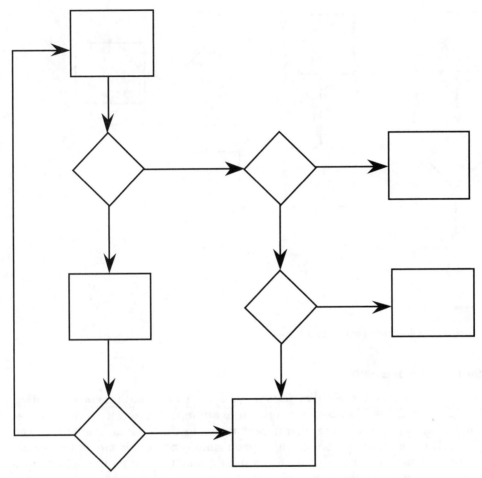

Figure 3.3 Flow chart of traditional program.

The subject of processing flow and, specifically, how to simplify it, will be discussed at length in Part 4 of this book. It is worth noting that complex flow logic is not unique to distributed systems. It has always been a feature of operating system software and real-time software, for example.

A more recent example is the GUI-based application. Most GUI-based programs can be characterized as consisting of many little snippets of code that can be executed in any sequence and that communicate by manipulating data structures in memory. The reasons are different from those associated with distributed systems, but the need for a new type of program structure is the same in both cases. It is worth noting that the mental adjustment required has been a significant obstacle to developing GUI-based applications.

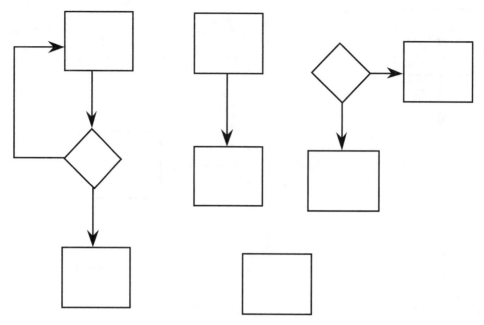

Figure 3.4 Flow chart of a distributed application.

3.5 Synchronization of Events

Because of attributes of a distributed system such as simultaneous execution and a multiplicity of states, it is natural to attempt to associate time information with events occurring in different nodes in the system. Sometimes the intention might be that something happen simultaneously in two or more locations. For example, a new policy for handling customer accounts might go into effect at noon throughout the network.

More often, we simply wish to determine the order in which two events occurred at different locations in the network. This is quite important in networks that accept bids to buy and sell things—currency, for example. The sale at a certain price should go to the bidder who bid first.

Unfortunately, it is not particularly easy to do either of these things. It is safe to assume that a program running on any modern computer can easily obtain the date and time from the operating system any time it is needed. The first IBM PCs had a clock that had to be set when the system was turned on. But now even the most inexpensive computer has a clock that keeps time even when the power is off. So in a monolithic system it is easy to relate events in time.

In a typical data network, however, it is safe to assume that the individual system clocks will *not* be set to the same time. They will probably be within a minute or so of each other, perhaps within a few seconds, but for some purposes this is not good enough. With specialized hardware, including a link to an official time service, it is possible to synchronize events to a billionth of a second or better over a wide area. In fact, the telephone companies do this in order to synchronize the clocking of their digital transmission equipment. The equipment is expensive, however, and is not usually provided in ordinary public or private data networks.

Since we cannot count on the system clocks to relate events in time, it is natural to think of sending messages from one node to another as a solution. The difficulty with this approach is that it takes time for messages to travel from one application to another elsewhere in a network.

Figure 3.5 illustrates this problem. This type of diagram is frequently used to illustrate interactions in a distributed system in which relative timing is an important factor. The vertical axis represents time; events toward the bottom happen later. The columns represent nodes or processes within the system. In other words, the horizontal axis represents space in one dimension. This diagram is useful if the interactions are along one dimension—for example, if just two nodes are involved. It is not very useful if the interactions occur in two or more dimensions.

In the diagram, we see that an event called X occurs at node A. About the same time, another event called Y occurs at node B. Node A sends a message to

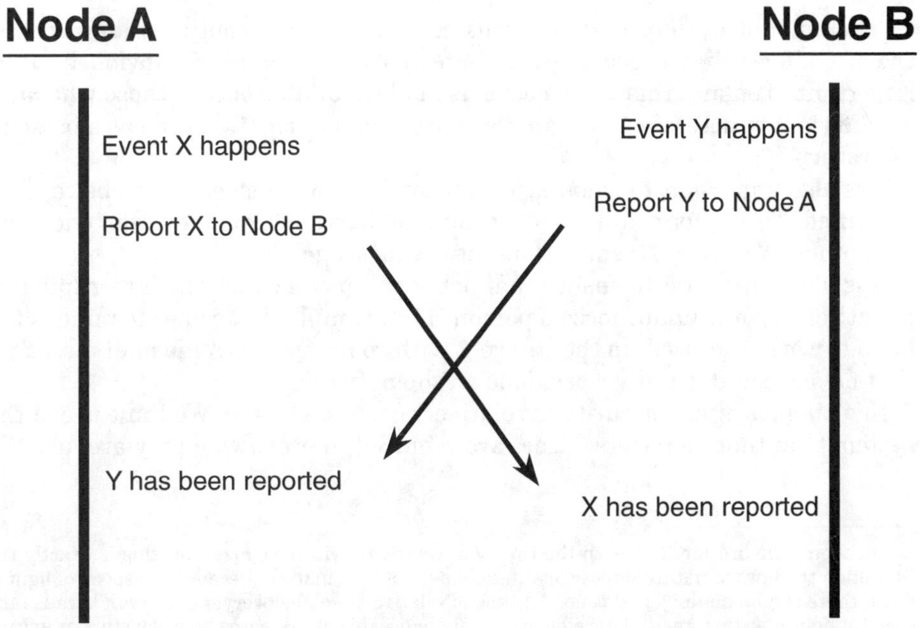

Node A

Node B

Event X happens

Event Y happens

Report X to Node B

Report Y to Node A

Y has been reported

X has been reported

Figure 3.5 Networks make timing uncertain.

B to announce event X. Node B also sends a message to A reporting event Y. Node A now believes that X occurred before Y, whereas B believes the opposite.*

Perhaps you are thinking that we still could synchronize events by exchanging messages if we simply account for the time it takes for the message to travel from one point to another. If we subtracted the delay, we would at least be able to determine which one of two events occurred first.

Unfortunately, this is not feasible either. The propagation delays in a network are neither constant nor predictable. First, data networks make efficient use of communications facilities by sharing them. This means that when there is a lot of traffic on the network, some messages will be delayed slightly to wait for other messages to accumulate. When the traffic is light, there will be no delay.

Second, for reasons of efficiency and reliability, many networks are capable of sending messages over more than one path between the same two nodes. The different paths may entail different delays. In addition, variable delays may occur even within a single computer because of the variations in the time until a process gets scheduled, for example, or in the time required to move the disk heads.

In summary, there has been no way to determine relative timing to a high degree of accuracy within most distributed systems.

3.6 Security Enforcement

As the amount of information entrusted to computers continues to increase, the need for reliable security mechanisms also increases. Obviously, it is important to ensure that information is made available only to those who have a valid right to access it. An example is personal information such as a person's tax return.

It is also important to ensure that the origin of a transaction can be reliably identified. Think, for example, of a command to transfer money from one bank to another. We better be sure who sent the message!

It is also important to ensure that network service cannot be interrupted by the action of some unauthorized person. The example that comes to mind is the famous worm that tied up the Internet with so many electronic mail messages that no one could get any work done on the network.

In a single system, security is relatively easy to enforce. We limit use of the system to authorized users. Users are required to prove who they are, usually

---

* Readers who are familiar with the theory of relativity will recognize that this is exactly the limitation the laws of nature impose on all exchanges of information. Because the speed of light is fixed, there can be no universal time. All time is relative to some observer. However, because the speed of light is so fast, relativistic effects are only noticeable at distances between stars or in time intervals associated with the interactions of subatomic particles. In distributed systems, we are instead limited by the much larger time intervals entailed in transmitting substantial amounts of data over links of limited capacity.

by typing in a password. Once in, users are limited in what they can do. They can only look at data that they have specifically been given access to, they cannot make changes to the operating system, they cannot change their own privileges or those of other users, etc. Certain people, such as operators or systems programmers who need more powerful privileges, are given special accounts that are closely guarded, and so forth.

Of course, many systems (practically all PCs) have no security mechanism in effect, and lots of people use the name of their child (or dog) for their password, or worse still, write it on a piece of paper somewhere on their desk. Still, if a single system needs to be made secure, the way to do it is well understood.

A distributed system is another matter. Requests can come in from users in the next room or the next country. All the features that make a distributed system convenient for legitimate users to use also make it convenient for unauthorized use. It is easy to get to data located anywhere. It is difficult to be sure who is making a request.

The features that provide uniformly easy access regardless of location make it difficult to determine where a user is physically located. A clever intruder may even be able to wreak havoc by using features provided for management and administration of the system.

The basic problem is knowing who to trust. Because a distributed system contains many computers, it is impossible to be sure that security has been properly enforced in any particular one. It is possible that a remote system being communicated with has been modified. In fact, since networks may run throughout a building or over telephone lines, the remote system could be a completely bogus system merely pretending to be legitimate. It may have intercepted previously transmitted passwords or other access information.

In short, security on a distributed system is a significant problem.

3.7 Performance Estimation Difficulties

The people who design distributed systems (or any other systems) are not usually the people who pay for them. Quite often, before those who pay agree to pay, they will want to know how much they are getting. They are also very likely to want to know whether a proposed system will operate with enough speed, reliability, and so forth to suit its intended purpose. (There is a well-known story of a system that could compute an accurate 24-hour weather forecast in about 72 hours.)

The people who pay usually ask the people who design to provide the answers to these questions. There may even be penalties associated with answers that later turn out to be incorrect.

Although this is perfectly natural and understandable, it is a big headache for designers of distributed systems. We have already seen how complex distributed systems can be, but that is not the root problem. Equally, a single monolithic system is far too complex to analyze rigorously. No one knows a magic formula for predicting the response time or capacity of a system that has not been implemented yet and, in fact, may not even have been completely designed. The point is that most systems are estimated by extrapolating to a proposed system from one that already exists.

When trying to apply this approach to distributed systems, however, we are at a double disadvantage. First, as distributed systems are relatively new, there are fewer existing systems to use as benchmarks. Second, because of the complexity of distributed systems, it is less likely that experience with an existing system will have a bearing on a new system.

This is most acutely true for estimating performance. So many variables can interact to limit the performance of a distributed system, it is difficult to know where to begin. A few to consider are:

- Capacity of the network media
- Capacity of network adapters
- Capacity of routers, bridges, or gateways in the network
- Efficiency of network protocols
- Processor speed of network nodes
- Memory capacity of network nodes
- Disk speed of network nodes
- Design of operating system on network nodes
- Pattern of network traffic generated
- Extent of overlap of network traffic and other operations
- Amount of network congestion due to other applications

This list barely scratches the surface. There are many more considerations that could be important in certain situations.

Performance itself is not a single measure. Depending on the requirements of an application, the most important factor may be response (how long it takes for something to happen), throughput (how much data can be processed per unit of time), or capacity (how many entities such as users, clients, applications, etc., can be provided with an acceptable level of service). To make things more complicated, usually it is impossible to optimize all three. The design of the distributed system will be a compromise that represents trade-offs among them.

A large body of technical literature exists on the subject of performance in distributed systems. Unfortunately, most of it is of little use to someone who actually needs to estimate the performance of a real system. A lot of it consists of theoretical studies of "pure" situations. Usually, in order to make analysis possible, it includes a number of simplifying assumptions. Therefore, the conclusions tend to be of the nature that doing X is faster than doing Y, but with no indication how fast X is.

The few rigorous experiments that have been done to measure actual performance also have been mostly based on "pure" situations. Very few studies have been published that report the actual behavior of production distributed systems. Because of the large number of variables affecting the performance of distributed systems, the odds are against being able to apply these findings to your system.

Estimating the reliability and availability of a distributed system is a little better understood. A system can be analyzed to identify the critical points of failure. The mean time between failure (MTBF) and mean time to repair (MTTR) of most production computer hardware can be obtained or estimated accurately. Given the statistics for each component and their dependencies, it is a fairly straightforward matter to calculate the expected reliability and availability of an entire system. Software exists that will do the numbers for a given configuration or propose adding redundant components to meet some specified level of reliability.

The bad news is that this is not all there is to estimating reliability. First, it ignores the network links. Certainly there are published figures for the bit-error rates of LANs and digital telephone lines. We can even estimate with some confidence the probability of someone driving a bulldozer through the wall of a building that has the Ethernet cable in it, or of the telephone company failing to notice they are running off batteries.*

The real problem is that no one knows how to estimate the MBTF or MTTR of a piece of software. If a program has been running (unmodified, of course) for a few years, maybe. But the reliability of a new program may have nothing to do with that of the last one. None of the techniques that hardware engineers use are available to us. Where they might say "CMOS failures are such and such compared to ECL," we cannot say "Pascal programs have fewer bugs than FORTRAN programs."

Furthermore, the mathematical models for calculating reliability and availability of hardware systems assume that failures are independent of each other. But it is obvious that software failures in different components running *the same code* are anything but independent. This was demonstrated in dramatic fashion in June of 1991 when California and Washington, D.C., experienced simultaneous failures in their separate telephone networks caused by a bug in identical switching software. (Conspiracy theorists forgot about JFK, at least for a few days.)

In order to be allowed to build a distributed system, one will probably have to be able to characterize its expected performance, and at present this is more of an art than a science.

---

* This is of course a reference to the AT&T network failure of 1991 in New York City, which occurred because network operations people failed to notice that a major switching center serving the city had been running on battery power, until about 20 minutes before the batteries were exhausted. It was too late to resolve the problem in time to avoid a major outage lasting several hours. The point of the story is not to flagellate AT&T (this has already been done by others), but to underline that such failures are both inevitable and unpredictable.

3.8   Complex Design Tradeoffs

One of the goals in designing any system is to optimize it. A complex system like the ones we are discussing will have many attributes to be optimized. The designer must consider cost, delivery date, risk, performance, reliability, and many other factors. Invariably, each of these requires some tradeoff against the others. For example, additional testing may increase reliability but result in more cost and a later delivery date.

When considering the design of a distributed system, the uncertainties involved in these tradeoffs are particularly acute, for three related reasons.

Again because distributed systems are relatively new, the requirements for factors such as risk, performance, and reliability are not usually easy to determine. Everyone wants a system that is more available, rather than less, but it is usually hard to quantify precisely what a given increment is worth.*

For example, a transaction processing system could be made more reliable by performing all transactions redundantly on two servers. The tradeoffs would likely be increased cost and slower processing. Suppose that it could be determined that this would reduce the downtime of the system from 12 hours a year to 1 hour a year and that it would increase the time to process the average transaction from 1.5 to 2.5 seconds and increase the total system cost by 21 percent. In most real-world situations, it would not be possible to say whether that was justified or not.

Of course, there are systems (like those flying the space shuttle) for which the need for 100 percent availability is obvious. Similarly, if a design alternative would result in an increase from 80 to 95 percent availability, no one would doubt the need for it. In practice, most systems are more like the example given earlier and no one, least of all the end user of the system, can define the requirements of the system with that much precision.

Second, it is very difficult to determine, during the design stage, the actual values for reliability, cost, response time, and so forth. Consider the example just given. The calculation of the hours of downtime is a complex one, even for the hardware components. Next, we must consider the effects of software bugs, environmental factors, human errors, etc. Even supposing we could come up with something as precise as "1 hour versus 12 hours of downtime per year," this would only represent a long-term average. The fluctuation from year to year might be enormous. Of course, it might average out over 50 years or so, but who is going to run an unmodified system for 50 years?

Third, in practice, the effect of tradeoffs must be judged from experience with similar systems. Even once an organization has built a few similar distributed applications, this knowledge may not be applicable to a new system

---

* I once observed a system used by a large bank to do interbank money transfers. It had been calculated that a single failure of two hours or more occurring around two o'clock in the afternoon would cost the bank $4 million in interest payments. This is the exception. Reliability requirements are rarely so well quantified.

that is different in some important way, because of the complexities involved in distributed systems. And because of the large number of possible designs, the newness of distributed systems, and the weakness of the theory, it is unlikely that most organizations will be able to find examples of systems built by others that will be usable as design models. The accumulation of experience relevant to any given design is likely to be slow.

Unfortunately, both vendors and end users may be reluctant to share relevant information for competitive reasons. On the other hand, some efforts are currently under way to form industry consortia to act as forums for sharing this kind of information.

3.9 Use of Multiple Technologies

Another factor that makes distributed systems more difficult to implement is their involvement of multiple technologies that are the result of the partitioning of computer technology into specialized areas. Each area deals with solving the problems of its own domain using concepts and terminology that have been developed to serve its specialized needs.

The worlds of systems analysis, computer languages, operating systems, CASE, database design, expert systems, communications protocols, transaction processing, and graphical user interface all overlap, but all have their own unique view of the world. The word "token" means very different things to a language expert and a protocol expert. Operating-system specialists say "virtual memory" where database experts say "hierarchical storage" to mean roughly the same thing. Nobody but GUI people has any idea what a "widget" is.

This is fine when dealing with the typical monolithic system that can be built using tools from just one of these specialties. Unfortunately, distributed systems invariably involve several of them. It is often difficult even to understand how a concept from one field works with a concept from another. It is often difficult even to reconcile the terminology found in the manuals for products based in different technology areas.

It is difficult to design a system that mandates an interface between two technologies when you cannot determine if they are even intended to be compatible. Yet most of the challenges of designing, implementing, and testing distributed systems arise in crossing these borders.

The other aspect of this problem is that of individual expertise. It takes time to master just one specialized area. Few have time to become expert in two or more. Although some individuals develop a superficial level of knowledge in a wide variety of specialties, frequently their knowledge is too shallow to be of much use in successfully designing a distributed system.

Of course, it is possible to gather together a bunch of experts in the relevant technologies and hope that they can solve the problem as a team. Often there is no better option available. But if each expert speaks a different language and sees the problem in different terms, progress will be slow and there will be a real risk of failure.

Furthermore, outside experts may not be able to help much either. Software vendors, systems vendors, and consultants all usually focus on one particular technology. Their people may have greater depth of knowledge in their chosen area than the staff of an end-user organization, but all too frequently they are equally at a loss when it comes to bridging distinct domains.

3.10   Frequent Component Incompatibilities

A related problem is that distributed systems usually use products from multiple vendors and, sad to say, more often than not they are found to be incompatible in some way. Sometimes the difficulty is fatal and either another product must be used or, if none is available, the project abandoned. Sometimes the incompatibilities are relatively minor, but the system does not function smoothly, or the users find its operation confusing, or some valuable feature is rendered unusable.

Perhaps the biggest drawback associated with incompatibility is that many times the problem is not discovered until a system is being tested or even after it has been installed. This tends to maximize the impact and particularly the cost of fixing the problem.

The best thing that can be said of the incompatibility problem is that it is much more widely recognized than many of the others discussed in this chapter. Any organization that has a variety of packaged software installed on a LAN has probably experienced it to some degree. If anything, a fear of the problem has led some organizations to completely avoid distributed systems and their attendant benefits.

There are several root causes of the problem. The usual scapegoat is "lack of standards." That this is true, especially when it comes to MS-DOS, goes without saying. But, in fairness, in many of the areas we are discussing there has been no consensus until recently as to how things should work together or even what the "things" were. It is not possible to have standards until there is broad consensus at least on the fundamental concepts involved.

Of course, some vendors have gone out of their way to do things that result in incompatibilities. Sometimes this has been from a deliberate intent to lock customers into proprietary technology. More often it has been prompted by a legitimate desire to differentiate a product by providing a special feature.

Most often, product incompatibilities simply result from the many ways components can be combined. We have already seen the multiplying effect that component combinations have, even in modest-sized networks belonging to a single organization. When this is extended across the many customers who will use a single software package, it is clear that no vendor can exhaustively test the many possible interactions that a product will encounter.

Although two products often can be made to work together, it may be extremely difficult to determine what combination of parameters and commands to use to achieve compatibility, often because each arises from a technology area that has its own concepts and terminology, as discussed in the previous section.

3.11 Testing and Debugging Difficulties

One of the biggest and most often ignored problems in developing distributed applications is that of testing and debugging them. For one thing, because of the large number of states possible, it is often difficult to create test scenarios that reproduce the conditions that will be seen in the live environment.

Even after a problem has been detected, it may be difficult to control the conditions well enough to reproduce the problem at will. This is because of the number of computers and other components that may be involved, as well as the fact that distributed systems usually involve both asynchronous events and concurrent execution. Because events are happening asynchronously, reproducing the exact situation (assuming that it is known) in which a bug is seen can be quite difficult.

Another reason is that testing and debugging tools generally provide little support for these conditions. Some debuggers offer some support for multithreading, but they are the exception. I know of no tool that allows for debugging a distributed application from a single point of control. The best that can be done today is to run a debugger on each node from a single windowing terminal. Testing tools also provide little help for that difficult task.

Another reason testing and debugging distributed systems is difficult is that, even when a problem can be reproduced at will, it can be very difficult to gather the information necessary to debug it. For one thing, many existing software products provide little access to information about internal states. This is typically true of communication protocol implementations as well as popular PC and workstation operating systems.

Often it is also difficult to gather information about what is happening in different nodes or even in different software components at the same time. Even when the information can be gathered, the lack of detailed documentation of the software's operation or the unfamiliar terminology used may make it difficult to interpret.

3.12 Multiple Configurations

A final but important obstacle to implementing distributed systems is that the software usually will be required to run on multiple hardware and network configurations. The environment in which an application is developed and tested typically consists of only a few machines isolated from the user's production network.

Once the system goes into production, the number and kinds of computers, network links, perhaps even operating systems and network protocols involved are likely to be quite different. It is not unusual for an application to be initially installed in a number of different environments. Certainly, over time, constant turnover and reconfiguration of the hardware, software, and networks can be expected.

True, in a traditional mainframe environment, applications are built and tested on a separate (typically smaller) test system, but the test system is usually only a different model of the same computer from the same manufacturer. The operating system and other software are likely to be identical. In the PC environment, developers often are fortunate enough to be able to test their product in exactly the same environment it will run in.

The large number of possible system variations, the potential for interconnecting practically every computer within an organization, and the trend toward constant reconfiguration to meet changing needs all conspire to ensure the distributed-systems designer of a moving target. The designer must try to anticipate not only what may occur when the system is installed, but what its behavior may be under future conditions.

3.13 Chapter Summary

If this review of the reasons distributed systems are difficult to implement has made you think of giving up on the whole thing, that was not my intention. Many distributed systems are in use today, providing great advantages to their owners and users. The problems discussed can be overcome, but not by wishing them away. We will return to this list of difficulties in later chapters of the book and examine how, with DCE and other means, we can overcome them.

The OSF Distributed Computing Environment (DCE)

We have now concluded our introduction to distributed applications, and it is time to examine OSF's Distributed Computing Environment (DCE). Chapter 4 presents a general overview of DCE. The goal of the chapter is not only to give the reader a feel for the capabilities of the technology, but also to explain how the features are intended to be used and the benefits that are derived from using them. These benefits result not merely from the technical merits of DCE, but from the business and economic climate of the computer industry into which OSF and DCE have emerged. Chapter 4 concludes with a brief introduction to each of the DCE components and a discussion of a number of important concepts that are meaningful in the context of more than one of the DCE components.

In succeeding chapters of Part 2, each of the DCE components is described in detail. These chapters present the terms and concepts related to each component. They describe all the important features and capabilities of each, emphasizing those most useful in typical distributed applications. These chapters explain why features have been included in DCE and include recommendations for and against the use of specific features. Example source code is introduced to illustrate the important features of each of the DCE components. The major goal of these chapters, however, is to provide an understanding of how the components work; with that understanding, it is a simple matter to look up required syntax. More-complete program examples are presented later in the book.

At the time this is being written, there are no production-quality, commercial versions of DCE available. Therefore, the information in this book is based on the documentation set from OSF and on the product Gradient SysV-DCE from Gradient Technologies, Inc.

Overview of the Distributed Computing Environment (DCE)

This chapter is an overview of the Distributed Computing Environment (DCE). The goal is to provide the reader with a general sense of what DCE is all about and what benefits can be derived from using it, from both the technical and nontechnical points of view.

This chapter provides an introduction to the components that make up DCE and describes how they relate to each other. It also introduces a number of general concepts, several of which are fundamental to understanding DCE as a whole. Other concepts that relate primarily to a single DCE component are described in the chapter on that component.

4.1 What Is DCE?

DCE is a set of software tools and services that make it much easier to develop and operate distributed computer applications. DCE does this in several ways.

4.1.1 DCE advantages

First, DCE provides services that can be found in other computer networking environments, but packages them so as to make them much easier to use. For example, the DCE Remote Procedure Call (RPC) facility provides a way of communicating between software modules running on different systems that is much simpler to code than older methods, such as using socket calls.

Second, DCE provides new capabilities that go beyond what was available previously. The DCE Security Service provides a reliable way of determining if a user of a distributed system should be allowed to perform a certain action, for example. This is very useful for most distributed applications, yet the design and implementation effort entailed in providing such a capability would be prohibitive for an individual developer.

Third, DCE integrates components in a manner that makes them more valuable together than separately. For example, the DCE RPC uses threads in such a way that a developer can implement a multithreaded server without ever explicitly creating or destroying a thread.

Finally, DCE supports both portability and interoperability by providing the developer with capabilities that hide differences among the various hardware, software, and networking elements an application will deal with in a large network. For example, the RPC automatically converts data from the format used by one computer to that used by another. Portability is a measure of the ease with which a piece of software that executes on one type of computer can be made to execute on a different type of computer. Interoperability is a measure of the ability of computers of different types to participate in the same distributed system.

Generally speaking, if the software modules of a distributed system are portable, interoperability can be achieved by porting them to other computers as required. The converse does not hold. It is perfectly possible to build a distributed application that interoperates among a number of different types of computers but that is not in the least portable.

4.1.2   DCE acceptance

There are many other ways of describing DCE. DCE is a standard. DCE is a piece of software. DCE is a product. DCE is brand new. DCE uses proven technology. DCE is open. DCE must be licensed from OSF. All these descriptions have some truth to them.

The Open Software Foundation (OSF), which provides DCE to vendors, is a consortium of more than 200 companies. Membership is open to any organization, although it is not cheap. Guided by input from its members, OSF issued a Request for Technology (RFT) that invited any party to submit software components for a distributed computing environment. After a lengthy process, during which requirements were refined and various business and legal arrangements concluded, selections from among various vendors' submissions were announced.

All of the selected components existed as software in production use somewhere. The next step was to integrate the components into a cohesive system. In the process, some features were extended or changed. As a result, although the DCE components have been in use for various periods of time, DCE, as a whole, is a new piece of software.

DCE is a standard in several senses of the word. First, it conforms to a published specification for distributed computing called the *Application Environment Specification* (AES). AES documents both the software programming interfaces and also the communications protocols employed by DCE. Thus, it would be possible, in theory, for someone to build a compatible implementation without using the code from OSF.

Further, the X/Open Company, Ltd., has agreed to make the AES specification part of its Common Application Environment. Therefore, any vendor that wishes to identify its product as compliant with the X/Open Portability Guide (XPG) will have to provide a conforming implementation of DCE. Compliance with the XPG is generally considered to be a requirement for any product claiming to be an open system.

DCE's status as a de facto standard is even stronger. Almost every major hardware and software vendor has committed to providing DCE on its platform. These vendors include not only OSF stalwarts such as IBM, DEC, and H-P, but also other key vendors such as UNIX System Laboratories and Novell, Inc. In addition, a number of major user organizations (e.g., the European Economic Community) have already embraced DCE as their standard for distributed applications.

DCE implementations will not be limited to UNIX-like operating systems either. Such diverse systems as IBM's MVS and DEC's VMS will be able to run servers in a DCE environment. The popular desktop platforms—IBM-compatible PCs running Microsoft Windows and Apple Macintoshs—will also provide DCE support, although these systems will probably be limited to client-only implementations. In short, it is reasonable to predict that DCE availability will be nearly universal within the next few years.

DCE represents a departure from past standards efforts in two respects. First, in the past, many standards have served to codify existing technology. DCE provides functionality that is unavailable in any previous commercial product. Second, whereas most standards emerge as specification documents, DCE is a working implementation.

The latter point can be viewed negatively as well as positively. DCE licensing is open to anyone on an equal basis and the fee is certainly far less than what it would cost to replicate the functionality. Still, OSF controls the code and licensing terms. OSF's position is that it will work with anyone who wishes to reverse-engineer DCE from the AES, but that a vendor cannot label a product OSF DCE without having purchased a license. On the other hand, this is not so different in practice from the situation with some international standards that have been implemented by only a handful of vendors; most other vendors choose to license from those vendors rather than start afresh.

From these circumstances one can conclude that OSF DCE will be the dominant environment for distributed systems in the 1990s and beyond. To adopt DCE will be beneficial to end-user organizations, software vendors, and hardware vendors alike.

End-user organizations will benefit from the ability to choose from a broad range of software and hardware products that will be DCE-compliant and from the lower prices of a competitive market. They also will benefit from the advantages of portability and interoperability mentioned above. If they build their own applications to run over DCE, they will gain not only the technical advantages described above, but also an increased ability for their applications to interoperate with off-the-shelf software packages.

Software vendors who build applications that run over DCE will benefit from the ability to operate in many environments, thus gaining a much larger potential market. They also will benefit from being able to make use of the DCE technology to solve technical problems that they would otherwise have to deal with themselves.

In addition, they will benefit from the ability to interoperate seamlessly with popular products from other software vendors. Most importantly, DCE will give them opportunities to introduce totally new categories of products that were not previously feasible because of the lack of a standard distributed systems environment in sufficiently widespread use. It is difficult to predict what the distributed system's equivalent of the spreadsheet will be, but it will surely run over DCE.

Hardware vendors will benefit from providing DCE on their platforms because it will enable a large body of existing software to run on their systems and networks with no additional development effort. They can avoid the risk of spending a lot of money to develop DCE-like services only to find that a competitor's scheme has become the de facto standard. Hardware vendors also will have the opportunity to differentiate themselves by creating extensions to DCE and tools for using DCE, beyond those provided by OSF.

4.2   DCE Components

DCE consists of a number of distinct components. These can be thought of as services or subsystems. Each component is relatively distinct from the others and can be understood in isolation. Although the components are integrated, they can generally be used alone. However, the greatest benefits from DCE come when the components are used in combination.

4.2.1   The DCE Remote Procedure Call

The DCE *Remote Procedure Call* (RPC) facility is at the heart of DCE. RPC makes distributed application development easier by modeling two distributed processes as a subroutine and the caller of that subroutine. RPC is a syntactic model that embodies the client/server flow model. The subroutine is the implementation of the server, and the caller of the subroutine is the client. The subroutine parameters represent the data passed from the client to the server or returned from the server to the client.

The DCE RPC provides three basic services that the application developer would otherwise have to implement. First, it provides the communications facilities required to communicate between the client and the server. Second, it provides the mechanism that allows the client to locate the server within the network. Third, it transports the data across the network and converts it from one format to another as needed. This is an important feature, given the different internal formats for data such as integers, floating-point numbers and characters that are in use in different computers.

4.2.2 The DCE Directory Service

The DCE *Directory Service* provides a reliable mechanism by which distributed applications can associate information with names. Its primary purpose is to allow clients to locate servers. Its capabilities, however, are general-purpose, and it can be used in any application that needs to make names and their attributes available throughout a network. Some examples would be applications that associate user names with addresses and telephone numbers, printer names with location, and software products with vendor and licensing information.

The DCE Directory Service consists of two components: the *Global Directory Service* (GDS) and the *Cell Directory Service* (CDS). Each implements a hierarchy of names, that is, a set of names arranged in a tree structure in which every item has exactly one parent and zero or more children. The CDS provides naming within a local set of nodes called a *cell*. The GDS provides global naming services over multiple cells. Each CDS appears as a branch somewhere in the GDS tree. This is illustrated in Fig. 4.1.

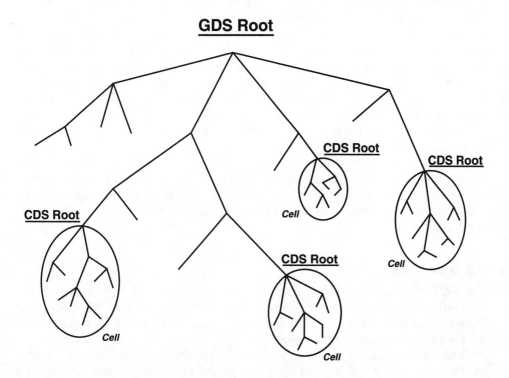

Figure 4.1 Each cell is a branch in the global directory tree.

The GDS complies with the X.500 international standard for a naming service. That means that organizations that use DCE can connect their networks to other private or public networks to access services that conform to X.500, without having to make any changes to their own software. Ultimately, most of the computers in the world may be interconnected, providing easy access to an enormous range of services, but with each organization still able to control its own resources.

Currently, the Internet uses a set of naming protocols known as the *Domain Name Service* (DNS). In DCE, the CDS can use DNS as a global directory service instead of GDS. This allows DCE users to participate in computer communities that exist today and to make an easy transition to X.500 once its use becomes more widespread.

The DCE Directory Service implementation is designed for use in production distributed systems. Although all users see a single consistent tree of names, or *namespace,* the actual directories are distributed and replicated and make use of caching, because if the Directory Service became unavailable there would be no way for users to locate services in the network.

As a distributed namespace, the Directory Service actually consists of multiple independent database files, located on different computers, implementing different parts of the tree. This means that portions of the namespace are autonomous and can continue to function even if a hardware failure partitions the network.

Replication means that multiple copies of the same naming information are stored on different nodes. The Directory Service protocols provide mechanisms to ensure that the copies remain identical as changes are made. Administrators can control the number of copies and their location. Replication provides reliability, as it eliminates a single point of failure. It also improves performance because naming information can be read from the nearest copy, reducing both network traffic and the load on any given database file. It does increase the work required to update, but this is a favorable tradeoff because, normally, reading is far more common than writing.

The caching capability means that Directory Service clients can retain the results of a query. If the same name is referenced again, there is no need to consult the directory server again; the name is immediately available in the cache. This results in performance gains in the common case of repeated references to the same items.

4.2.3   The DCE Security Service

The DCE *Security Service* provides mechanisms to ensure that services are made available only to properly designated parties, without inconveniencing legitimate users. The need for this is obvious, especially as interconnection of networks becomes more widespread.

There are basically three parts to the security problem. First, it is necessary to establish with certainty that users, dispersed at various locations in a network, are the persons they claim to be. Second, it is necessary to securely determine what kind of security privileges are associated with those users. Third, it is necessary to check those privileges against the operation the users wish to perform. For example, suppose a user asks to read an accounting database. The Security Service determines: the user is John Smith; John Smith is an auditor; auditors are allowed to read the accounting database. These steps are called *authentication, authorization,* and *access control,* respectively.

Of course, computer operating systems provide such services for their own local users, but a distributed system entails many new problems. For one thing, we want the user to be registered just once for the whole network, rather than having to be entered individually on every computer in the network. For another thing, the nature of the network makes it difficult to know for sure where a message is coming from. Therefore, it is possible for an unauthorized user to send a message that appears to come from a legitimate user.

Further, a knowledgeable user can easily capture messages from a network, read confidential data and passwords, and even retransmit messages, with or without alteration, in order to fool clients or servers or even a security system itself.

Everything said previously about the need for a directory service to be robust and reliable goes double for a security system. If a distributed security system is correctly designed, there should be no way to access the other services on the network unless the security system is running.

The DCE Security Service solves all these problems with a robust set of capabilities. Like the Directory Service, the Security Service is distributed and replicated. It authenticates users and determines what they are allowed to do. It is immune to various kinds of attacks involving the capture and replay of messages. It never transmits passwords over the network. It provides a finer degree of control over access to resources than many other popular schemes.

4.2.4 The DCE Distributed Time Service

The *Distributed Time Service* (DTS) performs two basic functions. It keeps the clocks on all the computers within the network reasonably close to the same time, even when their hardware clocks do not run at exactly the same rate. Second, if any of the nodes in the network are connected to a public time service, such as the United States government's, DTS will keep all the clocks in the network reasonably close to that time.

The DTS operates largely behind the scenes, exchanging messages between nodes and adjusting the system clocks as needed. This is valuable for several reasons. The most important is that the protocols used by the Security Service assume that all the nodes on a network keep the same time. Certain types of Security Service messages include expiration times; if the system clocks disagree, then the messages may expire prematurely.

Aside from the Security Service requirements, it is an enormous convenience to have all the clocks synchronized. For example, programs such as "backup" or "make," which are controlled by comparing the creation times of different files, would not behave correctly in a distributed environment without universal time. Or consider a distributed application that is controlling a nuclear reactor. It might be vital to know if an increase in pressure caused a valve to close or if it was the other way around. It would be impossible to tell, unless the clocks of the computers used to read the pressure and close the valve were synchronized.

4.2.5 DCE Threads

DCE *Threads* provides the ability to create, control, and synchronize threads. Threads are lightweight processes that are independently scheduled but share the same address space. DCE Threads is not a distributed service, in the sense that threads operate entirely on a single computer system. But the threads capability is an extremely useful one for developing distributed applications.

The most common use of threads is in a server. Each request handled by a server can be given its own thread and therefore proceed at its own speed. This allows the server to overlap I/O operations and make use of multiple processors, if they are available, thus improving response to client requests. Multiple threads can be used in other ways by distributed applications. For example, a multithreaded client can distribute portions of a compute-intensive problem to different servers, speeding the calculation.

Some operating systems provide threads as a native service. The DCE Threads implementation is provided by OSF for use with those that do not. The application programming interface (API), based on the POSIX.4a draft standard, ensures portability of DCE applications. Obviously, threads can be used to implement nondistributed applications as well as distributed applications.

4.2.6 The DCE Distributed File Service

The *Distributed File Service* (DFS) provides programs the ability to access files located on a file server just as if they were located on the local system's disk. The application does not have to know where the files are located or even that they are not local.

In concept, DFS is similar to Sun Microsystem's popular NFS found on most UNIX-like systems. It also resembles the many so-called network operating systems, such as Novell NetWare, Microsoft LAN Manager, Banyan VINES, and Apple AppleTalk. DFS, however, provides a number of additional features.

Possibly the most significant addition is DFS's single, consistent, global namespace for all files, provided by virtue of its integration with the Directory Service. This means that every node in the network identifies the same file by the same name and sees it located in the same directory. In other schemes, each client may see different device or directory names.

Another powerful DFS feature is data replication. DFS files can be replicated on two or more server nodes and DFS will maintain consistency between the copies. The number and location of the copies is controlled by the systems administrator.

DFS supports the full set of file operations, including file and record locking. DFS uses data caching at the client to improve performance and it provides a very rich access-control mechanism. It has an efficient mechanism to take a snapshot of the file system at any time, thus allowing complete tape backup even while the server is in use. DFS uses a logging mechanism to ensure file system consistency in the event of a system failure, without requiring the time-consuming rebuild operation typical of UNIX-like systems.

DFS is implemented on top of the DCE services described above. This means that DFS has all of the DCE portability and interoperability characteristics. Aside from its intrinsic value to users, DFS provides an excellent example of many techniques that are useful in the implementation of distributed applications.

4.2.7   The DCE Diskless Support Service

The DCE *Diskless Support Service* (DSS) provides the mechanism necessary to support nodes that have no local disk. Diskless systems provide advantages in lower purchase and maintenance costs, increased security, and simplified administration. Although diskless systems have been available for some time, no vendor-independent means of supporting them is currently in widespread use.

DSS consists of several different capabilities designed to meet the requirements of diskless systems. First, it supports the need for a diskless node to request and receive a copy of its operating system over the network and to receive the system parameters unique to the node over the network.

DSS also provides a mechanism by which a server can manage multiple sets of executable binary programs for use on client nodes that have incompatible processors. This allows all clients to access the same programs under the same names, even though the actual binary files are specific to the machine type.

DSS also allows diskless systems to perform swapping across the network and lets the DFS client cache use local main memory instead of local disk space.

It must be noted that the actual availability of these capabilities depends on hardware manufacturers to support DCE bootstrap protocols in PROM. There is no particular difficulty in doing this, so widespread availability seems likely.

Because DFS and DSS are not application development services, they are not discussed any further in this book.

4.2.8   Integration of DCE components

One of the major advantages of DCE is the integration of its components. In several cases, the normal use of a component is not explicit, but indirect, through another component.

A good example of this is Threads. Although there is a Threads API that allows the explicit creation and deletion of threads, the most common way to use DCE Threads is as an implicit consequence of using RPC. RPC automatically uses threads in servers. All the programmer has to do is to specify the maximum number of threads needed and to deal with data interactions, if any. As all the other DCE services are based on RPC, they all use Threads as well.

RPC was the basis for OSF's implementation of the Directory Service, Security Service, Time Service, and DFS. In turn, the Directory Service and the Security Service are seamlessly integrated into the RPC. The mechanism used by the RPC to connect a client to its server is the Directory Service. Client/server applications requiring security use the *authenticated RPC* implemented by the Security Service.

Figure 4.2 illustrates the dependencies among DCE components. The net result is a whole greater than the sum of the parts.

4.3   DCE Concepts

This section introduces a number of concepts that are important in DCE in the context of two or more DCE services. Some of them have other meanings in the context of other environments or products.

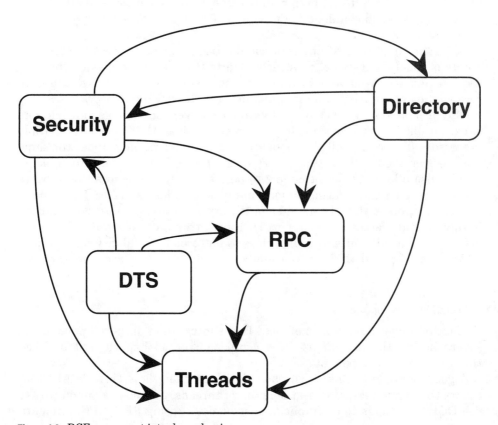

Figure 4.2 DCE component interdependencies.

Main Program

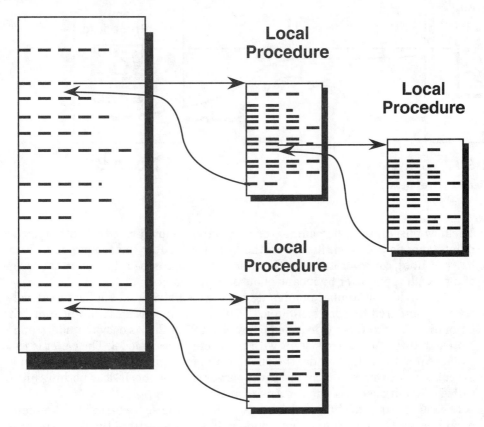

Figure 4.3 Local procedure calls.

4.3.1   Remote procedure call

A remote procedure call (RPC) is a syntactic model for developing a distributed application. An RPC mimics the syntax of a local (regular) procedure call in a programming language. Figure 4.3 represents the logic flow of a program that calls a local procedure. When the program reaches the point at which the procedure is to be called, control passes to the beginning of the procedure. Input arguments may be used, which have the effect of passing data from the calling program to the called procedure.

The statements of the procedure are executed and control is passed back to the point immediately after the procedure call. Data may be passed back from the procedure to the caller either as the value of the procedure or by means of output arguments.

In an RPC, the same general flow occurs, but the calling program and the procedure execute on different nodes. Figure 4.4 illustrates the flow of an RPC.

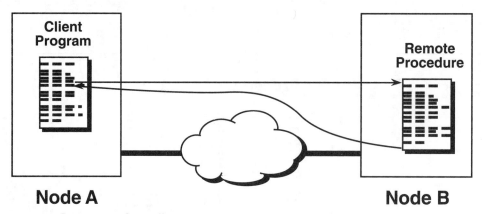

Figure 4.4 Remote procedure call.

The flow passes from the point of the call to the remote procedure. Input arguments may be provided, just as in the local case. After the remote procedure has executed, control returns to the caller. Results can be returned in the form of a procedure value or by means of output arguments.

RPC provides a number of advantages to the distributed application developer as compared to older techniques. It packages network communications in a familiar syntax. It provides a logic flow discipline that is easy to understand. Notice that the flow is consistent with the client/server model. The caller is the client. After the call is made, the client waits for completion before resuming execution. The remote procedure is the server component. It does nothing until called. Then it executes and returns results.

Because all the machinery necessary to locate the server, establish communications, and transport data back and forth is hidden within the RPC, the programmer does not have to deal with these complexities, and the same program can operate over many different types of network protocols. The programmer also can deal entirely with familiar data types without worrying that they are represented differently on different types of computers.

There are differences between local and remote procedure calls, however. The most important is that in a local call, global data is accessible to both the caller and the procedure, and other kinds of global state are also available. For example, any open files can be accessed by the caller or the procedure. In the case of an RPC, only those items that are explicitly passed can be shared.

Performance is another issue when using an RPC. An RPC consumes both time and network and computing resources in executing. It would be foolish to call a remote procedure so short that the calling process took longer than the execution of the procedure. The amount of data to be transferred must also be considered. Moving data within a computer is orders of magnitude faster than transferring it over a network, even a LAN.

4.3.2 Client, clerk, server, and manager

The client/server model has been previously described in Chap. 1. In DCE, the *client* specifically refers to an application program that requests services more or less directly at the behest of a human being. In many cases, the node containing the client also contains a program called a *clerk*. Like a client, the clerk requests services from a server, but a clerk usually operates autonomously. Typically, a clerk updates certain local information periodically, based on the passage of time. Or the clerk may act as the result of messages received from servers or other clerks.

In DCE, the term *server* is used in two ways. It is used to refer to the entire program that handles requests from clients (or clerks). This program consists of a portion that is responsible for the interactions with the DCE environment and one or more portions that actually implement the remote procedures. The portion that sets things up and interacts with the DCE environment is also called the server and the remote procedures are called *managers*. This terminology seems a bit arbitrary, but must be understood in order to follow the DCE documentation.

4.3.3 Cells and LANs

The *cell* is one of the most important concepts in DCE. A cell is a group of networked nodes managed as a unit. Every node must be in exactly one cell. DCE recommends, but does not require, that the elements of a cell be topologically contiguous. A cell is defined by the Directory Service. The Cell Directory Service (CDS) directory describes the elements of exactly one cell. The cell is also very important to the Security Service, which distinguishes between requests made by clients in the same cell and those made from a *foreign* (different) *cell*.

In some cases, DCE treats things according to their location on the same LAN versus different LANs. For example, the Distributed Time Service differentiates sources of time information by their LAN location. This is because transmission delays on a LAN are both shorter and more consistent than those experienced over a wide-area network.

4.3.4 UUID

A very important DCE concept is the *Universal Unique Identifier* (UUID). A UUID is simply a long number (bit string), generated in a manner that ensures it will never be duplicated. At OSF they like to say that UUIDs are "unique in time and space." This may sound a little metaphysical, but it describes how they are implemented. One part of the UUID is derived from the current date and time. This is done in such a way that even if two UUIDs are generated at nearly the same time they will be different values. The other part of the UUID is a number which is guaranteed to be unique to that node.*

UUIDs are used to label things so that they can be identified with certainty. Their most elementary use is to ensure that a client and server using RPC have exactly the same definition of their interface. They are also used to identify objects in the network, such as printers or databases. Internally, DCE uses UUIDs to identify everything that it deals with. UUIDs are used to identify users, groups, nodes, cells, etc.

The concept of a unique identifier is a very powerful one. As networks around the world become more and more interconnected, it is vital that it be possible to unambiguously distinguish one item from another, even though they may have been created by different people at different times. UUIDs are well suited to this purpose.

A DCE application development environment will provide a utility program and library routines that can generate UUIDs. UUIDs are conventionally written as a string of hexadecimal digits separated by dashes like this:

```
005E9AC0-486D-1B6C-B747-0000C07C3610
```

4.3.5 Access Control Lists

An *Access Control List* (ACL) is a data structure that controls the ability to perform an operation.† ACLs are a part of the Security Service, but also are used by DFS and other DCE components. The operation and use of ACLs is described in detail later on. The basic idea is that somebody wants to do something to some object. The "somebody" might be a person or a program. The object has associated with it an ACL. The ACL specifies the operations that can be performed by every class of user. For example, all users might be allowed to read; some particular user might be allowed to write; the owner of the object might be allowed to change the ACL. DCE defines and uses a number of types of ACLs and provides mechanisms to implement new types to protect new types of objects.

4.3.6 Handles

The concept of a *handle* will be familiar to some readers—simply an opaque piece of data (meaning we should not pay attention to what it contains) that is used to refer to something. Typically, we call a routine that returns a handle that refers to something. Later, we pass the handle to other routines that need to refer to the same something.

---

* Generally, this is the permanent hardware address built into the network adapter. There are already registration schemes in place to ensure that these addresses are never duplicated.

† ACL is often pronounced AK-el.

If you are comfortable with C language pointers, you may wish to think of a handle as a pointer. (This is how handles are usually implemented.) The difference is that we are only allowed to store and copy handles. We cannot perform other operations that we might perform on pointers, such as subtracting one from another or incrementing them. It is not even legal to compare two handles to see if they refer to the same thing. It is possible that the same object could have handles with different values.

4.4   Chapter Summary

The DCE is a set of vendor-supplied software tools and services for developing distributed applications. DCE has been integrated by the Open Software Foundation and is now licensed as source code. DCE goes beyond what has been available for developing distributed applications by providing new capabilities, integration of the services, and a standard to facilitate portability and interoperability that has received the backing of a range of vendors.

The seven components of DCE are the Remote Procedure Call, the Directory Service, the Security Service, the Distributed Time Service, Threads, the Distributed File Service, and the Diskless Support Service. These are structured upon the concepts of the remote procedure call, client and server, as defined by DCE, as well as a number of other concepts common to the integrated components, including the clerk, manager, cell, the Universal Unique Identifier (UUID), Access Control Lists (ACLs), and handles. The development services, the first five components, are discussed in detail in the following chapters. DCE is or will be available on practically every computer and operating system in widespread use today.

5

The DCE Remote Procedure Call

This chapter is the first of three describing the DCE Remote Procedure Call (RPC) facility of OSF DCE.* It begins by discussing the purpose and benefits of using RPC. Much of what is said applies to any RPC, not just the DCE RPC. Next, we will take a look at how the DCE RPC actually works at runtime, including the various components involved and their relationships to each other. At this point, a number of important RPC-related concepts are explained, as well as some specialized terms used throughout the DCE documentation.

The rest of the chapter, and Chaps. 6 and 7, deal with implementing distributed applications with the DCE RPC. First, we take an overall look at DCE RPC application development, including the process and the software components involved. A very simple application is presented to give a feel for what a DCE application looks like. Chapter 6 describes how to use the RPC tools: **uuidgen**, IDL, and ACF files. Chapter 7 describes the library facilities, first those used by clients and then those used by servers.

Throughout, the intent is to be extremely pragmatic. Capabilities most likely to be useful are described most fully. Features or options that are expected to be rarely used, or that are of limited value, are described briefly or omitted. As much as possible, the purpose or intended use of each feature is described. In certain instances, we recommend for or against using certain features.

5.1 Overview

In many ways, the Remote Procedure Call (RPC) is at the heart of DCE. The DCE RPC is the one service that a software developer must use to create a distributed application with DCE. RPC is the way that DCE implements the client/server model. RPC is the tool that was used to implement the clients and

---

* DCE RPC is based on NCS RPC, which was developed at Apollo Computer. (Apollo is now part of Hewlett-Packard.)

servers of the Cell Directory Service, Security Service, Time Service, and Distributed File Service. Developing distributed applications with DCE mostly involves the libraries and utilities associated with RPC.

The basic idea of the remote procedure call is simple. Any well-structured program is organized into *procedures*. These are also called *routines* or *subroutines*. In the C language they are officially known as *functions*, but in practice all four terms are used interchangeably. A program begins execution in a main program that calls subroutines that, in turn, call other subroutines. Figure 5.1 illustrates this.

Executable Program

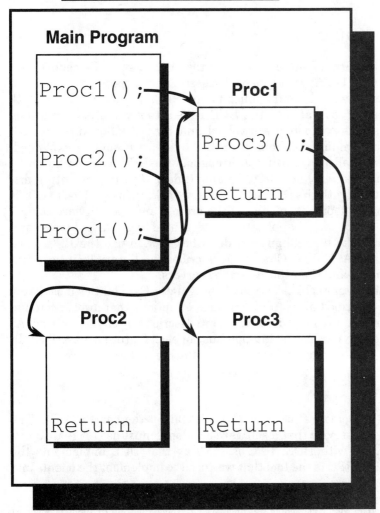

Figure 5.1   Local procedure calls.

A remote procedure works the same way, except that the calling program and the procedure execute on different network nodes. The logical flow of a remote procedure call is shown in Fig. 5.2. Just as in the local case, program execution transfers from the calling program to the remote procedure at the point of invocation. The procedure executes, and control returns to the point just after the call. Arguments provided by the caller work just as in the local case. Results can be returned by means of arguments or as the value of the function.

RPC is a syntactic model which implements the client/server flow model. This means that the RPC specifies the syntax or language that allows the client and server to interoperate. The language is deliberately chosen to be similar to some familiar programming language. In the case of DCE RPC, this language is C.

An RPC uses the same flow model as local procedure calls do. The caller (client) blocks or waits until the procedure (server) completes execution. The client and server are never executing at the same time. This is consistent with the client/server model. Of course, the server may be working on more than one client request concurrently. This requires special considerations in designing the server, which are discussed later.

To be sure, many clients and servers have been implemented without using any RPC; an RPC just makes it easier. First, as mentioned earlier, the software

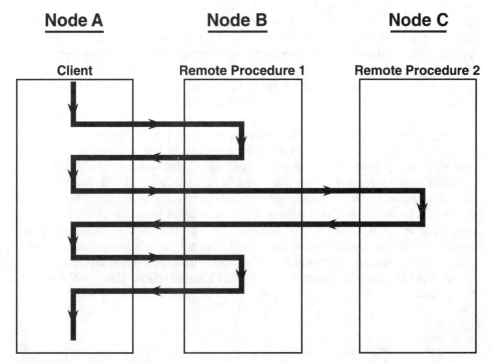

Figure 5.2 The flow of an RPC.

writer only has to deal with the simple logic flow of the familiar relationship between subroutines and their callers. This is an enormous simplification over other mechanisms for building distributed applications. For example, in many other environments, distributed application components must be designed to expect that messages may arrive from the network at any point in time.

In addition, an RPC simplifies client/server development and provides transparency in respect to the use of the network. Because it hides most of the mechanisms associated with use of the network, the application developer can largely ignore the network and focus on issues related to the application itself. This provides two kinds of benefits. First, there is less to think about, and fewer skills are required, thus reducing the learning required. Also, simplifying the application code reduces the potential for bugs, just as the use of higher-level languages eliminates some kinds of bugs.

RPC transparency means that the application developer is shielded from the details of the network type, computer hardware, and operating system being used. This means that the same application code will function correctly even if these change. This helps support the goals of portability and interoperability.

5.2   RPC Runtime Execution

In order to provide transparency, any RPC needs to perform three basic services at runtime. First, the client must be matched up with a compatible server somewhere in the network. Next, the RPC must invoke the communications mechanisms of the underlying network service in order to transfer data across the network. Finally, the RPC must take the data items used by the client and server and present them in the form expected by the program. Where dissimilar computers are involved, this may involve translating the data from one format to another.

The process by which a client locates an appropriate server is known as *binding*. Binding can be understood by analogy to the process of locating a business that provides some service, such as a gardening service.* First, the gardening service must advertise somewhere, such as in the yellow pages. Next, the person who wants the service must consult the listing. The information might be organized by the name of the company, type of service, location of service, or some other way. After looking through the listing, a particular gardening service company is selected. The listing contains information on how to contact the company—for example, its phone number. When the company is called, the call must be directed to the proper department. Each of these steps has an analog in the binding process.

---

* Fred Oldfield suggested this analogy.

5.2.1 RPC runtime components

Let's look at how DCE RPC operates. The server and the client each consist of a number of distinct parts. These are illustrated in Fig. 5.3. The client consists of the *client application code, client stub,* and *client runtime.* The client application is the program that the developer must write. It may or may not call various RPC service routines, but at some point it calls one or more operations that have been defined as the RPC interface. In other words, it makes the remote procedure call.

Of course, in a real application, the client might contain large amounts of other code that has nothing to do with RPC. For example, it might present the user with a graphical user interface, or perform complex mathematical calculations.

The stub, as we will see further on, is generated automatically by the RPC tools. The stub works together with the other component of the client, the client runtime, to provide the RPC services. Both are libraries that are linked together with the client application to create a single executable unit.

The distinction between the stub and the runtime is that the stub is specific to the particular client/server interface. For example, if the interface uses floating-point numbers, the stub will contain code to deal with them. In con-

Server

Client

Application Code
Client Stub
Client Runtime

Server Control			
Server Operation	Server Operation	Server Operation	Server Operation
Server Stub			
Server Runtime			

☐ *Provided by Developer*

▨ *Provided by DCE RPC*

Figure 5.3 DCE RPC components.

trast, the runtime is generic and provides capabilities needed by any client. One of the most important of these is the interface with the network software of whatever network is being used.

The server contains four major components. The *server stub* is generated automatically, just like the client stub. The server stub and the *server runtime* provide services of the RPC to the server just as the client stub and runtime do to the client. Note that the client stub and server stub for the same interface are usually quite different. This is because the typical interface is not symmetrical. Generally, the client passes certain data to the server and the server returns other, different, data as results.

The client and server runtimes are also different, because clients and servers require different services. For example, servers generally advertise over the network that they can do a certain thing and then wait for a client to make a request. Clients, on the other hand, ask to be connected to a server that can do a certain thing.

The other two components of the server are the *server control* and *server operations*. The server control code makes the calls to the RPC that are necessary for the overall operation of the server. These are usually fairly similar in any server, regardless of its function. In the OSF documentation, this component is referred to as the *server*. This seems potentially confusing, so this book uses the term *server control*.

The server operations provide the application-specific capabilities of the server. They are, in fact, the actual remote procedures. There is one for each procedure supported by the server. The operations may or may not make any calls to the RPC routines or other DCE routines. There is a separate procedure provided for each operation supported by the server. In the DCE documentation, these routines are called *managers*. This book uses the term *server operations,* to avoid confusion with several other things in DCE which are also called managers. Like the client, the server consists of a single executable unit created by linking together the stub, runtime, server control, and each of the server operations.

5.2.2   DCE RPC execution flow

Now let us take a look at the sequence of steps that occur when a remote procedure call is made. This section omits some details in order to give the reader a feel for the general process. Some of these steps occur only on the first call and some occur every time. Later, we will examine in detail what actions must be performed by the client and the server to make these steps happen.

Normally, the client and the server would execute on different nodes on the network. Figure 5.4 shows the steps involved.

The server is started first. In a production environment, it would be started automatically, probably when the node is brought up. Execution begins in the server control portion of the server with several initialization steps. These

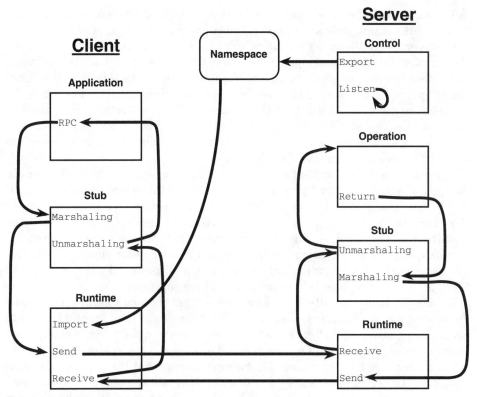

Figure 5.4 RPC execution steps.

include registering the server in the namespace. In DCE terminology, the server *exports its name*. This corresponds to our example of the gardening service advertising in the yellow pages.

At the end of initialization, the server calls a routine that causes it to wait indefinitely for requests from clients. Normally, the server control routine does not execute any further. It has done its job.

Sometime later, a client begins to execute somewhere in the network. It may perform many functions unrelated to DCE, but at some point it makes a remote procedure call. The stub and client runtime together must perform several actions before the server can be invoked. First, they must locate a server compatible with the client. This is referred to as *binding*. It is analogous, in our gardening example, to the person looking through the yellow pages and selecting a gardening service. The runtime routines that have to do with the use of the DCE Directory Service for the purpose of storing and retrieving binding information are collectively called the *Name Service Interface* (NSI).

As DCE can run over different communications protocols, it is also necessary to identify a protocol that both the client and server can support. Using the information that the server previously exported, the client stub and runtime locate all the compatible servers. If there is just one server, it is easy.

However, DCE allows for the possibility that there is more than one server that implements the same operations. One possibility is that several servers, equivalent in other respects, control different resources. In this case, the client needs to bind to the server that controls a particular resource. For example, the user might want to print on the printer just down the hall or access the database associated with the local region. DCE allows particular resources (objects) to be uniquely identified, so that clients can bind to the appropriate server. This is known as the *object model for binding*.

The other possibility is that there are multiple servers available that are in fact interchangeable. For this case, DCE provides the *service model for binding*. In this case it may be desirable to select the servers in a preferred order. For example, one may be on a node that is closer to the client's node or may be executing on a particularly powerful processor. DCE provides something called a *profile,* which allows servers to be assigned a priority for selection. Profiles can be associated with individual users, groups of users, all users on a given LAN, all users in a given cell, or whatever is appropriate.

If there is truly no difference between servers, one can simply be chosen more or less at random. It is also possible for the designer of an application to invent some other way of choosing a server. For example, servers could measure how busy they are and bindings could be directed to the least-busy server.

Once a binding has been selected, it simply means that the client knows how to contact the server. The next step is to actually establish communications with the server. There are some differences here, depending on whether the underlying network service is connectionless or connection-oriented, but the principle is the same in either case. A two-way communications channel is established between the client and server which allows them to exchange messages. This corresponds to calling up the gardening service in our binding analogy.

Now the data to be provided as input to the RPC is collected. This step is called *marshaling*. The data, along with information about its format and the actual operation requested, is packaged into a message and sent over the network to the server. The data transmission format used by DCE RPC is called *Network Data Representation* (NDR).

At the server, the runtime receives the message. The first step, called *unmarshaling,* is to unpack the data. Since the client and server may be running on machines that use different data formats, the data is converted if necessary. This conversion strategy is called *receiver makes it right.** It is very

---

* Technically, NDR is a multicanonical data format scheme. What this means is that there is a (short) list of formats in which data may be sent without necessitating any conversion. The goal was to include the native formats of most modern CPUs. It is possible that machines with unusual architectures might have to perform conversion during marshaling.

advantageous for the client and server to use the same representation, because no conversion needs to be done. (If data is always converted to a standard format, it may be necessary to do two conversions even when transmitting data between identical machines.)

A thread for the remote procedure to execute in is allocated, and control is passed to the particular operation that the client has requested. The mechanism used is called an *Entry Point Vector* (EPV). The EPV is simply a table of pointers to each of the server operation routines. The server operation routine does the required processing and writes any return data, just as any subroutine would.

When the routine exits, control returns to the server stub. Any data that should be returned from the procedure, including the function return value, is marshaled and transmitted back to the client. This is the end of processing at the server for this particular remote procedure call.

Back at the client, the data is unmarshaled and, if necessary, converted. Control is returned to the client at the point immediately following the call, as with any local procedure call. If the underlying network service is connection-oriented, the connection will be kept open for use on further calls to the server. Whichever type of network service is used, binding will not occur again.

Using RPC is like using a local procedure call in many ways, but there are important differences. Remote procedures can only use data that has been explicitly passed as routine parameters. Local procedures frequently access global data, file descriptors, environmental variables, and other kinds of data that cannot be used in a remote procedure call. For this reason it is usually not feasible to convert an existing program into a client/server application simply by converting the subroutines into remote procedure calls.

Another difference is that, as we have seen, calling a remote procedure involves a number of steps. These steps consume time. Therefore, there must be some benefit to having the client and server processing performed on different nodes. Otherwise, the only accomplishment will be to make the application take longer.

5.2.3 DCE RPC concepts

It is important to understand a few key concepts used by OSF RPC. One is the *interface,* already mentioned above. The interface is a set of remote procedure call operations and associated data. Every interface contains one or more operations. An operation is an actual remote procedure. Each operation may have input and output parameters associated with it, just like any procedure call.

A server may support more than one interface. A server that supports a given interface, however, must implement all of the operations contained in that interface. There are no such restrictions on a client. A client may call any number of operations within any number of interfaces. An interface usually contains a set of operations that are related in some way. For example, an interface might contain operations to open, close, read, and write a database.

The RPC's use of the DCE concept of the Universal Unique Identifier (UUID), introduced in Chap. 4, is also important to understand. A UUID is a 32-digit hexadecimal number (128 bits) which is guaranteed to be unique for all time. That is, if the proper procedure is used to create a UUID, no other person (or the same person at a later time) will ever create the same UUID. The UUID is written in this form:

XXXXXXXX - XXXX - XXXX - XXXX - XXXXXXXXXXXX

where the Xs are the hexadecimal digits 0,1,2,3,4,5,6,7,8,9,a,b,c,d,e,f.

UUIDs can be used for anything, but they have two main uses with RPC. First, every RPC interface is identified with a UUID. The UUID is known to all clients and all servers that support that interface. The UUID is part of the information exported by the server. In the discussion of binding, it was said that the client stub locates all compatible servers. The UUID (combined with a version number) is the key to determining that a client and server are compatible.

When the object model is used for binding, UUIDs are used to identify the objects. The server associates a UUID with each unique resource that it controls. When a client makes a request, it specifies the UUID of the particular object that it is interested in. DCE ensures that binding selects the server associated with that object.

Another RPC concept is the *server endpoint*. When binding to a server, it is necessary to identify a protocol that both the client and server can support and the node where the server is located. This information is relatively static and will not change even though the server and the node may restart.

In addition, it is necessary to identify which program running on the node is the server. This address-within-node is called the server endpoint. The endpoint corresponds to a concept provided by the underlying network protocols. In TCP and UDP, it is called a *port;* in DECnet, an *object number*. In the garden service analogy, the endpoint is like the telephone extension of a particular department.

One way for the client to find the endpoint is to arrange for the server to always use a certain prearranged endpoint. This is referred to as a *well-known endpoint*. This is all right for servers that are system or network utilities present on every node. However, it would be extremely wasteful to reserve endpoints for the thousands of application servers that might exist within an organization's network. Only a couple might reside on any given node. Further, an administration would have to maintain a central registry to avoid conflicts.

DCE's simple solution is to use *dynamic endpoints*. All this means is that the server is assigned an endpoint whenever it starts executing. A special service on each node, called the *endpoint mapper,* keeps track of the endpoints the servers on that node are currently using. This eliminates the need to update the distributed namespace every time a server is initialized. During the binding process, the endpoint mapper is consulted by the client to locate the endpoint. Once it has been discovered, further binds can occur without the help of the endpoint mapper.

5.3 RPC Development Process

Now we will consider the steps involved in actually developing a DCE application. This process is depicted in Fig. 5.5. First the interface is defined by creating a file called an *interface definition*. This ensures that the client and server will work properly with each other. Then the client and server are imple-

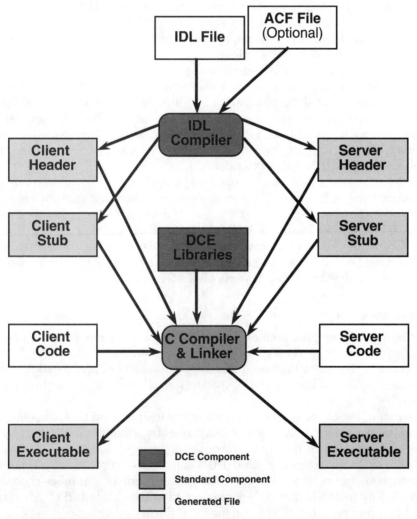

Figure 5.5 DCE RPC development process.

mented. These are two separate steps, which can be done in either order and on different computers that possibly have different hardware architectures. Typically, the server is implemented once and many different clients are implemented over a period of time.

5.3.1   Defining the interface

The first step in defining a new interface is to obtain a UUID. DCE provides a utility program called **uuidgen** to create a UUID for you. **uuidgen** puts the UUID in a text file that is in the proper format for an interface definition.

The next step is to use a text editor to create a complete interface definition. This is done by using a language called the *Interface Definition Language* (IDL). The IDL is a language that uses C-like syntax to declare the attributes of the interface, its operations, and parameters. IDL does not contain any executable statements, only declarations.

The interface definition is compiled using an IDL compiler. The compiler generates an **#include** (.h) file that contains function prototypes for all the operations and other data declarations defined in the interface. This file can (and should) be used by both the client and the server. The IDL compiler also generates a client stub file and a server stub file. Depending on the attributes specified, the IDL compiler may also generate client and server auxiliary files, which are conceptually part of the stubs.

The interface definition can be modified by optional use of an *Attribute Configuration File* (ACF). An ACF controls aspects of the interface that are purely local to the client or the server. Different ACFs (or none) can be used on the client and the server. Different ACFs can be used on clients or servers that run on different hardware platforms. In other words, all compatible clients and servers must be built from the same IDL file, but each client environment and each server environment can have its own ACF.

5.3.2   Implementing the client

The client is a C program created and compiled in the usual way. The program must include the .h file created by the IDL compiler. This contains the function prototypes for the actual remote procedure calls (server operations) defined in the interface. This is the only DCE-specific item that *must* appear in the client source file.

The rest of the client is an ordinary application program that, at some point during its execution, makes one or more remote procedure calls that, by and large, look and act just like local procedure calls.

Of course, there are many other DCE capabilities that the client can take advantage of. For example, the client can use any one of a number of sophisticated binding methods, multiple threads, and authenticated RPC. All of these useful features require calls to various DCE library routines.

Once the client program has been compiled, it is linked with the client stub files created by the IDL compiler and with the client runtime library. When this has been done, the client is complete and ready to execute.

5.3.3   Implementing the server

Implementing the server is a little more complicated than implementing the client. Like the client, the server is a C program that incorporates the outputs of the IDL compiler. The server source code must include the .h file generated from the interface definition. The server will ultimately be linked with the server stub generated by IDL and with the runtime libraries provided for servers.

The server control is usually the main program of the server. It contains a number of calls to DCE library routines that are necessary to initialize the server and inform the world of its existence. The server control may also contain other utility routines, such as routines to clean up failed sessions (called *context rundown* routines).

The server contains a server operation routine for every operation defined in the interface. These routines actually implement the operations and need not contain any special DCE-specific code. Their main potential complication is that each call to the server will generate a separate thread. This means that care must be taken about any data that might be accessed by more than one thread at a time. This subject is discussed in detail in Chap. 12.

5.4   A Simple Client and Server

Now let us take a look at a simple RPC application, just to get an idea of what it looks like. For now, we will ignore most of the details; they are covered later. This application simply takes a number typed into the client and sends it to the server. The server adds 1 to it and sends it back. Then the client prints out the result.

Figure 5.6 shows the IDL file for the application. The name of the interface is "simple." The interface is identified with a UUID and version numbers. The interface supports just one operation, called "simple_operation." There are just two parameters, one input and one output.

Figure 5.7 shows the client. All it does is take a number as an argument, pass it to the remote procedure and print the number that is returned. Notice that except for the line:

```
#include "simple.h"
```

it looks like a nondistributed application program.

Figure 5.8 shows the server. The server also contains:

```
#include "simple.h"
```

```
/* SIMPLE.IDL */
[
uuid(004C4B40-E7C5-1CB9-94E7-0000C07C3610),
version(1.0)
]
interface simple
{
    void simple_operation(

        [in]  long x,
        [out] long *y
    );
```

Figure 5.6 Example IDL file.

```
/* SIMPLE_CLIENT.C */

#include <stdio.h>
#include "simple.h"

main(int argc, char *argv[])
{
idl_long_int x;
idl_long_int y;

if   (argc < 2 )
    {
    x = 1;
    }
    else
    }
    x = atol(argv[1]);
    }

simple_operation(x, &y);           /* This is the Remote Procedure Call
*/

printf("The answer is: %ld.\n",y);
```

Figure 5.7 Example RPC Client.

```
/* SIMPLE_SERVER.C */

#include <stdio.h>
#include <dce/rpc.h>
#include "simple.h"

#define ERR_CHK(stat, msg) if(stat != rpc_s_ok)\
    { fprintf(stderr,"Error: %s in file: %s at line %d.\n",msg,__FILE__, __LINE__);
        \ exit(1); }

/***** Server Control *****/

main()
{
error_status_t      status;
rpc_binding_vector_t *bindings;
unsigned_char_t      *name = "/.:/applications/simple";

rpc_server_register_if(simple_v1_0_s_ifspec, NULL, NULL, &status);
ERR_CHK(status,"Could not register interface");

rpc_server_use_all_protseqs(rpc_c_protseq_max_regs_default, &status);
ERR_CHK(status,"Could not use all protocols");

rpc_server_inq_bindings(&bindings, &status);
ERR_CHK(status,"Could not get binding vector");

rpc_ns_binding_export(rpc_c_ns_syntax_default, name, simple_v1_0_s_ifspec, bindings,
                      NULL, &status);
ERR_CHK(status,"Could not export bindings");

rpc_ep_register(simple_v1_0_s_ifspec, bindings, NULL, NULL, &status);
ERR_CHK(status,"Could not register endpoint");

printf("Listening for requests\n");

rpc_server_listen(rpc_c_listen_max_calls_default, &status);
}

/***** Server Operation *****/

void simple_operation(idl_long_int x, idl_long_int *y)
{
*y = ++x;
```

Figure 5.8 Example RPC Server.

near the beginning. Error checking is done using a macro called "ERR_CHK". For simplicity, the name of the server in the namespace is hard-coded to be:

```
"/.:/applications/simple"
```

The server control portion of the server is the main routine. It performs six steps, each of which is a call to an RPC library routine. In each routine call, the last argument is a status variable that indicates success or failure. This is immediately checked using the "ERR_CHK" macro.

The first step is to register the interface that was defined in the IDL file with the RPC runtime. The trick here is that the symbol "simple_v1_0_s_ifspec" has been generated by the IDL compiler, using the name of the interface and the version number.

Step two is to get the RPC runtime to generate binding information for one or more available protocols. We could have specified some particular ones but, instead, we chose to use all available ones.

The third step is to get binding handles for each of these protocol sequences. Handles are the way that DCE manipulates binding information. Since there may be more than one set of binding information, multiple handles may be needed. This is done by using a one-dimensional matrix (vector) of binding handles. Amazingly enough, this is called a *binding vector*. In practice, the whole binding vector is treated as an opaque data structure, just like the handles themselves. It gets filled in by one library routine and passed on to other routines.

Step four is to make the server known to the world. This is done by putting all the binding information in the namespace, under the name of the server. In DCE terminology, we *export our bindings*. Notice that "simple_v1_0_s_ifspec" is passed in addition to the binding vector. This ensures that the server's UUID will appear in the namespace so that only compatible clients get connected. As was mentioned previously, we chose to hard-code the name of the server. Other alternatives include using a command-line argument or environmental variable.

Actually, in step four we did not quite export all the information necessary for a client to find us. The missing piece, the endpoint, identifies the server within a particular node. Therefore, step five is to make a call to register our endpoint with the endpoint mapper.

The sixth and final step is to wait for client requests. The call to **rpc_server_listen()** will never return under normal circumstances. Instead, the thread will be used by the runtime to initiate new threads to service client requests by executing the server operation routine. The first parameter specifies the maximum number of threads that will be concurrently active servicing requests. In this example, we have chosen to use the default.

Near the bottom of Fig. 5.8 is the server operation. Notice that the name of the routine is the one specified in the IDL file. It looks just like a local procedure call and works the same way. In our example, it does something trivial, but in a real application the server operations might be the major part of the code. Notice that because the server operation uses no data except for its arguments, it can safely be run in multiple concurrent threads.

5.5   Chapter Summary

This chapter is the first of three explaining how DCE RPC works and how to use it. RPC is the foundation on which the other components of DCE are built as well as the means of developing new distributed applications. RPC implements the client/server flow model by mimicking the syntax and general behavior of a local procedure call.

The runtime components of DCE RPC are the client application code, the client stub, the client runtime, the server stub, server runtime, server control, and server operations. Working together, they allow a client to connect to a server (binding), transfer data across the network, and present it to the application software in native format (marshaling). DCE allows binding to occur based on the identity of the server (service binding model) or based on the objects the server implements (object binding model).

The process of developing a distributed application consists of creating an Interface Definition Language (IDL) file and of coding the application portions of the client and server. The example application shown in this chapter illustrates the necessary code. The next chapter describes IDL in greater detail. The following chapter discusses the library routines used by clients and servers.

6

Defining the RPC Interface

In the previous chapter, we presented an overview of the steps involved in implementing a client and a server, and presented a simple program to give a general feel for the elements involved. A key step in building a DCE RPC application is to define the interface between the client and server. This is done by means of the Interface Definition Language (IDL) and an optional Attribute Configuration File (ACF). This chapter describes IDL in detail and explains when to use each of its features. The chapter also describes how an ACF may be used to tailor the interface for a particular client or server. The use of the **uuidgen** utility, which generates UUIDs, and the IDL compiler, which processes IDL and ACF files, is also explained.

6.1 The Interface Definition Language

The Interface Definition Language (IDL) is the key to building client/server applications using DCE RPC. The IDL file for each RPC defines the interface between the client and server and ensures compatibility between them. The IDL compiler reads the IDL file and creates the .h and stub files from it. However, it would be worthwhile to generate an IDL file even if it just served as documentation!

IDL has a syntax that is similar to C. It has many of the same rules as C about the construction of identifiers, separators, terminators, and comments. One important difference is that IDL has only declarations, no executable statements. The other difference is that IDL declarations can be preceded by attributes inside of brackets. A typical IDL declaration looks like this:

```
[attribute1, attribute2] type name { declaration1; declaration2 }
```

or like this:

```
[attribute1, attribute2] type name ( declaration1, declaration2 )
```

Attributes are special properties associated with the thing being declared. Generally, they specify something that DCE needs to know to make the RPC operate correctly. (A number of attributes are intended to provide backward compatibility with NCS Version 1. All of these attributes begin with **v1_**, for example **v1_string**. These attributes are not discussed any further in this book.)

6.2   The UUID Generator

Usually, the first step in building the IDL file will be to employ a utility program DCE provides, **uuidgen**, that generates UUIDs and provides the essential content of the interface declaration. This needs to be done only when an interface is defined for the first time, but it is important that the UUID is created in such a way that it is unique.

On a system with a POSIX.2 (UNIX-like) human interface, the command would be:

```
uuidgen -i -o simple.idl
```

where "simple" is the name of the interface to be defined. This would generate a file called simple.idl, containing something like this:

```
[
uuid(005E9AC9-486D-1B6C-B747-0000C07C3610),
version(1.0)
]
interface INTERFACENAME
{
}
```

The next step is to edit this with a text editor to create the rest of the IDL file. The text INTERFACENAME is replaced by the actual interface name, "simple" in the example.

The **uuidgen** utility can generate UUIDs in a couple of other formats as well. It can generate them all by themselves, or in the form of a C language initializer. Creating an IDL template is the most common use of **uuidgen**.

UUIDs can also be created from within a program by calling the library routine **uuid_create()**. This would be useful in a server that creates objects dynamically and uses UUIDs to identify them, for example.

6.3   The IDL File

The IDL file is constructed with five declarations, which make up the *interface definition*. They are the *interface declaration, constant declaration, typedef declaration, import declaration,* and *operation declaration.* Each of the IDL declarations is described below, along with its attributes and other considerations for its use.

6.3.1 The interface declaration

An IDL file begins with the *interface declaration*. Usually it will be generated using the UUID generator, as described above. After editing it looks like this:

```
[
uuid(005E9AC9-486D-1B6C-B747-0000C07C3610),
version(1.0)
]
interface simple

{
  more declarations...
}
```

The interface declaration begins with attributes, followed by the keyword **interface** and the name of the interface. It is followed, within braces, by the other declarations.

The interface name can be any valid identifier, but should be descriptive. The recommended convention is for the IDL file to have the same name with an extension of **.idl**.

The **uuid** attribute is the first attribute of the interface. As we have seen, it is usually generated using the UUID generator. As described earlier, the RPC runtimes use the UUID to ensure that the client and server are compatible. Binding will never occur between a client and server that have different interface UUIDs.

Another important interface attribute is the **version**. The version consists of two numbers separated by a dot. The first is the major version and the second is the minor version. Like the UUID, the version is used in the binding process. A client and server are compatible only if their major versions are the same. In addition, the minor version of the server must be newer (higher) or equal to that of the client.

The logic behind this is that in some sense the server "owns" the interface. That is, it implements the service and determines how it works. The client must take it or leave it. Thus, the server is never modified to respond to changes in the client, but the client may need to be modified if incompatible changes are made to the server. So when modifying the server, the rule is: if the changes are upwardly compatible (old clients will still work), increment the minor version number only. If the changes are not upwardly compatible, increment the major version number and set the minor version to zero.

There are three other interface attributes in IDL. The **local** attribute is mutually exclusive with the UUID attribute. It specifies that the call is not a remote procedure call at all. No stub code is generated. This attribute does not seem very useful. Presumably it is intended for testing purposes, but it is perfectly possible to test a client and server on the same system.

Another interface attribute is the **endpoint** attribute. This is intended for the case where a well-known endpoint is used and therefore does not apply to most interface definitions.

The last is the **pointer_default** attribute. DCE RPC provides two distinct types of pointers, *full pointers* and *reference pointers*. These are discussed later on in this chapter. This attribute establishes a default pointer type for the interface definition as a whole. If this attribute is not specified, it is necessary to declare the type of each pointer when it is defined.

6.3.2   The constant declaration

Four kinds of declarations are allowed within the body (between the braces) of the interface definition. The first of these is the *constant declaration*. Constant declarations look like this:

```
const int BIG = 999999;
const boolean BOGUS = FALSE;
const char TAB = '\t';
const char* HELLO_STRING = "Hello, world\n";
const void* NULL_PTR = NULL;
const int LARGE = BIG;
```

This is the same syntax as ANSI C. Constants are used to give mnemonic names to values used elsewhere in the IDL file. They are particularly useful when the identical value must appear in several places—for example, in several arrays that need to be the same size. By assigning the value to a constant, you ensure that all the values will be the same.

Constant declarations also improve the readability of code, either C or IDL. Prior to ANSI C, the standard technique was to use macros (**#define**) to accomplish the same thing. Constants are better for several reasons. In IDL, the most important reason is that there are no macros.

The only allowed constant declarations in IDL are integer (8, 16, and 32 bits, signed or unsigned), boolean, character, string, and null pointers. The usual C language syntax is used for specifying values. The names of the constants can be any valid IDL identifiers, but it is recommended that all capital letters be used. This is consistent with standard C programming style. Note that the value of a constant can also be a previously defined constant.

6.3.3   The typedef declaration

The next kind of declaration that can appear in the body of an interface definition is a *typedef*. A typedef declaration is a way of creating a new data type and giving it a name. Later, actual data objects of this type can be declared. This is similar to a C typedef.

The main reason for using a typedef in IDL is because you have some kind of special data type that you plan to use in several operations. For example, suppose the interface being declared contains operations to read and write payroll records. First, you would define the format of payroll records using a typedef. Then each of the operations would have parameters that were declared to be counted strings.

Here are some examples of typedefs:

```
typedef int number_t;
typedef struct {
  long int date;
  int employee_id;
  long int pay_amount;
} payroll_record_t;
typedef [string] char name_t[21];
```

The syntax is like C except that, as usual, there can be attributes in brackets. One attribute is the **handle** attribute. This is provided for sophisticated applications that for some reason find the built-in handle type **handle_t** unsatisfactory.

Another typedef attribute is **transmit_as**. This is used when you want to provide your own routines to convert between the data formats used within the client and server and the data format used over the network. You might want to use this if you were manipulating large sparse arrays, for example. In sparse arrays, most of the elements are zero. Therefore, you might want to implement your own scheme for transmitting just the nonzero elements.

Other attributes are **context_handle**, **ref**, **ptr**, and **string**. Context handles are used to maintain the state associated with a client from call to call. The **ref** and **ptr** attributes indicate which of the two types of RPC pointers is being declared. The **string** attribute indicates that the array contains a string. All of these attributes are discussed more fully later in this chapter.

After the attributes comes the actual declaration. As in C, there are two flavors of types: *base types* and *constructed types*. They mostly correspond to familiar C types, with a couple of additions: **byte** and **handle_t**. Since different C compilers generate different-size variables for built-in C types like **int**, RPC provides a set of declarations that are guaranteed to be compatible with the corresponding IDL types. These are listed in Table 6.1.

Just as in C, the characters [ ] can be used to declare arrays and * can be used to declare pointers to the data types. There can be multiple [ ]s and *s that follow the usual rules of precedence and can be grouped using parentheses. What is not allowed is using () to define a function. Functions within an interface must be explicitly defined as operations, which are described later in this chapter.

The IDL constructed types are: **struct**, **union**, **enum**, and **pipe**. The first three are similar in concept to the C constructs with the same name. Pipes are a mechanism provided in DCE RPC to transfer data that does not fit conveniently in a single data structure. All four constructed types are discussed later in this chapter.

6.3.4 The import declaration

The *import* declaration makes declarations from other IDL files available in the current IDL file. It looks like this:

```
import "complicated.idl"
```

import looks like **#include**, but it is not the same. It imports only the constants and typedefs from the named file. The interface declaration and the operations are not imported. Import declarations can also be nested, so any constant or typedef declarations that were imported by the file we imported will also be available.

The import declaration is intended to allow different interfaces to share data-structure definitions. It should be used only when there is a strong need, as the excessive use of the import declaration, and especially of nested import declarations, could lead to a confusing tangle of file dependencies and the potential for inadvertently creating bugs when an innocent change to some upstream IDL file is made. If two interfaces are very closely related in their use of data structures, maybe they should be combined into a single interface. If an import declaration is going to be used, the safest approach is to create a definitions-only dummy IDL file that is never compiled, only imported by other IDL files.

6.3.5 The operation declaration

The most important and the most complex declaration is the *operation declaration*. This declares the actual operations (remote procedures) that make up the interface. The form of an operation declaration is similar to a function prototype in C, with the addition of attributes. Here are a couple of examples:

```
void simple_operation(
  [in] long x,
  [out] long *y
  );

[context_handle] void * open_database(
  [in, ref, string] char * database_name,
  [out] long * status
  );
```

Six operation attributes may be specified. Three of them—**ptr**, **context_handle**, and **string**—apply to the value returned by the procedure. In each, the declared "type" of the procedure must be an appropriate data type to go with the attribute. In RPC, if an operation returns a pointer it must be a full pointer (as opposed to a reference pointer). If the default pointer type in effect is reference, because of the value of the interface attribute **pointer_default** being **ref**, the **ptr** attribute must be specified on any operations that return pointers.

The **context_handle** attribute specifies that the operation returns a context handle. The operation must be declared to be of type: **void***. The string attribute indicates that the routine returns a string. The data type must be a **char** or **byte** array or pointer. Pointer types, context handles, and strings are discussed more fully later in this chapter.

Idempotent attribute.   The **idempotent** attribute is the first of three operation attributes that control what is called *execution semantics*. Execution semantics is a fancy name for the behavior provided by RPC when the remote procedure is actually invoked. If none of the three attributes is specified, the operation is said to have *at-most-once semantics*. This means that RPC will ensure that the operation will never be executed more than once for a given client call. If an error occurs, it will be reported, but there will be no attempt to automatically retry the operation.

This is useful, because often it would be a bad idea for an operation to be repeated inadvertently. For instance, if we are adding $10 to a bank account and an error occurs somewhere, it is clearly better to just give up and report an error than to run the risk of adding $20 to the account. Even if the operation has only partly executed, there is no way for RPC to tell how far it got. The safest strategy is to give up.

On the other hand, some operations will cause no harm if they are repeated. For example, consider reading the current balance in the bank account. If this fails, it would be nice to have the RPC automatically retry the operation. Such operations are called *idempotent*. (Idempotent comes from Latin roots meaning "same power.") The idempotent attribute tells RPC that it is safe to retry the operation. The concept of idempotent operations is very useful in distributed applications and is discussed at length in Chap. 16.

Broadcast attribute.   Normally, when a client binds to a server, the runtime establishes communications with exactly one server. If the operation has the **broadcast** attribute, the runtime will send the remote procedure call to every node on the same LAN. If there is a server on the node that supports a compatible interface, it will execute the operation. If there are any outputs returned, the runtime will deliver to the client only the results of the first response it receives. Responses received from any other server will be discarded. There is no way for the client to tell if the call succeeded or failed at other servers or how many servers there were.

Broadcast operations have several potential uses. As one example, imagine that there are some management servers that keep track of the current status of certain utilities programs. The utility programs might periodically report on their progress by sending a broadcast to all the management servers. If a server happened to miss one call, that would not be too serious; its table would be a little out of date, but could be updated at the next broadcast.

Another way to use broadcast would be in a situation in which a client needs a piece of information known to all of the servers. Suppose the client wishes to get the answer as quickly as possible and that the amount of network traffic is not a concern. The client could broadcast the request for information and simply use the answer from the first server that responds.

RPC always assumes that broadcast operations are idempotent. This makes sense, because the normal at-most-once semantics assume that the application will somehow recover if the operation fails. However, we cannot tell at which servers broadcast has succeeded or failed. Currently, broadcast semantics are supported only over connectionless protocols. In practice, that means the UDP protocol. While in theory this restriction could be lifted, it probably will not be any time soon.

Maybe attribute.   The final operation attribute is the **maybe** attribute. Operations with the maybe attribute cannot have any output parameters or return value. In fact, with a maybe operation, the client does not receive any response from the server at all. The call is not guaranteed to succeed. Even if it does succeed, the client cannot assume that it has completed at the time the remote procedure returns.

Maybe operations are useful for providing advisory information to servers, where there is no concern about lost messages. They can provide performance advantages, because the client does not have to wait for a response from the server. Like the broadcast operations, maybe operations are implicitly assumed to be idempotent.

Following the attributes is a data type specifier. This specifies the type of value returned by the routine. The type specifier can be a base type or a previous typedef. If the routine does not return a value, **void** must be specified. As mentioned previously, the operations attributes—**ptr**, **context_handle**, and **string**—all affect the interpretation of this declaration.

6.3.6   Parameter declarations

After the name of the operation, the formal parameters of the routine are declared in the style of ANSI C. It will come as no surprise that operation parameters can have attributes, which are specified inside brackets, prior to the type specifier. Here are some examples:

```
[in] long x,
[out] long *y,
[in, ref, string] char * database_name,
[in, out] complex_structure * cs
```

Two of the operation attributes, **in** and **out**, are generic to all parameters. They specify the direction the data is passed, from the point of view of the remote procedure (server). In other words, **in** parameters are passed from client to server and **out** parameters are passed from server to client. Parameters may also be declared as **[in, out]**. Every parameter must be declared as **in** or **out** or both. The other parameter attributes are specific to certain data types and will be discussed in conjunction with those data types.

The usual rules of the C language apply. All routine parameters are passed by value. Therefore, for output parameters to work properly, they must be in fact pointers to the item to be manipulated. This means that they must be declared as pointers or as arrays and when the remote procedure is called the argument must be either an explicit pointer or the address of the item.

Base data types. All parameters are either *base types* or *constructed types*. This section describes them as if they are being declared as operation parameters, but they could also be declared as typedefs.

The base types are listed in Table 6.1. The integer and floating-point types work just the way you would expect. The integer types can be declared to be unsigned, just as in ANSI C. (IDL does not allow the keyword **signed**, however, only **unsigned**.) These values are treated as numbers and are converted, if necessary, to match the native hardware that the program (client or server) is running on.

TABLE 6.1 IDL Base Data Types

IDL declaration	C declaration	Size in bits
small [int]	idl_small_int	8
short [int]	idl_short_int	16
long [int]	idl_long_int	32
hyper [int]	idl_hyper_int	64
unsigned small [int]	idl_usmall_int	8
unsigned short [int]	idl_ushort_int	16
unsigned long [int]	idl_ulong_int	32
unsigned hyper [int]	idl_uhyper_int	64
float	idl_short_float	32
double	idl_long_float	64
char	idl_char	8
boolean	idl_boolean	8
byte	idl_byte	8
void*	idl_void_p_t	
handle_t	handle_t	
error_status_t	error_status_t	

IDL will always generate variables of the number of bits indicated in the table. Unfortunately, in C, the sizes of types like **int** or **short** may be different on different machines. For that reason IDL provides its own set of type declarations, guaranteed to be the same as the corresponding IDL type. These types all begin with **idl_** and are listed in the table. They should be used in C programs whenever variables that will be used as arguments to remote procedure calls are declared. It is equally important to use these to cast constants to the appropriate type.

The **char** data type in IDL is like **char** in C, but it is assumed to contain characters in the native machine's character set. Therefore, the characters may be converted, from ASCII to EBCDIC, for example, by RPC. Boolean is an 8-bit quantity which is either zero or nonzero. It should not be assumed that any particular nonzero quantity will be preserved by RPC. If you want an 8-bit quantity to be sent as is, by RPC, use **byte**. IDL also provides **void**, which is usually used to declare generic pointers, for example:

```
void * p
```

The data type **handle_t** provided by IDL is the handle type used by all RPC routines that use handles. Finally, IDL provides an **error_status_t** data type for use with RPC library routines that return or manipulate an error status.

Arrays.   Like C, IDL allows the declaration of arrays by using [ ] after the identifier of a base data type. Multidimensional arrays can be specified by using multiple [ ]s. The syntax of IDL differs from C in two ways. First, as usual, the declaration can be preceded by attributes. Second, IDL allows upper and lower array bounds to be specified by separating them with **. ..** Here are some examples:

```
long x[12]
float y[-20..20]
[length_is(a)] short z[1000]
[string] char c[201]
```

The way arrays work in RPC, however, is quite different from the way they work in local procedure calls. In a local procedure call, only a pointer to the array is passed to the local procedure. The caller and the procedure both can operate directly on the same copy of the data. This, obviously, is not possible in an RPC. Instead, all of the data must be transferred across the network and a pointer provided to the local copy of the data. For this reason, DCE RPC provides several ways of specifying array elements.

The names of the array types are shown in Table 6.2. The simplest to use is the *fixed array*. The bounds of a fixed array are determined at compile time and the entire array is transferred over the network. This also involves the least

TABLE 6.2 IDL Array Types

Array types	IDL attributes
Fixed	\<none\>
Conformant	max_is size is
Varying	first_is last_is length_is

overhead for marshaling and unmarshaling. Arrays of less than 500 bytes or so should always be fixed. Currently, IDL requires that the lower bounds of all arrays must be zero. This is sufficient for C, but this restriction will be lifted in the future to allow the use of other languages, such as FORTRAN, which permit the use of nonzero lower bounds.

The size of a *conformant array* is determined at runtime. The basic technique is to use another variable to specify the length. The other variable must either be another parameter to the same operation or be a member of a structure of which the array is also a member. In IDL, conformant arrays are declared using either the **max_is** or the **size_is** attribute. They specify a variable used at runtime to determine the last element or number of elements, respectively. Conformant arrays are intended for situations in which the nature of the application dictates that the size of the array is unknown at compile time.

In contrast, *varying arrays* are used when a large array is in use locally (within the client or server), but only a portion of the array needs to be passed across the network. As with conformant arrays, additional variables are used to specify at runtime which elements of the array should be transferred. The rules for varying arrays boil down to the fact that the parts of the array that are transmitted must be contiguous in memory. That is why only the first dimension of a multidimension array may vary.

The attributes **first_is**, **length_is**, and **last_is** are used to specify the lower bound, the number of items, or the upper bound, respectively. Note that these attributes do not affect the indexing of the array. For example, consider this declaration:

```
[first_is(low), last_is(high)] long x[20]
```

If at the time of the remote procedure call, "low" is 3 and "high" is 12, ten elements of the array will be transferred across the network and they will be known to both the client and server as x[3], x[4], ... x[12].

The fourth kind of array provided by RPC is called an *open array* and is a combination of the conformant and varying types. It is a little difficult to imagine a practical situation that would require the use of an open array.

The other way of handling array length in RPC is by use of the **string** attribute. The string attribute is only used with one-dimensional arrays of characters or bytes. The idea is that the array can contain a variable-sized string and that RPC will determine the length of the string at runtime, using a method appropriate to the system and language type. At the present time, DCE RPC really only supports the C scheme of having a **NULL** byte terminate the string. For this reason, the array should be declared to be one item bigger than the largest string to be stored.

Pointers.   IDL also allows the declaration of pointers. As with arrays, the syntax is similar to that of C, with the addition of attributes. However, pointers in RPC are very different from their C counterparts. In C, a pointer is a convenient way to allow a procedure to access some data without having to copy the data. It is also the best way to manipulate data structures that are inherently dynamic, for example, linked lists.

With RPC, in order to make pointers work as operation parameters, it is necessary to transmit the data that the pointer points to across the network, store it somewhere in memory, and create a local pointer that points to it. This has a number of implications, the most important of which is that the declared type of a pointer will determine exactly what gets transferred.

Many C programmers are used to being fairly careless about declaring pointers to be of the proper type. Sometimes all pointers are declared as **void** *. Some compilers do not enforce type checking of pointers or, if they do, the tendency is simply to cast the pointer to the correct type when it is used. When using RPC, pointers must be declared properly.

Since the use of pointers in DCE RPC results in data copying, just as does the use of arrays and structures, the question arises: When should pointers be used? Pointers should be used when the data being pointed to is dynamically allocated. For example, consider a linked list of items created using **malloc()** and passed to a remote procedure one by one. Using a pointer is the only way to locate them in memory. On the other hand, if the data was stored in a static array or structure, it would be simpler and require less overhead to declare the data item as a parameter and pass it directly.

Another complication in using pointers in IDL arises from RPC's support of the two types of pointers: reference pointers and full pointers. The kind of pointer is selected by using the attributes **ref** or **ptr**. Reference pointers have less overhead associated with them and are intended to be used in the normal case where we simply want to pass some dynamic data item. Reference pointers have some restrictions as compared to full pointers. Reference pointers can never have a **NULL** value. Reference pointers cannot change in value during the remote procedure call. Also, it is impossible to tell if two reference pointers that are parameters to the same operation are the same by comparing their values. In other words, RPC treats each reference pointer separately, even if they point at the same data.

Full pointers do not have these restrictions. Full pointers can have a **NULL** value. If the remote procedure changes a full pointer value that is an output parameter or routine value, the change will be reflected back to the caller. Full pointers that point to the same data will have the same values, and full pointers can result in the return of dynamically allocated data. Full pointers cannot be declared as **out** only. If you want to use a full pointer as an operation parameter to return a value, declare it with the attributes **in**, **out**. In the client, before making the remote procedure call, set the value of the pointer to **NULL**.

Full pointers also require some care in handling of memory allocation. First, consider the server. In general, there is a problem with returning any dynamically allocated data in a remote procedure call. If the space is deallocated in the operation routine, the data cannot be returned to the caller. If, on the other hand, it is not deallocated, it will become unavailable for any future use.

The solution is to allocate the space by calling **rpc_ss_allocate()** instead of **malloc()**. (The **ss** stands for stub support.) Space allocated by **rpc_ss_allocate()** will automatically be freed up after marshaling has been done. Any dynamically allocated space used for inbound parameters will also be obtained from **rpc_ss_allocate()**. In the rare case that the operation needs to explicitly free space allocated by **rpc_ss_allocate()**, it can call **rpc_ss_free()**.

Now consider the memory allocated in a client in conjunction with a full pointer. The client should allocate the items to be passed using the standard memory allocation method, e.g., **malloc()**. The stub routines will deallocate this space using the standard routine, e.g., **free()**. When a full pointer has the **out** attribute, the stub routines will allocate space for the pointed-to items. It is the responsibility of the client application code to deallocate that space.

In contrast, a reference pointer simply points to a particular piece of memory which is big enough to hold the item in question. If a reference pointer has the **in**, **out** attributes, on return from the remote procedure it will point to the same place in memory, which will now contain the updated values. Similarly, in the server a reference pointer points to a particular piece of memory (allocated by the stub using **rpc_ss_allocate()**), which can be updated in place.

In general, use reference pointers when you simply want to pass some dynamic piece of data from server to client. Use a full pointer when the client and server both need to be able to manipulate some complex, dynamic data structure. When using a reference pointer, ensure that it points to valid storage (is not **NULL**) at the time of the remote procedure call.

Structure declaration. IDL provides four constructed data types: **struct**, **union**, **enum**, and **pipe**. The struct data type works just as in C. As usual, the members of the structure can have attributes. Here is an example declaration:

```
struct
{
handle_t hdl;
long vect[100];
[string] char msg_text[80];
[ignore] char * cp;
} strange_structure;
```

The **ignore** attribute is applied to a pointer to keep RPC from passing the pointer and the data it refers to across the network. This is very useful in the case that the structure is one item in some kind of list linked with pointers. If the ignore attribute was not specified, RPC would follow the pointers and pass the entire list. By using ignore, it is possible to pass just one item, without having to make a copy of it before the remote procedure call.

The other structure member attributes are the ones that apply to particular datatypes, such as pointers or arrays, and are described in the relevant sections. Generally structures work just the way you would expect. Structures are very useful for grouping together data items that relate to each other, for example, a pointer to some data buffer and the amount of data in the buffer. Putting these items in a structure is much clearer than making each a separate operation parameter.

There are some restrictions in defining structures in IDL. A structure may not contain a pipe. If a structure contains a conformant (variable-size) array, it must be the last member in the structure.

Union declaration.   In C, the purpose of a union is to be able to store any one of a number of data types in the same place. The program is responsible for keeping track of the type of data currently being stored. IDL also provides unions for the same purpose, but the mechanism for determining the current data type must be specified explicitly. This type of union is called a *discriminated union.* Here is an example:

```
union switch(small id_type) ui
  {
  case 1: long num;
  case 2: char name[8];
  } usr_id;
```

The basic idea is to generate a structure that contains both the discriminator variable and the actual union. In this way, the client and server will always be in agreement on which type of data is being passed. This technique is very useful for the common case in which the same operation can accept (or produce) several different record types, each of which has a field at the beginning in the same location that indicates which record format is being used. (This is similar to the use of the REDEFINES clause in COBOL.) For example, a banking server might read and write account records, customer records, and summary records. Note that in a real application, each of the cases would most likely be a structure rather than a single data item.

Unfortunately, the way this has to be done in C results in somewhat obscure syntax. The identifier that follows the switch ("ui" in our example) is used to create the structure that contains the discriminator and the union. The identifier after the braces ("usr_id" in the example) is the name of the union. Thus the code to test what type of data is in the union looks like this:

```
if (ui.id_type == 1) ui.usr_id.num ... \      /* its a number */
else if (ui.id_type == 2) ui.usr_id.name ... /* its text */
else                                          /* error */
```

The actual operation parameter would be the name of the structure, in this case "ui" (or a pointer to "ui"). The switch/case construct enables the stub routines to properly handle the transfer of data, but the client and server are still responsible for testing the value of the discriminator to determine the data format.

It would generally be a good idea to use an enum declaration to give mnemonic names to the cases, instead of using numbers. The enum declaration is described next.

Enumeration declaration. The enumeration declaration in IDL is almost the same as in C. It creates a new data type whose values can only be one of a list of identifiers. The first identifier is associated with the value zero, the second with one, and so on. In the union example given above, we could have used an enumeration like this:

```
typedef enum { NUM_TYPE, NAME_TYPE } USR_ID_t;
```

Then, later on, the operation parameter definition would look like this:

```
union switch(USR_ID_t id_type) ui
  {
  case NUM_TYPE: long num;
  case NAME_TYPE: char name[8];
  } usr_id;
```

IDL does not allow the use of = in the enumeration list the way ANSI C does.

Pipe declaration. The final constructed data type in IDL is the pipe. This should not be confused with the pipe facility found in POSIX.1 and other operating system environments. The general intent of RPC pipes is similar, but the details are quite different.

The basic idea of a pipe in RPC is that it provides a way of transferring data from client to server in pieces, instead of all in one lump as is usual for a remote procedure call. The pipe data type is constructed out of other data types: base or constructed. It does not have to be a series of bytes, but could be a series of numbers or structures or arrays. (It cannot be constructed from pointers or pipes.) Note that pipes must be declared using a typedef declaration.

Like any other operation parameter, pipes can be **in** (client to server) or **out** (server to client) or both. In either case, the process that is the source of the data must define a C routine that, whenever it is called, will provide the next bunch of data. The process that is the destination of the data must call a routine, provided by the stub, that collects the next bunch of data. In addition, the client must provide a routine that allocates buffers, regardless of whether it is an **in** or an **out** pipe.

When an **in** pipe is used, the flow of data from client to server is known as *pull;* when an **out** pipe is used the data flow is called *push.* Therefore, for an **in** pipe, the routine provided by the client and the routine called from the server are called the *pull routine.* Conversely, for an **out** pipe, the client calls and the server provides a *push routine.* These routines are what is known as *callback routines.* While it appears to the client and server as if they are calling across the network, the push and pull routines operate only locally.

Figure 6.1 illustrates the operation of these routines in conjunction with the stubs and runtimes. It is important to understand that the operation of the callback routines at each end and the transfer of data over the network is completely asynchronous. In fact, there is no guarantee that the chunks that the pull routine provides are the same size as the chunks that the push routine receives. All of the data will be received in order, however.

Eventually, the routine at the data source will provide an empty buffer, indicating the end of the data. Once all of the data has been delivered, the server will return from the remote procedure call. There are also facilities for controlling the state of the pipe and for raising exceptions in the event of an error. The use of asynchronous callback routines allows for efficient transfer of data, while at the same time potentially taking advantage of the data conversion capabilities of RPC.

RPC pipes are quite elegant. In spite of this, I recommend thinking twice before using them. There are two major categories of application for pipes. The

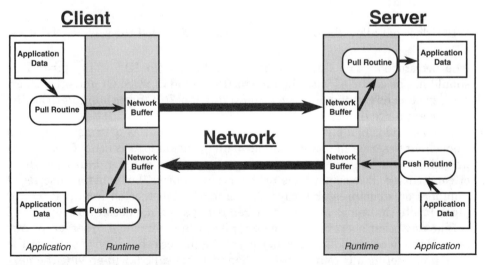

Figure 6.1 Operation of pipe data type.

first is to transfer files too big to fit in a single buffer.* In this case, rather than writing an RPC application at all, it will usually make more sense simply to use the file transfer capabilities provided by the network. (Any network protocols robust enough to support DCE will come with a file transfer utility.)

The other category of application in which pipes might be used is where data is being generated more or less continuously from some outside source. An example would be a device that measures temperature changes. The problem with this type of example is that it really does not fit the client/server model very well. Consideration should be given to using something other than RPC for an application of this type. Client/server and other distributed processing models are discussed further later in this book.

Context handles.   Quite frequently a server will need to associate some state information with a particular client. Usually this is because the server implements a number of operations that have some relationship to each other. For example, consider an interface that supports the operations open, close, read, and write. The open call specifies what object the other calls operate on. The server needs a way to locate some information that tells what has happened so far. This type of state information is called *context*.

It is not trivial for the server to identify the proper context for a given call, because it is serving multiple clients who may issue requests in any order and because the requests will be assigned different threads at random. With DCE RPC, the solution is to associate the context with a context handle. When the first call is made, the server allocates some kind of data structure that describes the current state of processing associated with that particular request and sets the context handle to point to it. When the call returns, the context handle is returned as an output. The client then provides the handle on all subsequent calls. This allows the server to find the appropriate context.

In IDL, context handles are declared by using a **void** pointer and the **context_handle** attribute:

```
typedef [context_handle] void * context_hdl_t;
```

The operation that should be called first would return a context handle either as the routine value or as an output parameter. The subsequent routines would be declared to have the context handle as an input parameter. The last operation should declare the context handle parameter to have both the **in** and **out**

---

* Ideally, it is better not to copy disk files from one node to another. It is better simply to access the data required and process it directly. As soon as you copy a file, you have two copies. The problems begin immediately. Which one is the authoritative version? What if both get modified in different ways? When can you safely delete one copy? What should they be named? How do you detect and handle errors that occur at various points in the process of transferring and processing the data? In spite of this, I recognize that in many cases, because of the need for compatibility with existing systems, file transfer is the best approach.

attributes. When this operation completes, the server should clean up whatever resources are associated with the context and set the context handle to **NULL**. When the client stub sees the context handle returned with the value of **NULL**, it will clean up at the client end. The operation declarations might look like this:

```
void first_op(
  [in, string] char * obj_name,
  [out] context_hdl_t * ctx);
void next_op(
  [in] context_hdl_t * ctx,
  ... );
void last_op(
  [in, out] context_hdl_t * ctx,
  ... );
```

It is important to know that context handles are associated by the runtime with specific servers. In DCE terminology, context handles carry binding information. In our example above, when "next_op()" is called, the runtime will ensure that the call goes to the same server that handled "first_op()". The different methods of binding by clients are discussed later.

A server that uses context handles should provide a context rundown routine. This routine will be called by the RPC runtime if the connection to the client is broken. The purpose of the routine is to clear up any resources associated with the context. Otherwise, the server would accumulate obsolete context information and perhaps eventually run out of memory or some other resource. The context rundown routine is identified by its name, which must consist of the context handle type name followed by **_rundown**. In our example, that would be "context_handle_t_rundown".

The rundown routine has one parameter, which is the context handle to run down. Naturally, the type of the parameter is the declared context handle type. If the server uses more than one type of context handle, it should provide a rundown routine for each one.

6.4   The Attribute Configuration File

When the IDL compiler is run it looks for a file that has the same name as the **.idl** file and an **.acf** extension, called an Attribute Configuration File (ACF). If the **.idl** file has any import declarations, IDL will also look for **.acf** files that correspond to the imported **.idl** files. An ACF is never required.

ACFs affect only the interaction between the local program (client or server) and the local stub and runtime. The use of an ACF allows an application to have a single interface definition that is the same for all clients and servers and, at the same time, to handle special cases that occur only in certain environments.

The syntax of an ACF* has the same style as that of IDL. The basic idea is that there is an interface header (which can be preceded by attributes) followed by an interface body. The interface body can contain typedefs, operations, parameters, and the **include** statement. The IDL import and constant declarations are not permitted. The typedefs, operations, and parameters are the ones from the IDL file that have some special ACF attributes. If the item has no special ACF attributes, there is no need to have it in the ACF.

Some of the ACF features control certain optimizations of the local stub; the others provide miscellaneous capabilities.

6.4.1 ACF optimization features

Several of the ACF attributes provide control over optimization. That is, they do not modify the way the application functions, only execution speed or memory utilization. The use of these features does not require changing the source code in any way. This means that you can decide whether or not to use them at a late stage in development, perhaps even after initial debugging.

Code / nocode. The **code** and **nocode** attributes make it possible to selectively suppress the generation of stub code for operations the client does not use. This could result in a (slightly) smaller executable program. These attributes have no effect on the generation of the server stub. **Code** and **nocode** can be used as either an interface attribute or an operation attribute.

The default is that stub code will be generated for all operations defined in the interface. If **nocode** is used as an interface attribute, it suppresses the generation of stub code for all operations which do not have the **code** attribute. If the **nocode** attribute is applied to an operation, it suppresses that operation. Obviously, it is illegal to use both attributes in the same declaration. Here is an example of the use of **code** and **nocode**:

```
interface database_access
{
[code] db_open();
[code] db_close();
[code] db_read();
[nocode] db_write();
[nocode] db_ioctl();
}
```

The **[code]** attributes are not strictly needed (in fact those operations could have been left out entirely), but it is better practice to clearly document what

---

* OSF uses the term "Attribute Configuration Language," but never abbreviates it to ACL because of the potential for confusion with Access Control List.

is going on. The fact that these attributes have no effect on server stubs is consistent with the notion that the server "owns" the interface and must implement all of it, while clients are free to use only those operations they need.

In_line / out_of_line.   The **in_line** and **out_of_line** attributes affect the stub code generated for marshaling and unmarshaling nonscalar* parameters. Normally, the IDL compiler generates marshaling code for all parameters in line. This means that if the same data type is used repeatedly, the identical code will appear in multiple places. If **out_of_line** is specified, the marshaling and unmarshaling code will be provided as a subroutine, which is called from wherever it is needed.

These attributes can be applied to either the interface declaration or to a typedef. They are applied in the same way as **code** and **nocode** and, like them, are mutually exclusive.

It makes no sense to use **out_of_line** unless the same type is used repeatedly. In theory, there is a performance penalty to using a subroutine (not so much the extra instructions associated with the call and return as the effect on the cache), but in practice this penalty is negligible as compared with the time required for a remote procedure call. Therefore, in most cases the savings in code size will not be worth the trouble entailed in using the **out_of_line** attribute.

Heap.   The **heap** attribute can be applied to either a typedef or parameter declaration. It causes space for the parameter to be allocated from the heap rather than the stack. This could be useful when large data structures are being used in an environment where stack size is limited. The heap attribute applies only to the server.

6.4.2 Other ACF features

The other ACF features are used for a number of different reasons. What they all have in common is that they affect only operations on the local system and are invisible to processes built using other ACFs.

Binding options.   Three attributes, **auto_handle**, **explicit_handle**, and **implicit_handle**, control the method of binding used by the client. All three may be used as interface attributes. In addition, **explicit_handle** may be used as an operation attribute. These attributes specify the method of binding to be used by the client. The three methods of binding are discussed in Chap. 7 in the section on client facilities. Automatic binding (**auto_handle**) is the default.

---

* Scalar data types are ones like **int**, **float**, or **char** that have a single value. Nonscalar types include arrays and structures that have multiple values. In C, a pointer would be a scalar, but recall that in RPC the use of a pointer implies that the parameter includes not only the pointer, but whatever it points to as well. Therefore, pointers are considered nonscalars.

Error-handling options.   Normally, in RPC, runtime errors in the server or in the network are reported to the client by raising an exception. An *exception* is a mechanism whereby control is transferred directly to a previously specified exception-handling routine instead of resuming immediately following the remote procedure call. Exceptions are sometimes called *traps* or *interrupts.*

In some cases it may be desirable to handle an error in a way that is specific to the particular call during which it occurs. This can be done by means of the **comm_status** and **fault_status** attributes. The **comm_status** attribute controls the reporting of communications failures and the **fault_status** attribute controls the reporting of server errors. Using these attributes in the ACF file causes the error to be returned either as the routine value or as an output parameter, instead of raising an exception.

If these attributes are used as an operation attribute, the error status will be returned as the value of the procedure. The procedure should be declared as **type error_status_t**. If the attributes are used as parameter attributes, they cause either an existing parameter defined in the IDL file or a new parameter to be used to return error status. The handling of errors by clients is discussed more fully in the section on client facilities.

Represent_as.   The **represent_as** attribute allows a client or server to treat a parameter as a local data type different from the type defined in the IDL file. The ACF specifies the local data type to be used. Routines must be provided to convert back and forth from the local type to the IDL-defined type. **Represent_as** is a typedef attribute that specifies a base or constructed data type to be used as the local representation. Here is an example:

```
typedef [represent_as(special_record_t)] record_t;
```

This capability is similar in concept to the **transmit_as** attribute in IDL. The difference is that **transmit_as** is intended for situations in which all of the clients and servers use a data type that, for efficiency or other reasons, is transmitted over the network in a different format. An example is a sparse array that has a large number of cells that are zero. It would be more efficient to transmit only the nonzero cells.

In contrast, **represent_as** is intended for situations in which a certain local system needs to represent some data in a different way from all of the other systems. Usually, this would be because the local hardware or operating system makes a certain data format more convenient or efficient to use. For example, suppose the local system has vector-processing hardware that expects vectors to be stored in a certain format.

Enable_allocate.   The **enable_allocate** operation attribute ensures that the server stub initializes the memory allocation routines. If the server operation routine calls **rpc_ss_allocate()** and **rpc_ss_free()**, it is necessary for them to be initialized before use. If the operation uses either a full pointer or any type with the **represent_as** attribute, then the initialization will occur, even if **enable_allocate** is not specified. However, it is still good practice to use the attribute as a form of documentation.

Include statement.   The ACF **include** statement does not do what you might think it does. The include statement does not cause anything to be included in the ACF or IDL file. Instead, it causes an **#include** statement to be placed in the source of the client and server stub files. The reason for using the include statement is that a **represent_as** or **implicit_handle** attribute refers to a data type that has not been defined in the IDL file. In this case, it is necessary to provide a **.h** file that contains the appropriate C typedef. The include statement looks like this:

```
include "special_defs";
```

Do not include the **.h**; the IDL compiler will tack it on to the end of the name. (Someday, IDL may support languages other than C.) Also, do not specify the directory where the file is located; this can be controlled by means of command-line options to the IDL compiler.

6.5   Running the IDL Compiler

The syntax of the command to invoke the IDL compiler depends on the local operating environment. In a POSIX.2 (UNIX-like) environment, the command would look something like this:

```
idl simple.idl -server none
```

This command causes IDL to compile the file "simple.idl" and generate a header file called "simple.h" and a client stub file called "simple_cstub.c". IDL will invoke the local C compiler facility (including any preprocessor) to compile the stub into "simple_cstub.o". Depending on the definitions in the IDL file and ACF, it may also generate an auxiliary file called "simple_caux.c", which will be compiled into "simple_caux.o".

In the example, the "-server none" suppresses the server stub files. If they were being generated, they would be named "simple_sstub.c" and "simple_saux.c". If your system has limits on the length of file names, when choosing the name of the IDL file keep in mind that the compiler will be creating the stub file names in this way.

The IDL compiler has a large number of options that modify its behavior in various ways. Here are some of the most useful.

client, server	Suppresses the generation of client or server stub or auxiliary files.
cstub, sstub, caux, saux, header	Specifies names for stub, auxiliary, and header files other than the defaults.
I	Specifies directories to be searched for import files.
no mepv	Suppresses the automatic generation of a server EPV (entry point vector). This is useful when using the object model for binding. If the server implements the operations for two or more object types, it must provide an EPV for each object type. In this case, the server will provide its own EPVs, rather than use the one generated by IDL. This is described in detail in Chap. 8.
syntax only	Causes IDL to check the syntax of the IDL file, but does not generate any output.

Other IDL options are available to modify the interaction with the local C compiler and preprocessor and to control the messages generated by the IDL compiler.

6.6   Chapter Summary

The principal tool for using DCE RPC to build distributed applications is the Interface Definition Language (IDL). The developer creates an interface definition, or IDL file, which defines the interface between a client and a server. The IDL compiler processes the IDL file and, if present, the Attribute Configuration File (ACF), and generates a header file and client and server stubs. IDL has a syntax similar to C, but consists entirely of declarations. There are no executable statements. As a result of the nature of distributed systems, many IDL constructs behave differently from their C counterparts.

There are five declarations in IDL. The interface declaration specifies properties of the interface as a whole. (The **uuidgen** utility can be used to create an initial interface definition template, which can then be edited like any program source code.) The import declaration provides the means to reuse definitions from other IDL files. The constant declaration specifies compile-time constants. The typedef declaration, like its C counterpart, creates new data types, which can then be used repeatedly.

The operation declaration is used to specify the characteristics of the remote procedures in a form similar to C function prototypes. IDL supports a rich set of data types that may be used in either the typedef declaration or as operation parameters.

The scalar data types, such as integer and floating-point numbers, correspond closely to their C counterparts and should be used in the same ways. The aggregate and constructed types, such as arrays and structures, are useful for statically allocated data. Because of the nature of remote procedure calls, they cannot be passed by reference but instead must be transmitted over the network between client and server. IDL provides a number of different ways to control which portion of an array is actually transmitted over the network.

Two kinds of pointers are used for passing dynamically allocated data. The reference pointer provides an efficient, but restricted, means of referencing some item of data. The full pointer provides the full generality of a C pointer and allows complex data structures, such as lists or trees, to be passed and to be restructured by the server.

IDL supports a pipe data type, which allows the transmission of a stream of data via callback routines, but which is not well matched to the client/server flow model. IDL has several special-purpose data types, including the error-status variable and the context handle, which are used to control the processing of the remote procedure call.

In addition to the IDL file, an optional ACF can be used to further modify the characteristics of the interface definition. The ACF allows the developer to specify certain local optimizations, how errors will be reported to the client, what method of binding the client will use, and other specialized aspects of the interface.

7

The RPC Runtime Services

The previous chapter explained the tools available to the programmer designing an application to use RPC. It explained how they work, how to use them, and when and when not to use them in creating the IDL file that defines the interface required by RPC to carry out a remote procedure call. This, our third chapter on RPC, explains the runtime facilities provided in DCE, how they work, and the circumstances in which they are used. The chapter first covers those facilities accessible at the client end. Then it explains the facilities available to aid the programmer in the greater amount of work required on the server side.

7.1 Facilities Used by a Client

As we have seen, the client can largely ignore the fact that it is calling a remote procedure. Once the interface definition has been created, the client simply includes the header file and calls the routines, just as if they were local library routines.

There are two areas, however, in which it is possible for the client to exercise considerable control over how RPC operates. The two areas are in the way that binding is done and in the way that errors are handled.

7.1.1 Binding methods

DCE allows clients to bind to servers by using the Directory Service or not. When the Directory Service is not used, the technique is called *string binding*. The basic idea is that the client obtains the name of the server and other binding information by some means, such as a user command or disk file. The information is converted to a string, and a special library routine is called to obtain a binding handle from the string.

This method is not recommended for production applications, because the ability to locate servers from a distributed directory service is one of the major advantages of using DCE. When the Directory Service is used, binding can be managed and administered effectively in a large-scale network. Properly designed clients and servers will continue to operate correctly in spite of changes to the configuration of the network.

To use the Directory Service, a client chooses one of three methods of binding to a server: *automatic binding, implicit binding,* or *explicit binding.* This choice is not visible in any way to the server; it affects only the client. The server initializes and exports its binding information to the namespace and waits to receive requests. The client binding method has to do only with how the client selects the binding information that it will use. In fact, different clients can use different methods to bind to the same server.

Automatic binding is the simplest to use. The RPC runtime is responsible for identifying compatible servers and selecting one. Not only is automatic binding simple to use, but if the call to the server should fail, the runtime will attempt to recover if possible. If the failure occurs before the server begins to process the call or if the operation is declared to be idempotent, the runtime will try to send the request to another compatible server, if one exists.

Automatic binding is recommended, unless there is some reason it cannot be used. The disadvantage to automatic binding is that the client has no control over how binding is done and cannot alter the method that the runtime uses to pick the server it will bind to. Another possible reason for choosing an alternative is that, in DCE Version 1.0, it is impossible to use automatic binding when using authenticated RPC.

Implicit binding and *explicit binding* allow the client to control the binding process. However, more code is required. The basic idea is that the client makes a series of calls to the RPC runtime to obtain binding information about servers that support the interface. The client decides which server to bind to and then uses the appropriate binding information to establish the connection.

The difference between implicit and explicit binding is that in implicit binding the client establishes a global variable containing the binding information, which is used by the runtime whenever it is needed. In the common case, where all the operations of an interface are supported by the same server, this is very convenient. All code dealing with binding can be located in one place in the client; the client sets up the binding information and then forgets about it.

With explicit binding, the binding information is passed to the runtime as a parameter to each operation. Explicit binding is useful in unusual cases, such as one in which different calls will be directed to different servers. For example, applications that perform a distributed computation would use this technique.

OSF provides a sample application of this kind with DCE, called *timop.* There is just one client. It breaks the calculation into little pieces and calls a number of servers, running on different computers, to do the work. The servers work simultaneously and, because it is multithreaded, the client can accept the results as soon as each arrives. The client gathers all the pieces together into a single result, which in theory has been calculated more quickly than if a single computer had been used for the server. The ability to explicitly bind each operation to different servers on different computers is critical.

Automatic binding and implicit binding are mutually exclusive, because they both affect all of the operations in the interface. In other words, either there is an implicit binding handle defined or there isn't. Explicit binding, on the other hand, can be used on any operation, regardless of how the other operations bind. Also remember that context handles, when used as input parameters, carry binding information.

Keeping all of this in mind, here are the rules for binding.

1. If the first parameter in an operation definition in the IDL file is a binding handle (has the type **handle_t**), explicit binding will be used for that operation. Use this method if all clients will use explicit binding for this operation.

2. If **explicit_handle** is specified (as an interface or operation attribute) in the ACF, then the client must pass a binding handle as the first parameter to the routine, in front of the other parameters defined in the IDL file. Use this method when explicit binding is only used by some clients.

3. If an operation has a context handle as a parameter, with the **in** attribute, the binding information associated with the context handle will be used to do explicit binding. (Rules 1 and 2 take precedence over this, but if the call contains a binding handle and a context handle that point at different servers, it is probably a bug.)

4. If the ACF contains the **implicit_handle** interface attribute, the client must set the specified handle variable to point at binding information before invoking any operations. When the operations are called, implicit binding will occur unless rules 1, 2, or 3 apply.

5. If nothing is specified, or if the ACF contains the **auto_handle** interface attribute, automatic binding will be done unless rules 1, 2, or 3 apply.

The use of an implicit or explicit binding handle requires the client to obtain binding information. The way to do this is to use one of two sets of routines designed for the purpose. Either call:

rpc_ns_binding_import_begin()

rpc_ns_binding_import_next()

rpc_ns_binding_import_done()

or:

rpc_ns_binding_lookup_begin()

rpc_ns_binding_lookup_next()

rpc_ns_binding_lookup_done()

In either case, the **_begin** routine is called first to initialize. Then the **_next** routine is called repeatedly, until an appropriate binding is found or until the routine returns a status of **rpc_s_no_more_bindings**. Then the **_done** routine is called to clean up.

The difference between the two sets of routines is that **rpc_ns_binding_import_next()** always returns exactly one binding. Use this call if you expect to use one of the first servers you find. The routine **rpc_ns_binding_lookup_next()** returns a vector containing multiple bindings. It is useful in the case where you expect to need multiple bindings, because you are calling multiple servers, for example.

How to select the appropriate binding is up to the application designer. Some of the possible methods are: choose the first one, use information provided by the user, use information from some file or database, use information stored in the namespace by the servers, choose one at random.

In summary, use automatic binding if you can. If you can't, use implicit binding, unless you need to access several different servers from a single client.

7.1.2   Error handling

The other area in which the client has flexibility in handling remote procedure calls is error handling. The basic choice is between handling errors by means of exceptions or by means of a returned error-status variable. This choice applies only to remote procedure calls. All of the RPC library routines return a status variable and cannot be made to generate an exception.

By default, remote procedures will report all errors as exceptions. The Attribute Configuration File (ACF) error-status attributes enable the use of error-status variables. The **comm_status** attribute governs the reporting of communications errors, for example, the error: **rpc_s_comm_failure.** The **fault_status** attribute applies to server errors, such as **rpc_s_fault_addr_error.** If these are used as operation attributes, then errors will be returned as the procedure value. Alternatively, **comm_status** and **fault_status** can be used to declare an output parameter to be an error-status variable. In either case, the result returned will be of type **error_status_t**.

When an error-status variable is used to handle errors that occur during a remote procedure call, processing flow resumes immediately after the call, whether or not there has been an error. The code must immediately check the value of the error variable and take action if an error has occurred. If no error has occurred, the variable will contain the value **rpc_s_ok**. This approach is most useful if there is a specific way to recover from specific types of errors. For example, if a call returns **rpc_s_comm_failure**, the client might immediately try to bind to another server. The program logic might go like this:

```
rpc_ns_binding_import_begin( ..., ctx, &sts);
ERR_CHK(sts,"Can't do binding");
```

```
do
{
rpc_ns_binding_import_next(ctx, bnd, &sts);
ERR_CHK(sts, "Can't find server binding");

sts = remote_op(bnd, arg1, arg2);

} while (sts != rpc_s_ok);

rpc_ns_binding_import_done( ... );
```

In this example, we are doing explicit binding and have declared the remote procedure **remote_op()** to return error status as its value. If the call fails, we get a binding to another server and try again.

When errors are handled by means of exceptions, then if an error occurs during a remote procedure call, processing flow does not resume immediately following the call; instead, it is transferred directly to a previously declared exception-handling routine. If no handler for this type of exception has been declared in the local scope, the current block or routine will be exited and a handler from the next level up invoked. This process is repeated until a handler of the proper type is found. This is known as *propagating the exception*. If no handler has been declared anywhere, the thread will be canceled. (In a single-threaded program, the process will be killed.)

Different kinds of exceptions can be handled separately, but there is no way to tell which call caused the exception. Exceptions should be used when the response to a certain kind of error is always the same. For example, if the client always prints an error message and exits when there is a communication error, it is convenient to declare an exception handler once, rather than check a status variable after each remote operation.

DCE provides a set of macros for handling exceptions.* The way they are defined somewhat limits the flexibility allowed to the programmer, but they are the only portable mechanism available in DCE for exception handling.

To use these macros, first insert **#include <pthread_exc.h>**, replacing **#include <pthread.h>** if it is present. (The actual macros are defined in **exc_handling.h**.) There are two general forms that can be used. The first uses CATCH macros.

```
TRY

    code which could raise exceptions
```

---

* The DCE exception-handling macros are based on and similar in operation to the TRY, CATCH, and FINALLY clauses in the Modula 3 language.

```
CATCH (exception type 1)

   code to handle exception type 1

CATCH (exception type 2)

   code to handle exception type 2

CATCH_ALL

code to handle any other exception types

ENDTRY
```

The second uses the FINALLY macro.

```
TRY

   code which could raise exceptions

FINALLY

   code to be executed whether or not an exception occurs

ENDTRY
```

It is unnecessary, but harmless, to put braces around each block of code. The TRY and ENDTRY macros mark the beginning and end of that location at which exceptions are detected and handled. Typically, they might occur at the beginning and end of a routine. The code following the TRY macro but preceding any CATCH, CATCH_ALL, or FINALLY macro is called the *TRY block*. In the same way, we refer to *CATCH blocks* and *FINALLY blocks*.

In the first form, the CATCH macro permits the handling of specific exceptions. If the exception specified as an argument to CATCH is raised anywhere in the TRY block, the CATCH block will be executed. The CATCH_ALL macro works the same way, except that it handles any type of exception that has not been handled by a previous CATCH block. Both the CATCH and CATCH_ALL macros are optional. The CATCH_ALL macro should always appear last. If there is no CATCH_ALL, any exceptions that are not handled by CATCH blocks will be propagated.

There is also a RERAISE macro, which can be put at the end of the CATCH or CATCH_ALL block. This is useful when you want to take some action when an exception occurs, and to propagate it as well.

Notice that the CATCH macro takes only one argument. This means if you want to handle two or more exceptions the same way you must write a subroutine and call it from both places. You cannot stack CATCH macros like **case** labels.

The second form of the TRY block uses the FINALLY macro. The FINALLY block will always be executed whether or not an exception occurs in the TRY block. The usefulness of the FINALLY macro is quite limited for two reasons. First of all, the two forms cannot be mixed. Therefore, if you wish to handle any exceptions you cannot use FINALLY.

Second, there is no way for the FINALLY block to determine where in the TRY block the exception occurred. This is a problem, because the FINALLY block may have to perform different cleanup actions, depending on how far the TRY block got before the exception occurred. Consider this example:

```
TRY
    op1();
    op2();
    op3();
FINALLY
    {cleanup code}
ENDTRY
```

Suppose that **op2()** allocates some data structure. The FINALLY block cannot tell whether or not it should deallocate it, because it cannot tell when the exception occurred.

There is also a RAISE macro, which allows a client or server to explicitly raise a particular exception. Normally, this is not necessary, because the RPC runtimes will detect communications or server failures and raise the proper exception.

Every error condition recognized by RPC has a symbolically defined error-status code and exception code. The form of these codes is **fac_?_error_type**, where "fac" represents the facility, such as **rpc**, **ept**, or **uuid**, and "?" is **s** for status codes and **x** for exceptions, and "error_type" describes the error. For example, if a remote procedure call takes too long, the exception **rpc_x_call_timeout** is generated or the status **rpc_s_call_timeout** is returned.

7.2 Facilities Used by a Server

We have already seen that the server has two kinds of routines that are generated by the application developer: server operations and server control. The server operations correspond to the operations declared in the IDL file. These are the actual remote procedure calls. By and large, these routines will consist of C language statements and standard library calls. Since servers are usually multithreaded, operation routines need to take special care in their use of data that might be accessed by more than one thread. This subject is discussed in Chap. 12.

Server operations generally need to be aware of the special characteristics of certain data types used as RPC operation parameters. In particular, arrays, pointers, and unions have characteristics that differ from their corresponding C language types. Server operations that need to maintain state from one call to the next should make use of context handles. These issues were discussed previously (Chap. 6).

Except for these considerations, server operations can largely ignore the fact that they are being executed as a remote procedure. The server control portion of the server, on the other hand, is devoted to dealing with the issues specific to the DCE RPC environment. The steps performed by the server control are discussed in the following sections, in the order in which the programmer will normally deal with them.

7.2.1 Registering the interface

The first thing the server control routine must do is to register the interface with the RPC runtime. This is done by calling **rpc_server_register_if()**. The purpose of this call is to tell the local runtime what interfaces are supported by this server and how to find the server operation routines. This call does not make the information accessible to any other clients or servers.

When the service model of binding is used, there will be exactly one set of routines that implement the server operations. When the object model of binding is used, there will be multiple sets of operation routines to support multiple object types. The rule is: call **rpc_server_register_if()** once for each object type supported for each interface supported. In the most common case it is called once.

There are three input arguments to **rpc_server_register_if()**. The first argument is a handle that specifies the identity of the interface. This handle is automatically generated by IDL and will have a name such as "simple_ v1_0_s_ifspec". In this example, "simple" is the name of the interface, "1" is the major version, "0" is the minor version (0.0 is the default), and "s" indicates server ("c" for client).

This handle refers to the following attributes of the interface:

- The UUID
- The major and minor version numbers
- The transfer syntaxes supported (currently DCE supports only NDR)
- Well-known endpoints (if the interface has the endpoint attribute)
- The default EPV (entry point vector)

The second argument specifies an object type, and the third argument specifies an EPV other than the default. These arguments are used with the object binding model, which is described later in the section on the Directory Service. When the service model is being used, these arguments should be **NULL.** The only output from **rpc_server_register_if()** is a status variable, indicating success or failure.

7.2.2   Establishing protocol bindings

DCE allows pairs of clients and servers to communicate over (potentially many) different protocols. However, for a client to successfully call a server, they must both use the same protocol. Fortunately for us, it is not necessary to implement the protocols; they are provided by the DCE vendor. But it is necessary for the server to specify the protocol or protocols it is willing to use.

The simplest way to do this is to call **rpc_server_use_all_protseqs()**. This causes the runtime to create binding information and the associated binding handle for every supported protocol. Clients using any of those protocols can then make calls to the server. An actual call will, of course, use only one. This routine has one input argument, which specifies the maximum number of simultaneous calls that can be handled on this protocol. Currently, DCE ignores this argument, so it is a good idea to use the default value, **rpc_c_protseq_max_reqs_default**, in order to ensure future compatibility.

The other alternative is to specify use of a particular protocol by calling **rpc_server_use_protseq()**. This would be necessary, for example, in the case of a broadcast operation that can occur only over a connectionless protocol. This routine takes an argument that specifies the protocol to be used. Like the previous call, it accepts (and ignores) an argument specifying the maximum number of calls. This routine can be called repeatedly to support more than one protocol.

Rather than just guess, the server may want to find out which protocols the local runtime supports. DCE provides two routines for this purpose. Call **rpc_network_inq_protseqs()** to get a list of supported sequences. Call **rpc_network_is_protseq_valid()** to test if a particular protocol is available.

If you are using well-known endpoints, there are three routines provided for creating protocol information. Use **rpc_server_use_all_protseqs_if()** to use all protocols and register the well-known endpoints specified in the IDL file. Use **rpc_server_use_protseq_if()** to use a particular protocol and register the well-known endpoints specified in the IDL file. Both routines take the interface handle as an argument (just like **rpc_server_register_if()**). The routine **rpc_server_use_protseq_ep()** lets you specify a well-known endpoint as an argument. When well-known endpoints are used, the endpoint mapper is not called, because clients are expected to know what the well-known endpoint is.

None of the five routines beginning **rpc_server_use_** return any handles; they simply cause the runtime to create the information. All of them return a status variable.

When the server is finished setting up the information for all the protocols to be supported, it calls **rpc_server_inq_bindings()**. This routine returns a vector containing all the binding handles that the runtime has created. This vector is used only to pass these to other library routines.

7.2.3 Exporting binding information

The next step for the server is to export the binding information to the Directory Service so that clients can locate the server. This is done by calling the **rpc_ns_binding_export()** routine. This routine takes five input arguments. The first argument specifies the syntax of the entry name for the server. Its value should be **rpc_c_ns_syntax_default**.

The second argument is the name in the Directory Service that the server entry will have. It is a character string. The format of directory entries is discussed in Chap. 8.

The third argument is our old friend the interface handle. This ensures that only clients with the same interface will bind to the server. The fourth argument is the protocol binding vector we obtained above. The fifth argument is used only with the object model of binding. Its use is discussed in Chap. 8. When using the service model, it should be **NULL**. The only output of **rpc_ns_binding_export()** is a status variable.

DCE RPC also provides a routine, **rpc_ns_binding_unexport()**, that removes an entry from the Directory Service. This should not normally be done, but the routine might be used if binding information changed for some reason.

7.2.4 Registering the endpoint

It is also necessary for the server to register with the local endpoint mapper. Recall that if the server is using dynamic endpoints, it will get a new endpoint every time it starts up. The Directory Service does not maintain the endpoint information. Instead, the endpoint mapper keeps track of the endpoints. Of course, if well-known endpoints are used, the client is expected to know the endpoint and this step is not necessary.

The call to register with the endpoint mapper is **rpc_ep_register()**. This routine takes four input arguments. The first two are the interface handle and the binding vector, just as in the previous call. The third argument is used with the object-binding model, which is described in Chap. 8. When the service model of binding is used, it should be **NULL**.

The fourth argument is a string of up to 63 characters that documents the purpose of this particular mapping. This string is not used by the endpoint mapper. It is intended to be displayed by management programs when listing the contents of the endpoint map.

Note that the currently assigned dynamic endpoints associated with each of the specified protocols are implicit arguments to this call. This means that only a server can register its own endpoints; no other process can do it. Like the other routines, **rpc_ep_register()** returns a status variable to indicate success or failure.

Another routine, **rpc_ep_register_no_replace()**, takes the same arguments and has the same purpose. The only difference is that if the interface already appears in the endpoint map, this routine adds the information instead of replacing it. This is useful if there are several servers supporting the same interface, running on the same node.

When a server shuts down, it should call **rpc_ep_unregister()** with the same arguments that it previously used in calling **rpc_ep_register()**. This will ensure that no invalid entries remain in the endpoint map. If this is not done, the endpoint mapper will eventually notice and remove the entry, but it is good practice to unregister before exiting.

7.2.5   Waiting for calls

Once all of these preliminaries are out of the way, the server can begin to accept remote procedure calls. It does this by calling **rpc_server_listen()**. This call does not return until the server is shut down. Incoming remote procedure calls are directed to the appropriate server operation routine via the EPV.

This routine has one input argument, which specifies the number of remote calls that can be in process concurrently. If the value specified is one, only one remote procedure will execute at any given time. The advantage of this is that it is not necessary to worry about synchronizing data access among threads. The disadvantage is that remote procedures will take longer, as there will be no overlap between I/O and processing. Also, it will be impossible to take advantage of multiple processors if they are available.

If the value of the argument is greater than one, then multiple calls may be in progress at the same time. This means that the server operation routines will have to provide synchronization of data access. The methods of doing this are described in Chap. 12. Note that data synchronization must be considered even if there is only one operation, because multiple calls from different clients could be in progress at the same time.

It is recommended that the value passed to **rpc_server_listen()** be quite large. By allowing all the pending calls to execute concurrently, the potential for overlap of processing an I/O is maximized. The value should be larger than the expected maximum number of concurrent calls. If more calls arrive at any given time than the specified maximum, they will be queued up and execute in the order they arrived. The size of the queue is implementation-dependent.

A server can arrange to shut down gracefully. The way this is done is for one of the server operation routines to call **rpc_mgmt_stop_server_listening()**. At this point, any new remote procedure calls to the server will fail. Any calls that are queued up or already executing will run to completion. Once all have completed, the call to **rpc_server_listen()** will return. At this point, the server control routine can perform any cleanup, such as calling **rpc_ep_unregister()**, before exiting.

7.3   Chapter Summary

A client and server obtain services from DCE RPC by calling library routines at runtime. The developer of a client can exercise control over how binding is done and how errors are reported. A client using automatic binding leaves it up to the RPC runtime to select the server. With implicit binding, the client selects a server binding, which is then used for every remote procedure call. With explicit binding, the binding is specified on each call. At the developer's option, remote procedure call errors can be reported to the client either as exceptions or via error-status variables. Exceptions can reduce the complexity of error-handling code, particularly when whole classes of errors can be handled in the same way.

Servers must perform a number of steps in order to make their services available to clients. For the most part, these are performed just one time, when the server first starts up. The server must register the interfaces it supports with the runtime in order to specify the location of the server operation routines. The server must establish the protocols that may be used to communicate with it. The server must export its interface to the namespace and to the endpoint mapper. The server must call **rpc_server_listen()** in order to begin accepting remote procedure calls.

The DCE Directory Service

One of the most valuable attributes a distributed system possesses is network transparency. Network transparency means that every resource within the distributed system looks just the same regardless of where it is accessed from. A user in Boston and one in San Francisco not only can access the same database on a server in Chicago, but can refer to it in exactly the same way. The benefits of this are enormous. The potential for various kinds of errors is greatly reduced, user training is simplified, network reconfigurations are invisible to users, users who travel can easily access the network from wherever they are, software design is easier, and on and on. Most people would agree that this is the natural way that things ought to work.*

Sadly, today, very few distributed environments provide much transparency. Frequently users must issue commands that depend on the current configuration of the network (e.g., sign on to X, then access gateway Y, etc.). The most popular schemes for sharing files across a network, such as NetWare or NFS, permit each node in the network to use a different name to refer to shared file directories.

One of the most important prerequisites for network transparency is a single distributed directory service that encompasses the entire distributed system. A distributed directory service allows processes to access a single consistent set of names that apply to every resource. Programs, users, databases, nodes, printers can all be identified by a name that is the same to everyone. Applications are freed from having to worry about propagating naming information and maintaining its consistency, because the directory service takes

---

* It is important to remember that sometimes transparency is not desirable. If I print out a memo, I want it to come out on the machine down the hall, not on the other side of the continent. The point is to hide the attributes of the distributed system that do not matter. Once transparency has been achieved, it is simple to make attributes, such as location, visible when it is appropriate.

care of it. Alone, a distributed directory service does not ensure network transparency, but having one represents a major and necessary step toward the goal.

DCE provides a distributed Directory Service that is integrated with its other components, particularly RPC and the Security Service. The Directory Service is replicated and designed to allow organizations to maintain and administer their own name service and, at the same time, seamlessly participate in interorganizational directory services such as the Internet Domain Name Service or private or public directory services based on the X.500 international standard.

As developers of distributed applications, we will use the Directory Service mainly as a means of allowing clients to bind to servers. However, in order to make best use of the Directory Service, it is useful to understand how it works. Further, the Directory Service is itself a distributed application, so we may find that some of the techniques used in its implementation are applicable to the systems we design.

8.1 Directory Service Concepts

The DCE Directory Service consists of a *Cell Directory Service* (CDS) and a *Global Directory Service* (GDS). A cell is simply a number of nodes (minimum of one) that are administered as a unit. A cell could encompass a company, a department, or a lab. The GDS is the glue that connects cells together. Both CDS and GDS implement collections of arbitrary names and associated data arranged in a tree-structured hierarchy. Every cell appears as an entry somewhere in the GDS. This is illustrated in Fig. 8.1.

CDS is tailored to the needs of the other DCE components and provides advanced functionality such as replication and caching. The DCE GDS is one of the first implementations of the X.500 international standard for providing naming service between organizations. It is expected to gradually become the most widely used service as it becomes available from more and more vendors. However, CDS is also compatible with the use of the Internet's *Domain Name Service* (DNS), currently used by a large number of networks that use TCP/IP protocols. Therefore, CDS cells can be integrated into larger public or private networks based on either GDS, some other X.500 implementation, or DNS.

8.1.1 DCE name syntax

What matters to us is that each of these three services thus incorporated into DCE—CDS, GDS (X.500), and DNS—uses a different syntax for naming things. CDS uses a syntax similar to UNIX file names. For example, a CDS name might be:

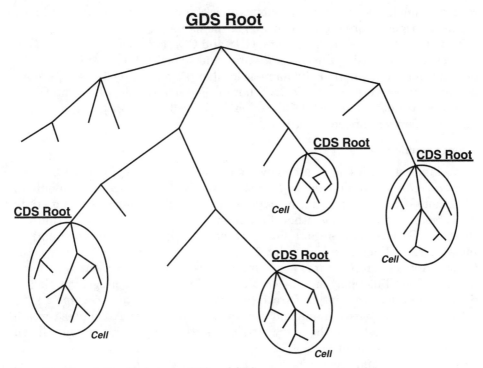

Figure 8.1 The relationship between GDS and CDS.

```
/.:/subsys/magic/server_01
```

The */.:/* indicates that the name is a cell-relative name. The global name of the cell depends on which GDS is employed. An example of an X.500 name that might refer to the same entry as the previous example is:

```
/.../C=US/O=Onsett International Corp./OU=padded/subsys/magic/server_01
```

A DNS version looks like this:

```
/.../padded.onsett.com/subsys/magic/server_01
```

In both cases the name of the local cell is "padded." The */.../* indicates that it is a global name. The use of the */.:/* and */.../* prefixes helps to avoid confusion with file names. Notice that in CDS syntax and X.500 syntax names go from left to right, from global to local. The DNS-specific part of the name in the second example goes from right to left. In DNS the cell name is first; in X.500 it appears right before the local portion of the name.

From the DCE user's point of view, GDS and CDS form a single service. References are made using the correct syntax and the Directory Service does the rest. It figures out whether the name is local or not and contacts the appropriate directory servers automatically. There is just one set of calls to the Directory Service, not two. In fact, DCE can be configured with a CDS only, in which case all references are cell-relative.

8.1.2   Name service entries

Three kinds of entries maintained by the Directory Service are of most interest to us: *directories, objects,* and *soft links.* (Actually, soft links are found only in CDS, not GDS.) Directories are *container objects.* Their purpose is simply to hold objects, soft links, and other directories. Objects are the "things" that the Directory Service names. Soft links are entries that point to other entries somewhere in the name hierarchy. This allows the creation of *synonyms* or *aliases.* Application programs are allowed to create only object entries. Directories and soft links may only be created by administrative programs. Collectively, all of the entries in the Directory Service are called the *namespace.*

Entries always have a name and usually have attributes. Attributes contain the data associated with the entry. Attributes have values and in general can be single-valued or multivalued. For example, a marital status attribute would be single-valued and have some value like "married," "single," "divorced," etc. A children's names attribute would be multivalued and contain zero or more names. Every attribute has a type (e.g., integer, string). Entries that have the same attributes are said to belong to the same *class.*

Because the GDS has a schema, specified by OSF, based on X.500 guidelines, there is a preset structure to the hierarchy and the attributes of various entry types. In contrast, the CDS has no preset schema. Applications can, in principle, create objects with arbitrary combinations of attributes and extend the namespace however they want. Care must be taken, however, because certain DCE components, such as RPC and the Security Service, expect the namespace to be used in certain ways.

Figure 8.2 shows the CDS namespace as it is configured when DCE is installed. OSF recommends use of the directory **/. : /subsys** to contain the exported binding information associated with servers from third-party products. Products should create a directory in **/ . : /subsys** which is the name of the product and then create whatever hierarchy they need below it. DCE follows this convention. Its server entries are found under **/ . : /subsys/dce.**

OSF recommends that end-user applications create a directory at the cell root level, with a name such as "/. : /applications" to contain server binding information for applications they develop themselves. Each application would have its own directory, with names such as "/. : /applications/general_ledger" or "/. : /applications/MRPII". Generally, entries used by DCE components, such as

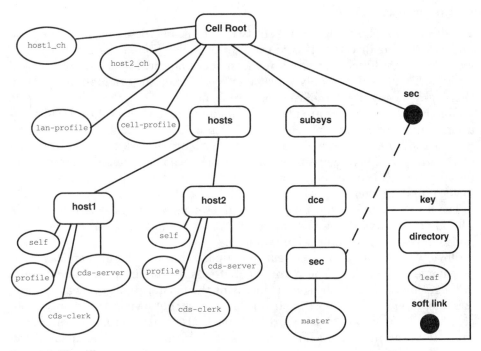

Figure 8.2 The cell namespace.

the server bindings used by RPC or the entries used by the Security Service, should not be manipulated directly from the Directory Service but only by the APIs provided by those services.

Another kind of entry in CDS is called a *junction*. A junction is referred to as if it were a directory entry, but it is actually a separate namespace maintained by a different server. The junction contains binding information that allows that server to be called. When an entry in the junction namespace is referenced, the junction server is invoked and passes the part of the name to the right of the junction name, known as the *residual*. The junction server interprets the residual and performs the request on the indicated entry.

This technique allows other DCE components to be conveniently integrated with CDS. A good example of a junction is **/. : /sec,** which is a junction implemented by the Security Service. If a reference is made to "/. : /sec/principal/ cell_admin", the Security Service will be called to interpret the residual "principal/cell_admin".

The ability to create, read, modify, or delete entries in the namespace is controlled by the DCE Security Service. Every item in the namespace has associated with it an Access Control List (ACL) that controls who can do what to it. (There also may or may not be an ACL associated with the object itself.) ACLs and other security mechanisms are described in Chaps. 9 through 11.

8.1.3   Replication concepts

The directory is the name service entity that contains the items making up the namespace. The directory is also the unit of replication of the Directory Service. For every directory, there are one or more physical instances of it called *replicas.* There is always only one *master replica,* i.e., the original. In addition, there may be any number of read-only replicas.

Changes to a directory are always applied to the master replica. Read operations can occur against any replica. This provides two benefits. First, if the master replica is unavailable because of a node or network failure, processing can continue, using a read-only replica. Second, read performance is improved, because the read can be done from any replica, thus avoiding network delays, disk contention, etc.

The directory replicas located on any given node are physically located in a file called a *clearinghouse.* The directory server reads and writes the clearinghouse in response to application requests.

Obviously, when the master replica is updated, the read-only replicas must be changed to match it. There are two methods. In the first, called *immediate propagation,* whenever the server that owns the master replica gets an update, it immediately sends a message to all the servers that own the read-only replicas. This is done on a best-effort-only basis. In other words, if a server is unavailable or unreachable for some reason, its replica will not be updated and no error indication is given. Immediate propagation is intended to keep replicas up to date within seconds or minutes.

The second method for keeping read-only replicas up to date is called a *skulk.* In a skulk, all the changes to the master replica since the last skulk are gathered together and then applied to the read-only replicas. If any of the replicas are not available, that fact is logged and the update is retried later on. Skulks are intended to keep replicas up to date within hours or days.

All of the replicas that are supposed to be the same are marked with a timestamp called an *epoch.** If during the skulk it is found that the replicas have different epochs, the skulk aborts. The reason for this is that if the master becomes permanently unavailable for some reason, the cell administrator can make one of the read-only replicas into the master replica. Now suppose the original master came back on line. The next skulk instituted from either master would flag this potentially disruptive situation.

The cell administrator can control the number and location of read-only replicas as well as the occurrence of immediate propagation and the frequency of skulks. Skulks can occur (1) on a scheduled basis; (2) as a side effect of any of a number of administrative actions, such as defining a new replica; or (3) on command of the administrator. The existence of replicas and of the mecha-

---

* This should not be confused with the standard use of the term *epoch* on UNIX-like systems to refer to a specific date/time: namely, 00:00:00 January 1, 1970.

nisms for keeping them matched is invisible to an application that uses the Directory Service, except for the fact that it is possible to get information that is out of date, in between skulks.

In order to speed access to Directory Service operations, every CDS client node maintains a cache of recently accessed entries. The process responsible for managing the CDS cache is called the CDS *clerk*. Requests go through the clerk so that if they can be satisfied from the cache the server will not be consulted. When requests must go on to the server, the entries obtained are saved in the cache for future use. The cache is maintained in main memory, but periodically it is saved on disk as well.

As with replicas, the cache is not guaranteed to be up to date. Applications should be prepared for this possibility. For example, if an attempt to contact a server fails, it may just be that the cache entry is out of date and the binding information has changed.

8.2   How RPC Uses the Directory Service

The main reason the Directory Service is a part of DCE is to allow clients to bind to servers. The RPC calls that make this possible are called the *Name Service Interface* (NSI). The library routines that make up the NSI all begin with **rpc_ns_**. Some of them, for example, **rpc_ns_binding_export,** were discussed in the section on RPC. One group of routines, which provide management functions, begins with **rpc_ns_mgmt**.

NSI works by creating certain directory object types with special attributes that it interprets in order to provide the desired functionality. The three types of entries used by NSI are *server, group,* and *profile*.* A server entry normally corresponds to a single server. If there are several servers running on the same node and supporting the same interface, they can share the same entry. In this case, they are called *interchangeable servers.*

The NSI server entry is created and removed by the calls **rpc_ns_binding_ export()** and **rpc_ns_binding_unexport()**. The entry contains the information identifying the interface supported by the server, the associated binding information, and the objects the server supports, if any. It is this entry that allows a client to get the information necessary to bind to a server.

If several servers running on different nodes support the same interface, each will have its own NSI server entry. To make it easy for a client to locate all those servers, NSI implements the concept of a *group entry*. A group entry is identified by the interface UUID and contains pointers to server entries. A group entry can also point to another group entry. A group entry is illustrated

---

* Technically, all three are the same type of entry. They simply make use of different attributes. However, the mixing of, say, group and profile attributes in a single entry is unsupported, so it is simpler to think of them as three different types.

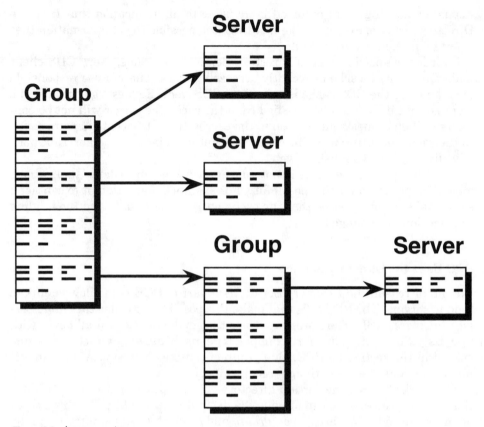

Figure 8.3 A group entry.

in Fig. 8.3. When a client begins searching for bindings with a group entry and calls **rpc_ns_binding_import_next()**, the routine returns the server bindings in random order. (This is done by the runtime when automatic binding is used.)

The third kind of entry, the *profile,* contains one or more *profile elements.* Each profile element is associated with a particular interface and points to a server entry, group entry, or another profile entry. Each profile element has a priority. Figure 8.4 illustrates a profile. When a client calls **rpc_ns_binding_import_next()**, having begun with a profile entry name, the priority is used to determine which item to select from among those that support the specified interface.

A profile is intended to allow users to control the order in which servers are selected. For example, we might want to use a nearby server under normal circumstances and only a remote one if the nearby one is unavailable. Typically the lowest-priority profile element would point to another profile as the default.

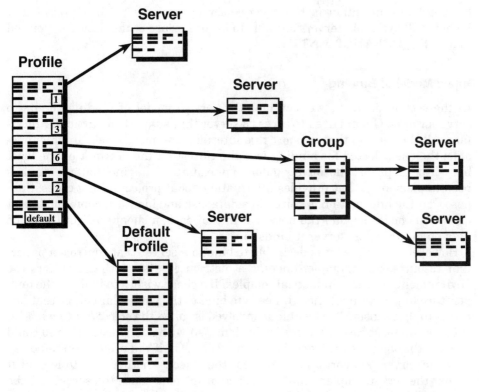

Figure 8.4 A profile entry.

When DCE is installed, it comes with a cell default profile and a LAN default profile. Users and administrators can create others as they are needed. Unfortunately, the administrative tools provided by OSF with DCE make this an excessively cumbersome procedure. Currently, to create a profile element it is necessary to discover and then successfully type in the interface UUID and other information associated with the server or group—hardly a user-friendly task. Hopefully, DCE vendors will eventually provide better tools: something that lets you view existing entries and "point and click" to create an element would make a big difference.

NSI provides for the use of profiles (and groups) in the following way. The second argument to **rpc_ns_binding_import_begin()** and **rpc_ns_binding_lookup_begin()** is the name of a directory entry to begin the search. Of course, the name of a server or group entry can be provided. However, if the value of this argument is **NULL,** then the contents of the environmental variable (or equivalent) **RPC_DEFAULT_ENTRY** will be used as the starting point of the search. (This is done by the client runtime in the case of automatic binding.) The intention is that every user be provided with a profile that includes all available servers suitable to his or her use of the network, pointed to by **RPC_DEFAULT_ENTRY.**

8.3 The Object Model of Binding

In the section on RPC, we saw how the service model of binding clients to servers works. Clients need to access a server that supports a particular interface. All the servers that support this interface are more or less interchangeable; the one selected for binding was the closest on the network or the least busy or perhaps just chosen at random. For example, imagine that a server has been implemented that provides information about project billing codes. Suppose that the information is stored in a database and identical copies of it exist on various nodes around the network. In that case, a client will get the same data no matter what server it binds to.

However, sometimes it is desirable to bind to a server that controls a particular resource. For example, imagine a distributed system that monitors the environment in a large industrial complex. If a client wishes to find out the temperature in a certain location, it needs to bind to the particular server that has access to that sensor. The technique involved is called the *object binding model.*

In the simplest case, each server is identified with a single object. You could think of the object as the "identity" of the server. Or, if you prefer, you could say that the server "supports" or "provides" the object. Another way to look at it is that the server "implements" the object or in some sense the server "is" the object. This last view is consistent with object-oriented design principles. The operations provided by the server can be seen as the object's "methods." (An overview of object-oriented principles and how DCE relates to them can be found in Chap. 23.)

Instead of just one object, each server, however, could be associated with multiple objects. Each server can include one or more objects along with the other information it exports. The client will specify the object it wishes to bind to, and the runtime binding routines will consider only servers that have advertised that object. Conversely, in some applications, the same object might be accessible from more than one server. Figure 8.5 illustrates these possibilities. DCE permits both of them.

As we are talking about a single interface definition, the implication is that all of the servers implement the same operations. That is, they have the same names and parameters and, unless we are quite foolish or perverse, the operations will be equivalent, from a commonsense point of view. However, it may be that the objects themselves differ and that implementation of the operations will have to take this into account. Extending our previous example, let us imagine there are different kinds of devices that measure the temperature. The operation of reading the temperature is the same, but different code is required to read it from different devices.

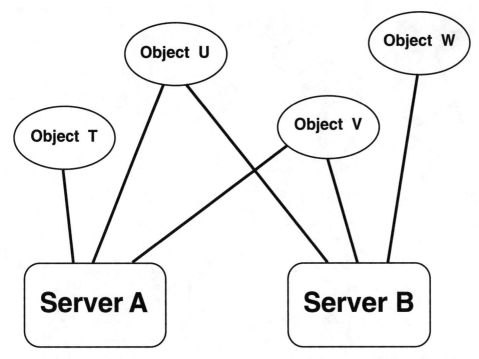

Figure 8.5 Possible server-to-object relationships.

DCE allows for this as well. Servers can specify to their runtime that different sets of operation routines are to be used for different object types. When binding occurs, the runtime will ensure that the proper implementation is called. DCE allows free choice for grouping object types with servers. Each server can support just one type, or certain servers can support certain types, or all servers can support all types. This is illustrated in Fig. 8.6.

The object binding model is a little confusing at first, but it is not difficult to use once the underlying mechanisms are understood. The first principle is that DCE identifies everything by using UUIDs. Therefore, every object that we wish to specify must be associated with a UUID. In fact, the only thing about the object that DCE cares about is the UUID associated with it. From DCE's point of view, the UUID is the object. DCE also uses UUIDs to identify object types. Again, the UUIDs have no special meaning; they just let the server runtime distinguish one object type from another.

The other confusing thing about using the object binding model is that three different entities have to be told about the objects that the server supports. The Directory Service must be informed so that clients can bind to the node on which the server is running. The endpoint mapper must be informed so that it can complete the partial binding and map to the proper server. The server run-

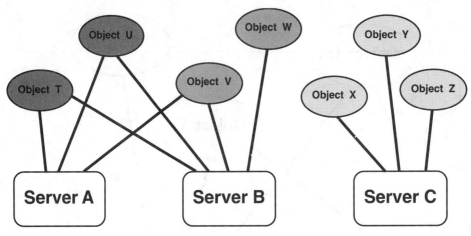

Figure 8.6 Associating object types with servers.

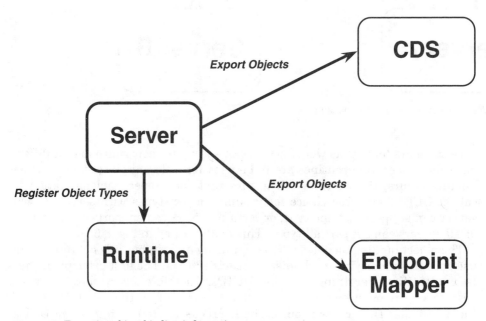

Figure 8.7 Exporting object binding information.

time must be informed not only about the objects supported, but also about which set of operation implementations go with which object types. Figure 8.7 depicts these three steps.

Actually, as we saw previously in the section on RPC server facilities, these steps are performed in the reverse order to that sequence of their use. The first step for the programmer is to tell the runtime which objects are of which type. This is done by calling **rpc_object_set_type()** once for each object. Next,

rpc_server_register_if() is called once for each object type to associate an entry point vector (EPV) with each. As multiple EPVs are required, they must be created explicitly, rather than using the one generated by the IDL compiler.

Next, each object is registered with the endpoint mapper by calling **rpc_ep_register()** with a vector containing the UUIDs of all the objects supported. Finally, the objects are exported to the namespace by calling **rpc_ns_binding_export()** with the same vector of UUIDs.

8.3.1 Object binding example

Now let's use an example (shown in Fig. 8.8), to look at the details. In the interest of clarity, parts of the example code have been left out. Some declarations and all of the error checking have been omitted.

In this example, the server will support three object types: red, blue, and green. There are several objects of each type:

RED	sunset, flag
BLUE	sea, eyes, bell, moon
GREEN	grass, money, leaves

1. Twelve UUIDs are needed, one for each object, plus one for each object type. They could be generated on the fly, by calling **create_uuid()**, but it is better to define them in advance; if we run multiple servers, we want the same UUID to refer to the same object. UUIDs are stored in a data type named **uuid_t.** The **uuidgen** utility has an option (**-s** in POSIX.2 environments) that will generate a UUID as a structure initializer corresponding to the **uuid_t** data type. Therefore, the first thing we do is create 12 UUID variables containing our 12 UUIDs. (The first few are shown.) As an alternative to compiling the UUIDs into the program, we could store them in a file or database and read them in when the server starts up.

2. The routines **rpc_ep_register()** and **rpc_ns_binding_export()** both expect a UUID vector. This is the data type **uuid_vector_t,** which is actually a structure with two members. The first, **count**, is the number of UUIDs and the second, **uuid**, is an array of pointers to UUIDs. Accordingly, we declare and initialize a vector called "obj_vec" with the nine object UUIDs. For convenience in calling **rpc_object_set_type()**, we declare a parallel vector containing the object type UUIDs corresponding to each object.

3. As there are three object types, three EPVs are needed. Assume that in the IDL file, the name of the interface is "object_example" and that three operations are defined: op1, op2, and op3. The actual server operation routines are named according to the object type they work for: "op1_red", "op2_red", "op3_red", "op1_blue", "op2_blue", and so on. The IDL compiler creates a typedef for the EPV from the interface name and version number. Since the interface is "object_example" and the version is 1.0, the type for the EPV is "object_example_v1_0_epv_t". This is used to declare three EPVs, which are initialized with the appropriate routine addresses.

```
#define NUM_OBJECTS 9

uuid_t sunset_uuid = { /* 005E9AC0-486D-1B6C-B747-0000C07C3610 */
        0x005e9ac0,
        0x486d,
        0x1b6c,
        0xb7,
        0x47,
        {0x00, 0x00, 0xc0, 0x7c, 0x36, 0x10}
      };

uuid_t flag_uuid = { /* 005E9AC1-486D-1B6C-B747-0000C07C3610 */
        0x005e9ac1,
        0x486d,
        0x1b6c,
        0xb7,
        0x47,
        {0x00, 0x00, 0xc0, 0x7c, 0x36, 0x10}
      };


        .
        .
        .


uuid_t red_type_uuid = { /* 005E9AC9-486D-1B6C-B747-0000C07C3610 */
        0x005e9ac9,
        0x486d,
        0x1b6c,
        0xb7,
        0x47,
        {0x00, 0x00, 0xc0, 0x7c, 0x36, 0x10}
      };


        .
        .
        .


uuid_vector_t obj_vec = { /* vector of object uuids */
      NUM_OBJECTS,
      { &sunset_uuid, &flag_uuid,
         &sea_uuid, &eyes_uuid, &bell_uuid, &moon_uuid,
         &grass_uuid, &money_uuid, &leaves_uuid }
};

uuid_vector_t obj_type_vec = { /* vector of object type uuids */
      NUM_OBJECTS,
      { &red_type_uuid, &red_type_uuid,
       &blue_type_uuid, &blue_type_uuid, &blue_type_uuid, &blue_type_uuid,
         &green_type_uuid, &green_type_uuid, &green_type_uuid }
};

          /* Entry Point Vectors for each object type */
```

Figure 8.8 Object binding example code.

```
object_example_v1_0_epv_t red_obj_epv =
      { op1_red, op2_red, op3_red };

object_example_v1_0_epv_t blue_obj_epv =
      { op1_blue, op2_blue, op3_blue };

object_example_v1_0_epv_t green_obj_epv =
      { op1_green, op2_green, op3_green };

/*************   Execution begins here   ***************/

/*  Register the type of each object   */

for (i=0; i < NUM_OBJECTS; i++)
            rpc_object_set_type( obj_vec.uuid[i],
                                 obj_type_vec.uuid[i],
                                 &status);

/*  Associate each object type with the appropriate EPV   */

rpc_server_register_if(object_example_v1_0_s_ifspec,          /* Red */
                       red_type_uuid,
                       (rpc_mgr_epv_t) &red_obj_epv,
                       &status);

rpc_server_register_if(object_example_v1_0_s_ifspec,          /* Blue */
                       &blue_type_uuid,
                       (rpc_mgr_epv_t) &blue_obj_epv,
                       &status);

rpc_server_register_if(object_example_v1_0_s_ifspec,          /* Green */
                       &green_type_uuid,
                       (rpc_mgr_epv_t) &green_obj_epv,
                       &status);

/*** Get the bindings - same as the service binding model ***/

rpc_server_use_all_protseqs(rpc_c_protseq_max_reqs_default, &status);

rpc_server_inq_bindings(&bindings, &status);

/*** Register interface and list of objects in the namespace ***/

rpc_ns_binding_export(rpc_c_ns_syntax_default,
                      name,
                      object_example_v1_0_s_ifspec,
                      bindings,
                      &obj_vec,
                      &status);
```

Figure 8.8 *(Continued)*

```
/*** Register interface and list of objects with Endpoint mapper ***/

rpc_ep_register(simple_v1_0_s_ifspec,
                bindings,
                &obj_vec,
                NULL,
                &status);

/* Wait for requests */

rpc_server_listen(rpc_c_listen_max_calls_default, &status);
```

Figure 8.8   (*Continued*)

4. Now the executable code begins. The first thing to do is to tell the runtime which objects are which type. The **for** loop containing **rpc_object_set_type()** does this.

5. Next, we tell the runtime which EPV should be used with each object type by calling **rpc_server_register_if()** three times. Notice that the EPV is cast as type **rpc_mgr_epv_t**.

6. Now we register our interface, bindings, and list of objects with the Directory Service and with the endpoint mapper. Note that both routines expect a pointer to a vector of object UUIDs. The **NULL** argument to **rpc_ep_register()** is the character string annotation.

7. Finally, we call **rpc_server_listen()**, just as in the service binding model.

We could also have called **rpc_server_register_if()** a fourth time with **NULL** for the object UUID vector. This would in effect create a "default" EPV to be used if a client called one of the operations with either a **NULL** object UUID or with an object UUID that was not in our list. Of course, we would have to provide an EPV and a set of operation routines to handle this case.

8.3.2   Adding objects dynamically

The example assumes that all of the objects to be supported are known in advance. But what if the application must provide for adding new objects after the server has been started? Of course, it is not reasonable to expect to be able to add a new object type—"yellow," for example—on the fly. A new object type would require us to provide a new set of operation routines, which would require rebuilding the server or adding a new one.

It would be reasonable, however, to want to add a new object of an existing type, say "green emerald." Unfortunately, this is not so easy to do. Suppose a management program is implemented to allow an administrator to add new objects. The administrator would provide the object UUID and object type UUID, but what would the program do with them?

The management program could, in principle, add the object to the name-space, as that is accessible to any suitably privileged program. However, the endpoint mapper and the runtime both present problems. When a server calls the endpoint mapper, an implicit argument to the call is the endpoints associated with protocol sequences for that server. Therefore, only the actual server process can make the call to **rpc_ep_register()**. Similarly, the run-time is part of the server process and there is no way for the management program to communicate with it directly to register the EPV associated with each object type.

The way to solve this problem is to create a management interface in the server. This should be defined as a separate interface with its own set of oper-ations, because normal application clients will not be calling the management operations. Figure 8.9 illustrates this approach.

The management program is a client of this interface and makes a call such as "add_objects()". The parameters of the operation would be the object UUID being added and its object type UUID. The server would then make the calls to the Directory Service, endpoint mapper and runtime in order to add the object. If desired, it would be possible to implement a "remove_object()" operation as well. This would require the server to call **rpc_ns_binding_unexport, rpc_ep_unregister()**, and to call **rpc_object_set_type()** with a **NULL** object type UUID.

This method would allow objects to be added dynamically, but managing a large number of servers that implement many objects could become quite com-plex in practice. Also, at this time it is unknown to what extent the object bind-ing model will scale up. Clearly, supporting dozens of objects poses no problem.

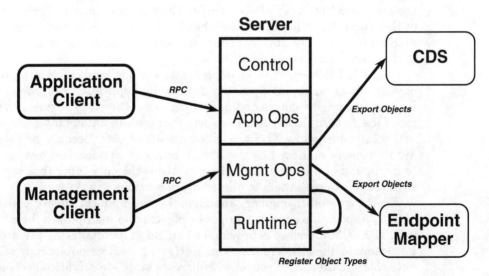

Figure 8.9 Implementing dynamic objects.

In all probability, it will never be reasonable to have a server support a million objects. Between these extremes, no one knows where the practical limits lie.

8.4   Accessing the Directory Service Directly

As was previously stated, the DCE Directory Service's primary purpose is to permit RPC binding. However, the cell directory and global directory are generalized, replicated, distributed databases that can be used for other purposes by applications. To aid this, DCE provides the X/Open Directory Service (XDS) interface and the *X/Open Object Management* (XOM) interface.

A complete discussion of programming with the XDS and XOM interfaces is beyond the scope of this book. But it is worth knowing generally how they work. In XDS/XOM terminology, an object is a generalized data structure with one or more attributes that have values. Attribute values can be simple (e.g., string, integer) or can themselves be objects.

In XDS/XOM, objects do not have methods (code), but they do belong to classes that form an inheritance hierarchy. In other words, it is possible to create classes of objects that inherit some of their attributes from their parent classes. A "table" object and a "chair" object might inherit some of their common properties from a "furniture" object.

In C code, objects are actually implemented as arrays of structures of the type **OM_descriptor**. Each descriptor represents an attribute of the object. The descriptor contains the attribute type, syntax, and value. If the value is an object, it is implemented as a pointer to the object, which of course consists of the same kind of array of structures. The first attribute is always the class of the object. Its value indicates what kind of object it is and therefore what attributes it has. The object's other attributes follow. A null entry in the array of structures marks the end of the object.

The DCE Directory Service implements various kinds of objects, but these objects can never be manipulated directly by application programs. Instead, applications create objects and pass them to the Directory Service via the XDS interface. In turn, XDS returns objects that contain data of interest.

Objects returned by XDS are called *private objects*. Because private objects are in memory managed by the library routines, applications are not allowed to manipulate their attributes directly. About the only thing that can be done with them is to pass them to other library routines.

Objects created in memory managed by the application are called *public objects*. Applications can create public objects and manipulate their values at will. The XOM interface is provided as an aid in manipulating private objects. For example, the XOM routine **om_get()** will create a public copy of any private object. Other XOM routines will create or delete private objects and read and write their values.

The XDS routines are used to manipulate the directory itself. Calls are provided to create and delete entries and modify their values. Generally speaking, the application is unaware of whether the CDS or GDS is being accessed; the entry name determines which.

DCE comes with many header (**.h**) files containing definitions of the object types of interest to DCE applications. There are definitions having to do with the interface itself, for example, a directory entry name. There are definitions having to do with the X.500 directory schema, for example, a country. There are definitions having to do with the X.400 Email standard, for example, an originator/recipient address.

Programming XDS/XOM requires, first, figuring out what kinds of objects need to be manipulated. Next, the input objects are created and the appropriate XDS routines are called. The XOM routines are called as needed to manipulate the objects returned by XDS. The code tends to look quite formidable, as it consists of lots of object declarations and a few routine calls.

There are two limitations in using the CDS that are important to know about. First, directories can be created only by the directory administration program. Applications can create entries in existing directories, but not new directories. Specifically, the **ds_add_entry()** call will fail if the specified object is of the directory class and the name is a CDS name.

The other restriction is that searches cannot be done on CDS. That is, the **ds_search()** call always fails on CDS. In other words, if you know the name of an entry, you can find it, but you cannot ask for all of the entries that meet some criterion. The reason is that, unlike X.500, CDS does not have any built-in schema of entry attributes. Without such an attribute schema, the search routine cannot understand how to search for given criteria because it has nothing to check against.

8.5   Chapter Summary

A distributed directory—in DCE, the Directory Service—contributes to the transparency of a distributed system by providing programs, users, databases, nodes, printers, and other components of the system each with a name that is the same to everyone using the system. It has many benefits, including the elimination of worries about maintaining consistency of names for elements of the system that may be propagated by individual applications, as in today's file-sharing schemes, and permits the user to use a network resource from any location without having to negotiate a path to its location.

The DCE Directory Service is composed of a Cell Directory Service (CDS), used for collections of nodes administered as cells and integrated with the other DCE components, and the Global Directory Service (GDS), which contains the names of all cells and may be an X.500-based global service, as is OSF's, or one using the Internet Domain Name Service. The Directory Service uses a single consistent syntax for referring to all directory entries, whether local to the cell or global.

Developers of distributed applications will use the Directory Service mainly to bind clients to servers by means of the RPC Name Service Interface (NSI). There are three types of NSI directory entries. A server entry contains the interfaces, protocols, and objects supported by a server. A group entry identifies a number of equivalent servers. A profile entry allows servers and groups to be selected in prioritized order.

The most sophisticated use of the NSI permits the implementation of the object model of binding. With the service model of binding, discussed in Chap. 5, clients select the particular server they wish to bind to. In the object model of binding, servers advertise their ability to support objects of different types. Clients request objects and are directed to the appropriate operation routines within the appropriate server. While the scheme is oriented toward statically defined objects, it can be adapted to support the dynamic creation of objects as well.

Some applications may need to use the Directory Service for purposes other than binding. The DCE Directory Service may also be accessed via the X/Open XDS and XOM APIs. While these use a somewhat unfamiliar coding style, they can be mastered by any competent C programmer. It should be noted that DCE does impose some restrictions on the use of XDS. The major ones are: (1) only leaf nodes can be created, not directories; (2) generalized searches on attribute values are not permitted; and (3) asynchronous operations are not supported.

The DCE Security Service

Interlude

The suspicion that he was walking into a trap crossed Edward Duke's mind once again as he made his way through seedy-side Istanbul's maze of alleys and passageways. Still, the obviousness of the trap suggested it was not one, as crude tricks were not Professor X's style. In any event, M had reliable information that it might be possible to obtain some extremely valuable documents in Istanbul, so here he was.

Suddenly he was at his destination, facing a heavy wooden door. Wtihout a word, an unsmiling servant ushered him into the presence of Professor X. Duke knew very well that the Professor was a shadowy figure, dealing with parties on both sides of the fence. His ways were mysterious and secretive, but his success at the dangerous game he played owed to the fact that he always delivered on his promises.

"You are looking well, Edward," he said, waving a hand at the chair across from him. "I believe I have some property your people would like to acquire. One million pounds sterling in my Zurich account and it is yours. My time is limited and I am not interested in dickering."

"Done," said Duke. "When do I take delivery?"

"The materials are in my safe in Athens. However, I have other pressing business and cannot go there at this time."

"Just give me the combination and I will take care of the rest," Duke said.

"Not so fast," said the Professor, with a smile, "I am just selling you this one package. I would not like to have the British Secret Service rummaging through my things every time you get the notion. My cousin Constantine will provide you with the documents. I will give you a letter to carry to him. It is too dangerous to send him a message by any other means."

"How will he know the letter is genuine?"

"It contains a phrase Constantine and I have previously agreed upon."

"But, my dear Professor, once I read your letter, what is to keep us from using your phrase whenever we please?"

"Now, Edward, don't you think I trust your honor as a gentleman?" the Professor said in mock protest. "But, in fact, the letter is written in the secret language of an extinct tribe of gypsies, known only to the male members of my family, so you will not be able to read it."

"Well then, suppose the opposition were to obtain the letter and use an imposter to present it to your cousin?"

"I certainly hope that does not occur, for it would mean that they had ended the career of Commander Duke. But it would do them no good, for the letter instructs Constantine to challenge you by making this sign with his hands, and you must reply just so," said the Professor, demonstrating. "If you fail to do this correctly, you will not leave Constantine's establishment alive."

"You certainly seem to have thought of everything," Duke remarked.

9.1   Introduction

The DCE Security Service provides the means to ensure that distributed system resources are accessed only by those who are authorized to do so and only in precisely the ways that they have been authorized to do so. DCE Security Service depends, however, on the presence of certain conditions in order to deliver on this promise of protection. Foremost among these conditions is adherence to proper administrative and operational procedures in the distributed computing environment.

This is the first of three chapters devoted to the DCE Security Service, how it works, and how to use it. The confusion that often surrounds the subject of security usually stems from misunderstanding the objectives and assumptions of a given security system. Therefore, this chapter discusses some of the basic principles of computer security and the kinds of occurrences a security system tries to prevent. This is followed by a description of the assumptions that the designers of DCE Security Service made about the environment in which DCE will operate. The requirements and desirable characteristics of the DCE Security Service are then considered.

This background sets the stage for examining, in Chap. 10, the three major services comprising the DCE Security Service: *authentication, authorization,* and *access control*. The reader can see how the mechanisms of the Security Service provide the required and desirable capabilities in the assumed environment. The chapter describes how each of these services operates to control access to resources. It also discusses options available under DCE security and suggests circumstances in which it is appropriate to use them.

Chapter 11, the final chapter on the Security Service, describes exactly how to use DCE-authenticated RPC to employ authentication, authorization, and access control to build secure applications.

9.2   First Principles

Security is often thought of as preventing access to something. The word *security* conjures up images of padlocks, barbed wire, and guard dogs. Paradoxically, computer security is mostly concerned with allowing access. After all, if we wish to prevent access to a computer, we can lock it in a safe, turn it off, or even disassemble it! The point is to allow the "right" folks to use it and keep the "wrong" folks from using it.

The next thing to notice is that security makes sense only when a system has two or more users.* If you are the only one who can ever access the system, then security is both pointless and ineffective. It is pointless because there are no unauthorized users to guard against. To see why it is ineffective, consider this. Suppose you can give a command that prevents you from accessing some part of a system. If there is some way that you can reverse the command, then clearly it provides no additional security. If, on the other hand, you cannot reverse the command, it is obviously not a very desirable feature.

In any security environment the existence of authorized and unauthorized users implies that there is somebody who can specify which is which. Obviously, a user who can specify what other users can do can easily acquire the ability to do anything. A little reflection leads us to the conclusion that there is nothing a security system can do to protect against such users. It is necessary to assume that they are trustworthy.

Any analysis of computer security must consider what an unauthorized user might try to do. Security specialists refer to the possibilities as *threats*. As it is not practical to build a system that prevents unauthorized access under all possible circumstances, the idea is to make such access more trouble than it is worth. For any given threat, the cost of penetration should be greater than the value derived from it.† Seen in this light, security is an economic function.

Although there are many different techniques that can be used to breach a security system, there are really only five threats. They are *data access, modification of data, theft of services, denial of services,* and *impersonation.* The first three correspond to the file permissions found on many multiuser operating systems: read, write, and execute. Obviously, a security system must ensure that these actions can be taken only by those authorized to do them.

Denial of services means preventing valid users from making use of the system. An example would be unauthorized action that sends hundreds of print requests to every printer in a system. In practice, this can be the most difficult

---

* I am not saying that single-user systems such as PCs and workstations do not need security; any passerby is a potential unauthorized user. Instead, imagine you and your computer alone on a desert island.

† This mode of analysis breaks down in the case of the individual who wants to break into a system or disrupt service for the thrill of it. Here, it is necessary to use judgment and historical experience to decide what precautions are required to make it more trouble than it is worth.

threat to deal with, because it is often difficult to draw the line between normal and abusive use of resources.

Impersonation refers to misrepresenting the identity of the originator of a request. For example, an embezzler might send a message to a banking system to transfer a million dollars into his or her own account. Of course, impersonation can be used to achieve one of the other threat objectives; by pretending to be a valid user, someone could get unauthorized access to data. In the security context, however, impersonation usually refers to producing an effect external to the system.

Multiuser computer systems generally have mechanisms to thwart these threats. These are referred to as *local security*. DCE Security Service provides *distributed systems security*. It does not replace local security. In fact, in certain respects it depends on the correct operation of local security mechanisms.

Both local security and distributed security depend on proper execution of administrative and operational procedures. This makes security different from the other DCE services. If RPC or the Directory Service are improperly configured, the effects are likely to be limited to a single application or a single node. Once the error is rectified, the problem is gone.

In contrast, security is like a fence. If there is a hole in the fence anywhere, it will not help to put more padlocks on the front gate. Also, once an unauthorized user has penetrated a computer system, he or she may be able to make unobtrusive changes that either cause damage in the future or allow the user to break in at will.

Because proper operation is so important, design of a security system must take practical considerations into account. If security requires users or administrators to perform procedures that are inconvenient, cumbersome, or too difficult to understand, they will simply find ways to bypass them. A system in which security has been bypassed is actually less secure than a system that has no security at all! The reason is that a system recognized as having no security will be treated as such, whereas the fact that security has been bypassed may not be known to some users who will continue to depend on the system's presumed protection.

9.3   Design Considerations

Given these general principles, we now examine the assumptions the DCE Security Service makes about the environment in which it operates and the problems it attempts to solve.

9.3.1   Assumptions

The DCE Security Service assumes that the network will contain single-user systems (i.e., PCs and workstations) that are insecure. In other words, the Security Service cannot assume that these systems are running software or operating systems that will guarantee that no security breach can occur. This assumption is necessary because it is so easy to modify or bypass the operating system of a single-user system.

A user can easily bypass the operating system of a PC by booting off the floppy disk drive. Even if this is somehow disabled and local security provided, the user, being also the system manager, can easily modify or replace the operating system, network driver, application, or any other software component. Of course, the Security Service cannot prevent the user from causing the PC to malfunction, but it has to protect itself by assuming that the PC could be running a program designed deliberately to breach security.

DCE also assumes that any node on the network can intercept any message transmitted over the network. This means an intruder can read any message sent by any node. This assumption reflects the reality on current networks. Data transmitted over wide-area telephone lines is subject to interception at many points. The necessary equipment for interception is relatively inexpensive and widely available.

LANs are even worse. LAN technology is inherently multiaccess. That is, the electrical signals that carry a message are normally available to every node on the LAN. A typical LAN running through a building provides scores of locations where an unauthorized user could connect a system without anyone noticing. Although it is true that each LAN adapter normally filters out messages that are not addressed to its node, this feature can easily be disabled. It is trivial to change a communications driver to collect any network message (that is how LAN analysis programs work).

The Security Service also assumes that it is possible for an intruder at any node to generate a message in an effort to fool other nodes. This is called *spoofing*. The node might pretend to be a valid and highly privileged workstation. Or it could pretend to be a server in an effort to get client systems to send it their data. It might even wait until a valid station signed on and then pretend to be the same station.

The potential for spoofing is as much a reality on present networks as interception. Spoofing on a WAN is not difficult and on a LAN it is trivial. Although LAN adapters come with a predefined origination address, popularly referred to as the *hardware address,* this can easily be overridden in the software.

These possibilities lead the Security Service to the assumption that there is no way to be certain of the true identity of the node from which a message originates. Nor is it possible, from another node, to discover the physical location of the source of a message.

The foregoing makes the task of the Security Service sound very difficult. If a malicious user can modify the software of systems to capture traffic and send messages that mimic other nodes, how is it possible to be sure of anything that happens throughout the distributed system? Actually, as stated, the problem is impossible to solve. DCE, however, depends on a couple of other assumptions that at least make its task possible, although far from easy.

The first and most important assumption is that server nodes are secure. Server nodes, including especially the one that runs the Security Service, must be free from tampering. It must be impossible for an unauthorized user to modify the software or to read any passwords stored on a server node. Typically, this would be done by physically securing the server and preventing ordinary users from logging into it.

DCE Security Service also assumes that multiuser systems are secure. That is, that local security mechanisms are in use to prevent ordinary users from reading password files, modifying the operating system, or accessing the files of other users. There are two reasons for this assumption. First, multiuser systems will often be used as server nodes. Therefore, they must be secure for the same reasons as stand-alone server nodes. Second, if users can access the resources of other users, they may be able to capture passwords or do other mischief.

The Security Service also assumes that it will not guard against certain occurrences. For example, it is not possible to prevent a node from sending garbage messages over a LAN at such a high rate as to make a network unusable. A low-level hardware mechanism prevents sending infinitely long messages, but a burst of messages in rapid succession could well be legitimate and should not be prohibited. It is not worth worrying about, because if it does occur it is relatively easy to detect and to identify the source of the problem with a LAN monitor.

9.3.2 Requirements

The assumptions outlined above frame the set of problems DCE Security Service must address. What are the design requirements?

First of all, the determination of what can or cannot be done will be based on the identity of the initiator of a request. In other words, it will not be based on the node from which the request originates or its physical location or any other criterion. This is desirable, because it means that, wherever I log in on the network, I will be allowed to do the same things. It is also a practical restriction, because, as was pointed out previously, there is no way to be sure of the identity or location of the node from which a message originated.

Another DCE Security Service requirement is that a typed password will be the only means of verifying the identity of a user. Although many devices are commercially available to otherwise establish user identity,* all involve additional cost and none are in widespread use. In theory, a DCE vendor (that is, someone who licenses the source code and sells binaries) could add support for

---

* Some examples of devices of this type include "smart cards" (banking cards with embedded microprocessors), devices that measure human hand geometry, devices that record the pen strokes used to write a signature, devices that compare voiceprints, devices that analyze the patterns on the human retina, and devices that compare fingerprints.

one or more of these devices as an enhancement. But, to ensure that DCE security can be used widely in present distributed systems environments, the password is its standard basis for verifying identities to the DCE Security Service.

DCE security accepts that someone who knows the password associated with a valid account is by definition a valid user, which places some problems outside its scope. Nothing can be done about users who tell their passwords to others or attach them on the front of their PCs. DCE also does nothing about people who use their account names or their own first names or the word "password" as a password. However, password-checking utilities to detect such easy-to-guess passwords can be used on some systems.

Another DCE requirement is that users need only log in once to access any service in the network.* In other words, the user logs in to the distributed system, not to an individual node. There are several reasons for this. First, it is a major convenience to users not to have to log in over and over again in order to access different services. Second, it is desirable and necessary to treat users in a uniform way regardless of where they log in. If something is legal for a user to do, then it should be legal from any node. Conversely, a user should not be able to circumvent security restrictions just by accessing the network from a particular node. Finally, it makes administration much simpler if a change in security can be made just once.

Given these conditions and requirements, it is clear that the DCE Security Service must provide absolute assurance of the identity of users. That is, the only way to get access rights is to log in properly. It must be impossible to fool the Security Service by capturing messages, sending bogus messages, or any other trick.

A final requirement of the DCE Security Service is that control of access must be very fine grained. It would not be sufficient for users to be classified as authorized or not authorized. It must be possible to selectively allow or prevent access to individual operations. It must also be possible to specify with great flexibility the categories of user with the rights to carry out particular operations.

The security system must not restrict the way access rights are assigned. For example, some systems assume that users fall into a hierarchy in which more-privileged users can do everything less-privileged users can do and more. This is not sufficient for many real-life situations. For example, consider accounting records. A clerk may be permitted to read and modify just certain databases, but an auditor must be able to read every database, and yet modify none.

---

* DCE users may be required to log in to their local node before running a separate DCE login program. In particular, this will be true in environments where most users do not use DCE. Eventually, as distributed systems access becomes the standard, DCE vendors may combine the steps. The DCE source code kit includes tools designed to keep the local and network users' attributes matched up, at least on UNIX-like systems.

Furthermore, as the security system will have to protect services that do not yet exist at the time it is implemented, it must be possible for system developers to extend the access control mechanism when necessary. It must be possible to do this in a manner consistent with the rest of the security system and in a manner that does not compromise security in areas that remain unchanged.

9.3.3 Desirable features

In addition to these requirements, some other features are highly desirable. For one thing, modern operating systems usually do not store actual user passwords on disk. Instead, passwords are encrypted before they are stored on disk, using an algorithm that cannot easily be reversed. When a user logs in, the typed password is encrypted and then compared to the ciphertext stored previously. The reason is that, in spite of all precautions, an unauthorized user may obtain access to the password file. An encrypted password is much less useful for breaking into accounts. It is desirable for DCE security to follow the same practice and not store unencrypted passwords.

Another desirable feature is that the Security Service alone accesses password files and other security-related databases. Even though application servers are ultimately responsible for allowing or prohibiting access to the resources they provide, they should not deal directly with the security mechanisms that identify users. This makes it easier to design application servers and also reduces the risk of a security breach. It also allows for DCE security mechanisms to be changed in the future without impacting existing servers.

Even though the Security Service must authorize users for the benefit of application servers, it is desirable to avoid direct communication between the security server and other servers. Instead, the security server should provide the client with information that the client can present to the application server to demonstrate that it is authorized. This reduces the complexity of the security server and allows application clients and servers to communicate however they wish. It also helps prevent the security server from becoming a performance bottleneck, by reducing the number of times it has to interact with other processes.

Finally, it is desirable for the use of the DCE Security Service to be optional for any server. As distributed systems probably will make some services available to all users without restriction, it is convenient to be able to omit the security mechanisms in those cases.

9.4 Chapter Summary

Many misconceptions about computer security stem from a lack of understanding of the problems a given system is trying to solve, the assumptions it makes about the environment in which it operates, and the limits it accepts to the scope of its responsibilities. As preparation for the chapters that follow on the mechanisms used by the DCE Security Service and the means by which a developer may employ them, this chapter lays the groundwork for understanding why DCE security works the way it does.

All computer security systems have the objective of allowing authorized uses and preventing unauthorized uses. This implies the existence of one or more users who are allowed to specify what is authorized. Security systems are designed to counter threats. The most common kinds of threats are data access, data modification, theft of services, denial of services, and impersonation.

The Security Service differs fundamentally from the other DCE services. While the others try to ensure that something will happen in the face of predictable types of failures, the Security Service attempts to ensure that certain things do not happen in the face of maximal human ingenuity. Any gap in the security renders the entire system ineffective. Security also must depend on proper administrative procedures being carried out correctly.

DCE assumes that single-user systems are inherently insecure and that their software and hardware may have been modified in order to breach security. DCE also assumes that any message sent over the network might be captured and that an attacker is able to generate any message he or she wishes. The consequence is that there is no inherent way to be sure of the validity of the originator of any given message. DCE does assume that server systems can be made secure by means of local security mechanisms. It also assumes that users of multiuser systems are protected from each other by local security.

DCE security is based entirely on who makes a request rather than on the location, type of computer, or any other consideration. DCE security assumes that a requestor's identity can be determined by his or her knowledge of a password. DCE security is a network service; therefore, it must only require a user to log in one time in order to do the same things regardless of where or when the login occurred. The Security Service must reliably determine the identity of a user and permit a very fine-grained control of what is authorized.

It is desirable for the security system to encrypt passwords before storing them on disk. It is also desirable that only the components of the Security Service interact directly with the security databases. The Security Service should be able to authorize access to application servers without having to communicate with them directly. The designers of distributed applications should be free to decide which, if any, security mechanisms are appropriate for a given application.

How the DCE Security Service Works

This chapter discusses how the Security Service functions to fulfill the DCE security design requirements outlined in the preceding chapter and to provide some of the desirable features within the assumed distributed system environment, as discussed in that chapter.

Although this is a book on development, this chapter deals predominantly with how the DCE Security Service works. This should help the software developer judge how to use the Security Service in a particular application. It also recognizes that the software developer is likely to be called upon to justify and explain the security characteristics of a given distributed system to others who have less technical background. Quite a bit on administrative considerations is included as well, because, in practice, administrative and operational personnel are likely to look to the developer to specify the necessary administrative environment.

10.1 Concepts

The DCE Security Service's three components—authentication, authorization, and access control (the three As)—work together to provide security in DCE. *Authentication* means validating the user's identity. DCE authentication is based on Version 5 of Kerberos, the authentication protocol developed in Project Athena at MIT. *Authorization* means determining what sort of user this is. *Access control* means deciding if this sort of user should be allowed some particular thing. DCE access control is based on *Access Control Lists* (ACLs) as defined in POSIX.6 Draft 12. The DCE Security Service also provides a variety of other services, such as user login, administrative utilities and services, and programs to display various kinds of information. As developers, we are most interested in the three As.

The DCE Security Service uses the concept of the *cell*, just as the DCE Directory Service does. In fact, it is the Cell Directory Service that establishes the definition of the cell used by the Security Service. Every cell contains exactly one Security Service. The cell is the unit of administration for DCE security.

The cell is especially significant for access control. Users are classified as being from the local cell or from some other cell. Figure 10.1 illustrates local and intercell references. Each security server communicates with security servers in other cells to coordinate access across different cells. Kerberos documentation refers to the unit of administration as a "realm." In the context of DCE, this is identical to the cell.

Principal refers to any party to an interaction secured by DCE security. Normally, principals are either users or servers. The term *principal* is used to indicate a distinction from an intermediary that is doing something on behalf of some other party.

Encryption is an important concept in the field of security generally. Although most people understand the notion of encoding and decoding a message, let us look at the concepts and terminology associated with encryption a little more carefully. In encryption terminology, a piece of information that needs to be protected is referred to in its natural form (e.g., letters, numbers, images) as *cleartext*. When the information is changed into another form, the result is called *ciphertext*.

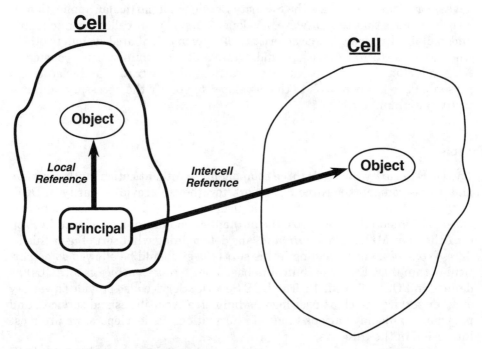

Figure 10.1 Local and intercell references.

The transformation process is called *encryption* and the process of reversing it is called *decryption*. The algorithm used to encrypt and decrypt information is (remarkably enough) called an *encryption algorithm*. Many encryption algorithms exist and new ones are invented all the time. A very well known one is the Data Encryption Standard (DES), which is a U.S. government standard.

The point is that the encryption algorithms are not secret. What protects the ciphertext from being decrypted is that the encryption algorithm is supplied with a *key*. A key is just a piece of information (usually much shorter in length than the cleartext) that is used by the encryption algorithm. Without knowing the key, it not possible to decrypt ciphertext.

In *secret key* encryption algorithms, the same key is used to encrypt and to decrypt. Therefore, it is important that the key is known only to those who should have access to the information.

In *public key* encryption, there are two keys, one used to encrypt and another used to decrypt. Once a message has been encrypted, it cannot be decrypted using the encryption key. Further, knowing the encryption key provides no clue about the decryption key. This has definite advantages.

For example, I can publish my encryption (public) key in the newspaper or the telephone directory or electronically and anybody can send me a message that only I can decrypt. I never have to tell anyone my decryption (secret) key. If somebody else does the same thing (using a different pair of keys) we can securely exchange messages back and forth.

Actually, a pair of public and secret keys can be used interchangeably; ciphertext created by one can be decrypted by the other. If I write something such as "This is my last will and testament . . ." and encrypt it with my secret key, anyone can look up my public key, decrypt the message and know with certainty that only I could have written (and encrypted) the message. Thus, public keys can be used to "sign" things.

The DCE Security Service is currently based entirely on secret key encryption. As we will see, it is used in several ways.

10.2 Authentication

Authentication is the foundation of DCE security. Only if we can be sure of who we are talking to can other security features be of any value. Authentication is also the DCE mechanism most different from mechanisms used in monolithic systems, the most complex part of DCE security, and the most difficult to understand.

We have already seen that the requirements placed on authentication make its task quite formidable.* It must make certain of the identity of principals, but it cannot be sure from which system or location a message has

---

* Actually, when I first thought about the problem, I thought it was impossible.

come. An intruder potentially can capture any message that is sent and create any kind of bogus message in an effort to fool the Security Service. Authentication must be based on passwords, but they cannot be stored or sent over the network.

10.2.1   Our noncomputer illustration

In spite of these difficulties, DCE authentication can reliably certify the identity of principals to each other. The episode featuring the secret agent at the beginning of the preceding chapter serves to illustrate how it does this.

Edward Duke represents the principal (client) who desires access to a resource (in his case, materials in a safe in Athens). Professor X represents the Security Service. The Professor wishes to give Duke access, but he is not willing to travel to Athens.

> *"Just give me the combination and I will take care of the rest," Duke said.*
>
> *"Not so fast," said the Professor, with a smile, "I am just selling you this one package. I would not like to have the British Secret Service rummaging through my things every time you get the notion. My cousin Constantine will provide you with the documents. I will give you a letter to carry to him. It is too dangerous to send him a message by any other means."*
>
> *"How will he know the letter is genuine?"*
>
> *"It contains a phrase Constantine and I have previously agreed upon."*

Constantine represents an application server. The letter instructing him to give Duke the secret papers contains a phrase that lets Constantine know the letter is genuine.

> *"But, my dear Professor, once I read your letter, what is to keep us from using your phrase whenever we please?"*
>
> *"Now, Edward, don't you think I trust your honor as a gentleman?" the Professor said in mock protest. "But, in fact, the letter is written in the secret language of an extinct tribe of gypsies, known only to the male members of my family, so you will not be able to read it."*

The letter is written (encrypted) in a secret language. Since the British cannot read the letter, they cannot make up other, fake letters, because the letters would not contain the phrase known to the professor and Constantine.

> "Well then, suppose the opposition were to obtain the letter and use an impostor to present it to your cousin?"
>
> "I certainly hope that does not occur, for it would mean that they had ended the career of Commander Duke. But it would do them no good, for the letter instructs Constantine to challenge you by making this sign with his hands, and you must reply just so," said the Professor, demonstrating. "If you fail to do this correctly, you will not leave Constantine's establishment alive."

The final touch is to ensure that Constantine knows that the person presenting the letter is the one to whom it was given—that it was not stolen. This is done by teaching Commander Duke a secret set of hand signs, which are described to Constantine in the letter. The result of this procedure is that Edward Duke can get what he wants because: (1) Constantine knows what is required, (2) Constantine knows the request is genuine, (3) Constantine knows that Duke is the authorized bearer of the request, and (4) the process does not give the British the ability to create other, forged requests.

10.2.2   Special techniques

Now let us consider how DCE security operates to provide the same kind of assurances. The entire process is easier to understand by first considering several special techniques it employs.

The first one is to use a principal's password to create a secret key to encrypt and decrypt messages. The password itself is not used. Instead, it is changed to a different form using a "one-way" encryption algorithm just like most operating systems use. This is then that principal's permanent secret key.

A second technique is the use of short-term *conversation keys*. Although each principal has a permanent password (key) which is known to the authentication service, it is used only to set up a secure exchange. For an authenticated interaction (conversation) between two principals, the Security Service provides both principals with a key that they will use for the duration of the conversation. This has two advantages. First, no principal ever learns the permanent key associated with another principal, thus reducing the chances that it will fall into the wrong hands. Second, if the conversation key should become known to an intruder, it will be of no value once the conversation is over.

A third technique is to encrypt a message and give it to a principal that does not have the key to decrypt it. Although the principal cannot read the message, it can pass it along to another principal who *can* decrypt it. The Security Service transmits conversation keys to an application server through the client in this manner. When an encrypted message of this type is an authenticated request directed to a server, it is called a *ticket*.

A variation of this technique is also used in which the ticket is encrypted with one key and then the resulting ciphertext, along with additional information, is encrypted with a second key. This technique is illustrated in Fig. 10.2. It allows the entire message to be passed to a principal who has the "outer" key, but not the "inner" key. That principal can access the added information in the outer wrapper, but only pass along the inner ticket to a principal who knows the key used for the first encryption of the ticket.

A fourth technique is used by DCE security to allow an application client to prove to an application server that a message it is using to gain access to a resource was not stolen, but was actually given to the client by the Security

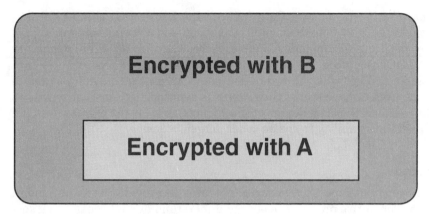

Figure 10.2 Double encryption—inner and outer keys.

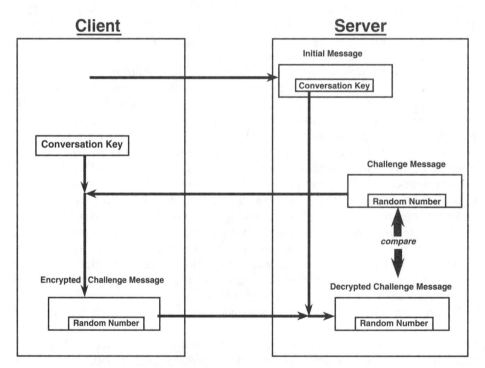

Figure 10.3 Authentication challenge message.

Service. Figure 10.3 shows the steps. A conversation key known to the client is sent to the server within the resource request message. When the server gets the request, it generates a random number and sends it to the client. The client encrypts it (using the conversation key) and sends it back to the server. The server uses the conversation key inside the original message to decrypt the number, thus proving that the client knows the conversation key and therefore is the rightful originator of the message and not someone who copied it off the network.

10.2.3 Putting it all together

Now let us look at the authentication process from beginning to end. The steps are shown in Fig. 10.4. The process begins with a user login. First, the account name is typed. This is sent, as cleartext, to the security server. The security server (using authorization procedures explained in the next section) creates a ticket for the principal corresponding to the account and encrypts it, using a key stored in the security database that has been derived from the user's password. Also in the encrypted message is a conversation key generated by the security server just for its own conversation with this principal.

Because the ticket will later be used by the principal to ask the security server for tickets that authorize access to application servers, it is referred to as a *Ticket-Granting Ticket* (TGT). The encrypted TGT is sent to the principal's node. After it has been received, the user is prompted for a password. The password is immediately converted to the new key and that copy of the password is destroyed.

Now the derived key is used to decrypt the message. By examining certain fields, the login program can tell if the decryption succeeded and, therefore, if

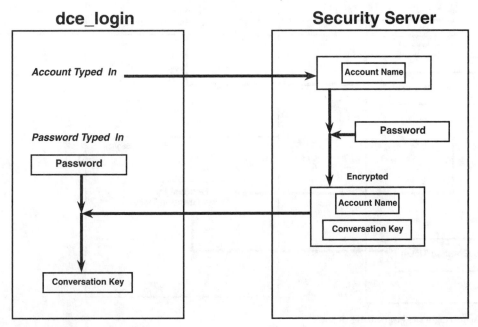

Figure 10.4 Initial login process.

the correct password was typed. If so, the principal now has a TGT and a conversation key that can be used to communicate with the security server.

In order to communicate securely with an application server, the principal must obtain a *Privilege Attribute Certificate* (PAC) from the security server. The PAC contains information on the principal's authorization, in other words, what sort of principal this is. The PAC is obtained from a part of the security server known as the *Privilege Service*. Figure 10.5 illustrates this process.

Because the privilege service is architected as a separate service within the security server, a two-step process is necessary. The principal first requests a ticket to the privilege service from the authentication service and then requests a ticket containing the PAC from the privilege service. In each step, the principal uses the TGT and conversation key previously obtained. The ticket containing the PAC is called the *Privilege-Ticket-Granting Ticket* (PTGT).

Normally, all of the above steps take place as part of the DCE login process. The results, including the tickets and conversation keys, are known as the *login context*. The login context is stashed away somewhere in the environment where it can be accessed by applications as needed.

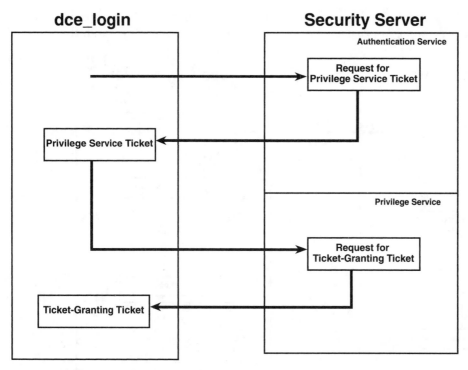

Figure 10.5 Acquiring a ticket-granting ticket.

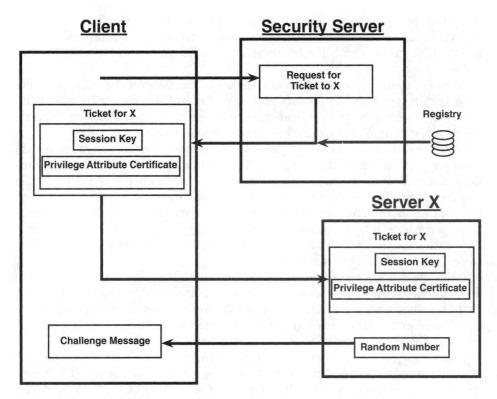

Figure 10.6 Authenticating to an application server.

The next step is for the application client to authenticate itself to an application server. This process is illustrated in Fig. 10.6. First, the client obtains a binding handle to a server that supports a compatible interface, matching object UUIDs, if any, and so forth. The method of doing this was discussed in Chaps. 5 and 7 on RPC and in Chap. 9 on the Directory Service.

Once the client obtains a binding handle, it can determine the principal name of the application server. It then sends a request to the security server to obtain a ticket to access the application server. This request includes the principal name of the server and the PTGT, which, as noted above, contains the PAC. The request is encrypted with the conversation key.

If the application server is a properly registered principal, the Security Service will know its password. (More precisely, it will know the key derived from its password.) The Security Service creates a new conversation key for the application client and server to use. This application-session conversation key and the client's PAC are combined to create the ticket to the application server, which is then encrypted with the application server's password (key). Then this ciphertext plus a copy of the new application-session conversation key are encrypted using the client's conversation key previously established for the client conversations with the security server. The whole thing is sent back to the client.

Since the client knows its conversation key, it can decrypt the outer package. As a result, it learns the conversation key that will be shared by it and the application server for the application session. As it does not know the server's password, it cannot decrypt the application server ticket.

When the client makes a request of the server, the server must decide whether or not to perform the request. The first thing it does is generate a random number, as discussed previously, with which to challenge the client.* The client encrypts the random number with the application-session conversation key and sends that ciphertext, along with the encrypted ticket, to the server. The server uses its own password (key) to decrypt the ticket. Using the new application-session conversation key, the server decrypts the random number to see if it matches what was sent.

If the check is successful, then the server knows that the client is a properly authenticated principal whose authorization is described by the PAC. Further, both the client and server are now in possession of a session conversation key that they can use for various purposes. For example, they can use it to encrypt the data they send to each other.

In summary, notice the key points. Each principal starts sharing one piece of knowledge with the Security Service—namely, its own password. The client proves its identity to the Security Service by using its password to decrypt a message. The Security Service never communicates directly with servers. Instead, on request, it provides the client with a ticket that the client cannot decrypt. The server then uses its own password to decrypt the ticket. At the end, the client and server have been authenticated to each other and are in possession of a session conversation key for use in further communications.

10.3 Authorization

Once the authentication process has verified the identity of a principal, the Security Service must determine what sort of principal it is (that is, what kinds of things it is allowed to do). This is called *authorization*. Compared to authentication, authorization is quite easy to understand.

We have already described how a client principal obtains from the security server a privilege authorization certificate, or PAC, which becomes part of the resource request message it sends to an application server. The PAC is gener-

---

* The random number helps to ensure that another node on the network cannot simply capture and replay the messages that the client sends, and use them to obtain unauthorized access.

ated by the security server by consulting the *registry,* a database that is the major element of the Security Service concerned with authorization.

The registry contains entries for *principals, accounts, groups,* and *organizations.* The password associated with a principal's account is used in the authentication process as described previously. When the PAC is generated by the Security Service, it contains the name of the principal and the identity of all of the groups to which the principal belongs.

The meaning of a principal has been discussed previously. A principal is something that can participate in authenticated communications—users, servers, machines (nodes), or cells. Cell principals are used for authentication between different cells. Machine principals are used by the login program to verify the identity of the security server. This chapter confines its attention to user and server principals.

The difference between server principals and user principals is the way that passwords are treated. Figure 10.7 illustrates this difference. Remember that authentication depends on a password shared between the Security Service and the principal. The Security Service copy of the encrypted password is kept in the registry. Users can memorize their passwords, but this will not work for servers.

Servers ought to run as distinct principals, but for production use they should be started automatically. For two reasons, it would be a poor idea to compile a password into a server or to store it in a batch command file. First, it

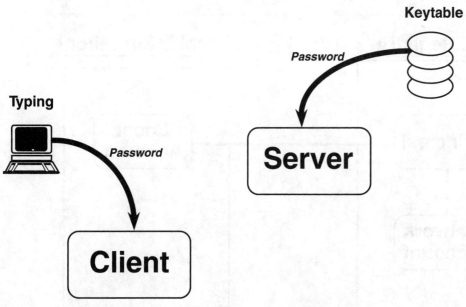

Figure 10.7 Server passwords come from a key table.

would increase the risk that the password would become known to unauthorized users. Second, it is very desirable to change passwords from time to time, so there must be a reasonably convenient way for an administrator to change both copies of a server password simultaneously.

DCE solves this problem by using key tables. Key tables are local files that are protected so that they can be read only by the server. The key tables contain the (encrypted) server password. In contrast to the registry database, which is collocated with the Security Server, the key tables for each application server must be located on all the nodes where it can run.

Every principal in the registry has associated with it local account information and network account information. The reason the two are distinct is that DCE runs over many different operating systems, each of which may organize local account information differently. The local account information is maintained by the local operating system. The principal entry in the registry contains one field, which is the name of the local account. (The DCE documentation refers to this as the *UNIX name*.)

The network account information associated with a principal is kept in the registry in an account entry. Every account entry is associated with both a principal and a group. Every principal is identified by a UUID different from that of any other principal. The relationship between principals and their local and network accounts is illustrated in Fig. 10.8.

A *group* is simply a named collection of principals which is used for access control, as described in detail in the next section. The idea of groups is that they contain principals allowed to do the same things. When an authorization

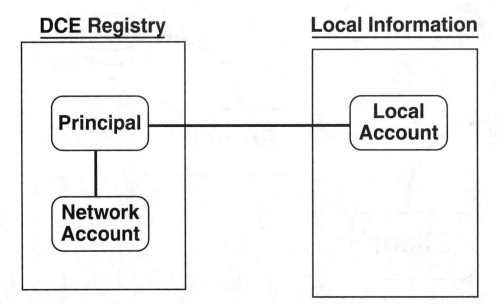

Figure 10.8 Principals: local and network accounts.

change is made, it can be applied to a group as a whole instead of necessitating a change of each principal's authorization.

A principal can belong to any number of groups. Associated with every group is a list of principals belonging to that group. Associated with every principal is a list of the groups to which it belongs.

An *organization* is a named collection of principals that is simply an administrative convenience. For example, policies such as the minimum length for passwords can be specified for a whole organization. DCE organizations are intended to correspond to real-world organizations. In the registry, it is actually the account that is associated with the organization. Every account (and, therefore, every principal) belongs to just one organization. The relationship between principals, groups, and accounts is illustrated in Fig. 10.9.

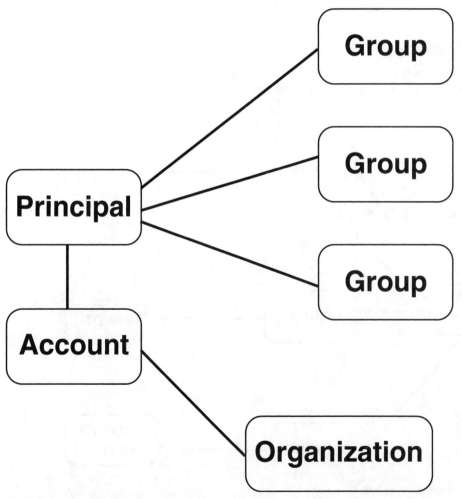

Figure 10.9 Principals, groups, accounts, and organizations.

DCE permits the use of *aliases*. An alias is a special type of principal that has the same UUID as another principal, but a different name. An alias has the same local account (UNIX name) as its principal, but a different network account. An alias can therefore have a different password and belong to different groups. Aliases are intended to be used with user principals to allow a person to log in with different attributes for different purposes. For example, the same person might be both a cell administrator and an ordinary user. Figure 10.10 depicts the relationship between principals, aliases, and their accounts.

That is all there is to authorization. When a principal logs in to the cell, the Security Service consults the principal's account entry in the registry to learn its password. Once authentication has taken place, the registry is consulted to identify the groups the principal belongs to. The identity of the principal, the groups it belongs to, and its home cell are all incorporated in the PAC for use by access control.

10.4   Access Control

The responsibility for DCE security now passes to the server to exercise access control. Access control is implemented using Access Control Lists (ACLs). An

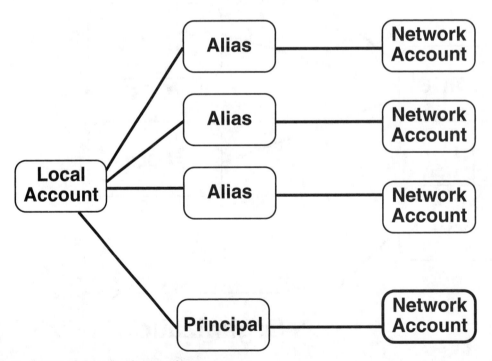

Figure 10.10 Principals: aliases and accounts.

ACL can be associated with any object or resource that needs to be protected. What an ACL is associated with is entirely up to the application. An ACL could apply to a hardware device, a single item of data, a whole file, or even an entire computer system.

Figure 10.11 shows a typical ACL. Notice that the word *list* in the name is very appropriate. An ACL is a list that specifies who is allowed to do what operations on the object that the ACL refers to. Each line (list element) in the ACL is called an *entry*. The three parts of an ACL entry are called the *entry type,* the *key,* and the *permissions.* Some ACL entry types do not have a key. The way that an ACL is interpreted is discussed later in this section.

10.4.1 Different kinds of ACLs

There are a number of different kinds of ACLs, which play different roles in DCE security.

First of all, suppose we have an object that we wish to protect with an ACL. The simplest way to make this ACL accessible is to register the object in the namespace. However, the Cell Directory Service (CDS) always creates an ACL to protect each entry in the namespace. Therefore, two overall kinds of ACLs may be associated with the same object, one protecting the directory entry for the object and one protecting the object itself.

Second, consider that objects can be either simple objects or container objects. Container objects, as the name implies, are objects that can contain other objects. A disk file directory is a good example of a container object. Note that a container object could, in principle, contain both simple objects and container objects. Now, when a new object is created, it is desirable for it to start life with an ACL, and there should be some way, administratively, to specify the default values for this new ACL.

To meet this requirement, DCE security provides for *Object ACLs, Initial Object Creation ACLs,* and *Initial Container Creation ACLs.* The ACL APIs

```
user_obj:chsjp
user:lily:sjpk
foreign_user:/.../cabot.edu/julie:sj
group_obj:hsjpk
group:musicians:sp
group:dancers:hjk
group:clowns:j
foreign_group:/.../bigelow.edu/singers:
p
other_obj:k
any_other:jk
```

Figure 10.11 A typical access control list.

refer to these ACLs, collectively, as **sec_acl_type,** and, respectively, as **sec_acl_type_object, sec_acl_type_default_object,** and **sec_acl_type_default_container.** Object ACLs are the regular kind used to control access to the object. Simple and container objects each have one of these.

Only container objects have initial object creation and initial container creation ACLs. They are never used to control access; their only role is to provide default values when new objects are created within the container. Initial object creation ACLs provide the default values for simple objects and initial container creation ACLs provide the default values for container objects. A new container object also needs its own creation ACLs. The default values for them come from the corresponding creation ACLs of its parent container.

Figure 10.12 shows how this works. Big Box is a container object that can contain trinkets or other boxes. It has three ACLs called BB (Big Box), TD (Trinket Default), and BD (Box Default). If we create a trinket in Big Box, it will have one ACL and its default values will come from TD. If we create a Little Box (a container) inside of Big Box, its ACL default values will come from BD. The default values for its initial object creation ACL will come from TD and those for its initial container creation ACL will come from BD.

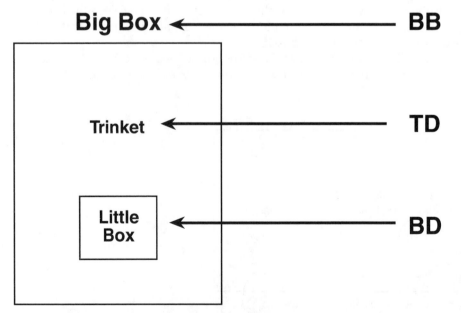

Figure 10.12 Object, default container, and default object ACLs.

ACLs can also be considered as coming in different flavors. This is because ACLs are used to protect different objects for which different operations, and therefore permissions, are appropriate. An ACL for a file might have permissions corresponding to read, write, and create. A printer ACL might have permissions such as print, get status, and so on. These ACLs may not support all of the ACL entry types either.

OSF calls such variations *ACL manager types,* referring to the ACL manager or managers that every server protecting resources with ACLs must provide. This is potentially misleading, because not only are the managers different, but so are the ACLs. ACL managers are discussed further in Chap. 11.

10.5   Interpreting ACLs

Although every server must implement its own ACL managers, all ACLs have the same entry types and are supposed to be processed in the same general way. There are two basic ACL entries: *privilege attribute entries* and *mask entries.* Privilege attribute entries specify a principal, group, or other category that has a certain set of permissions. Mask entries are used to limit the permissions given to a class of users. The term *mask* comes from the common programming technique of performing a bitwise **AND** (**&** in C) of a field with a mask.

The next section first describes the general meaning of privilege attribute entries, and then describes mask entries. Following that, the entire process of interpreting an ACL is presented.

10.5.1   Privilege attribute entries

There are nine privilege attribute entry types. They are listed in Table 10.1. Every ACL has associated with it a home cell. The term *local* is used to refer to principals and groups belonging to the same cell as the object. The term *foreign* is used to refer to principals and groups from other cells. The object that the ACL protects may also have an owner principal and an owner group associated with it. These determine the interpretation of certain ACL entry types as described below.

TABLE 10.1   Privilege Attribute Entry Types

Entry type	Description	Key	May appear in ACL
user_obj	owner principal	none	once
user	specific principal	principal	multiple times
foreign_user	specific principal	cell/principal	multiple times
group_obj	owner group	none	once
group	specific group	group	multiple times
foreign_group	specific group	cell/group	multiple times
other_obj	other local principals	none	once
foreign_other	other foreign principals	cell	multiple times
any_other	other principals	none	once

The owner principal need not be a member of the owner group. Neither do the owner principal or the group principal have to be registered in the home cell, and the home cell need not be the same as the cell in which the object is located. However, normally these conditions will be true.

Notice that the entries with no key are exactly those that can appear only once in an ACL. If an entry type does not appear, it means that principals of that class are granted no permissions.

Here are what the entry types refer to:

user_obj	The one specific principal that "owns" the object
user	A particular local principal identified by the key
foreign_user	A particular principal from a particular foreign cell identified by the key
group_obj	The one specific group that "owns" the object
group	A particular local group identified by the key
foreign_group	A particular group from a particular foreign cell identified by the key
other_obj	Any other local principal not identified by any other entry
foreign_other	Any other foreign principal from a particular foreign cell identified by the key, not identified by any other entry
any_other	Any other principal not identified by any other entry

Notice that if an **other_obj** entry is present, then the **any_other** entry will refer exclusively to foreign principals. If there is no **other_obj** entry, then the **any_other** entry may refer to both local and foreign principals.

The format of an ACL entry is <entry name>:<key>:<permissions>, or, for the **user_obj, group_obj, other_obj** and **any_other** entries that do not have a key, <entry name>:<permissions>. The entry name is, of course, one of the nine keywords.

The key field is either a principal name, group name, cell name, or a combination of these. Principal and group names are simple text identifiers. A cell name is specified as it would be in whichever choice of Global Directory Service (GDS) is used.* That is, it starts with / . . . / followed by the fully qualified cell name. The cell name does not have a / at the end. An example cell name, using X.500, would be:

```
"/.../C=US/O=Onsett International Corporation/OU=padded"
```

If DNS is used, the cell name would look like this:

```
"/.../padded.onsett.com"
```

---

*ACL managers actually identify principals, groups, and cells by their UUIDs. Both the UUIDs and string names are stored in the ACL data structure, but the strings are only for human-readable display.

The **foreign_user** and **foreign_group** entries have keys that contain a cell name, then /, followed by a principal or group name, respectively. Assuming that "lockhart" is a principal and "programmers" is a group, the DNS syntax would look like this:

```
"/.../padded.onsett.com/lockhart"
```

and

```
"/.../padded.onsett.com/programmers"
```

The permissions field of an ACL entry specifies what the class of principal is allowed to do. The permissions are single alphabetic characters, meaningful to the particular ACL manager type. The permissions are usually written one after another without any spaces. Permissions are implemented as bits that are on if the permission is present. The characters used and their meanings are different from one flavor of ACL to another.

Most flavors of ACL use the **c** (control) permission to indicate that a given class of principals can modify the ACL itself. The reason this works is that the ACL managers contain the code to create and modify the ACLs that they manage. If the **c** permission is used, then the ACL manager must ensure that at least one entry in an ACL contains the **c** permission. Otherwise, it might be possible to create an ACL no one could modify. An alternative to using the **c** permission would be to allow only the object's owner to change its ACL.

10.5.2   Mask entries

ACL mask entries are used to limit the permissions that would otherwise be granted to a class of principals. There are two ACL mask entry types: **mask_obj** and **unauthenticated.** Each type can appear only once in an ACL. The format of the mask entries is just the same as that of privilege attribute entries that do not specify a key: <entry name>:<permissions>.

The **mask_obj** entry limits the permissions granted by any privilege attribute entry or combination of them, except for the **user_obj** and **other_obj** entry types. In other words, if the principal in question matches the **user_obj** or the **other_obj** entry, then the **mask_obj** entry is not used. Otherwise, the procedure is to first calculate the permissions allowed for the principal and then eliminate any that do not also appear in the **mask_obj** entry. If there is no **mask_obj** entry in the ACL, then the permissions will not be limited. If there is a **mask_obj** entry with an empty permission field, however, then no permissions will be granted (except as specified by the **user_obj** and **other_obj** entry types).

The **unauthenticated** entry limits the permissions granted to a principal whose claimed identity matches one or more of the ACL entries, but whose identity has not been certified by the Security Service. If the **unauthenticated** entry is not present or contains no permissions, it means an unauthenticated principal is allowed no permissions.

The exact role played by the mask entries will become clearer in the next section as the entire process of interpreting an ACL is described.

10.5.3 ACL access checking

ACL access checking answers the question: Should this principal be allowed to perform this action on this object? A slightly different way of asking essentially the same question is: What actions is this principal allowed to perform on this object? This discussion is geared toward answering the second question, as that will allow us to easily answer the first question.

To answer the question, the following items associated with the object are needed: the ACL, the owner principal of the object, the owner group of the object, and the home cell of the object. Also needed are the following items associated with the principal (and contained in the PAC): the identity of the principal, the list of groups to which the principal belongs (also called the *principal's project list*), and the principal's home cell.

The ACL entries are always processed in a particular order, regardless of the order in which they appear in the ACL. The first entries processed are those that identify a particular principal: **user_obj, user,** and **foreign_user.** Next come all the group entries: **group_obj, group,** and **foreign_group.** Last are the residual entries: **other_obj, foreign_other,** and **any_other.**

Generally speaking, as soon as a match is found, the indicated permissions are accepted and no further processing is done. The exception is the group entries; all the group entries are checked and the permissions combined. However, the general principle still applies: if at least one matching group entry is found, then no further ACL entries will be examined.

After a match has been found, except in the cases of the **user_obj** and **other_obj** entries, the **mask_obj** entry will be applied to limit the permissions. Further, if the principal's credentials have not been certified, the **unauthenticated** mask will be applied as well.

Figures 10.13, 10.14, and 10.15 show the three steps in flowchart form. To simplify the presentation, several checks are combined into a single step. Each time a check is performed to see if the principal matches a particular entry type, it should be understood that a match will occur only if the entry of that type is present, the principal meets the criteria, and the principal's cell meets the criteria.

Figure 10.13 shows the checking of principal entries. First **user_obj,** then **user,** then **foreign_user**, are checked. The processing for each is the same except that the **mask_obj** is not applied when the **user_obj** entry is used.

The processing of group entities is shown in Fig. 10.14. Note that if processing gets this far (because there was no match in the previous step), all group entries will be checked and all permissions from any matching groups will be combined. This makes sense, because a principal can belong to any number of groups. Notice that, because every principal belongs to a particular cell, it may match the **group** entries or a subset of the **foreign_group** entries, but not both.

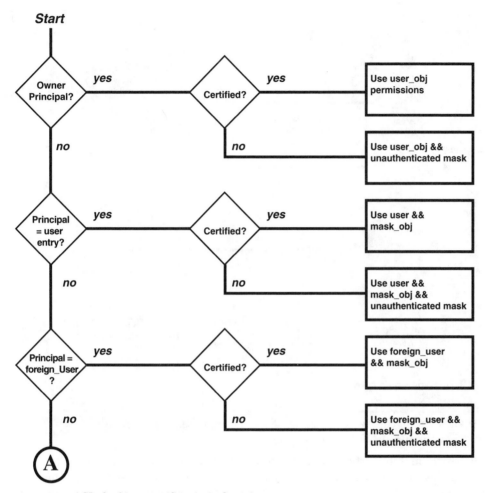

Figure 10.13 ACL checking: specific principal entries.

Figure 10.15 shows the processing of the residual entries. Once again, the processing for each step is similar, except that, if the **other_obj** entry is used, the **mask_obj** is not applied. The final entry checked, **any_other**, will match anything, so this match will fail only if the entry is not present. In that case, no permissions will be granted.

10.5.4 ACL checking example

Here is an example of how the checking would work for a variety of principals. Table 10.2 shows a set of users, their home cells, and the groups they belong to. Table 10.3 shows the principal owner, group owner, and home cell of something called object X, which is protected by an ACL. Figure 10.16 shows the ACL protecting object X. Table 10.4 shows the permissions that would be available to each of these users.

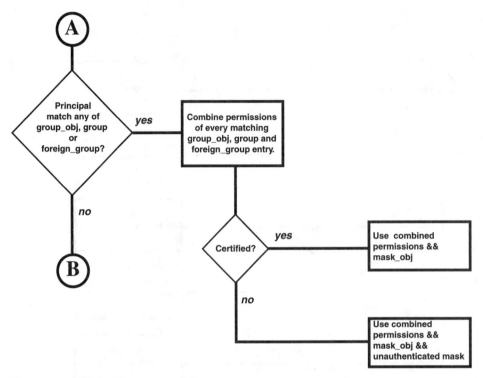

Figure 10.14 ACL checking: group entries.

- Groucho is the owner of object X, so he matches the **user_obj** entry. Notice that the **mask_obj** is not applied.

- Chico matches the **user:chico** entry. Because the **mask_obj** entry is applied, Chico does not actually get the "k" permission. Notice that because an entry matched, the group entries are not checked, even though Chico would match them.

- Harpo does not match any of the particular principal entries, but he matches two groups. He therefore gets all of the permissions in both (limited by **mask_obj**).

TABLE 10.2 ACL Example: Users

User	Cell	Groups
groucho	hollywood	clowns
chico	hollywood	clowns, musicians
harpo	hollywood	clowns, musicians
zeppo	hollywood	straightmen
charlie	london	clowns, dancers
harold	kansas	clowns

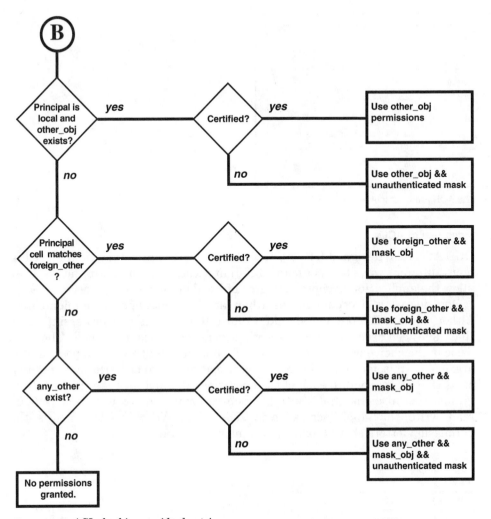

Figure 10.15 ACL checking: residual entries.

- Zeppo does not match any of the individual or group entries, but because his cell is the same as that of object X, he matches the **other_obj** entry. As the **mask_obj** is not applied, he gets the "k" permission.

- Charlie matches the **foreign_user** entry. Note that if this entry were not present, Charlie would not match any of the group entries, because he is from a different cell.

- Harold is in either the wrong group or the wrong cell to match any of the previous entries, so the **any_other** entry is applied. Because the **mask_obj** is applied, he gets only the "j" permission.

```
Object X's ACL-possible permissions: chsjpk
user_obj:chsjp
user:chico:sjpk
foreign_user:/.../london.com/charlie:sj
group_obj:hsjpk
group:musicians:sp
group:dancers:hjk
group:clowns:j
foreign_group:/.../kansas.com/musicians:p
other_obj:k
any_other:jk
```

Figure 10.16   The ACL protecting object X.

10.5.5   Intended use of ACLs

DCE ACLs are designed for very flexible use. Potentially, they can be used in many different ways to meet many different access control requirements. They allow the application designer a degree of freedom in several respects.

One degree of freedom arises when an ACL manager is implemented. Although an ACL manager should conform to the rules and processing steps that have been described, there are still several decisions to be made. The most basic is the choice of permissions and of what they control. Some possibilities are: one permission that allows all server operations to be performed; permissions that correspond to each of the operations defined for the interface; fine-grained permissions that control suboperations; generic permissions (e.g., read, write) that apply across several operations. Whatever the choices, the permission letters should have some mnemonic value.

**TABLE 10.3   ACL Example:
Object X Attributes**

	Object X
Owner user	groucho
Owner groups	producers
Home cell	hollywood

TABLE 10.4   ACL Example: The Effective Permissions

Principal	Entries matched	Apply mask_obj?	Effective permissions
groucho	user_obj	No	chsjp
chico	user:chico	Yes	sjp
harpo	group:musicians group:clowns	Yes	sjp
zeppo	other_obj	No	k
charlie	foreign_user:	Yes	sj
harold	any_other	Yes	j

The developer must also decide how the owner principal and owner group will be identified. One approach is to disregard these entry types altogether. Any of the entry types can be eliminated from an ACL manager. The ACL manager must have a means of limiting the ability to change the ACL. If the **c** permission is used for this purpose, the ACL manager must ensure that at least one entry has the **c** permission at all times. Otherwise, it would be possible to create an ACL that no one can modify. An alternative scheme would be to allow only the owner principal to modify the ACL and not use the **c** permission at all. In any event, the **c** permission should never be used for any other purpose, because it would lead to confusion.

A second degree of freedom arises when the actual ACL entries are set up. The number of ways that ACL entries can be used is limited only by the imagination of the person doing it. However, ACL processing takes place as it does because entry types were intended to be used in a certain way. Generally, things will work better if the following guidelines are followed.

First, because ACL processing ends once a matching entry is found, the entries that are processed first usually should have the most permissions. For example, if the **user_obj** entry had fewer permissions than some **group** entries for groups that the owner principal belonged to, then the owner would be unable to do things that his or her group membership ought to entitle the owner to do.

The **user_obj** and **group_obj** are intended to identify a user and a group as having some special relationship to the object. Typically, the **user_obj** entry would have the **c** permission if it is implemented. The **group** entries are the normal way that most permissions are granted. Users should be assigned membership to groups based on some common reason for accessing the system. Groups normally correspond to natural real-world groupings. Auditors, students, chess players, and mothers are examples of natural groups.

The fact that group attributes are combined fits this model well, because individuals can be members of more than one group (e.g., a mother and a student). The same considerations apply to **foreign_group** entries. The main difference is that users in other cells might have fewer permissions than local users.

The **user** ACL entry is intended for the relatively rare situation in which a particular user needs a special permission. Generally, if a permission is even potentially generic, it is better to create a group, even if it has only one member at the outset. The **user** entry could also be used to grant an individual fewer permissions than group membership would normally allow. If a large number of **user** entries are created, they will be a headache to administer.

The residual entry types, **other_obj, foreign_other,** and **any_other,** are intended to provide some low level of permissions available to unidentified local and foreign users. It would not make a lot of sense for these entries to have more permissions than principals and groups that are specifically identified.

The **mask_obj** entry is, strictly speaking, unnecessary. That is, any assignment of permissions that can be achieved by using **mask_obj** can be done by changing other entries.* However, the **mask_obj** entry is a great convenience. When a complex ACL with many entries has been created, it is easy to lose track of who can do what. The **mask_obj** can help ensure that the general run of users is not accidentally given more permissions than intended.

The **unauthenticated** mask normally will not be used at all. Generally, there is no point in going to the trouble (and processing overhead) of using authentication to begin with if unauthenticated users are given permissions. However, in certain cases it may be desirable to allow unauthenticated users to get certain services.

Note that although the ACL processing steps treat each case separately, there is really no reason to treat an unauthenticated user who claims to be a certain principal any differently from one who claims to be another. In other words, there really is no difference between an unauthenticated **user_obj** and an unauthenticated **any_other.** The conclusion is that, if used at all, the **unauthenticated** mask should not be a superset of any entry's permissions.

Finally, the **c** (control) permission should be granted with great caution. In effect, having the **c** permission is equivalent to having all permissions. This is because a principal with the **c** permission could simply run the **acl_edit** program (or equivalent) and give itself any permission it wants.

10.6   Chapter Summary

The DCE Security Service provides authentication, authorization, and access control. Parties to secure interactions are referred to as principals. Authentication means determining that a principal is who he or she claims to be. Authorization means determining the attributes of the principal. Access control means deciding if a principal is allowed to perform a certain action on a certain object.

DCE authentication is based on secret key encryption. Starting with a key known only to a given principal and the Security Service, the principal can obtain a special message, called a ticket, which will allow the principal to request services and exchange messages securely with any DCE or application server. The design of these protocols is such that even if another party captures all of the messages transmitted it is not possible to impersonate the legitimate principal.

If the principal represents a human user of the system, the secret key is derived from the password that the user types. If the principal is a server, it obtains its key from a local file called a key table. DCE cannot protect against security breaches caused by users telling other people their passwords or by unauthorized access to key tables.

---

* In point of fact, as this was being written the **mask_obj** entry was eliminated from the most recent POSIX.6 revision.

DCE principals may be members of one or more groups and are identified with a home cell. They may also be identified with an organization for purposes of policy and administration. Once users are authenticated and request access to some server, the information about their identity is encrypted into a message called a Privilege Attribute Certificate (PAC). The PAC is presented to a server along with a request for service.

Access control is implemented by means of Access Control Lists (ACLs). Every protected object has an ACL associated with it. An ACL specifies the operations allowed to various categories of principals. Principals are identified individually, as members of groups, local cell, and specified other cells. DCE specifies a standard algorithm for processing an ACL, but it is the responsibility of the developer of a server to properly implement the ACL manager that manipulates and evaluates its ACLs.

11

Using the DCE Security Service

The previous two chapters described the DCE Security Service. We have examined the design assumptions and requirements and how each of the components—authentication, authorization, and access control—works to meet the requirements while incorporating a number of desirable features.

The developer gains the use of the Security Service by implementing authenticated RPC. This chapter explains how to do this. It also discusses some of the options offered by the Security Service and recommends when to use them.

As we have seen in the previous chapter, the Security Service functions in essentially three stages. The first, establishing a user's identity, takes place as part of the login process in which communications between a principal (typically a user) and the security server conclude in the user being granted a Privilege Attribute Certificate (PAC) contained within a Privilege-Ticket-Granting Ticket (PTGT). Respectively, they describe the user in terms of a principal identity with a set of privileges and give that user the means to request that those privileges be granted in terms of the resources of an application server. Together with session encryption keys, they are filed as a security identity associated with the user, known as a *login context*.

Once this has been done, it is possible for the components of a distributed application to communicate securely. First, the client and server establish an authenticated exchange that concludes with the server accepting a resource request. The server then performs access control by matching the principal's authorization privileges against the server's protection of the resource in question, as represented by an Access Control List (ACL).

This chapter explains what the application developer must do to make all this happen. It assumes an understanding of the concepts introduced in the previous chapter. As in earlier chapters, the client is discussed first, then the server.

11.1   Security Facilities Used by a Client

Using authenticated RPC does not require adding a great deal of code to a client. The mechanisms described in the previous chapter are executed by routines provided by DCE. The client must merely make calls to the RPC runtime to indicate which security options are desired.

11.1.1   Authenticated RPC
with automatic binding

Figure 11.1 shows a simple client using the automatic binding method. It was created by adding security calls to the client program introduced in Chap. 5.

In this example, it is assumed that the person running the client program has already logged into DCE by using **dce_login** or some equivalent program. The client then uses the security identity created by the login program. This is the normal procedure, whether or not authenticated RPC is being used.

The first thing the client does is to call **sec_login_get_current_context**() in order to obtain a pointer to the login context previously set up by the login program. This call does not require any input arguments. It returns a handle to the current login context and a status variable.

Next the client calls **rpc_if_register_auth_info**() to tell the runtime that it wants to use authenticated RPC and to specify security options. The first argument is the handle of the interface to which the specified security options will be applied. The RPC runtime will automatically associate this security information with each binding created for operations in this interface. In the example, the symbol is "simple_v1_0_c_ifspec". Notice that the symbol the IDL compiler generated contains **_c_** (for client). It would be **_s_** for a server.

The second argument is a pointer to a string that is the principal name of the server. This can be provided to the client in many ways. It could be passed on the command line, stored in a file, or derived in some way from the directory name of the server. In our example, it is a compiled-in string. The name can be freely chosen, but the client and servers must be in agreement as to what it is. If there is to be only one instance of the server, then the principal name of the server can be the same as the name it exports to the namespace.

In the probably more common case in which there are several servers in the network offering the same service, the servers should be given different names. (This is required if the servers run on different nodes and recommended even if they run on the same node.) The same principal name, however, should be used for all identical servers. Among the reasons is that the client needs to be able to specify the principal name even though it does not know in advance which server it will bind to. It follows that when there are multiple servers, the principal name cannot be identical to the directory name.

For convenience of administration, however, it is desirable for the principal and directory names to be similar. For example, the directory name could be

```
/* SIMPLE_SEC.IDL */
[
uuid(004C4B40-E7C5-1CB9-94E6-0000C07C3610),
version(1.0)
]
interface simple
{
    boolean simple_operation(

        [in]  long x,
        [out] long *y
    );
}
----------------------------------------------------------------
/* SEC_CLIENT_AUTO.C */

#include <stdio.h>
#include <dce/rpc.h>
#include <dce/sec_login.h>
#include "simple_sec.h"

#define ERR_CHK(stat, msg) if(stat != rpc_s_ok)\
    { fprintf(stderr,"Error: %s in file: %s at line %d.\n",msg,__FILE__, __LINE__);\
    exit(1); }

main(int argc, char *argv[])
{
sec_login_handle_t login_context;
error_status_t status;
unsigned_char_t *princ_name = "/.:/simple_server";

idl_long_int x;
idl_long_int y;

if  (argc < 2 ) x = 1; else x = (idl_long_int) atol(argv[1]);

sec_login_get_current_context(&login_context, &status);
ERR_CHK(status,"Could not get current security context")

rpc_if_register_auth_info(
        simple_v1_0_c_ifspec,              /* Interface handle */
        princ_name,                        /* Server principal name */
        rpc_c_protect_level_pkt,           /* Protection level - every packet */
        rpc_c_authn_dce_secret,            /* Authentication service */
        (rpc_auth_identity_handle_t) login_context,
        rpc_c_authz_dce,                   /* Authorization type (PAC) */
        &status);
ERR_CHK(status,"Could not register security information")

        /* This is the Remote Procedure Call */

if (simple_operation(x, &y)) printf("The answer is: %ld.\n",y);
                    else printf("RPC failed\n");

return(1);
}
```

Figure 11.1 A client using authenticated RPC with automatic binding.

TABLE 11.1   DCE Security Protection Levels

Symbol	Meaning
rpc_c_protect_level_default	Use the default protection level
rpc_c_protect_level_none	Do not provide any protection
rpc_c_protect_level_connect	Verify identities when the client first connects
rpc_c_protect_level_call	Verify identities on each call to the server*
rpc_c_protect_level_pkt	Verify identities whenever data is sent
rpc_c_protect_level_pkt_integrity	Ensure that data sent has not been modified
rpc_c_protect_level_privacy	Encrypt the data that is sent

*Applies only to connectionless protocols. If used with a connection-based protocol (e.g., **ncacn_ip_tcp**) it will automatically be converted to **rpc_c_protect_level_pkt**.

the principal name plus the node name (e.g., "acct_serv_pluto"). Selecting the principal name for servers is an important development task, just as devising the naming scheme is.

The next argument selects the desired level of protection for the RPCs that will be used on this interface. Table 11.1 shows the options available and their symbolic names. Recall that the DCE authentication process reliably establishes the identity of the client and server to each other and also provides each with a session conversation key known only to the two of them. This key can be used to provide various levels of security on the data passed between client and server in the course of the RPC.

The level **rpc_c_protect_level_default** simply uses whichever of the other values is the local default. This value generally should not be used, because there is no way of knowing what protection is in effect, and because the default may vary with DCE implementations. The symbol **rpc_c_protect_level_none** is provided for completeness and should not be used. If security is not required, just don't bother with authentication at all.

If **rpc_c_protect_level_connect** is used, the identities of the client and server are verified only when the initial connection is established. This is generally insufficient, because an unauthorized user could send bogus data following the initial message exchange.* It might be acceptable, however, for certain applications with minimal security requirements.

Selecting **rpc_c_protect_level_call** causes the security system to use the session conversation key to attach an encrypted field to each RPC, which allows the client and server to confirm that the message came from the expected party. This is about the minimum choice that provides any useful protection. Because of differences in the RPC protocols used with connectionless versus connection-based transport protocols, this level will be applied only when a connectionless protocol (e.g., **ncacn_ip_udp**) is used. With a

---

* This is not merely a theoretical possibility. In 1992 a program that used this technique to fool a Novell NetWare server was demonstrated.

connection-based protocol (e.g., **ncacn_ip_tcp**), DCE will use **rpc_c_protect_level_pkt** instead. Because of this, unless the application has some specific reason for using a connectionless protocol only, it is better to specify **rpc_c_protect_level_pkt.**

Therefore, for most applications the choice of protection will be between **rpc_c_protect_level_pkt, rpc_c_protect_level_pkt_integrity,** and **rpc_c_protect_level_pkt_privacy.** They provide successively higher levels of security, but with increasing processing costs. The distributed application designer should select the lowest level that provides the functionality required by the application. Performance measurements available at the time this book is being written indicate that performance characteristics are just what would be expected. The performance cost is almost entirely in node processing time, the cost is linearly proportional to the message size, and the cost increases as the level of protection increases. Special-purpose encryption hardware or very fast general-purpose processors could conceivably eliminate the differences. In that case, it would make sense always to choose the highest protection level, even without a clear-cut requirement for it.

If **rpc_c_protect_level_pkt** is chosen, DCE attaches an encrypted verification field to each packet that is transmitted across the network. This differs from **rpc_c_protect_level_call** because a single RPC can result in the transmission of multiple network packets for several reasons. For example, multiple packets can result when the size of the data is greater than the maximum packet size permitted by the transport protocol, or because the pipe data type is being used.

The use of **rpc_c_protect_level_pkt** ensures that the source of the data is as purported. It does not guarantee that the data is unaltered, and it does not prevent any other node on the network from reading the data. It should be used in situations where minimizing delay is important, and where the likelihood of data being altered is small or the consequences of altered data being received can be ignored.

When **rpc_c_protect_level_pkt_integrity** is chosen, the Security Service calculates a checksum over the data in each packet and encrypts the checksum. This means that if a third party tries to alter the data, the checksum will no longer be correct. As the unauthorized party does not know the conversation key, it is not possible to correct the checksum to match the altered data. This choice would be useful in an application such as a transfer of funds, in which it is vital that the amount of money being transferred has not been changed. This level of protection does not prevent someone from reading the data. Its cost in processing is intermediate between the previous and next level.

The highest level of protection available is **rpc_c_protect_level_pkt_privacy.** This means that every packet is encrypted using the conversation key for the session. It provides all the protections of the previous levels and, in addition, prevents the data from being read. Although it carries a higher processing cost, the situations where it is needed are usually clear-cut. If the data

TABLE 11.2   DCE Authentication Services

Symbol	Meaning
rpc_c_authn_none	No authentication
rpc_c_authn_dce_secret	Use shared-secret key authentication
rpc_c_authn_dce_public	Use public key authentication (not implemented)
rpc_c_authn_default	Use the default type of authentication

being transmitted should not be disclosed, this level of protection should be used.

The next argument to **rpc_if_register_auth_info()** specifies the authentication service to be used. The possible values of this argument are shown in Table 11.2. The value **rpc_c_authn_dce_secret** should be used. The reasons are simple and similar to those given above in the discussion of protection level.

If you don't want to use authentication, just omit the security routine calls; there is no need to specify **rpc_c_authn_none.** DCE currently does not support public-key-based authentication, so **rpc_c_authn_dce_public** should not be used. Therefore, **rpc_c_authn_default** is equivalent to **rpc_c_authn_dce_secret.** It is better practice to specify **rpc_c_authn_dce_secret** explicitly, because it better documents the code and, as mentioned above, relying on the default could lead to unanticipated results if the code came into use with a future version of DCE in which the default has been changed.

The next argument is a handle to the principal's security information. In this case, the login context handle that was obtained from the previous call to **sec_login_get_current_context()** is passed. The cast is used because of the slightly different ways in which RPC and the Security Service libraries define a typeless pointer.

The next argument to **rpc_if_register_auth_info()** specifies the type of authorization to be used. Table 11.3 lists the possible values for this argument. The value that should be used is **rpc_c_authz_dce.** This means that authorization is based on a PAC and enables the use of ACLs for access control. The alternative, **rpc_c_authz_name,** is intended only for interoperability with non-DCE applications that use Kerberos. The value **rpc_c_authz_none** should not be used for reasons discussed previously.

The final argument is the usual status return variable. Once the call to **rpc_if_register_auth_info()** has executed successfully, every call made on the specified interface using automatic binding will perform authentication as specified.

TABLE 11.3   DCE Authorization Services

Symbol	Meaning
rpc_c_authz_none	No authorization
rpc_c_authz_name	Authorization based on client principal name
rpc_c_authz_dce	Authorization based on PAC

The example program contains one other difference from the example shown in Chap. 5. The IDL file has been changed to allow the routine to return a boolean value indicating success or failure. This could have been done in the example using RPC without authentication, but was left out to keep the example as simple as possible. Here, the primary reason that the routine might return an error is a security failure.

In summary, the use of authenticated RPC does not add much complexity to a client using automatic binding. The application designer must decide what the appropriate level of protection is. Other than that, it is simply a matter of making two calls to the runtime, using relatively static arguments.

11.1.2 Authenticated RPC with explicit binding

Using authenticated RPC in a client that uses implicit or explicit binding is very similar to using it with automatic binding. Early versions of DCE did not support the **rpc_if_register_auth_info()** and therefore did not permit automatic binding with authenticated RPC. An example of using authenticated RPC with explicit binding is shown in Fig. 11.2.

The main difference, compared to automatic binding, is that the security information is associated with a binding handle rather than with an interface. In the example, a binding handle is obtained by calling **rpc_ns_binding_import_begin()**, **rpc_ns_binding_import_next()**, and **rpc_ns_binding_import_done()**. Then the same call as in the automatic binding example is made to **sec_login_get_current_context()** to get a handle to the login context. In this case, **rpc_binding_set_auth_info()** is called instead of **rpc_if_register_auth_info()**. The two routines take almost the same arguments, with all the same semantics. The considerations are the same as were previously discussed. Only the first argument is different: instead of an interface handle, the previously obtained binding handle is passed.

In the example, the binding handle is then used as the first argument to the remote procedure call. If implicit binding is being used, the binding handle would be stored in the variable identified by the **implicit_handle** attribute in the ACF file. In either case, calls made using that binding handle will provide authenticated RPC with the specified characteristics.

11.2 Security Facilities Used by a Server

Implementing authenticated RPC requires more work on the part of the server than the client. There is also more freedom to decide what security checks should be made. The server must perform four basic steps. The first two take place in the server control routine when the server is initialized. They are:

- Register security information with the runtime.
- Log in under the principal name allocated for the server.

```
/* SIMPLE_SEC.IDL */
[
uuid(004C4B40-E7C5-1CB9-94E6-0000C07C3610),
version(1.0)
]
interface simple
{
    boolean simple_operation(

        [in]  rpc_binding_handle_t *binding,
        [in]  long x,
        [out] long *y
    );
}
-----------------------------------------------------------------
/* SEC_CLIENT_EXPLICIT.C */

#include <stdio.h>
#include <dce/rpc.h>
#include <dce/sec_login.h>
#include "simple_sec.h"

#define ERR_CHK(stat, msg) if(stat != rpc_s_ok)\
    { fprintf(stderr,"Error: %s in file: %s at line %d.\n",msg,__FILE__, __LINE__);\
    exit(1); }

main(int argc, char *argv[])
{
error_status_t status;
rpc_ns_handle_t binding_context;
rpc_binding_handle_t binding;
sec_login_handle_t login_context;
unsigned_char_t *princ_name = "/.:/simple_server";

idl_long_int x;
idl_long_int y;

if  (argc < 2 ) x = 1; else x = (idl_long_int) atol(argv[1]);

/*********** Get a binding to a compatible server ***********/

rpc_ns_binding_import_begin(rpc_c_ns_syntax_default,
                            NULL,
                            simple_v1_0_c_ifspec,
                            NULL,
                            &binding_context,
                            &status);
ERR_CHK(status,"Could not import binding context")

rpc_ns_binding_import_next(binding_context, &binding, &status);
ERR_CHK(status,"Could not find any bindings")
```

Figure 11.2 A client using authenticated RPC with explicit binding.

```
rpc_ns_binding_import_done(&binding_context, &status);
ERR_CHK(status,"Error releasing binding context")

/*********** Associate security information with the binding ***********/

sec_login_get_current_context(&login_context, &status);
ERR_CHK(status,"Could not get current security context")

rpc_binding_set_auth_info(
        binding,                        /* Binding handle to secure */
        princ_name,                     /* Server principal name */
        rpc_c_protect_level_pkt,        /* Protection level - every packet */
        rpc_c_authn_dce_secret,         /* Authentication service */
        (rpc_auth_identity_handle_t) login_context,
        rpc_c_authz_dce,                /* Authorization type (PAC) */
        &status);
ERR_CHK(status,"Could not associate security information with binding")

        /* This is the Remote Procedure Call */

if (simple_operation(binding, x, &y)) printf("The answer is: %ld.\n,y");
                                else printf("RPC failed\n");

return(1);
```

Figure 11.2   (*Continued*)

The next two steps are performed by every server operation, whenever a remote procedure call is made. They are:

- Check the security options used by the client.
- Enforce access control by calling the ACL manager.

11.2.1 Server initialization security steps

Figure 11.3 shows an example of a server that implements authenticated RPC. It is based on the example server introduced in Chap. 5. The first difference to notice is that the server must use a binding handle in the remote procedure. This is because in the server, just as in the client, security information is associated with the binding.

This can be done in several ways. In the example, the IDL file declares the binding handle as the first argument in the operation signature. This method would work well when the client uses explicit binding. If the client uses automatic binding, the server could use an ACF file with the **explicit_handle** attribute to override the automatic binding for the server. Another method would be to use an ACF file with the **auto_handle** attribute when building the client.

```
 /* SIMPLE_SEC.IDL */
[
uuid(004C4B40-E7C5-1CB9-94E6-0000C07C3610),
version(1.0)
]
interface simple
{
    boolean simple_operation(

        [in]  rpc_binding_handle_t *binding,
        [in]  long x,
        [out] long *y
    );
}
-----------------------------------------------------------------
/* SEC_SERVER.C */

#include <stdio.h>
#include <dce/rpc.h>
#include <dce/binding.h>
#include <dce/sec_login.h>
#include <dce/keymgmt.h>
#include <dce/daclif.h>
#include <dce/dce_cf.h>
#include "simple_sec.h"

#define ERR_CHK(stat, msg) if(stat != rpc_s_ok)\
    { fprintf(stderr,"Error: %s in file: %s at line %d.\n",msg,__FILE__, __LINE__);\
      exit(1); }
#define CND_CHK(cond, msg) if( (cond) )\
    { fprintf(stderr,"Error: %s in file: %s at line %d.\n",msg,__FILE__, __LINE__);\
      exit(1); }

unsigned_char_t       *name = "/.:/applications/simple"; /* Server CDS name */
unsigned_char_t *princ_name = "/.:/simple_server"; /* Server principal name */
unsigned_char_t full_princ_name[50];  /* Server principal name including Cell */
const unsigned32 simple_perm = sec_acl_perm_write; /* Overload CDS write */


/***** Server Control *****/

main()
{
error_status_t          status;
rpc_binding_vector_t    *bindings;

rpc_server_register_if(simple_v1_0_s_ifspec, NULL, NULL, &status);
ERR_CHK(status,"Could not register interface")
```

Figure 11.3 A server implementing authenticated RPC.

```
rpc_server_use_all_protseqs(rpc_c_protseq_max_regs_default, &status);
ERR_CHK(status,"Could not use all protocols")

rpc_server_inq_bindings(&bindings, &status);
ERR_CHK(status,"Could not get binding vector")

setup_auth();   /**** Initialize Security ****/

rpc_ns_binding_export(rpc_c_ns_syntax_default, name, simple_v1_0_s_ifspec, bind-
ings,
                      NULL, &status);
ERR_CHK(status,"Could not export bindings")

rpc_ep_register(simple_v1_0_s_ifspec, bindings, NULL, NULL, &status);
ERR_CHK(status,"Could not register endpoint")

printf("Listening for requests\n");

rpc_server_listen(rpc_c_listen_max_calls_default, &status);
}

/******************** Initialize Security ********************/

void setup_auth()
{
sec_login_handle_t login_context;
void *key_ptr;
boolean32 expired;
sec_login_auth_src_t auth_src;
char *cell_name_p;

rpc_server_register_auth_info(princ_name, rpc_c_authn_dce_secret,
                             NULL, NULL, &status);
ERR_CHK(status,"Could not register security information")

sec_login_setup_identity(princ_name, sec_login_no_flags,
                        &login_context, &status);
ERR_CHK(status,"Could not obtain login context")

sec_key_mgmt_get_key(rpc_c_authn_dce_secret, NULL, princ_name,
                    (unsigned32)0, &key_ptr, &status);
ERR_CHK(status,"Could not obtain password")

sec_login_validate_identity(login_context, (sec_passwd_rec_t) key_ptr,
                           &expired, &auth_src, &status);
ERR_CHK(status,"Could not validate identity")
CND_CHK(expired,"Password has expired")
CND_CHK(auth_src != sec_login_auth_src_network, "Network identity not available")

sec_login_set_context(login_context, &status);
```

Figure 11.3 *(Continued)*

```
dce_cf_get_cell_name( &cell_name_p,
                      &status);
ERR_CHK(status,"Could not obtain cell name");

sprintf((char *) full_princ_name, "%s/%s", cell_name_p, princ_name);
free((void *) cell_name_p);
}

/***** Server Operation *****/

void simple_operation(
    rpc_binding_handle_t *binding,
    idl_long_int x,
    idl_long_int *y)
{
if (sec_ok(binding, simple_perm)) {
    *y = ++x;
    return(TRUE);
    }
    else return(FALSE);
}

/***** Check if Client is Authorized *****/

boolean sec_ok(
    rpc_binding_handle_t binding,
    sec_acl_permset_t permissions)
{
unsigned_char_t            *server_name;
sec_id_pac_t               *pac;
unsigned32                 protect_level, authn_svc, authz_svc;
error_status_t             status;
sec_acl_handle_t           acl_h;
unsigned32                 size_used;
unsigned32                 num_types;
uuid_t                     mgr_uuid;
sec_acl_posix_semantics_t  pos_sem;


rpc_binding_inq_auth_client(binding, (rpc_authz_handle_t *) &pac, &server_name,
      &protect_level, &authn_svc, &authz_svc, &status);
if (status != rpc_s_ok) return(FALSE);

if(strcmp(server_name, full_princ_name) != 0) {
    rpc_string_free(&server_name, &status);
    return(FALSE);
    }
    else rpc_string_free(&server_name, &status);
```

Figure 11.3   (*Continued*)

```
if (authz_svc != rpc_c_authz_dce) return(FALSE);

sec_acl_bind(name, TRUE, &acl_h, &status);
if (status != rpc_s_ok) return(FALSE);

sec_acl_get_manager_types_semantics( acl_h, sec_acl_type_object,
        (unsigned32) 1, &size_used, &num_types, &pos_sem, &mgr_uuid, &status);
if (status != rpc_s_ok) return(FALSE);

return (sec_acl_test_access_on_behalf(acl_h, mgr_uuid, pac,
                                    permissions, &status));
```

Figure 11.3   *(Continued)*

In the example, for clarity, all of the added security calls performed when the server starts have been put into a subroutine, "setup_auth()". The location of the call to "setup_auth()" is somewhat arbitrary. It could be performed at almost any point before the call to **rpc_server_listen()**.

The first step in setting up security is to register with the runtime by calling **rpc_server_register_auth_info()**. The server must specify its principal name and the authentication service to be used. The value **dce_c_authn_dce_secret** should be used for the reasons discussed earlier. The next two arguments allow the server to specify its own routine to provide encryption keys as a function of the principal name from either the default key table or a specified one. The **NULL** arguments cause the DCE-provided routine and table to be used. As usual, the routine returns a status variable.

Notice that the server does not specify either the protection level or the type of authorization service. These are specified only by the client. As we will see shortly, the server will have the opportunity to check what values the client has specified and accept or reject them. This is intended to provide the maximum flexibility for a server to permit any one of several choices or even for the client and server to negotiate a set of mutually acceptable values. We recommend, however, that this not be done. Instead, we recommend that the application designer decide upon one appropriate protection level and use it in both client and server. For reasons discussed previously, the values **dce_c_authn_dce_secret** and **dce_c_authz_dce** should be used for the authentication and authorization services, respectively.

The second step in security initialization is to log the server in under its appropriate principal name. Unlike the client, which is typically run under the direct control of a user (human being), the server process usually will start up when the node is initialized. As was discussed previously, the server logs in to its own principal name by obtaining its password from a local file known as a key table. This process requires four calls to the runtime.

First, a login context is created and initialized with the principal name by calling **sec_login_setup_identity()**. Next, a password (key) is obtained from the key table using the principal name as the index into it. The call to **sec_key_mgmt_get_key()** does this. Then the login context is validated by calling **sec_login_validate_identity()**. The server must determine that the password has not expired and that the authentication was done by Kerberos (as opposed to locally). Finally, **sec_login_set_context()** is called to tell the runtime to use this new login context as the default. This completes the processing associated with initializing the server.

11.2.2   Server operation security steps

The remaining work to implement authenticated RPC in a server is to provide for checking at the time each server operation is called. As most of the code will be the same for every operation, the code can be put in a separate routine that can be called from each operation. Such a routine is sometimes referred to as a *reference monitor*. Generally speaking, the only required arguments to this routine are information identifying the client and indicating the operation the client is requesting. In most cases, the client will be identified by its binding handle, which has security information associated with it. The requested operation is generally represented as an ACL permission or set of permissions.

In the example in Fig. 11.3, the security-checking routine is called "sec_ok()". It takes a binding handle and a permission set as an argument. It returns TRUE if the client is authorized for that permission and FALSE if it is not. Notice that in calling the security initialization code from the server control routine, if we encountered an error we were willing to treat it as a fatal error and exit from the server. Of course, in a production server, there might be attempts to retry some of the operations and to work around the problem, but, generally, errors during initialization are probably a result of a misconfiguration of the environment that will require human intervention to correct.

In contrast, once a server operation routine is called by a client, any errors that occur in the process of checking security should result in a refusal to perform the operation. They should not result in shutting down the server. This is logical, because if a DCE runtime security routine returns an error at this point it is because the client has not properly complied with the necessary security procedures. It is necessary, because otherwise an unauthorized user, by selecting invalid security options, could create a simple client that caused servers to crash at will. Of course, in addition to returning an error to the client, we could take other actions, such as noting the error in a log file or sending a message to the system operator. For the sake of simplicity, this example simply returns FALSE as the value of the remote procedure.

When "sec_ok()" is called, first the client's binding handle is passed to the routine **rpc_binding_inq_auth_client()**. It returns the security information associated with the binding. The items returned are the PAC, the server principal name (according to the client), the protection level, the authentication service, the authorization service and, as usual, a status variable. If we were using name-based authorization (**rpc_authz_name**), the second argument would return a pointer to a string that was the client's principal name. Because of this, the operation signature specifies the type **rpc_authz_handle_t*** (which is actually **void***) for this argument. Because we know we will receive a PAC, we declare the variable as a **sec_id_pac_t*** and cast it to **rpc_authz_ handle_t*** for the call.

After checking the status variable to make sure that the routine was successful, the server tests each of the other returned values to ensure that the client has selected the correct security options. First, the server principal name specified by the client is compared to the actual server name as known to the server. Then the protection level is checked to see if it is as expected (**rpc_c_protect_level_connect** in this case). Then the authentication service and the authorization service are checked. If any of these checks fail, it is considered to be a security failure, so an error is returned.

Checking client security is the area in which the designer has the greatest flexibility of action. The server can omit any of the above steps or perhaps allow the client to use any one of several protection levels. However, as was discussed previously, it is recommended that the application designer select the security options (protection level) that meet the requirements of the particular application and that the server enforce their use.

Enforcing access control is the final step for the server. This is done by testing the PAC against the ACL to see if an operation is allowed. In general, the two parts of this process are to obtain a handle to the ACL and call the ACL manager to perform the test. The other data items we need—the PAC and the requested permissions—were obtained earlier.

There are two general ways to obtain the ACL handle. If the ACL protects an object identified entirely within the server, some internal data structure can be used to obtain a handle that identifies the ACL to its ACL manager. If, on the other hand, the object that the ACL protects has been exported to the namespace, the routine **sec_acl_bind()** can be used to obtain the ACL handle.

As for calling the ACL manager, the recommended procedure is for a server to implement an ACL manager that is a part of the same process as the server control and server operations. The implementation of an ACL manager is discussed in the next section. In order to simplify our example, the server makes use of the ACL manager in the CDS server.* In other words, the meaning of the ACL manager that protects the entry in the CDS is overloaded.

If the recommended procedure of implementing an ACL manager in the server had been followed, there would be two ACL managers associated with the object. One, provided by the CDS server, protects the entry in the directory. The other, located in the application server, protects the actual object. The sec-

---

* This method was suggested to me by Clay Boyd.

ond argument to **sec_acl_bind()** permits this distinction to be made. If the argument is TRUE, the returned handle refers to the object's namespace entry. If FALSE, it refers to the object itself.

This scheme can be implemented by piggybacking on any object in the namespace. The server can export objects to be used for this purpose. In the example, the NSI entry for the server itself is used. One way to view this scheme is that the server implements a single object.

In the example, **sec_acl_bind()** is called with the second argument set to TRUE. First, **sec_acl_get_manager_types_semantics()** is called in orderto obtain the UUID of the CDS ACL manager. Second, **sec_acl_test_access_on_behalf()** is called. This invokes the ACL manager located in the CDS server. It checks the PAC against the ACL for the specified permission and returns TRUE if the operation should be allowed. The second argument to **sec_acl_test_access_on_behalf()** specifies which of several possible ACL managers associated with this ACL should be used. The status return variable is not checked, because the routine is guaranteed to return FALSE if any error occurs, and we are not interested in identifying the particular error.

This trick of using the CDS server's ACL manager has the advantage of simplifying the development of a secure server. Unfortunately, it has several disadvantages that make it unsuitable for use in a production server. First, only the permissions implemented by the CDS ACL manager can be used. These are **r** (read), **w** (write), **d** (delete), **t** (test), and **c** (control). Control determines who can modify the ACL, so it should not be used for anything else.

A second disadvantage to this scheme is that giving a user the ability to perform operations in the server also means that the user can perform operations on the directory entry. A malicious user could exploit this to cause problems. For instance, in our example we reused the **w** permission. This would allow a user to overwrite the directory entry for the server, thus making the server unavailable to clients. The third disadvantage is that if many servers used the CDS ACL manager, the CDS server would become a major performance bottleneck. In spite of these disadvantages, the technique is a useful one, especially for test or demonstration servers.

11.2.3   Implementing an ACL manager

As stated previously, a server that supports authenticated RPC is expected to provide its own ACL manager routines. This is intended to allow designers maximum flexibility in defining their own scheme for access control, consistent with the rules for ACLs described previously. An ACL manager consists of a set of routines that conform to interfaces predefined by OSF.

When designing an ACL manager, three basic decisions have to be made. The first step is to determine what ACLs are to protect. The simplest scheme is to construct a single ACL that protects the server's capabilities as a whole. For example, a server that provides access to an industrial robot might have one ACL controlling that access. It might have permissions that allow users to read the status of the robot, control the robot's operations, and run diagnostic procedures on the robot.

Alternatively, a server might provide multiple ACLs to protect objects that correspond to natural categories in the application. A bank account server might provide an ACL for every type of account (e.g., savings, checking) or even an ACL for every individual account. In this case, every operation would somehow identify the object on which the operation was to be performed. For example, one argument might be the account number. A server using the object binding method might provide an ACL corresponding to each object exported to the namespace. In this case, each object would be identified by a UUID. The server operations would call **rpc_binding_inq_object()**, with the binding handle as an argument, in order to obtain the object UUID specified by the client.

Once the ACLs have been decided upon, the designer must determine what the permissions should refer to and how they should appear when printed. One scheme would be for each permission to correspond to one of the operations defined for the interface. If a user has that permission, he or she can do that operation. Another scheme would be to protect generic capabilities, such as read, write, delete. There might be several calls that require read permission, and so on. There could be operations that require different permissions depending on their arguments. The goal should be to make permissions correspond to natural categories within the application.

Currently, DCE displays permissions as single characters concatenated without any separation (e.g., "wrtc"). This is consistent with UNIX-style file permissions and provides a compact format in which a lot of information is being displayed. On the other hand, it is not particularly user-friendly. The ACL manager interface allows an ACL manager to provide printable "help-strings" that describe the permissions, but that does not help with remembering whether **r** means "read" or "reset" or "remove." The ACL manager interface also permits the use of multicharacter strings to represent permissions. The ACL manager also can specify that the permissions must be separated (tokenized) when printed, rather than run together. Currently, however, **acl_edit** does not support the latter. Whichever style is chosen, the permission identifiers should have some mnemonic value.

Third, application designers must decide where to store the ACLs. ACLs have no real utility unless they are stored on some nonvolatile medium so that they will still be around after the node has rebooted. Usually this means storing them on disk. One obvious scheme is to create a separate file for the ACLs, and to read and write it from the ACL manager. Alternatively, a server that provides access to a database could store its ACLs in the database along with the application data. In any event, the file containing the ACLs must be protected from access by other programs, as with any of the resources that the server protects. Otherwise, if users could modify the ACLs or read the database just by bypassing the server, there would not be much point in implementing authenticated RPC to begin with.

Once the basic design decisions have been made, the ACL manager can be implemented. There are three sets of interfaces associated with an ACL manager. Figure 11.4 shows how they relate to one another. The calls beginning with **sec_acl_** are used by a client program that wishes to access the ACLs. The **acl_edit** program provided by OSF uses this interface, as do ACL management programs provided by vendors. If an ACL manager is properly implemented, users and administrators will be able to use standard utilities to display and modify the new ACLs. An application client (or server) program could also use this interface to access ACLs provided by a manager located in a different process. This technique was used in the example described previously.

The server, however, actually does not implement the **sec_acl_** routines. The **sec_acl_** routines bind to stub routines provided by DCE. They in turn call routines that begin with **rdacl_**, and it is these routines that the ACL manager implements. They are built using the header file **rdaclif.h**, which was created by compiling **rdaclif.idl**. It is important not to change the interface UUID in

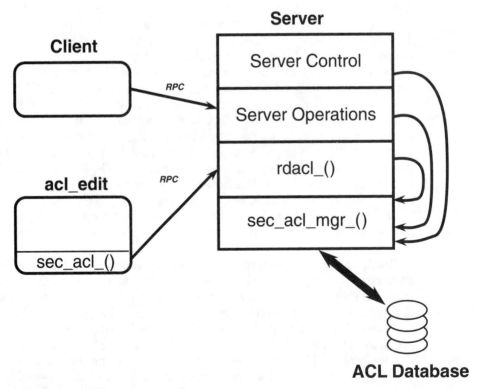

Figure 11.4 The ACL manager interfaces.

TABLE 11.4   ACL Manager rdacl_ Routines

Routine	Purpose
rdacl_get_access	Identify the permissions available to a principal
rdacl_get_manager_types	Identify all the ACL managers protecting an object
rdacl_get_printstring	Get the printable representation of the permissions
rdacl_get_referral	Locate the server with the writable copy of the ACL
rdacl_lookup	Read an ACL
rdacl_replace	Write an ACL
rdacl_test_access	Test if the calling principal has some permission
rdacl_test_access_on_behalf	Test if another principal has some permission

these files. This will allow clients, such as **acl_edit,** which call the **sec_acl_** routines to bind to it. Table 11.4 lists the **rdacl_** routines.

The third set of interface routines associated with an ACL manager is used by the server operations to call the ACL manager implemented within the same server process. The names of these routines begin with **sec_acl_mgr_**. They are listed in Table 11.5. Any of these calls that are not needed can be left out and, as these routines are called entirely within the server, there is no need to use the routines listed; any convenient set of calls may be used. A typical server operation might call only **sec_acl_mgr_is_authorized()**, to check if the client is authorized to perform some operation. The server-control routine might call **sec_acl_mgr_configure()** to perform initialization. If the objects protected by ACLs can be created dynamically, then **sec_acl_mgr_replace()** would be used to create an ACL whenever an object is created.

To aid developers, OSF has provided a sample set of ACL manager routines. Most vendors include this sample code in their DCE development kits. These routines implement the **rdacl_** and **sec_acl_mgr_** routines. A complete example of an ACL manager based on these sample routines is described in Chap. 22 of this book. A future version of DCE will contain a library designed to make it easier to implement an ACL manager.

TABLE 11.5   ACL Manager sec_acl_mgr_ Routines

Routine	Purpose
sec_acl_mgr_configure	Create or initialize an ACL database
sec_acl_mgr_get_access	Identify the permissions available to a principal
sec_acl_mgr_get_manager_types	Identify all the ACL managers protecting an object
sec_acl_mgr_get_types_semantics	Identify all the ACL managers protecting an object and their POSIX semantics
sec_acl_mgr_get_printstring	Get the printable representation of the permissions
sec_acl_mgr_is_authorized	Test if a principal has some permission
sec_acl_mgr_lookup	Read an ACL
sec_acl_mgr_replace	Write an ACL

11.3 Chapter Summary

In order for a distributed application to make use of the DCE security mechanisms, both the client and server must perform certain steps in addition to those required for unauthenticated RPC. For an interactive client, which will be run by a user who has already logged in to DCE, the only additional step required is to inform the runtime of the security options required. This is done by calling **rpc_if_register_auth_info()** when automatic binding is being done, or **rpc_binding_set_auth_info()** when implicit or explicit binding is used.

Applications using DCE security should specify DCE secret-key authentication and PAC-based authorization. Developers should specify the protection level appropriate for a given application. The higher the level, the more performance penalty incurred. In most cases, the choice will be between packet integrity, which ensures that the transmitted data has not been modified, and packet privacy, which encrypts the data so that it cannot be read.

The server has to perform several steps in order to implement DCE security. These break down into initialization actions and actions taken when remote procedures are called. During initialization, the server, like the client, must inform the runtime of the security options it wishes to use. Like the client, the server should specify DCE secret-key authentication. The other part of server initialization is to log in the server to DCE. Because a server typically starts up without human intervention, it obtains the necessary key (password) from a local file.

The other part of the work of the server is to decide whether or not to perform requests made by clients. This consists of performing general checks and consulting the ACL manager to see if requested operations should be allowed. The general checks include determining if the client has specified the proper server principal, authorization service, and protection level and confirming that the client is properly authenticated.

The most extensive task is to implement an ACL manager. This requires implementing a local interface used within the server and an RPC interface that may be called by programs such as **acl_edit**. The ACL manager must store and retrieve ACLs, test the permissions available to a specified principal, and perform utility functions such as providing printable representations of the permissions.

The implementer of an ACL manager must decide what the ACLs should protect, what the permissions should represent, how to store the ACLs, how to determine the owner principal and owner group of objects protected by the ACLs, if and how to handle the default ACLs associated with containers, and how to identify the objects protected.

A complete example implementation of an ACL manager is described in Chap. 22. A shortcut, suitable for nonproduction servers, is to piggyback on the Cell Directory Service (CDS) ACL manager. A future version of DCE will provide libraries for building an ACL manager.

12

DCE Threads

DCE Threads is a facility that allows developers to create multithreaded programs. The facility is based on the interface specified by POSIX 1003.4a, Draft 4. Because of this POSIX origin, the library routines all begin with **pthread_** and are collectively referred to as *Pthreads*. The threads package provided to vendors by OSF is a nonkernel library called CMA* as originally developed by Digital Equipment Corporation; many of the symbols and header file names contain **CMA** or **cma.** Some vendors who already have a Pthreads-compliant facility in their operating system may provide it, in place of CMA, with their DCE implementation.

DCE Threads is different from the other DCE facilities in the sense that threads have inherently nothing to do with networking. Threads are a local service that affects the operation of a single program on a single node. Threads, however, are a very useful tool for the development of distributed applications, providing an efficient and portable way to handle asynchronous events and concurrent processing, which are both characteristic of network software.

As threads are a local service, facilities similar to DCE Threads are provided by some vendors as a native service in their operating systems. In this chapter, discussion of threads concepts applies to implementations generally, and many of the terms are in common use.

The concept of threads was introduced in Chap. 1. In this chapter, we discuss how threads work, in general, and, specifically, how the application programmer will encounter DCE Threads in using DCE RPC. We present examples of

---

* Depending on which header file comments you believe, CMA stands for Concert Multithread Architecture or Common Multithread Architecture.

pitfalls and how to avoid them. As threads are essentially a refinement of processes, we begin with a review of the concepts of process that carry over into threads.

12.1   Introduction to Threads

In order to understand how threads work, it is first necessary to understand how an operating system manages and schedules processes. This was discussed earlier, in Chap. 1, and is reviewed here.

12.1.1   Processes

A running computer program does two things. First, it interacts directly with the computer processor to get machine instructions executed. Second, everything else a program can do (e.g., write a disk file, operate an elevator, dial a telephone) is done by calling the operating system. When it is executing on the processor, the program is called a *process*. Every computer and operating system has the notion of a process. In some systems it may be called a *task* or a *job*.

A single-tasking operating system such as MS-DOS has just one process. On such a system, a program executes machine instructions until it needs to access an I/O device, at which time the processor waits until the device completes what it has to do and the program resumes executing instructions.

In a multitasking operating system, several processes can be concurrently active. Assuming there is only one processor, only one process can actually be executing instructions at any one time, but the operating system can switch from one process to another, giving several processes a chance to use the processor.

In addition to allowing several programs to execute concurrently, this can reduce the total time required to perform a given quantity of work by allowing one process to use the processor while other processes are waiting for I/O operations to complete. Better still, on a multiprocessor system, several processes can actually execute at the same time on different processors, thus reducing elapsed time even further.

Operating systems provide multitasking transparently to application programs. Each process sees an environment that appears just as if it were the only process running on the computer. Several techniques make this possible. Hardware mechanisms provide each process with a memory address space distinct from that of any other process. If a program changes its data, crashes because of an error, or even modifies its own instructions, no other process will be affected.

Second, the operating system is able to switch the use of the processor from one process to another because it can save the information associated with the current state of a process and later restore it so that the process can resume where it left off. This is called *context switching*. The action of selecting a process to execute is called *scheduling*.

The process state is made up of a number of categories of information. One important category records the current state of the processor. Much of this is machine-specific, but every machine has a *program counter* and *stack registers*. The program counter identifies the instruction currently being executed. Even when a program has called the operating system, although this typically involves a large number of instructions in the operating system, the call appears to the program as a single instruction and the program counter points to the call location until control is returned from the operating system to the process. Stack registers point to the stack, which is located in main memory.

Another part of a process's state is its *address space*. This contains code, other read-only memory, and writable memory. There are three categories of writable memory: *automatic, static,* and *dynamic*.

Automatic storage, which exists only within the program block in which it is declared, is allocated on the stack. This is necessary to allow for recursive calls. Function arguments are another form of automatic storage, also located on the stack. Less obviously, **register** variables are also a form of automatic storage.

Static storage is present for the entire time a program is executing and exists in a fixed location within the process address space. In C, static storage is created by declaring data outside of any procedure (function) or by using the keyword **static.**

Dynamic, or *dynamically allocated, storage* can be obtained and released by a process at any time by calling routines such as **malloc()** and **free()**. Dynamic storage is allocated from the pool of memory called the *heap*. Dynamic storage is manipulated by means of pointers that themselves must reside either in automatic or in static storage.

When the operating system carries out a context switch, it saves the information associated with the processor state—such as the program counter and stack registers—in memory associated with the process. Then it loads the same information associated with some other process and lets that process run.

Generally, a context switch will take place for one of two reasons. Either the program has done something that causes it to wait, such as initiating an I/O operation or putting itself to sleep, or the operating system decides that the process has been running long enough and it's time for another process to run. The first case is referred to as a process *blocking*, or *yielding*, and the second is called *timeslicing*. If timeslicing can occur, the scheduling is called *preemptive*. *Nonpreemptive scheduling* means that timeslicing will not occur.

With nonpreemptive scheduling, a program can be written with the knowledge of exactly when its execution might be interrupted. With preemptive scheduling, a process could be interrupted and other processes could execute at any point (between any two instructions) in the program. When processes are timesliced, this does not cause any difficulty, because the processor state has been saved and each process's memory is distinct from that of any other process. Therefore, nothing another process does can affect the process it interrupted.

12.1.2   Threads

Threads exist within a process. Like a process, a thread has a program counter and other state information associated with the processor. The thread executes the instructions of the program. Unlike processes, all of the threads in a process share the same address space. Since static storage exists in a fixed location, all the threads in a process will be able to access it. The stack also exists in memory, but because the stack pointers are part of the processor state associated with each thread, automatic variables will be private to each thread.

The following example illustrates this. Imagine that the routine "foo()" is being executed by two different threads in the same process. Each thread will see its own version of the automatic variable "a". Both threads will see the same static variable "s".

```
static int s;

void foo()
{
auto int a;

/* do some processing with a and s */

}
```

Dynamic storage is a little more complicated. Like the stack, the heap is located in memory and thus potentially accessible to all threads. Just as with the stack, a thread cannot use heap storage unless it can reference it. If the pointer to the dynamic storage is an automatic variable, only the thread that allocated it will be able to access it. If the pointer is placed in static storage, the dynamic storage will be available to all threads.

Pthreads provides two other data storage capabilities. First, the variable used for error reporting, **errno,** is implemented in such a way that each thread sees its own copy. Second, three of the Pthreads library routines implement storage that is static but only accessible to a single thread. This allows different routines executing in the same thread to share data that is not available to any other thread. The routines are:

pthread_keycreate()

pthread_setspecfic()

pthread_getspecific()

The disadvantage of having threads share address space is that, like processes, threads are preemptively scheduled. Since threads can change data visible to other threads, timeslicing is not transparent. Threads must specifically take into account the possibility that other threads may change shared data at any point. Code that will function correctly when executed by multiple concurrent threads is called *thread-safe*.

One advantage of having threads share address space is that it makes communication between threads much easier than between processes. Another advantage to using threads rather than processes is that there is much less overhead associated with using them. As each thread has very few resources unique to it, the process of context switching is much faster. Benchmarks using DCE have demonstrated that using threads requires less processor time and reduces the elapsed time to perform a task involving concurrent execution, as compared to using processes.

12.2   Using Threads in Distributed Applications

There are two ways to approach the design of multithreaded applications. One way is to understand exactly how threads operate and think through each situation from first principles. If you can do this, by all means do so. The previous section contains all the necessary information.

Most people, however, find this difficult to do, at least when they first begin to use threads. The next sections describe some common situations that arise when using threads and some standard ways to deal with them. Following this "cookbook" approach will not allow you to exploit all the possible uses of threads, but it will help you avoid hard-to-debug errors in these situations.

This book takes the view that the main reason for using threads in the context of distributed applications is to implement multithreaded servers. While there are many clever ways of using threads in nondistributed applications, they will not be discussed here. It is also true that there are situations in which it is advantageous to design a multithreaded client. However, it is my belief that, in general, these situations are rare and only occur when an algorithm is available that has certain specific characteristics. This is discussed further in Chap. 17.

12.2.1   Creating and destroying threads

DCE Threads provides routines to create and destroy threads. When a routine is passed to **pthread_create()**, a new thread is created that begins executing that function. When the routine exits or **pthread_exit()** is called, the thread terminates. A thread can cancel another thread by calling **pthread_cancel()**. The resources associated with a thread can be deallocated by calling

pthread_detach(). A thread can wait for another thread to terminate by calling **pthread_join**().

Implementing a multithreaded server does not require calling any of these routines. Simply calling **rpc_server_listen**() with an argument value greater than 1 will cause each invocation of a server operation to run as a distinct thread. Unless the server operation needs to create additional threads for some reason, there is no need to explicitly call the **pthread_**routines. Since each server operation executes as a result of an RPC, there is generally no need to synchronize their termination, and thus no need to call **pthread_join**().

12.2.2 Preventing data access conflicts

Implementing a multithreaded server, however, does require protecting against conflicts between different threads accessing the same data. Conflicts can occur because a thread can be timesliced at any time. Whenever a thread accesses data that can be modified by another thread, there is a potential for inconsistent behavior. Consider the following C code where x and y are in static storage. Assume that y is initially 2.

```
x = y;
y = x + 1;
```

If this code is executed twice, the value of y will be 4 at the end. Now suppose it is executed by two threads. If the first thread is timesliced right after it has executed the first statement, the value of y will be 3 at the end. In general, the value of y will depend on the luck of how the threads get scheduled. This situation is sometimes called a *race condition,* because the result depends on which thread wins the race to execute. Not only is this a bug, but it may be a very hard bug to find. It might never show up during testing, but cause a failure in production.

I can already hear you thinking that no one codes that way. You would write:

```
y = y + 1;
```

or even

```
y++;
```

When the compiler generates machine instructions for either of these statements on most machines, however, the resulting code will actually be more like the first pair of statements. For example, in some imaginary assembly language it might look like this:

```
LOAD  Y
ADD   1
STORE Y
```

As the thread could be timesliced after the first or second instruction, the same potential for a race condition exists.

Here is another common case. This fragment grabs the first item off a linked list.

```
p = baseptr;
baseptr = p->nextptr;
```

If two threads execute this concurrently, they may both end up with the same item.

The only kind of write operation that is safe from a race condition is a single atomic write. For example, on most machines, this is safe:

```
y = 6;
```

It might be thought that read operations are always safe, but, when one thread reads data that another thread is writing, it may see inconsistent results any time the write operation takes more than one step. Consider this example:

Thread A executes:

```
last_item = last_item + 1;
list[last_item] = x;
```

Thread B executes:

```
y = list[last_item];
```

In this case, thread B may end up with invalid data. Sometimes this can be avoided by careful coding. For example, if the two statements executed by A are reversed, B will never see invalid data.

The only case that is always completely safe is when all of the threads are only reading data. In general, the potential for a race condition occurs anytime one or more threads perform a write operation that may take more than one instruction to complete or in which two data items are written that must be consistent with each other in some way.

12.2.3 Mutexes

Notice that in all of the examples given above, the problems could be prevented if all other threads could somehow be prevented from accessing the data item until the writer finishes both steps. The standard way of doing this is to use a *mutex*. Mutex is short for mutual exclusion. Other names for a mutex are a *lock* or a *semaphore*.

A mutex is a data object that is in one of two states: locked or unlocked. Once a thread has locked a mutex, no other thread can use it or lock it until it has been unlocked. A thread can lock a mutex by calling **pthread_mutex_lock()** and unlock it by calling **pthread_mutex_unlock()**. If the mutex has already been locked by another thread, **pthread_mutex_lock()** will not return until the mutex becomes available. Our previous example will always work correctly if we change it to this:

```
pthread_mutex_lock(&m);
x = y;
y = x + 1;
pthread_mutex_unlock(&m);
```

Sometimes, instead of waiting indefinitely for a return from **pthread_mutex_lock()**, it is desirable to have the thread test whether a mutex is currently locked. The routine **pthread_mutex_trylock()** does this. It always returns immediately. If the mutex is unlocked, it locks it and returns 1. If the mutex is already locked, it returns 0. Notice that this is different from all of the other **pthread_mutex_** calls, which return 0 to indicate success.

A program can create any number of mutexes. To create a mutex, call **pthread_mutex_init()**, which returns a pointer to the newly created mutex. To make the pointer available to multiple threads, remember that it will have to be kept in static storage. A mutex is not deleted when the thread that created it finishes. This allows other mutexes to go on using it. To get rid of a mutex, call **pthread_mutex_destroy()**.

In DCE Threads, mutexes can be one of three kinds. (These are an extension to the POSIX.4a draft standard.) The three kinds are called *fast, recursive,* and *nonrecursive.* Here is how they work.

- *Fast.* It is the default mutex and the fastest to lock and unlock. But, if a thread calls **pthread_mutex_lock()** when the mutex is already locked, it will wait forever.

- *Recursive.* A thread can lock the same mutex repeatedly. The mutex will not become available to other threads until it has been unlocked just as many times as it was locked.

- *Nonrecursive.* Like a fast mutex, it can be locked only once. However, if a thread attempts to lock a nonrecursive mutex that is already locked, it will receive an error instead of waiting indefinitely for a return. An error will also be returned if a thread other than the one that locked it tries to unlock it.

Fast mutexes are the type most often used in production applications. Non-recursive mutexes are very convenient for debugging, because it is often easier to trace the problem to its source if the program can halt immediately on an error, rather than running on for a while and muddying the waters.

Recursive mutexes are rarely used. They are used when a routine needs to lock a mutex and then later call another routine that also locks the same mutex. One reason this can occur is if an application is designed to avoid dead-locks by locking mutexes in a specified order. Deadlocks are discussed in the next section.

Here is a simple way to avoid race conditions in a multithreaded server. First, identify any data structures that can be modified from different threads. Don't forget that the same operation may be called from different clients at the same time. Therefore, you must consider conflicts between different threads running the same operation as well as conflicts between different server operations.

Now consider the operations on the data structure. For example, suppose the server maintains some kind of list of items. The server might add things to the list, take things off the list, report how many items are in the list, and so forth. Write an access routine for each operation. Don't access the data structure directly from anywhere else. Always call an access routine. This, of course, is a use of the object-oriented principle of encapsulation. The advantage is that each access routine is responsible for locking and unlocking the mutex associated with the data structure before it returns. This makes it simple to understand and debug the interaction between different threads.

It may be that these access routines are, in fact, the server operations defined in the interface. Or, it may be that the data structure is accessed from various places, in which case the access routines should be a separate package of routines. Either way, the use of mutexes is not visible outside the access routines. There is no danger that some piece of code will forget to lock the mutex. If some routines (e.g., read number of items) do not need to lock the mutex, this is invisible to the rest of the program. If the nature of the data structure or the use of mutexes changes later, this is also invisible.

Another advantage to this approach is that it avoids locking mutexes for long periods of time. On some systems, mutexes are implemented as spin locks. This means that **pthread_mutex_lock()** will test the mutex over and over again. This can consume a lot of processor time. Therefore, it is a good idea to use mutexes in the way that has been suggested here, to protect a data structure only for the duration of a handful of instructions.

12.2.4 Avoiding deadlocks

When two or more mutexes are used, it is possible for two (or more) threads to fall into a *deadlock*. A deadlock is a situation in which the threads involved will make no further progress. Figure 12.1 illustrates a simple example of how a deadlock can occur. Thread A locks a mutex called X. Then thread B locks a mutex called Y. Now thread A attempts to lock Y. Since Y is locked, A must

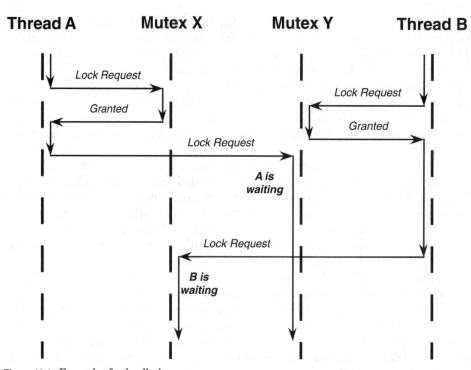

Figure 12.1 Example of a deadlock.

wait. So far, there is no real problem. But next, B tries to lock mutex X and now A and B will never stop waiting for each other. This situation is also known by the rather melodramatic name of *deadly embrace*.

A large body of computer science literature addresses avoiding and detecting deadlocks. The best-known and simplest method is to assign each mutex a unique number* (or priority). Then every thread must obey a simple rule: mutexes must be locked in numeric order. This guarantees that a deadlock cannot occur. This is shown in Fig. 12.2. In this example, low-numbered mutexes must be locked before high-numbered mutexes. Thread A has locked mutex 2. It can safely try to lock mutex 6. Because thread B has mutex 6 locked, B is not allowed to try to lock a lower-numbered mutex (2, in this case).

This rule is simple, but it can create major complications in coding. If a thread has already obtained some locks and needs a lower-numbered mutex, it must release any that are higher-numbered and reacquire them in the correct order. This can be quite inconvenient if the mutexes have been acquired in different routines. It can also cause anomalous delays in execution if another thread sneaks in and grabs a mutex that has just been unlocked. There is no complete solution to this problem.

---

* DCE does not need to know what the number is—it is just used by the application logic.

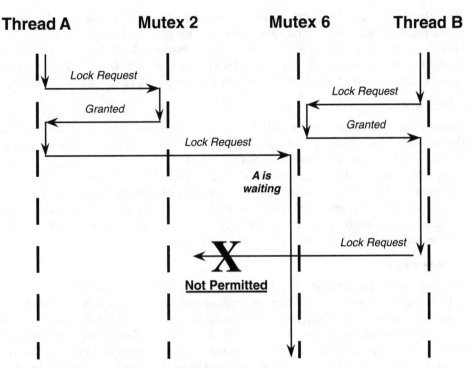

Figure 12.2 Avoiding a deadlock by ordering mutexes.

This is an example of the situation mentioned earlier in which it may be useful to use a recursive mutex. Suppose a program knows it will call a subroutine "sub_lock_two()" that locks mutex 2. But before doing this, it must do something that requires it to lock mutex 6 and keep it locked until after "sub_lock_two()" is called. Assume it is not an option to move the locking of mutex 2 out of "sub_lock_two()". If mutex 2 is made a recursive mutex, it can be acquired prior to locking mutex 6 and then be redundantly locked by "sub_lock_two()". The code would look like this:

```
pthread_mutex_lock(&mutex_2);
pthread_mutex_lock(&mutex_6);

/* do something which requires mutex 6 */

sub_lock_two(); /* locks and unlocks mutex 2 */

/* do something else which requires mutex 6 */

pthread_mutex_unlock(&mutex_6);
pthread_mutex_unlock(&mutex_2);
```

Note that although the mutexes are locked and unlocked in reverse order, this is not required. As long as they are locked in the proper order, no deadlock can occur, regardless of the order in which they are unlocked. Also note that all these complications can be avoided by locking only one mutex at a time and by using mutexes to protect short sequences of code, as was previously suggested.

12.2.5 The global mutex

Sometimes it is necessary to call libraries or systems routines that are not thread-safe. The only way to do this without conflicts is to ensure that only one thread at a time executes the libraries in question. Because there may be many such libraries, and they may call each other, DCE Threads provides a *global recursive mutex*. To lock the global mutex, call **pthread_lock_global_np()**; to unlock it, call **pthread_unlock_global_np()**.* Using the global lock is not efficient, because all other threads will be blocked from entering the libraries, but, in some cases, there may be no alternative.

12.2.6 Condition variables

Pthreads provides another mechanism to coordinate the actions of threads, called *condition variables*. Whereas mutexes allow two threads to access the same data without conflict, condition variables allow one thread to wait until another thread has generated some work for it to do. Condition variables are most useful when a task is being performed by the combined efforts of several threads. Although this is not the case in the typical multithreaded server, it is worth understanding how condition variables work.

The basic idea is that the threads have some application data that one thread sets to indicate that there is work for the other thread to do. Typically, the second thread resets it when the work is done. In the example in Fig. 12.3, thread A puts items in a list and thread B removes and processes them as they appear. Thread B uses a condition variable to wait until the list has something in it. A mutex is used to protect the list. The code to initialize the mutex and condition variable is not shown. Also, to make the code easier to follow, the return values are not checked for errors.

Thread A locks the list, adds an item to it, signals the condition, and unlocks it. The last two steps could be done in either order. Thread B runs in an endless loop, waiting for items to appear and processing them. Thread B locks the list and calls **pthread_cond_wait()**. (The **while** loop is needed because, rarely, a thread may wake up from a wait condition even though it was not signaled.)

The routine **pthread_cond_wait()** unlocks the mutex and waits for the condition to be signaled. This allows thread A to acquire the lock. Once the condition has been signaled, the routine reacquires the lock, waiting if necessary, and returns. Thread B then takes the item off the list, releases the lock, and

---

* In DCE Threads, any symbol referring to a feature that is not part of the POSIX draft standard has "np," for nonportable, on the end of it.

```
Thread A executes:

pthread_mutex_lock(&m);                    /* protect access to the list */
list[++last_item] = x;                     /* put something on the list */
pthread_cond_signal(&c);                   /* signal work to do */
pthread_mutex_unlock(&m);                  /* make the list accessible */


Thread B executes:

for (;;)
    {                                      /* look for work forever */
    pthread_mutex_lock(&m);                /* protect access to the list */
    while(last_item < 0)                   /* test for spurious wakeups */
        pthread_cond_wait(&c, &m);         /* unlock, wait for signal, relock, return */
    x = list[last_item--];                 /* get item off list */
    pthread_mutex_unlock(&m);              /* make the list accessible */
    process_item(x);                       /* do something with it */
```

Figure 12.3 Using a condition variable.

processes the item. Note that A and B can modify the same data structure without conflict and B does not have to run in a tight loop looking for work.

Condition variables can be used as building blocks to create more complex thread control structures. For example, a condition variable can be used to create a *thread barrier*. A thread barrier allows one thread to cause a number of other threads to wait at a synchronization point and then release them all at once.

Figure 12.4 shows an illustration of how to do this. The master thread creates the worker threads and lets them go all at once. The worker thread is the same as in the previous example.

A condition variable can also be used to implement a *read/write lock*. A read/write lock is similiar to a mutex, except it has three states: *unlocked,* *read-locked,* and *write-locked.* If it is unlocked, it can be read-locked or write-locked. If it is write-locked, it is like a regular mutex; all requests for read or write locks must wait until it is unlocked. If it is read-locked, write-lock requests must still wait, but any number of other threads can also read-lock it. In other words, the write lock is exclusive and the read lock is shared.

A simplified implementation of a read/write lock is shown in Fig. 12.5. It consists of a structure declaration and seven routines. The caller of these routines is expected to allocate a structure of type **rwlock_t** and pass it to each of the routines. This gives the caller control of the type of storage used and allows any number of read/write locks to be used simultaneously. The **rwlock_t** structure contains a boolean indicating if any thread holds a write lock, and a counter of the number of threads holding read locks. It also contains a mutex and condition variable used to coordinate the threads using the lock.

```
Master Thread

last_item = -1;                    /* List is empty */
pthread_cond_init( &c,             /* Create condition variable */
                pthread_condattr_default);
for (i=0; i < num_threads; i++)    /* Create worker threads */
    pthread_create( th[i],
                pthread_attr_default,
                worker, 0 );
pthread_mutex_lock(&m);            /* protect access to the list */
for (i=0; i < num_items; i++)      /* put some items on the list */
    list[++last_item] = x[i];
pthread_cond_broadcast(&c);        /* signal work to do */
pthread_mutex_unlock(&m);          /* make the list accessible */


Worker Threads

worker()
{
for (;;)                           /* look for work forever */
    }
    pthread_mutex_lock(&m);        /* protect access to the list */
    while(last_item < 0)           /* test for spurious wakeups */
        pthread_cond_wait(&c, &m); /* unlock, wait for signal, relock, return */
    x = list[last_item--];         /* get item off list */
    pthread_mutex_unlock(&m);      /* make the list accessible */
    process_item(x);               /* do something with it */
    }
```

Figure 12.4 Implementing a thread barrier.

The routines **rwl_init()** and **rwl_destroy()** are used to initialize and destroy the read/write lock. Their operation is self-explanatory. Notice that a reader count of 0 means that the read lock is free.

The routine **rwl_read_lock()** obtains a read lock. A read lock may be obtained at any time unless the write lock is set. The routine tests for this and waits on the condition variable if necessary. Once the lock is available, the reader count is incremented to indicate that this thread has a read lock.

By calling **rwl_read_unlock()**, a thread can release a read lock it holds. If the count of readers goes to zero, the routine broadcasts on the condition variable. This allows any threads that might be waiting for the write lock to wake up and try to get it. If several threads are waiting, the one that will run first, and thus obtain the write lock, is determined by the scheduling policies and priorities of the threads. (These are described in the next section.) If the reader count is not 0, there is no need to do anything special.

The routine **rwl_write_lock()** is used to get the write lock. To get the write lock, no other thread must hold either a read or a write lock. The routine tests and waits until these conditions obtain and then sets the write-lock flag.

```
#include <pthread.h>

typedef struct                      /* Read/Write Lock Structure */
    {
    idl_boolean       write_locked;   /* TRUE if write locked */
    idl_short_int     reader_count;   /* Number of readers */
    pthread_mutex_t   rwl_mutex;      /* Mutex protects the lock vars */
    pthread_cond_t    rwl_cond;       /* Condition variable */
    }
    rwlock_t;                         /* Read/Write Lock Type */


/***** rwl_init - Initialize Read/Write Lock *****/

rwl_init( rwlock_t *lock);
{
pthread_mutex_init( &lock->rwl_mutex, pthread_mutexattr_default);

pthread_cond_init( &lock->rwl_cond, pthread_condattr_default);

lock->write_locked = FALSE;

lock->reader_count = 0;
}

/***** rwl_read_lock - Returns with read (shared) lock *****/

rwl_read_lock( rwlock_t *lock);
{
pthread_mutex_lock(&lock->rwl_mutex);

while(lock->write_locked) pthread_cond_wait( &lock->rwl_cond, &lock->rwl_mutex);

lock->reader_count++;

pthread_mutex_unlock(&lock->rwl_mutex);
}

/***** rwl_read_unlock - Releases read (shared) lock *****/

rwl_read_unlock( rwlock_t *lock);
{
pthread_mutex_lock(&lock->rwl_mutex);

if (--lock->reader_count == 0) pthread_cond_broadcast(&lock->rwl_cond);

pthread_mutex_unlock(&lock->rwl_mutex);
}

/***** rwl_write_lock - Returns with write (exclusive) lock *****/
```

Figure 12.5 A read/write lock.

```
rwl_write_lock( rwlock_t *lock);
{
pthread_mutex_lock(&lock->rwl_mutex);

while(lock->write_locked || (lock->reader_count > 0) )
    pthread_cond_wait(&lock->rwl_cond, &lock->rwl_mutex);

lock->write_locked = TRUE;

pthread_mutex_unlock(&lock->rwl_mutex);
}

/***** rwl_write_unlock - Releases write (exclusive) lock *****/

rwl_write_unlock( rwlock_t *lock);
{
pthread_mutex_lock(&lock->rwl_mutex);

lock->write_locked = FALSE;

pthread_cond_broadcast(&lock->rwl_cond);

pthread_mutex_unlock(&lock->rwl_mutex);
}

/***** rwl_demote_lock - Converts write lock to read lock *****/

rwl_demote_lock( rwlock_t *lock);
{
pthread_mutex_lock(&lock->rwl_mutex);

lock->write_locked = FALSE;

lock->reader_count++;

pthread_cond_broadcast(&lock->rwl_cond);

pthread_mutex_unlock(&lock->rwl_mutex);
}

/***** rwl_destroy - Deactivates read/write lock */

rwl_destroy( rwlock_t *lock);
{
pthread_mutex_destroy( &lock->rwl_mutex );

pthread_cond_destroy( &lock->rwl_cond );
```

Figure 12.5 (*Continued*)

A call to **rwl_write_unlock()** is used to release the write lock. The lock is freed and a broadcast is issued to wake all of the waiting threads. In this case, there may be threads waiting for both read and write locks. Once again, the scheduler will determine who wins the race. Notice that if one thread obtains the read lock, then all of the threads waiting to read will be granted read locks immediately.

The routine **rwl_demote_lock()** allows a thread that holds the write lock to convert it to a read lock without running the risk of having another thread grab the write lock in the middle. It frees the write lock, increments the reader count, and broadcasts to wake up the threads waiting for the read lock. There is no advantage to providing a routine to promote a read lock to a write lock, because it would likely have to wait for other readers to finish.

In order to make the code easier to follow, these routines do not provide any error checking. They implement the equivalent of a fast mutex, that is, if they are called under the wrong conditions (e.g., **rwl_write_lock()** twice in a row), they will hang. Either recursive or nonrecursive versions could be created by means of the thread-specific static storage mentioned earlier in the chapter. It also might be wise to add some basic consistency checks as well. Another improvement would be to provide nonwaiting lock routines analogous to **pthread_mutex_trylock()**.

Despite their usefulness, a typical distributed application will not use condition variables. In the standard DCE RPC server model, calling **rpc_server_listen()** causes a thread to be created to service each client call to a server operation. As these threads are serving different clients, their processing flow usually does not need to be coordinated. Therefore, condition variables will not normally be needed, unless the server operation explicitly spawns additional threads to perform part of the processing.

12.2.7 Thread scheduling

Active threads can be in one of three states: running, ready to run, or waiting. *Running* means the thread is actually executing instructions on the processor. (On a multiprocessor system, several threads can be in this state.) *Ready to run* means eligible to use the processor, but not currently doing so. Threads can be *waiting* for mutexes, condition variables, or for I/O operations to complete. Thread scheduling consists of selecting a thread to run from among those ready to run.

Pthreads provides the ability to exercise some control over scheduling of threads. Every thread has two scheduling attributes: *scheduling policy* and *scheduling priority*. Scheduling policy controls the algorithm used to schedule threads. Scheduling priority controls the treatment of a given thread relative to other threads.

Scheduling priority is an integer. It can be set to any value between minimum and maximum values defined as symbolic constants. There are distinct minimums and maximums for each scheduling policy. The symbols for the minimums and maximums are listed in Table 12.1. The general formula for setting a priority value is:

$$\text{minimum} + (\text{maximum} - \text{minimum}) * \text{priority-factor}$$

where minimum and maximum are the appropriate symbols from the table and priority-factor is a number between 0 and 1 which represents the priority desired. For example, a value of 0.8 would represent 80 percent of the range. Obviously, the minimum, maximum, and midpoint can be expressed more simply as:

minimum

maximum

(minimum + maximum) / 2

A thread can have four possible scheduling policies. (**SCHED_OTHER** and **SCHED_FG_NP** are the same thing.) For **SCHED_FIFO** and **SCHED_RR**, the treatment of threads of different priorities is the same. A lower-priority thread will never be run unless there are no higher-priority threads that are ready to run. If a higher-priority thread becomes ready to run while a lower-priority thread is running, the higher-priority thread will immediately get the processor.

The difference between **SCHED_FIFO** and **SCHED_RR** is in the way threads of equal priority are scheduled. If a thread has **SCHED_FIFO**, it will never be interrupted by a thread of equal priority. It will run until it goes into a wait. If the thread has **SCHED_RR**, it will be allowed to run for a while and then will be timesliced to allow another thread of equal priority to run. The amount of processor time it is allowed to use before being timesliced is called a *quantum*. The value of the quantum is implementation-dependent.

The DCE Threads default scheduling policy is **SCHED_OTHER**, which is the same as **SCHED_FG_NP**. **FG** stands for foreground and **NP** stands for nonportable. All the threads with this policy will be scheduled on a round-robin basis regardless of their priority. Higher-priority threads will get better treatment, but all will get some time to run. The intention is to provide some fair-

TABLE 12.1 Thread Scheduling Policies and Priorities

Scheduling policy	Policy symbol	Minimum symbol	Maximum symbol
First-in–first-out	**SCHED_FIFO**	**PRI_FIFO_MIN**	**PRI_FIFO_MAX**
Round-robin	**SCHED_RR**	**PRI_RR_MIN**	**PRI_RR_MAX**
Same as foreground	**SCHED_OTHER**	**PRI_OTHER_MIN**	**PRI_OTHER_MAX**
Foreground	**SCHED_FG_NP**	**PRI_FG_MIN_NP**	**PRI_FG_MAX_NP**
Background	**SCHED_BG_NP**	**PRI_BG_MIN_NP**	**PRI_BG_MAX_NP**

ness to low-priority threads. Threads with **SCHED_FG_NP**, however, can still be locked out by higher-priority **SCHED_FIFO** or **SCHED_RR** threads.

The last policy is **SCHED_BG_NP**. **BG** stands for background. This policy is just like **SCHED_FG_NP** except that background threads will be locked out by threads with any of the other policies. In other words, background threads round-robin among themselves whenever no other thread is ready to run.

SCHED_FIFO is the most efficient policy, because it minimizes the number of context switches that occur. It is also the best if all threads run only for a short time before blocking for I/O. If some threads run for extended periods, however, **SCHED_FIFO** can cause short-running threads to have to wait for long-running threads. Round-robin remedies this by timeslicing long-running threads of equal priority. **SCHED_FG_NP** takes this one step further by timeslicing across all priorities. **SCHED_BG_NP** is useful for threads that perform some kind of overhead function, such as garbage collection.

Experience has shown that simple scheduling schemes are the best. Complex multiple-priority schemes just don't work as expected. Either they have no effect on the actual execution profile of the threads or, worse, they produce some unfortunate side effect. Even experienced software developers are often poor at predicting the runtime behavior of their programs.* Usually it is best to use the same policy for all threads. And usually it is best to use a simple priority scheme, such as equal priorities for all threads or one high-priority thread and the rest equal.

12.3   Other Thread Features

Pthreads also provides some other features to facilitate the use of threads.

12.3.1   One-time initialization

Sometimes it is desirable to have multiple threads execute the same code, but to do some initialization the first time through. A routine called **pthread_once**() is provided for this purpose. It is called with an argument that points to an initialization routine. Only the first thread that calls **pthread_once**() will execute the initialization routine. Further, if any other threads call **pthread_once**() before initialization is complete, they will wait until the first thread returns from **pthread_once**(). This routine is most useful in libraries. It is not needed in multithreaded servers usually, because any necessary initialization can be put in the server control routine, which is executed by only one thread.

---

* This observation is based on experiences using program-counter sampling programs to locate "hot spots" for optimization. The results usually surprise everyone, including the program's designer.

12.3.2   Jacket routines

On most current operating systems, system calls are not designed to be thread-safe. For this reason, DCE Threads provides what are called *jacket routines*. Jacket routines take the name of a system call, but they call **pthread_lock_global_np()** to lock the global mutex before calling the actual system service. Of course, this means these calls are effectively single-threaded, but undesirable effects are avoided. In the future, more operating systems will provide full-kernel support for threads, and jacket routines will no longer be necessary. You can also use the same technique to protect existing libraries that are not thread-safe.

12.4   Thread Gotchas

Some facilities found in POSIX.1 (UNIX-like) environments should be avoided in multithreaded programs.

12.4.1   Use of fork()

Calling **fork()** from a multithreaded program can cause problems in all but a few specific cases. Generally, all threads but one should be terminated before calling **fork()**. About the only exception is when calling **fork()** is followed immediately by calling **exec()**.

12.4.2   Use of signals

Signals do not interact well with threads either. The reason is that signals and signal handlers are defined on a per process basis. Signals should not be used as an internal mechanism to coordinate between threads. Mutexes, condition variables, and the exception-handling macros described in Chap. 7 are provided for this purpose.

Two uses of signals in multithreaded programs are safe. The DCE Threads version of **sigwait()** has been extended so that a thread can wait for an asynchronous signal. For example, a thread can wait for **SIGQUIT**, which is caused by a user typing Control-C, and then perform cleanup before the process exits. The DCE Threads version of **sigaction()** can specify the handling of synchronous signals within a particular thread. For example, a thread could define a signal handler that recovers from a floating-point error when **SIGFPE** is signaled.

12.4.3   Runtime threads

Even a single-threaded client or a server that calls **rpc_server_listen()** with an argument of 1 will actually be multithreaded. The RPC runtime creates extra threads to perform various functions related to the communications protocols. Normally, these threads can be ignored because they do not interact or share any data with the application threads. These threads are most likely to be noticeable when a debugger is used. As most debuggers on the market today are not thread-aware, some unexpected behavior can result. Nothing can really be done about this except to be aware of the possibility. Hopefully, as the use of DCE Threads—and Pthreads in general—becomes more widespread, thread-aware debuggers will become more common.

12.5 Chapter Summary

DCE Threads provides a user-mode multithreading capability that conforms to the draft POSIX.4a standard referred to as Pthreads. Threads are lightweight processes that share the same address space but have distinct program counters and local variables. While threads are entirely local to a node, they are very useful for developing distributed applications—in particular, multithreaded servers.

Since DCE RPC generates the threads necessary for a multithreaded server automatically, it will usually not be necessary for the developer to create threads explicitly using the Pthreads calls. The developer does have to prevent data-access conflicts that may arise from the same data being accessed from multiple threads. The normal mechanism for doing this is to use a mutex to lock some resource while it is being modified.

DCE Threads supports three types of mutexes: fast, which do no error checking; recursive, which support recursive calls; and nonrecursive, which test against recursive calls. Careless use of mutexes can lead to deadlocks, which can either be prevented by the design or detected after they occur. DCE provides a global mutex, which is used to lock out library routines that are not thread-safe.

Pthreads also provides condition variables, which are used to synchronize the flow of distinct threads. Condition variables can be used to coordinate the activities of consumer/producer routines. Condition variables can be used to implement other synchronization constructs, such as a thread barrier or a read/write lock.

The Pthreads interface provides mechanisms to control the scheduling of threads, the ability to perform one-time initialization, a means to implement thread-specific static storage, and jacket routines around the most frequently used system library routines that are not thread-safe.

The use of threads also can create some special problems. The **fork()** call should not be used in a multithreaded program, except when immediately followed by a call to **exec()**. Signals should not be used for synchronization between threads. Mutexes or condition variables should be used instead. DCE RPC programs that appear to be single-threaded actually consist of several threads. This will not normally be visible to the application developer, but can cause problems when debugging.

13

The DCE Distributed Time Service

The main purpose of the DCE Distributed Time Service (DTS) is to keep the system clocks of all of the nodes in a network approximately in sync. It also has the capability of keeping the system clocks synchronized with true time, given the necessary additional hardware. DTS maintains time in a format compatible with the ISO 8601 (1988) international standard, but adds to it the notion of an inaccuracy component that expresses a range of uncertainty associated with the time.

Most of the machinery of the DTS is invisible to the software developer. The DTS synchronizes the system clock on each node by directly adjusting the time kept by the operating system. Under ordinary circumstances, this is done gradually so that there are no sudden jumps in the time. It is also done in such a way that the time never goes backward. If a system clock is too far ahead, it is slowed down until the time is correct. This is important, because it means it is possible to count on the fact that things like timestamps and file creation dates will reflect actual chronological order.

From a software development perspective, DTS provides a library of calls that retrieve the current time, convert time values between various formats, manipulate time values, and perform computations on time values. DTS library routines provide the ability to convert time values into a standard printable format or from printable to internal formats. The other software interface in DTS is to support connection of devices that can receive time signals transmitted by various standards bodies around the world so that they can become a source of time data to the DTS. This interface is primarily of interest to manufacturers of such devices.

13.1 DTS Operation

The components of the DTS are *clerks, local servers, global servers, couriers,* and *time providers.* Figure 13.1 illustrates their relationships. Every node in a

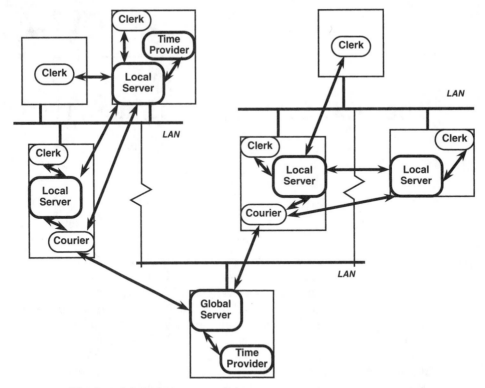

Figure 13.1 Distributed time service components.

DCE cell contains a DTS clerk. Based on configuration parameters, the clerk periodically determines whether a local system's clock has drifted out of synchronization with the correct time. If this has happened, the clerk queries several DTS servers for the correct time. Based on their answers, it calculates the most probable current time and an inaccuracy factor. It then adjusts the local node's clock as needed.

Every DCE cell contains a number of DTS servers. Ideally, there should be at least three on every LAN, running on highly available machines. DTS servers periodically exchange information with each other to keep their own clocks synchronized. The servers that provide time information to servers outside of their LAN are the global servers. The servers that request information from global servers on behalf of clerks are the couriers.

Notice that "global" has a very different meaning for DTS than for the Directory Service. The Global Directory Service connects different cells together. In contrast, the DTS operates entirely within a cell. In DTS terminology, *local* means within a LAN and *global* means between LANs in the same cell. The reason for this distinction between the same LAN versus a different LAN is because communications between LANs involves greater and more-variable time delays than communications within a LAN. This decreases the accuracy of the time information exchanged.

A time provider is a special-purpose server that provides access to a hardware device that receives standardized time information broadcast via radio, satellite, or telephone lines from a standards body or government organization. DTS servers query the time provider for the current time. DTS algorithms take into account the relative accuracy of different sources of time information. Time providers are considered to be the most authoritative source of time information. However, DTS servers do consider other sources of time information, so that they can detect a hardware malfunction. Ideally, in a large cell, there would be at least two time providers to provide redundancy in the event of failure of a node or communications link.

13.2   Representing Time Values

The international standard for time is called Coordinated Universal Time (UTC). Like the older standard, Greenwich mean time, UTC represents the time at the longitude of Greenwich, England. Local times around the world are represented as the UTC combined with a Time Differential Factor (TDF). The TDF can be positive or negative. The TDF is added to the UTC to obtain the local time. DTS maintains UTC internally using a format that is opaque. (Recall that opaque data types cannot be examined, only used as arguments to library routines.)

DTS uses several standardized formats for displaying different kinds of time values: *absolute time, relative time,* and *period of time.* An *absolute time* represents a particular moment in time. An absolute time has three components: the *calendar date and time component,* the *TDF component,* and the *inaccuracy component.* Here is an example:

```
1981-10-27-00:59:12.345+06:00I000.125
```

where   1981-10-27-00:59:12.345= the calendar date and time component
+06:00= the TDF component
I000.125= the inaccuracy component

This corresponds to 59 minutes, 12.345 seconds after midnight on October 27, 1981, 6-hour positive TDF, and an inaccuracy of plus or minus 0.125 seconds.

In accordance with the ISO standard, DTS also allows absolute times to be entered in this format:

```
1981-10-27T00:59:12,345+06:00±000,125
```

The differences are: a "T" separates the date from the time; "," is used to mark the decimal points; and "±" is used to separate the TDF from the inaccuracy component. In either format, the inaccuracy component may be omitted, indicating unspecified inaccuracy.

A *relative time* is a time interval that usually represents the difference between two absolute times. An example of a relative time is:

```
13-12:11:10.987I65.432
```

This means 13 days, 12 hours, 11 minutes, 10.987 seconds, with an inaccuracy of plus or minus 65.432 seconds.

A *period of time* represents a duration or frequency of events. Here is an example of a period of time.

```
P1Y3M1W6DT7H22M14SI1
```

This means 1 year, 3 months, 1 week, 6 days, 7 hours, 22 minutes, 14 seconds, with an inaccuracy of 1 second.

In this format, it is permissible to leave out elements. For example, a legal period of time is:

```
P5M2DT4H,
```

which means 5 months, 2 days, and 4 hours.

13.3 Binary Time Formats

DTS uses opaque binary data items called *timestamps* to represent UTC. DTS timestamps, which are stored in a structure called **utc,** have a resolution of 100 nanoseconds and a range of 30,000 years. This does not mean that all DCE nodes must measure time to this resolution, simply that the format allows values of that precision to be stored.

DTS supports conversion to and from two other binary time formats. Unlike **utc,** they are not opaque and may be manipulated directly. One is called **tm** and is defined in POSIX.1. It has a resolution of 1 second and a range of 30,000 years. It corresponds to the way the date and time are stored on most UNIX-like systems. The **tm** data type is defined as the following structure:

```
struct tm {
        int tm_sec;     /* Seconds in minute (0 to 61) */
        int tm_min;     /* Minutes in hour (0 to 59) */
        int tm_hour;    /* Hour in day (0 to 23) */
        int tm_mday;    /* Day in month (1 to 31) */
        int tm_mon;     /* Month in year (0 to 11) */
        int tm_year;    /* Years since 1900 */
        int tm_wday;    /* Day of week (0 to 6) 0 => Sunday */
        int tm_yday;    /* Day in year (0 to 365) */
        int tm_isdst;   /* ;ue0 =>daylight savings, =0 =>standard */
        };
```

The other binary time format is **timespec.** The **timespec** data format comes from the POSIX.4 draft standard and is intended for the high-resolution time measurement associated with real-time applications. The **timespec** data type has a resolution of 1 nanosecond, but a range of only 68 years. A **tm** and **timespec** data are frequently combined to represent a date and time with finer resolution than 1 second. The **timespec** data type is defined as the following structure:

```
struct timespec {
        unsigned long tv_sec;   /* Seconds since January 1, 1970 */
        long tv_nsec;           /* Nanoseconds */
        };
```

Closely related to **timespec** is **reltimespec,** which represents a relative time to the same resolution. The only difference in format is that the **tv_sec** field is signed.

```
struct reltimespec {
        long tv_sec;            /* Seconds */
        long tv_nsec;           /* Nanoseconds */
        };
```

13.4   DTS Library Routines

All of the library routines in DTS begin with **utc_**. Most of them provide conversion of time values from one format to another. Table 13.1 summarizes the provided conversions. The first row of the table represents routines that obtain the current time from the environment. XXXXXX indicates the null cases where the row and column formats are the same. Conversion between absolute and relative timestamps makes no sense and is marked N/A. Obtaining a relative time from the environment makes no sense either.

Notice that all of the conversions to and from DTS absolute and relative timestamps are provided. Some routines that are not in DTS but that are likely to be found in POSIX environments have been included in the table where appropriate.

The remaining DTS library routines fall into four categories. They are described briefly here.

Manipulations concerning the inaccuracy component

utc_boundtime()   Create a timestamp that encompasses the ranges of two ordered, input timestamps

utc_pointtime()   Create three timestamps: the earliest, most likely, and latest times represented by an input timestamp

utc_spantime()   Create a timestamp that encompasses the ranges of two unordered, input timestamps

TABLE 13.1 Time Format Conversion Routines

Source	Absolute timestamp	Relative timestamp	tm	timespec	ASCII string
			Destination		
Current time	utc_gettime() utc_getusertime()	N/A	time()+localtime() time()+gmtime()	getclock()	utc_ascanytime() utc_ascgmtime() utc_asclocaltime()
Absolute timestamp	XXXXXXX	N/A	utc_anytime() utc_gmtime()	utc_bintime()	
Relative timestamp	N/A	XXXXXX	utc_reltime()	utc_binreltime()	utc_ascreltime()
tm	utc_mkanytime() utc_mkgmtime() utc_mklocaltime()	utc_mkreltime()	XXXXXX		asctime() strftime()
timespec	utc_mkbintime()	utc_mkbinreltime()		XXXXXX	
ASCII string	utc_mkasctime()	utc_mkascreltime()			XXXXXX

NOTES: asctime(), gmtime(), localtime(), strftime(), and time() are defined in POSIX.1.
getclock() is defined in the POSIX.4 draft.

Comparison of timestamps

utc_cmpintervaltime	Compare two absolute or relative timestamps to determine their order or if they overlap
utc_cmpmidtime	Compare two absolute or relative timestamps to determine their order, ignoring their inaccuracies

Computations on timestamps

utc_abstime	Compute the absolute value of a relative timestamp
utc_addtime	Add two relative timestamps or a relative and an absolute timestamp
utc_mulftime	Multiply a relative timestamp by a floating-point number
utc_multime	Multiply a relative timestamp by an integer
utc_subtime	Subtract two absolute timestamps, two relative timestamps, or a relative from an absolute timestamp

Time zone operations

utc_anyzone	Get the time-zone label and TDF associated with an absolute timestamp
utc_gmtzone	Get the time-zone label and TDF associated with Greenwich mean time (constant outputs)
utc_localzone	Get the time-zone label and TDF associated with the local time zone

13.5 Chapter Summary

The Distributed Time Service (DTS) synchronizes all of the system clocks in the network. If a hardware device is available that can determine the true time, DTS will keep the system clocks synchronous with that. DTS performs this synchronization task behind the scenes by exchanging messages between its constituent servers and clerks. When a system clock's time must be reset, whether it is too fast or too slow, DTS ensures that its time will never run backward.

DTS uses time formats that conform to international standards. Because there is always some uncertainty associated with variable network delays, DTS can associate an inaccuracy factor with a time. This allows an application to know whether or not it can place two events in a definite time sequence.

For the convenience of programmers, DTS provides library routines to convert between a variety of time formats used by DTS and POSIX.1 systems. DTS also provides routines to manipulate the inaccuracy factor of a timestamp, compare timestamps, perform computations on timestamps, and manipulate time-zone information.

3

Distributed System Design Solutions

Now that we have completed our detailed examination of the DCE components and technologies, we return to the subject of developing distributed applications generally. In the first two chapters of this part, we revisit our discussion of the 12 major factors that make developing distributed systems difficult, which were presented in Chap. 3. Chapter 14 reexamines six of these problem areas to discuss how DCE helps solve or reduce them. We also describe some limitations and gaps in the solutions offered by DCE.

Chapter 15 discusses the six problems that are not addressed by DCE. Practical approaches are suggested for reducing or eliminating their impact. We also examine some emerging new products and technologies and predict what their effectiveness is likely to be in addressing these remaining problems.

The third chapter in this part, Chap. 16, discusses a number of issues and considerations that commonly come up in developing distributed systems. The intention is to make the reader aware of these topics and suggest some practical ways of thinking about the design of distributed applications. It is my hope that the chapter can help developers new to distributed systems avoid some of the mistakes frequently made. Most of the material in the chapter applies to the development of any distributed system, whether DCE is used or not.

14

Problems DCE Helps Solve

In Chap. 3, we discussed 12 reasons distributed systems are more difficult to design, implement, and operate than monolithic systems. Now that the DCE technologies have been described in detail, we return to take a second look at that list. This chapter examines how six issues from the list are addressed by DCE with considerable success. Some gaps in DCE design that limit its solutions are also discussed. We suggest methods of avoiding or minimizing the effects of these limitations.

14.1 Complex Processing Flow

In Chap. 3, it was stated that distributed applications have often been characterized by processing flows that are more complex than those of typical monolithic programs. DCE alleviates this problem to a great extent by supporting the client/server design model, implemented with DCE RPC. The model is much more tractable than the models used in distributed applications in the past. Paradoxically, it brings order to distributed applications by limiting the developer's range of choices in structuring an application. Although flexibility is limited, the model has been shown to be very effective in meeting the requirements of a broad range of applications.

The client/server model makes the processing flow of distributed applications easy to understand because it constrains each component to follow a specific pattern of logic. The client follows the familiar pattern of traditional computer programs, depicted in Fig. 14.1. It requests services by making a remote procedure call. Once the call has been issued, the client takes no further action until the call returns. Because of this, the remote procedure call is often described as blocking or synchronous.

The flow pattern is the same as for user-written subroutines, system library routines, and operating-system services. All issues of concurrency can safely be

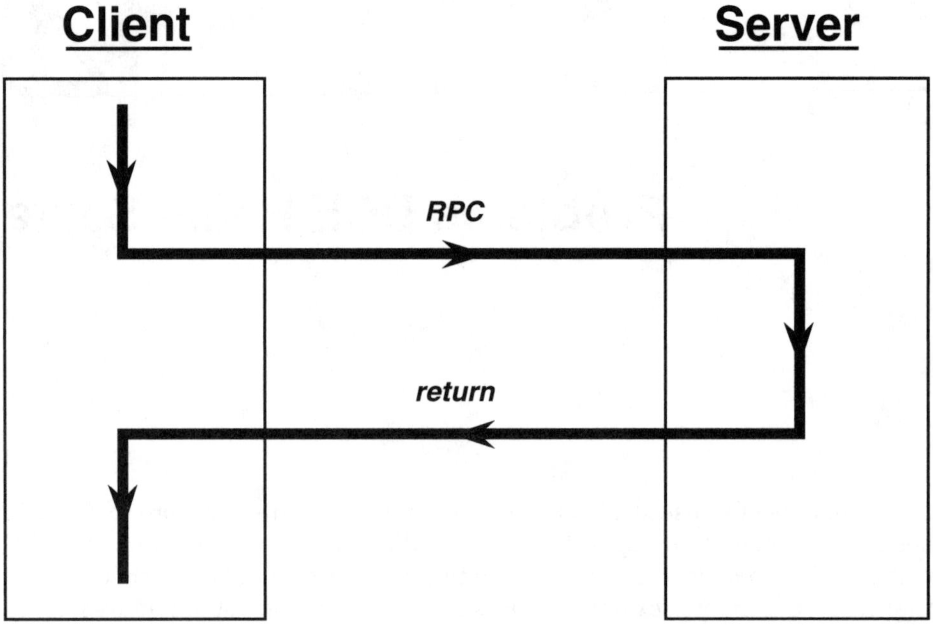

Client

Server

RPC

return

Figure 14.1 RPC processing flow.

ignored. The client logic must only check to see if an operation was successful. The entire structure of the client can be the typical linear, test-and-branch logic characteristic of so many traditional computer applications.

The use of the client/server model does not mean that DCE cannot tolerate additional complexity. Clients, for example, increasingly are built around a graphical user interface (GUI). GUI-based programs tend not to be structured in the classical fashion, but are often structured as semiautonomous snippets of code that respond to some user action, such as selecting a menu option or clicking on a button. Nevertheless, when the code snippet requires a remote service, the RPC allows it to request the service just as it would some local system function.

DCE also permits the design of inherently more-complex application logic. For example, RPC can be used merely to request initiation of a service and receive confirmation that the request was received. Then a later RPC can be used to determine that the requested work has been done and to obtain any results. This allows DCE applications to participate in asynchronous, queued-processing architectures.

Another, more complex, possibility is use of a multithreaded client. The client divides up the work to be done and distributes it to servers running on different nodes. This method is appropriate when the work is very compute-intensive and when there is a known algorithm for performing pieces of the computation independently of intermediate results obtained at other nodes.

Although a client of this type has a considerably more complex structure than that of the usual client, the use of RPC combined with DCE Threads simplifies designing it, as compared to implementing such a client from scratch.

DCE simplifies the flow logic of the server as well. Figure 14.2 depicts the structure of a typical DCE server. The server control routine executes sequentially, except for possible error handling, and then becomes dormant. The server side of RPC is almost as straightforward as the client side. The server

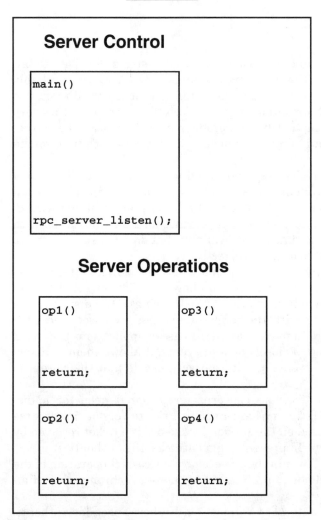

Figure 14.2 DCE server structure.

operations are coded as conventional subroutines, calling sequence–return values. What could be simpler? The only real complexity in implementing a server concerns data sharing between concurrently executing threads. This problem and its solution were discussed in Chap. 12 in the section on mutexes.

The basic DCE client/server model can be extended to several variant forms, some of which are described in later chapters. Alone or together with one or the other of these alternatives, the model will meet the requirements of a very large percentage of all distributed applications. Even considering all the variations, the model represents an enormous simplification over the range of possible flow structures that have been used to implement distributed applications in the past.

14.2 Synchronization of Events

In Chap. 3, it was stated that in most distributed systems deployed today, there is no way to determine the true time that an event occurred or to reliably determine the order of events that occurred at different nodes within minutes of each other. The DCE Distributed Time Service (DTS) remedies this very successfully. In fact, it seems to solve the problem as well as it can be solved, short of an organization equipping every node in its network with time source hardware.

The DTS keeps all system clocks synchronized to within seconds (or less) of each other. It updates the system clocks directly, without requiring any special action on the part of applications. It ensures that clocks never run backward, even if they get ahead of the correct time. It provides for synchronization with a hardware source of the true time if it is available, but does not require one to be present in order for DTS to operate correctly.

The DTS provides absolute and relative time information in an internal format, while providing conversion routines to allow it to be converted to and from other useful forms, including printable ASCII strings. DTS also provides a systematic way of dealing with the inherent uncertainty associated with time in a distributed system. In particular, in the case of applications that need to be certain about the order of closely spaced events, it allows them to determine the temporal order of events or, alternatively, decide that their order is indeterminate.

An interesting historical footnote concerns one original need for a distributed time service in DCE that no longer exists. Prior to Version 5, Kerberos used an "authenticator," based on the session key, to prove a ticket received by a server had not been stolen. To prevent replay attacks, the authenticator was timestamped to expire in a few minutes. Therefore, the correct operation of the authentication system depended on a reasonably close synchronization of all the system clocks.

The challenge-response protocol in Version 5 of Kerberos used for authentication in DCE eliminates that requirement. Security tickets do have an expiration timestamp, but they are good for eight hours or so, so precise synchronization is not an issue. Of course, all the other reasons for the DTS still exist.

14.3 Security Enforcement

As discussed in Chap. 3, the difficulty of providing consistent and reliable security mechanisms in distributed systems has been a major issue. The DCE Security Service probably does more to improve this situation than any other product or technology that has been introduced since people began to develop distributed systems.

The Security Service provides a reliable means of authentication that does not require specialized hardware. It implements a reasonable scheme for authorization and permits a reliable networkwide login. It allows applications the flexibility to strike a balance between performance and protection of the integrity and privacy of data transmitted over the network. It allows developers to implement access control tailored to the needs of their application, yet consistent with emerging standards and supported by the other Security Service mechanisms. In summary, a distributed system that correctly utilizes the mechanisms of the Security Service will be far more secure than one based on any other commercially available distributed computing environment.

That said, the Security Service, as it exists today, has some widely recognized shortcomings. Some of these can be remedied, and may well be in future versions of DCE. Others are outside the scope of DCE and therefore not so amenable to correction. Although it is possible to wish for any number of things from the DCE Security Service that it currently does not do, this section discusses some of the most generally agreed-upon deficiencies.*

14.3.1 ACL manager implementation

One significant obstacle to implementing even the most simple secure application is the considerable work required to write an ACL manager. Only DCE authentication based on a principal's PAC provides any real assurance of a principal's bona fides. Absent an ACL manager, however, what can a server do with a PAC? A related issue is that ACL managers are supposed to operate consistently with the standard DCE scheme, but nothing enforces that.

One possible solution to the first problem would be a distributed ACL manager product that relieved the developer of some of the work involved in writing an ACL manager. Such a product would provide a centralized store of ACLs from

---

* A variety of solutions to functional deficiencies in the Security Service can and will be created by DCE vendors and end users. Some examples include: enforcing various restrictions on passwords, such as keeping them out of the dictionary, expiring them periodically, permanently retiring old ones; enabling use of smart cards and biometric devices; integrating use of electronic signatures.

which ACLs could be configured to meet the needs of specific applications. It would need to ensure authentication and protection in all of its communications. For reliability it would need to be replicated, but to avoid becoming a bottleneck it would need to make use of caching. Such a product has been introduced by Atrium Technologies, Inc. If it is successful, it may attract competitors as well.

A future version of DCE will provide a library of routines that will simplify the development of an ACL manager. This library will implement the parts of the ACL manager that are generic, such as permission checking, while giving the developer control over other aspects of the ACL manager, such as the storage mechanism used. When available, this library should substantially simplify building an ACL manager.

14.3.2 Audit trails

Another deficiency of the DCE Security Service is the lack of well-defined mechanisms for generating audit trails. It is important to be able to log detected attempts to breach security. It is also desirable to be able to log routine changes to authorization and access-control information, so that, if a security breach occurs, the origin of changes can be tracked. A good audit-trail facility should ensure that it cannot be defeated by an unauthorized user intent on covering his or her tracks. It also should allow applications to log security information that is meaningful to them. The need for an audit facility has been recognized for some time, and OSF plans to add it to a future version of DCE.

14.3.3 Delegation

Currently, the Security Service does not permit controlled delegation of authorization. In other words, there is no satisfactory way for a server to request another server to do something on behalf of a client. In Fig. 14.3, a client makes a request to server A, which fulfills it by calling server B.

None of the current methods of dealing with this situation is satisfactory. The intermediary server principal (server A) can be authorized to do anything that any of its clients might want to do, but to do so it must duplicate the access-control checks that would normally be performed by the target server (server B). Another possible approach would be to have the client provide all the tickets necessary to access target servers, but this would require clients to know in advance all the servers that might be called.

Like the previous problem, this one has been recognized for some time and is among those OSF plans to address in a future version of DCE. The solution will involve extending the semantics of ACLs so that delegation can be both allowed and controlled.

14.3.4 Extended security model

The solutions for the deficiencies discussed above are foreseeable. As to otherwise enhancing the current DCE security model, there is little agreement,

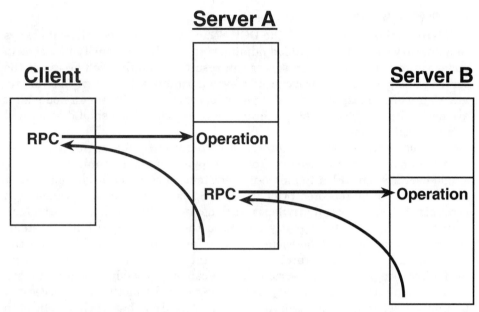

Figure 14.3 Use of intermediary server.

even though several other limitations are commonly brought up. As currently defined, the capabilities of ACLs are quite limited, for example. There is no way for access rights to depend on anything other than a principal's identity; they cannot depend on the time of day of the access, for example.

Frequently criticized is the Security Service's lack of support for public key encryption. Certainly the use of public keys would obviate the need for some of the machinery used in the current authentication process. DCE has reserved the symbol **rpc_c_authn_dce_public** for future use to indicate public-key-based authentication. However, this begs the question of whether a totally different approach based on public key technology is in order.*

Complicating the future of the DCE Security Service is that OSF's DME (Distributed Management Environment), which is dependent on DCE in other respects, has its own set of security requirements and proposed security models. At the time this book is being written, whether DME should depend entirely on DCE for security or should add its own on top of DCE is a matter of debate. As there is no agreement on these matters, it appears that the current DCE security model will not change significantly for some time.

---

*There is currently considerable debate about public key encryption. This encompasses both the technical merits of different schemes, including resistance to attack and computation speed, and legal issues such as ownership of certain algorithms and the applicable laws. On top of this, the U.S. government has announced a hardware-based encryption device called Clipper Chip, which has added a new level of confusion to the debate. As a result, very little can be said with confidence about the future evolution of DCE encryption.

14.3.5 Permanent security gaps

A different set of limitations to the DCE Security Service probably will always remain; they can only be handled administratively. Local security breaches in nodes running an application server can result in unauthorized access to the server principal identity. Breaches in a system running the security server create even more widespread risks. If possible, servers should run on nodes that are not multiuser systems but dedicated server nodes. They should be located in a physically secure place.

DCE also cannot prevent the theft of passwords due to local security breaches on multiuser systems or from fake login programs running on shared, single-user systems. Ideally, single-user systems should not be shared. If they are, they should be rebooted prior to login. Special care should be taken with accounts that have special privileges, such as those of network administrators.

In summary, DCE has greatly advanced the state of distributed systems security, but important deficiencies remain. For some of these, corrections can be expected in the near future; for others, the outcome is much less certain. Still others are permanent restrictions that can only be addressed administratively. Overall, the DCE Security Service provides the mechanisms necessary to provide security for distributed systems security, but their application requires vigilance and an understanding of their limitations.

14.4 Use of Multiple Technologies

The implementation of distributed systems will continue to entail combining many diverse components—communications protocols, databases, operating systems, compilers, GUIs, and security mechanisms. However, the advent of DCE helps with this in several respects, and it can confidently be predicted that because of DCE the challenge will continue to ease in the future.

First and most obviously, DCE has integrated the diverse technologies from which it was derived into an environment well suited to implementation of distributed systems. Furthermore, it has greatly simplified their use. Although no one would claim that using DCE is a trivial undertaking, most of the DCE facilities can be accessed simply by making a few calls to library routines to specify desired options. This is a vast improvement on having to master (or invent) the underlying mechanisms of a component such as CDS or Kerberos.

A second-order effect is that DCE itself presents a paradigm for the operation of distributed systems. As it becomes widely used, more individuals will become familiar with it and bring to it their own knowledge of other, related computer technologies. In the course of solving the problems of building tools and applications using DCE, they will help codify critical aspects of integrating these technologies.

Some of this is already happening. At the time this book is being written, a number of database vendors, working closely with OSF, are sorting through the issues associated with remote database access under DCE. I am aware of a half-dozen different projects to map existing language paradigms, from Visual Basic to C++, onto DCE. The subjects of these projects include reusable libraries and complete compiler systems, research prototypes, and code being used in production applications.

In the future, widespread use of DCE will drive other such efforts. Clearly, the techniques of building an X-Window-based DCE client will become better understood. The RPC is already understood to be an important mechanism for implementation of distributed transaction processing.

The existence of DCE will tend to focus such efforts. The potential for a large market will encourage the development of more powerful tools. In the long run, the distributed-system developer will no longer have to be the master of multiple technologies, creating solutions from scratch. Instead, using higher-level facilities that hide many of the underlying complexities and following existing patterns or templates to solve familiar problems will be the standard practice.

14.5 Frequent Component Incompatibilities

The most widely recognized problem in implementing distributed systems is that of component incompatibilities. DCE makes a major contribution in this area. Instead of the end user performing the integration of the software pieces from which the distributed system is constructed, OSF and its subcontractors have spent a number of years integrating the components of DCE. Interaction of the distributed environment with components on which it depends, such as operating systems and communications protocols, is now well understood.

Anyone who acquires a DCE implementation can be confident that additional effort will not be required to make DCE components work together. Also, because they all use the same source code, implementations from different vendors can be relied upon to interoperate.

Early results have shown these expectations to be justified. At the DCE Interoperability Festival (IFEST) at OSF in April 1993, more than 22 DCE implementations from more than 13 vendors were tested for interoperability. Only a few minor problems were found and were fixed on the spot. Although each product had been ported independently of the others and ran on a different operating system, including many non-UNIX-like ones, all succeeded in interoperating in a battery of conformance tests.

As DCE deployment increases, other products will be built to interoperate with DCE as well. Because of its existence on a wide variety of platforms, independent software vendors (ISVs) will want to build products that work with DCE. This will automatically benefit DCE users regardless of the platform they use. Since DCE is much richer than existing de facto standards, such as Netbios, vendors will be less inclined to invent their own mechanisms to make up for the inherent limitations of those environments. This will further tend to increase interoperability.

14.6   Multiple Configurations

Distributed systems need to be able to function in a much broader range of configurations than is typical of monolithic systems. DCE makes this easier by hiding many of the aspects of the configuration from the application software. DCE applications need not be aware of the processor type, operating system, communications protocols, or physical network they are using.* DCE clients find servers by name, simplifying network reconfiguration. The other technologies, such as the Security Service and DTS, are specifically designed to allow them to operate correctly over a wide range of configurations.

As new hardware and software technologies are introduced, the effect of a well-defined distributed computing environment will be to allow existing applications to take advantage of new configurations without modification, while enabling new applications to take advantage of capabilities that were not previously accessible. DCE is designed to scale up to a future in which public and private networks are highly interconnected, in which distributed applications span multiple enterprises (e.g., customer-vendor-bank), and in which DCE cells are managed by autonomous organizations.

14.7   Chapter Summary

DCE's impact on distributed systems is more significant than any other single product or technology. It has been shown that DCE directly addresses six of the most significant obstacles to development of distributed systems. As distributed system tools and applications begin to emerge, its effects will multiply.

DCE does not, however, represent the pinnacle of perfection. Already many additional needs, beyond those DCE can meet today, have been identified. As more DCE-based systems are developed, still other needs will doubtless emerge. Some will be satisfied by enhancements to DCE, some by new software products, still others by careful operational practice. The point is that many of these requirements could not even be identified before the advent of DCE. They are not so much a measure of DCE's weaknesses as an indication of the extent to which DCE has moved the art and science of distributed systems development to a new plateau, from which we can now dimly perceive the distant mountaintops.

---

* While it is true that some of this is due to other standards (e.g., ANSI C, POSIX.1), DCE does its part in shielding the application from operating-system differences such as network APIs (e.g., sockets versus TLI versus APPC versus QIOs).

Chapter 15

Problems DCE Doesn't Help Solve

Chapter 3 discussed 12 reasons distributed systems are more difficult to design, build, and operate than monolithic systems. In the previous chapter, we described how DCE, largely successfully, addresses six of these issues. This chapter takes up the other six issues, which are not addressed by DCE. It suggests how to minimize or avoid the problems entailed in these issues. In some cases, we can predict new products and technologies that may emerge to help alleviate them.

15.1 Multiple Failure Modes

Distributed systems can fail in many different ways because they are made up of so many independent components. There is nothing DCE can do to alter this fundamental fact. One thing that DCE (along with many other transport services) does do is to indicate clearly if a connection is up or down. In the past, for developers dealing with the prospect of intermittent failures, considerable ambiguity has surrounded the question of whether or not to continue. With DCE, using either connectionless or connection-oriented protocols, the client and server will see a definite error indication if a communications failure occurs.

To some extent, using the client/server model, at least in its simplest form, can reduce the number of failure scenarios the developer must consider. For example, take the basic case of a single client talking to a single server. Ignoring bugs and partial failures, the client can fail, the server can fail, or the network can fail. To the client or server, a network failure is indistinguishable from a failure of the other party. Therefore, there are really only two cases to consider.

In the case of the client, DCE provides automatic binding, allowing the runtime to rebind to another, equivalent, server. This will not work if the server uses a context handle, because, in that situation, the server has maintained information about the current state of the interaction that is not visible to an alternate server. Unless the server controls a unique resource, the client's basic failure strategy is the same. It must rebind to another server, even if it means that the session must be restarted from the beginning.

From the server's perspective, matters are also quite simple: if a client fails while the server is executing a server operation routine for the client, the application code will not be aware that anything has happened. When the operation routine exits, the runtime will discard any outputs and generally clean up. If for some reason the operation routine needs to deal with this case explicitly, it can use the **pthread_testcancel**() routine or enable asynchronous cancelability.

If a client fails at any time when it is not actually performing an RPC, the server is involved only if the client has some state information pointed to by a context handle. In that situation, DCE will perform a callback to clean up the context of the failed client. Servers that use context handles should provide a context rundown procedure for this purpose. If a client that has no outstanding context fails, the server does not need to take any special action.

Once the application design gets beyond this simple model, many more failure modes must be considered. Servers that share state with each other in order to provide redundancy need to consider various error scenarios and their potential effects on data integrity. Servers that call other servers or participate in more-complex flow models need to consider the consequences and recovery actions required in the event of failures at various points in the processing.

Two general principles apply. First, use the simplest design that will meet the requirements. For some reason, software developers and application experts alike tend to invent labyrinthine designs. Sometimes, however, it make sense even to accept a slight reduction in the functionality if that leads to a great reduction in the complexity of a design.

Second, pay attention to the design of error handling and recovery. There is a natural tendency to think exclusively about how things will work when everything goes normally. In part, this is because most people find it more interesting than thinking about failures. In part, however, it is because a conventional program can just print an error message and then exit. No special thought about error handling is required. In distributed systems, however, even if a problem occurs with one client, servers must continue to provide service to other clients. Therefore, they must be designed to handle errors and continue.

15.2 Simultaneous Execution

Distributed systems inherently entail simultaneous execution of software by multiple processors. DCE does not change this. To some extent, the client/server model reduces the application developer's need to think about it. DCE clients are single-threaded unless explicitly designed to be multithreaded. RPCs are blocking, so that the client and server do not execute at the same time.

The one case in which more than one piece of an application can be executing simultaneously is in a multithreaded server executing on a multiprocessor system. If the proper mechanisms to prevent race conditions among concurrent threads are used, they will serve to protect against interactions between simultaneously executing threads as well.

There is no getting around the fact, however, that when the distributed system, which may involve multiple applications, is viewed as a whole, things are happening on different nodes simultaneously. Figure 15.1 illustrates this phenomenon. This can manifest itself in a variety of ways; most of them have to do with shared state external to any server. For example, when data files or databases are directly accessed by multiple servers, care must be taken to avoid conflicts. Mutexes can control conflicts within a single process, but external locking mechanisms must be present to prevent conflicts among multiple processes on the same or different nodes.

One particular case of simultaneous execution is the application structure called a *distributed computation*. In this model the client distributes the work to multiple servers. The DCE example program "timop" is an example. We suggest that this approach be avoided unless the developer has a specific algorithm that is known to work well. The additional complexity will make it difficult to devise and debug a new algorithm successfully, while the extra overhead in communicating with multiple servers may easily outweigh any benefits of the approach.

15.3 Many Possible States

Distributed systems can assume a large number of distinct states. This also is something DCE cannot eliminate. The best that can be done is to isolate the complexity by limiting or eliminating the interaction between distinct applications. This may not always be possible. It is generally desirable to build

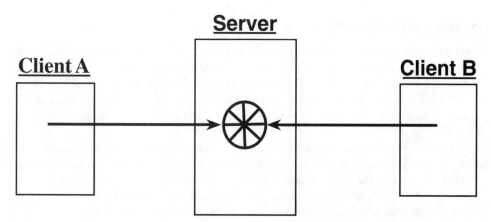

Figure 15.1 Simultaneous events.

reusable servers and amortize the cost of design and development over multiple uses. However, reusing a server for different purposes adds to the overall complexity of a system, because it means that the server will be a component in many different applications. The general advice is the same as was given above: make the design as simple as possible.

I was once involved in the design of a distributed system for processing bank loan applications. The system consisted of multiple nodes, each of which had a full or partial copy of the database. Data could be entered in the system at any node and then had to be propagated to the other nodes on a daily basis to keep the copies identical. The banking experts originally proposed functionality that included very complex rules concerning which node should update the others. The authoritative source of data could vary by data field, by record, even by day of the month!

The other members of the design team and I analyzed the requirements and determined that it would be extremely difficult to keep all of the nodes following the same rules and performing the proper updates. It also seemed to us that it would be extremely difficult to administer the system and keep the definitions straight. We also realized that, if it were ever necessary to restore the database of one of the nodes from backup, it would be nearly impossible to ensure that the data was correct.

We suggested (very firmly) that the application use a much simpler set of updating rules. Eventually, the system was developed using the rule that certain nodes "owned" certain fields and could update those fields on all nodes. When the system was deployed, the functionality was sufficient to meet the needs of every real customer who purchased it.

The point of this anecdote is that you may have to play the bad guy and press for the real requirements. Sometimes it may even be better to accept a manual process to handle some functions, rather than build a system that is inherently unreliable and cannot be administered or repaired.

15.4 Performance Estimation Difficulties

Performance estimation of distributed systems is barely an art, much less a science. Actually, almost all accurate performance estimation of any kind of computer system occurs in one of two situations. Either the problem has been simplified to some special case, or the application and configuration bear a close relationship to some existing system with well-known performance characteristics.

For example, given an existing mainframe-based transaction processing system, it is possible to make a reasonably accurate estimate of the effect of adding a certain number of additional users or supporting a new software package or upgrading the processor. But the behavior of distributed systems is so varied that it is usually impossible to make generalizations.

DCE does not attempt to address this problem. In fact, in the short run, DCE may make it more difficult to predict the performance of distributed systems. For one thing, DCE will encourage development of more-complex distributed systems that will be more difficult to characterize. For another, DCE contains many new components that applications must depend upon, but which have largely unknown performance characteristics.

In the longer run, the situation should improve. As more applications running over DCE are developed, more information will become available about the performance characteristics of different types of DCE applications. This will at least give us a feel for the characteristics of similar applications. Eventually, there may be enough data available to develop predictive models.

In the absence of data, or rigorous models, it is still possible to make some educated guesses based on rules of thumb. The three main measures of performance are *response, throughput,* and *capacity.* At the stage of feasibility assessment, response tends to be the major concern. This is because throughput and capacity often can be increased simply by buying faster processors, disk drives, etc.

One way to guesstimate *response* is to calculate roughly how long it will take for the data to move across the network. Figure all of the message flows, including responses, and estimate the message sizes. Add 25 to 50 percent to account for various kinds of overhead. Divide by the transmission speed of the network. The result will give an initial rough estimate for the response delay with a lightly loaded network and server node. One way to use the estimate is to treat it as a best-case number.

Throughput and *capacity* tend to depend more on the server or database. The vendor of the server system or DBMS may be able to provide information indicative of throughput, for example benchmarks indicating so many transactions per second or I/O operations per second on a certain system. As with the estimated response figures, these probably should be treated as a best case. Once the feasibility stage is passed, it may be possible to devise benchmarks that more closely model the real application.

Capacity tends to be very hard to estimate, because the amount of work associated with a client is usually highly variable. Usually, it is necessary to assume that if the response and throughput requirements can be met, then meeting capacity requirements is just a matter of money. In other words, up to some reasonable size, bigger server systems or more of them or faster disks will provide whatever capacity is required. Of course, if a server system under consideration is much larger than any currently in use, this assumption may not hold true.

In summary, the complexity of distributed systems makes their performance difficult to analyze. At the same time, each system is likely to be so different from others that it becomes difficult to extrapolate directly from one to another. As experience grows in developing different kinds of applications using DCE, some useful data points should emerge and, eventually, perhaps predictive models.

15.5 Complex Design Tradeoffs

Many of the same considerations that apply to performance estimation apply to design tradeoffs. The same complex interactions of the many components of a distributed system that make performance estimation difficult also make understanding design tradeoffs difficult. Nothing in the DCE technologies really helps this situation either.

As explained in Chap. 3, there are really two parts to the problem of design tradeoffs for a distributed system. The first part of the problem is to establish the metrics against which the design should be measured. Obviously, anyone would want a system that goes faster, stays up more, and is cheaper to build. Occasionally, a system can be optimized around just one requirement regardless of any other characteristics—for example, reliability. More commonly, it is necessary to trade off one characteristic for another. This requires a judgment that says, for example, that increasing availability from 95 to 98 percent is worth increasing development cost by 25 percent.

The second part of the problem is to determine what the actual tradeoffs are. As with performance estimation, this is very difficult to determine today. As more experience with DCE applications accumulates, the tradeoffs will be better understood.

Some work has already been done to benchmark DCE. More is planned. The objectives of the work so far have been (1) to identify areas where internal improvements to DCE would be most beneficial and (2) to provide data comparing different design choices. Studies of the second type are of potentially great value to application designers.

One study measured the effects of using multiple processes or threads. The results were as expected: using threads consumed less capacity than using processes, and using either increased throughput over using a single-threaded process. Another study showed that using packet privacy caused more delay than using packet integrity, which caused more delay than using per-call protection. In each case, the delay was a linear function of the message size. Neither of these results is surprising, but they represent a good starting point. More performance studies like these will help to quantify tradeoffs.

In contrast, the first part of the problem may never become any more clear-cut than it is today. Except in rare cases where a level of response time or availability has a direct economic consequence, the weighting of different attributes is likely to remain a matter of judgment or, at worst, prejudice.

15.6 Testing and Debugging Difficulties

Testing and debugging of distributed applications is currently a labor-intensive and error-prone process. DCE does not really help at all. Hopefully, its existence will spur vendors to build better tools.

It is not entirely clear that this will happen. The historical trends are unclear. The currently most popular network environment, NetWare, provides only very primitive tools for server testing and debugging. On the positive side, GUI-based applications have created a need for a whole new type of test program, and a number of vendors have responded with excellent new products. On the negative side, few vendors are willing to build software tools because the market for them is much smaller than for applications. Also, the willingness to pay for tools can be quite low, although this is not invariably so.

15.6.1 Debuggers

For what it is worth, here is what is needed. First of all, thread-aware debuggers are needed on every platform. This is particularly important, because in most DCE implementations both the clients and the servers are, in fact, multithreaded. Even when there is only a single application thread, the DCE runtime is using other threads for its own purposes. A thread-aware debugger will make debugging a program much easier.

A thread-aware debugger should allow breakpoints to be set on a thread-specific basis. It should allow the option of permitting other threads to continue or causing all threads to stop when a breakpoint is reached. Such a debugger should be able to display information about the states of all threads and identify threads. It should be possible to display information about other thread facilities, such as the states of mutexes, condition variables, exceptions raised, etc. It should provide facilities for watching specific data items for read or write access by selected threads or any thread.

The next step would be to provide a distributed debugger. Such a tool would use the facilities of DCE to coordinate the operation of debugging kernels located in processes on different nodes. It should allow the information collected to be gathered and coordinated from a single point. It should allow breakpoints to be set anywhere in the distributed application and provide coordinated control of processing in all of the components. It should be able to use timestamps to determine the temporal order of events on different systems. Naturally, it should be as unobtrusive as possible in its use of memory and communications bandwidth, so as to distort the behavior of the application as little as possible.

Another debugging issue relates to higher-level environments built over DCE. There is currently considerable interest in mapping high-level programming abstractions to DCE. These range from visual-programming paradigms to various object-oriented languages. As products, these tools will be successful only if they provide debuggers that allow the developer to deal in the high-level abstraction that the tool supports. Much of the benefit of a high-level paradigm is lost if the user must debug using the primitive of the underlying environment. Then, the user has to learn not only all the details that were supposed to be hidden, but also how the tool uses the lower-level facilities.

15.6.2 Test tools

Distributed test tools are also sorely needed. Here, the general functionality of current test tools is a good starting point. Some of the needs are for test scripts with the ability to fill in variables and constants, the ability to control timing, the ability to capture and perhaps recognize output, support for stress testing and regression testing, the ability to test against GUIs. In a DCE environment, it might be desirable to test servers directly, using a test client that binds to the interface and calls the server with different arguments. For some purposes, this might be more convenient than testing a client via its human interface.

Of course, a distributed test tool would do all these things in distributed fashion, controlled from a single point, using the facilities of DCE to communicate among its components. Like a distributed debugger, it should use timing information to allow it to coordinate and correlate events occurring on different nodes. Also like a debugger, it should create minimal distortion of the normal behavior of the application under test.

15.7 Chapter Summary

The six problems listed in this chapter are not directly addressed by DCE. In some cases, the existence of DCE will produce better tools or at least a better understanding of the problem. In others, it may be possible to apply common sense and rules of thumb until more precise models become available. In many cases, problems in developing and debugging distributed systems can be greatly reduced by sticking to standard application flow models and minimizing complexity wherever possible—even, if necessary, sacrificing nonessential functionality to do so.

16

Thinking About Distributed Systems

The existence of DCE will introduce many more designers to distributed systems. They will confront a number of issues common to distributed systems, with or without DCE, that require them to think differently about their applications. Some of these issues never arise when designing for a monolithic system. Others that had previously been only peripheral demand far greater attention in a distributed system environment. This chapter addresses some of these topics. The purpose is to help the reader who may be new to distributed systems avoid some of the mistakes that have been made by me and others in the past.

Some of the principles are general in nature and require experience and judgment to apply correctly. One of the most important choices that has to be made again and again is what to decide now and what to defer until later in the design process. There is no simple answer to this question, but here are some things to take into consideration.

Look for the fundamental invariants of the problem. For example, consider the entities or objects that are fundamental to the particular business or enterprise, such as customers, ovens, loans, classrooms, or tanks. These things will persist, while computer systems change. Do not design for a particular configuration or network. Assume that the scale of the application will change over time. The types of processors, their number, their geography and topology, the bandwidth of the network—all these things may change, except as they are dictated by the nature of the enterprise.

In terms of the design, in the early stages look for the properties that are inherent to the problem. Determine if some action can ever happen or never happen; don't worry about how frequently it occurs. Decide if an item can occur exactly once, or more than once. Group related functions and data physically as much as possible. This will not only increase efficiency of execution, but it will make the design more coherent and therefore easier to implement and modify. Where there are close relationships between different data items, cluster them together, preferably in the same server. This will make it much simpler to establish and maintain their dependencies.

Avoid casual duplication of data. Don't represent the same information in different places and expect to be able to keep it all consistent. If possible, avoid copying files. When you copy a file, you end up with two copies. This immediately creates the possibility that they may become different and raises the question of which is correct. If replication is required for reasons of reliability and availability, it should be explicitly provided, ideally in an application-independent way. At least, the rules for replication and updating should be specified, documented, and followed without exception.

In addition to these general guidelines, there are a number of specific issues that tend to crop up over and over again in distributed systems design. The following sections discuss them and suggest some practical approaches to dealing with them.

16.1   Thinking in Layers

Thinking in layers is one of the most productive habits a designer can bring to the challenge of designing distributed systems. The DCE design itself is a product of such thinking, as are many emerging technologies such as object-oriented paradigms. But one of the most instructive models for thinking in layers, for the distributed system designer, is the ISO's OSI (Open Systems Interconnect) communications model. This is not so much because of its use in network design, but because its organization suggests useful concepts for design of distributed systems.

The major elements of protocol layering are shown in Fig. 16.1. Each protocol layer has an upper and lower interface. (The exceptions are the topmost layer, which is an application, and the bottom layer, which is hardware.) Each layer provides a service to the layer above it via its upper interface, and is a user (or client) to the layer below it. Equivalent layers on different nodes are called *peer layers*. Peer layers communicate with each other using peer protocols. Even though the messages that constitute the protocol pass through other, lower, layers, only the peer layer will act upon it.

This approach has many desirable attributes. Layers encapsulate their internal state. That is to say, only a layer is aware of how it does its job. Other layers can only interact with it via its interfaces. The interfaces are carefully designed to represent a logical boundary between relatively separate functions, which only interact in limited ways.

Subdividing communications functions into layers makes it easier to focus attention on one part of the overall problem at a time and to get that part to work properly. Peer layers can work together to solve a particular set of problems and ignore all others. For example, a network protocol layer can concentrate on forwarding packets toward the right destination. It does not have to concern itself

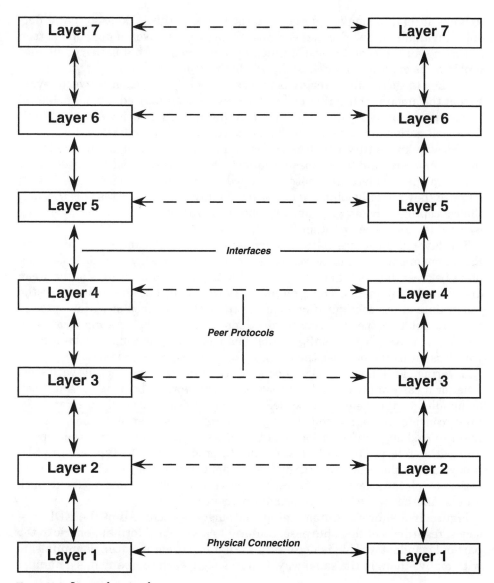

Figure 16.1 Layered protocols.

with what data is in the packets (the responsibility of upper layers) or how data gets transmitted over a LAN (the responsibility of a lower layer).

DCE RPC relieves the application designer from having to implement all the services performed by the communications protocol layers and hides their activities. Nevertheless, layering is a very useful way to approach the design of distributed systems. When the problem to be solved is complex, it makes sense to break it up into smaller pieces. In large projects, this is done so that different individuals can work independently of each other. Even if only one person is writing all the code, it is still much easier to deal with a series of smaller problems as opposed to tackling the whole thing at once.

The key to successful layering is to pick the point of division between layers so that the amount of interaction between layers is minimized. This is achieved by grouping closely related functions together into each layer. A system built from well-designed layers can be visualized as beads in a necklace. Each bead is a closely knit entity which is self-contained and difficult to subdivide. Its constituents are said to be closely coupled. On the other hand, the beads that make up the necklace are loosely coupled to each other and easily divided, because they are only joined in one place. Figure 16.2 illustrates this. Besides the conceptual advantages that are obtained from designing and developing isolated layers, there are other benefits as well.

The layered structure naturally lends itself to a distributed architecture. Each component, client or server, consists of one or more layers. The looser coupling between layers makes the layers the natural point of division between distributed components. The grouping of the layers can be chosen based on the constraints of the configuration, such as the size and speed of various processors, the relative speed of communications links, and the existing location of databases. Later, if the configuration changes, the grouping can be altered with less difficulty, because the coupling between each layer is low.

Layering can follow the OSI model of peer protocols interacting with each other or it can simply consist of breaking up the work to be done so that it can be handled by independent modules. A couple of examples will illustrate this. First, consider a system that links vendors and customers together to allow them to exchange information about products bought and sold—the type of application referred to as Electronic Data Interchange (EDI). Typically, an EDI link would be shared by several different applications. They might be an application to place orders, one to report deliveries, one to inquire about back orders, another to exchange information about payments.

Figure 16.3 shows a simple design for such a system. All of the EDI messages, regardless of their purpose, conform to a standard format generic to the particular industry. This is necessary so that each company can communicate with many others in the same way. In our design, each company has a number

Figure 16.2 Beads in a necklace.

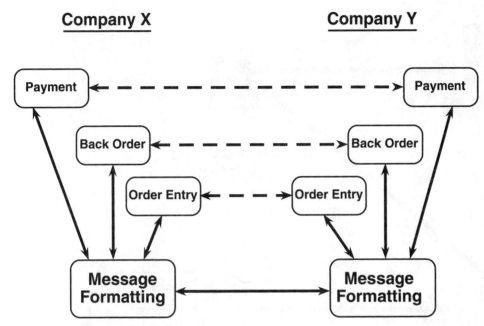

Figure 16.3 Layered design of an EDI system.

of application systems that can send and receive messages to corresponding applications at other companies. The inventory applications communicate, the accounting applications communicate, etc.

Since all applications need to format their messages according to the generic standard, our design has a separate message-formatting layer. It takes data from applications and builds messages in the standard format. It could perhaps perform other functions, such as locating the destination of messages or queuing them until they can be transmitted. At the receiving end, the message layer can unpack messages and direct them to the appropriate application. This design uses the peer layer concept. It simplifies the applications because they do not have to deal with issues related to message formatting.

Notice that even this simple design allows for several distributed configurations. Obviously, the software associated with each company is running on that company's own systems. Within each company, however, several configurations are possible. All of the applications and the message layer could be on a single node. The message layer could be on one machine and the applications on another. Each layer could be on a different node.

A second example illustrates layering without peer layers. In this case, the application controls operations of a manufacturing plant. A highly simplified design for such a system is shown in Fig. 16.4. At the lowest level, software directly controls the operation of factory floor machines. At this level, the soft-

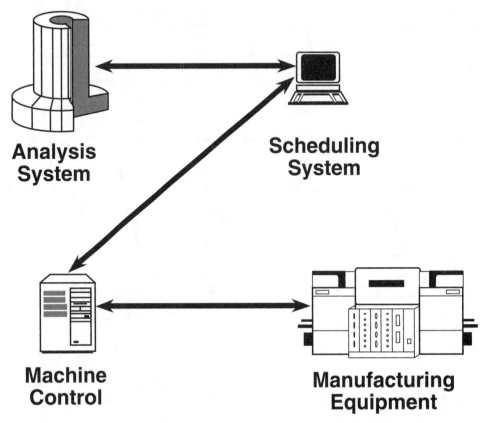

Figure 16.4 Layering in a manufacturing system.

ware can set up the machine to make some part, manufacture a certain number of the parts, and then switch over to make another kind of part.

At the next level, a scheduling system receives orders for goods. It knows what parts are needed, what machines can make what parts, how many machines there are of each type, how long it takes to switch over, etc. It schedules the order of different part runs, decides what machines to use, etc. It gives commands to the lower layer to run jobs. At this layer it is not necessary to worry about the details of how the machines operate, just as it is not necessary for the lower layer to think about what product a given part is being used in.

At the highest level, additional software takes a longer view of the manufacturing process. It might analyze the efficiency of the scheduling algorithm by measuring the average time to complete an order, the amount of time the machines are idle, or the average number of parts on hand. As a result, it might make changes that alter the way the scheduling layer does its job. Just like the other layers, it can ignore the issues that do not relate to the task that it performs.

In summary, layering is a useful and powerful technique that should be considered when approaching any distributed application design.

16.2 What Do Acknowledgments Signify?

The client/server model implies the use of a request-response protocol. That is to say, the client makes a request and gets a response (acknowledgment) indicating that the request has been satisfied or that an error has occurred. Normally, when a remote procedure call is used, the return from the remote procedure is considered to be the acknowledgment. In other words, the routine does not return until the requested work has been completely finished. This is the preferred design, because it simplifies many aspects of the problem, especially error handling.

There are several reasons why it may not be possible to use this approach, however. In many applications, the nature of the work to be performed is such that the remote procedure call is merely a request to initiate an action. There are many reasons why this might be done. The work may be something that occurs only on a periodic basis, e.g., every hour or every day. An example would be sending data over a dialup telephone line. Or the work may simply be something that takes so long to do that it is not reasonable for the client to wait until it has completed. For example, the request might be to fill a million-gallon tank.

Another category of application design, in which an acknowledgment does not necessarily indicate completion of an action, is one in which the work is performed by a series of independent processes calling each other in succession. Figure 16.5 depicts such a design. When the originator of the request (client) waits for the final step to complete and return an acknowledgment, this is known as *end-to-end acknowledgment.* In this example, because of the number of steps involved, coupled with the speeds of the processors and communications links involved, it may be necessary to return acknowledgments from some intermediate point.

In such cases, receiving an acknowledgment may signify that only part of the work has been done. An acknowledgment may merely mean that a request has been transmitted or perhaps only that it has been queued up to be transmitted. An acknowledgment may indicate that a request is syntactically correct, but still may fail. Even when the server has obtained the result and written it to disk, in most operating systems the result may not actually be physically written immediately. To carry that line of reasoning further, in order to guarantee that the result is not lost in the event of a head crash, it would actually be necessary to write it to multiple disk drives.

The point of this discussion is not to go into the issues of fault tolerance and transaction integrity, however. That would require another book.* The point is

---

* In fact an excellent book has been written on the subject. It is *Transaction Processing: Concepts and Techniques* by Gray and Reuter. (See "Recommended Reading" on p. 551.)

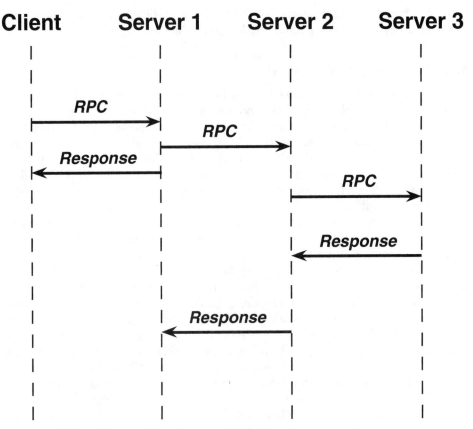

Figure 16.5 Acknowledgments do not imply completion.

that, depending on the application design, acknowledgments may mean different things. This does not matter most of the time when everything goes well, except that it may affect the way current status is displayed. The meaning of acknowledgments becomes most significant when errors occur. In order to correctly handle and recover from errors, it is necessary to be very clear on what state is implied by any acknowledgments that have been received.

There is no magic formula that will make every application behave properly. It is necessary to work through all of the possible cases and consider carefully what recovery steps are required. The main advice is to avoid falling into the trap of assuming that an acknowledgment means that a request has been completed or that all acknowledgments mean the same thing. This issue is another reason to use the simplest design that will meet an application's requirements.

16.3   The Resource Exhaustion Problem

One common problem in distributed systems is the resource exhaustion phenomenon; an application process (typically, but not necessarily, a server) continually consumes some resource but does not relinquish it. Colloquially, this is called a "core leak" or a "memory leak," since the resource is most often something stored in main memory.* Actually, it is a more general problem usually ascribable to a bug in the code or design that has created an imbalance between the calls to allocate the resource and calls to deallocate it. Typically, the program appears to work correctly at first, but eventually fails after running for some time.

One pernicious aspect to the problem is that the failure interval can be configuration-dependent. An application that appears to run fine on one system quickly dies on another. Of course, if the allocation/deallocation imbalance consists of excessive deallocation, the problem will be quickly found. What shocks me is that some people take the attitude that there is no need to spend a lot of time locating a bug like this. They just run a daemon to restart long-running programs whenever they die.

There are two approaches to finding and fixing such problems. I recommend that you use both of them. The first approach is to instrument allocation and deallocation routines to make detection and identification easier. (To "instrument" software means to add code which measures and reports information about its internal state for debugging and testing purposes.)

In this case, detection can be made easier by having the routines keep a count of resources in use that can be accessed easily in test mode. Watching the count as the process runs for a while will reveal any problems. It is normal for the process to maintain some nonzero level of allocation all the time, but if the count continually creeps up, you have a problem. The point is, it should not be necessary to wait for the program to crash before recognizing that there is a bug.

It is also a good idea to detect an attempt to deallocate something more than once. Here, there are two schools of thought. Some folks just ignore this as harmless. My preference is to indicate an error. After all, where there is one bug, there may be others. The one that is easy to detect may help you locate other, more subtle, ones.

Instrumentation can also be used to mark the items being allocated to determine where in the code they were allocated from. This can be very helpful in tracking down problems. The means of doing it are somewhat specific to the design of the application, but the basic idea is to leave enough room somewhere to indicate who called the allocation routine. It is also a good idea to leave the mark when deallocation is done, because it is sometimes helpful to know who allocated each item last, as well.

Instrumentation is a good idea, but the real solution is to get the design right in the first place. Usually, this kind of problem is caused by an ill-considered and overly complex allocation/deallocation scheme. Think through all of the code paths. Don't forget to deallocate when something unusual, such as an

---

* It amuses me that while many currently practicing software professionals are too young to have ever used a computer with a core memory, the term lives on in UNIX parlance.

error, occurs. It often helps to have a consistent rule about who is responsible for allocating and deallocating buffers shared between caller and callee.

Usually, it is most convenient to have the party that fills a buffer allocate it; otherwise, excessive data copying may be necessary. If a caller passes a full buffer and the callee does not return until it is empty, then it is convenient to have the caller deallocate it. This makes it easier to see that the allocates and deallocates match up. If the call returns while the buffer is still in use, however, then the callee must deallocate it. This is the kind of situation in which mismatches are most likely to occur.

If the callee passes data back to the caller, then the cleanest approach is to have the caller provide the buffer and get rid of it later. The same data-copying concern may require that the callee use its own buffer, however. In this case, the caller must deallocate, creating the opportunity for a mismatch. The main point is to have explicit rules and make them part of the specifications. If the situation is left ambiguous, bugs are likely.

In summary, resource allocation bugs should be eliminated just like any other kind of bug. They should be designed out, by careful analysis and explicit rules for allocation and deallocation. In addition, instrumentation should be provided to detect and locate them when they occur.

16.4   How to Think About Concurrent Execution

Concurrent execution occurs when the execution of a thread or process overlaps in time with execution of other threads or processes. Of course, that happens all the time on a timesharing system, for example. We care about concurrent execution when the concurrent threads share some state, that is, manipulate the same data. This is when there is a possibility of conflict.

Imagine that you had a spell cast on you that caused you to fall asleep at any time without warning. When you awoke, you could continue whatever you were doing from the point you left off, but while you were asleep, other people came into your house and moved your stuff around. That's what concurrent processing is like. (See Fig. 16.6.)

In the context of DCE, threads executing server operations in a multi-threaded server are the main concern. The techniques to avoid problems were described in Chap. 12. To review, static data is shared between threads. Threads are scheduled preemptively. Whenever a thread reads or writes data that is shared with other threads, consider the possibility of access conflicts. Remember that the other threads may be running the same code or different code.

Mutexes should be used to protect data that can be accessed from more than one thread. Create access routines that are the only code that will directly touch shared data and that are responsible for the correct use of mutexes. Avoid using complex schemes. The use of thread synchronization by condition variables or other means is not usually required. Don't try to control access conflicts by means of scheduling priorities.

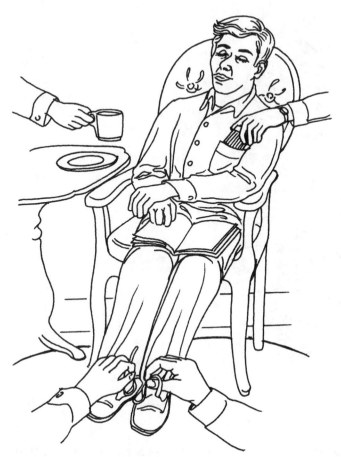

Figure 16.6 Concurrent execution.

16.5 How to Think About
Simultaneous Execution

Simultaneous execution is even harder to think about than concurrent execution. Simultaneous execution means that code is being executed at the same moment on different processors. As with concurrent execution, our concern is when the threads or processes share data. Imagine that you never fall asleep, but there are all these other, invisible, people running through your house, moving things around all the time. That's what simultaneous execution is like. (See Fig. 16.7.)

With DCE, simultaneous execution can occur in two cases. First, on nodes that are closely coupled multiprocessors, different threads can be executing simultaneously on multiple processors. Second, code executing on different nodes is actually executing simultaneously.

Figure 16.7 Simultaneous execution.

In the first case, the good news is that Pthreads has been designed so that the routines that prevent data access conflicts on a single processor will also work on a multiprocessor. The underlying mechanisms used to implement mutexes and condition variables are different on a multiprocessor than on a typical single-processor system, but this does not concern us, only the system vendor. If we have properly protected our shared data, the fact of simultaneous execution will not cause any problems.

On the other hand, some of the other Pthreads mechanisms, although defined to encompass multiprocessor systems, will behave differently in practice. For example, consider scheduling priority. On a single processor, a high-priority thread will lock out lower-priority threads completely, assuming the use of one of the "pure" scheduling policies (e.g., FIFO or round-robin). On a multiprocessor, the highest-priority thread will be scheduled first, but other threads will be scheduled on other processors. This is one of the reasons that priority should not be used in place of a mutex to guard shared data.

The other case of simultaneous execution, the execution of code on different network nodes, is far less likely to cause difficulties in the context of DCE applications. A distributed application with unrestricted flow logic would have to worry about occurrences such as the one shown in Fig. 16.8. Node A sends a message to node B. At almost the same moment, node B sends a message to node A. Node A cannot tell whether the message from node B was sent in response to its latest request or not. The protocol used by A and B must take this possible ambiguity into account.

Because of the restricted flow model of DCE RPC, two processes on different nodes can send messages (RPCs) to each other simultaneously only by using separate threads to run as both client and server.* Only in this type of design can this kind of problem arise.

In most situations the synchronous nature of RPC means that simultaneous execution can only manifest itself at another node by the execution of a thread. Thus, any data access conflicts that might arise will be manifested as the local simultaneous or concurrent execution cases described previously.

---

* Such a peer-to-peer design is described in detail in Chap. 21.

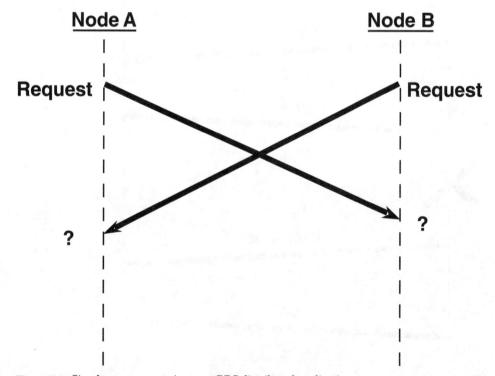

Figure 16.8 Simultaneous events in a non-RPC distributed application.

16.6   Atomic Operations

We have already seen how data access conflicts between threads can arise from write operations involving more than one step to complete—in other words, operations that are not atomic. Write operations that are applied to external objects such as data stored on disk fall in the same category. Nonatomic operations can result in conflicts between concurrently executing processes and can greatly complicate error handling because of the number of possible inconsistent, intermediate states that must be taken into consideration.

Therefore, whenever possible, atomic operations should be preferred over nonatomic ones. In some cases it may be possible to alter a design to produce atomic or quasi-atomic operations. A simple example is depicted in Fig. 16.9. The application manages a simple data file containing records pointed to by an index. Records can be located only by finding them in the index. The usual operations are supported: create a record, read a record, update a record, delete a record, etc. The file would be in an inconsistent state if there were any entries in the index that referred to a nonexistent data record.

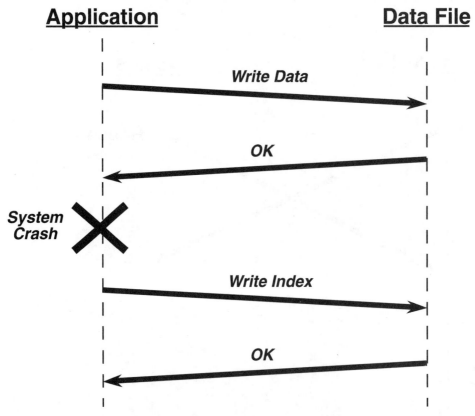

Figure 16.9 A quasi-atomic operation.

By arranging the file updates in the proper order, it is possible to avoid visible inconsistency in the event of a hardware or software failure. For the sake of this example, it is assumed that writing a single disk block is an atomic operation. When a record is added to the file, the application first writes the data record and then the index. If a failure occurs between the write operations, the record will be inaccessible, but there will be no visible inconsistency. (This is what was meant by a quasi-atomic operation.) The inaccessible records can later be removed by garbage collection. For the same reasons, the delete operation first removes the index entry and then the data record.

In summary, atomic operations will tend to reduce concurrency problems and simplify error recovery. In some cases it may be possible to order updating steps to convert nonatomic to quasi-atomic operations.

16.7   Idempotent Operations

An idempotent operation is defined as one which will have the same effect regardless of how many times it is performed. DCE RPC supports idempotent operations by means of the idempotent operation attribute. Operations labeled idempotent will be automatically retried by DCE if an error occurs during the execution of the operation.

Aside from their support by DCE, idempotent operations often simplify distributed system design. Frequently it is difficult to be absolutely certain if an operation occurred or not. If a remote procedure call returns an error, it may not be easy to decide if the error occurred before the critical step or after. The error could mean that the operation was not performed or that communications failed while the response was being transmitted. Being able to repeat the operation is a simple way to recover.

In many cases, the designer will not have any control over whether an operation is idempotent or not. When the choice presents itself, idempotent operations should be preferred. For example, instead of an operation to reverse the direction of a conveyor belt, define two operations, one to make it go forward and one for reverse. Either of these operations can be repeated as many times as necessary to accomplish the intended result.

16.8   How to Design the Server Interface

One important decision the designer of a client/server application must make is to choose the actual operations supported by a server. Given some set of application requirements, what should the operations be? How many operations should there be? What should their arguments be? How many IDL interfaces should the server support?

Most of the servers in production today have an interface based directly on some preexisting local program interface. For example, PC LAN servers, whether they use Microsoft's SMB or Novell's NCP, support the DOS file operations provided by software interrupt 21. That is, for every local file operation (e.g., read, write, delete) there is a corresponding server request. There is a similar correspondence between the requests supported by NFS servers and the UNIX system file operations. In the same way, SQL database servers provide functions that correspond to the primitives of SQL.

If your application is such that some set of primitive operations is already defined and familiar to developers of applications of this type, consider using them as the basis of your interface operations. If nothing of the sort exists, your design must strike a tradeoff between efficiency and reuse. Efficiency argues for making each operation as functionally rich and complete as possible. Every action that a client wishes to take should be handled within a single operation. This will reduce the number of calls required and correspondingly reduce the overhead and the delays associated with making multiple calls.

On the other hand, reuse considerations suggest exactly the opposite. It is very desirable to be able to use the same servers with multiple clients. The time and costs associated with designing, implementing, and debugging a server can be spread over several applications rather than having to implement a new server each time. However, if server operations are complex, they are less likely to be suitable for different uses. Extremely simple operations can be combined in many different ways to support many different applications.

In practice, the designer will have to use judgment and common sense to balance the tradeoff between these objectives. All known client requirements should be identified and the operations checked to ensure that they are sufficiently simple and flexible to support them. Some consideration should be given to undefined future requirements, although it is easy to overdo that. Given the constraints that result from these considerations, the operations should be as coarse-grained as possible to maximize network efficiency and to simplify the task of client implementation.

While we are on the subject, I will inject a more controversial opinion. At the time this is being written, many client/server applications are being implemented by having the client create an SQL statement that is passed to the server, which returns the results. In fact, work is currently under way to define a standard means for doing this using DCE RPC. Certainly this is the right approach when the user performs ad hoc queries using SQL or something conceptually similar. But when this method is used to retrieve data to support some business application function, there is a hidden disadvantage to this approach.

In order to make the SQL query properly access the appropriate data, it is necessary to understand the logical schema implemented by the database. This implies that the queries, by their very nature, have built into them a knowledge of the logical structure of the database. But it is possible or even likely that, over time, it may be necessary to restructure a database to better reflect the changing requirements of an enterprise. It may even be necessary to alter the way data is stored, dividing or combining databases. These changes may be necessary even if the functions of many existing applications do not change. If SQL statements are being used, then when these kinds of changes are made it may be necessary to modify most of the clients currently in production. Even ignoring the development cost, the operational cost of changing hundreds of applications distributed to thousands of nodes is very considerable.

If, instead, servers that provide access to databases and other corporate resources provide operations defined to correspond to business functions, then they stand a better chance of continuing to remain valid even in the face of changes of the underlying implementation. Clients that use these operations can continue to operate without modification. This approach allows implementation of servers that mask the database changes by supporting the same operations over the restructured databases.

On the subject of what the operation parameters should be, there is not a lot that can be said. The data should be represented in the form that is most natural and convenient for internal manipulation. DCE IDL provides a rich and extensible set of data types and they should be used freely. The convention for ordering first input, then input/output, then output-only parameters is well established and should be followed. Obviously, the DCE rules concerning special parameters such as binding handles must be followed.

As for the number of interfaces to be defined, here are some suggestions. An interface should define a cohesive set of related operations. Therefore, the number of operations defined in a single interface should not be too large. A dozen or so operations is probably the normal upper limit. Certainly 50 is too many.

Usually a server will support just one interface. If the server provides several distinct functions, then multiple interfaces are appropriate. If several different types of clients interact with a server it is reasonable to define an interface for each type. For example, if a server provides application functions and management functions it should probably export two different interfaces. This avoids cluttering up an application client with a lot of operation definitions it does not use (or having to suppress them with an ACF). It also allows each interface to have different security attributes—for example, different protection levels.

In summary, the design of server interfaces deserves careful consideration. If a functional model exists, use it. Otherwise, try to select a level of operation granularity that strikes a balance between the demands of efficiency and reuse. Prefer an interface defined by business functions rather than by its underlying implementation. It will still be valid when the technology of the underlying implementation changes.

16.9 Using Timers

Experience with distributed applications has shown that timers should be avoided as much as possible. The reason is that timers tend to be configuration-dependent. A reasonable time for a local server to respond may be way too short for a server in another country. Even if a timer is right today, the next reconfiguration of the network may invalidate it. If timers are too short, applications will report errors unnecessarily. If timers are too long, then it will take too long for applications to recognize the conditions they are trying to detect. A corollary to this is that if a timer must be used, it should be designed so that the exact value used is not critical.* That is, it should be able to use any of a range of values.

Timers get used for basically two purposes. One is to detect failures of nodes and links. The other is to determine some application state. The first use is unavoidable. There is really no reliable way to detect that a network component has failed except to notice that it is no longer sending messages. It is not practical to depend on the idea that any component that fails will send a message to that effect just before failing. Therefore, somebody has to maintain a timer and make an arbitrary decision that such and such part of the network is down. When using DCE, this is done for us. RPC will inform us when our network partner goes down. It uses criteria set by network management parameters, and applications are in no position to second-guess it.

On the other hand, using timers to determine application state can and should be avoided. The remote procedure call philosophy encourages an approach of returning an indication of success or failure with each call. In the terminology of IBM SNA, this is called *definite response mode*. As an example of the type of thing to avoid, imagine a server that keeps track of a number of clients that subscribe to its service. It would be a poor design for the server to keep a timer from the last time the client made a request and to cross the client off its list when the timer expired. A much better idea would be to have clients make specific requests to be on the list or off the list.

16.10   Design Flaws
versus Implementation Flaws

Something like the following scenario has happened to me and to other people many times. A distributed application is being debugged. It seems to mostly work; then, when some unusual conditions are tested, it behaves badly. A fix is applied and now it malfunctions under another set of circumstances. Another patch is put in and now one of the main functions of the application that was just working is broken. Any number of things can now ensue. More patches can be applied, resulting in code covered with overlapping bandages that will fall to pieces if anyone ever tries to modify it. Or all the fixes can be ripped out and the first bug documented as a permanent restriction.

---

* I first saw this idea expressed in a paper titled "Fault-Tolerant Broadcast of Routing Information" by Radia Perlman. (See "Recommended Reading" on p. 551.)

The point is that the problem occurred before the first bug was seen. It was the design that was in error, not the implementation of the design. In practice, the distinction is not always clear, but it is real. A scenario like this could happen with any type of application, but distributed applications seem particularly prone to them. The combination of the factors discussed previously—many possible states, multiple failure modes, concurrent and simultaneous execution—conspire to make it difficult to grasp the runtime behavior of the code.

The way to avoid as many of these problems as possible is to put in the time up front to think the problems through carefully. It is largely a matter of attitude. There is often an impatience to "get something working." In the long run, the time spent in hasty patching and fruitless debugging will be much greater than that spent on thinking the problem through in the beginning.

When you have a tentative design, write it down. This will help to ensure that there are no gaps or missing steps. Walk through the steady-state behavior—how it behaves once it gets going. Now walk through the start-up and shutdown sequences to make sure they work as expected. Then identify all the error cases, both expected errors such as bad data and unexpected errors such as a node crash. Check how the design behaves in all these cases. Peer review can be extremely useful in this process, if it is available.

Look for a simple scheme that handles many cases using the same mechanism. Use the simplest design structure that will do the job. If the design seems to be getting more and more complex and there are a large number of special cases, it is time to rethink it from the start.

A good test is to consider future modifications. What might someone want to add later? How hard would it be? Would the change be likely to introduce unexpected bugs?* Would it require dozens of small code changes all over the place? If so, rethink the design from the beginning.

16.11 Chapter Summary

In designing distributed systems, start by looking for the aspects of the problem that are fundamental and not likely to change, such as the business entities. Defer consideration of more transient considerations, such as the network configuration. Group interdependent functions and data. Avoid representing the same data in several places or copying files across the network. When redundancy is required, provide it via explicit rules.

Many problems in designing and debugging distributed systems come from unnecessary complexity or trickiness. It is generally best to stick to standard

---

* My own personal first law of programming is: Thou shalt not create heffalump traps. A heffalump trap is a piece of code that works, but will collapse like a house of cards if anyone ever tries to modify it.

models and use the simplest design that will meet the requirements. Consider a layered design and think carefully about what acknowledgments signify.

Be wary of concurrent and simultaneous execution. If they are unfamiliar, stick to familiar application designs. Prefer atomic and idempotent operations where possible.

Design the server operations to strike a balance between efficiency and reusability. Define an interface for each distinct use of the server. Avoid the use of timers.

Carefully walk through all error and normal cases before design completion. It will save time in the long run.

Four Model Distributed Systems Using DCE

OSF DCE represents a tremendous step forward in distributed systems development. DCE provides significant new capabilities needed by distributed applications, in an integrated environment more powerful than any previously available commercial product. DCE also represents a major step forward in standardization in an area where more robust standards have been sorely needed.*

Unfortunately, there are still significant obstacles to the development of distributed applications using DCE. One is the bewildering range of choices available to the developer. In part, this is because of the enormous range of application requirements awaiting solution by distributed systems. In fact, I believe we are moving toward a future in which nearly all computer applications are components in distributed systems. This implies that the full range of distributed systems requirements is identical to the full range of human information-processing requirements. This is certainly broader than the range of problems that DCE aspires to solve, but it does justify its very generalized capabilities.

The other reason for the number of design options presented by DCE is that its designers deliberately chose to give developers great flexibility in using DCE. Both the need to provide interoperability with existing systems that use the predecessors of the DCE technologies (e.g., NCS RPC, Kerberos) and the uncertainties about the nature of future distributed systems requirements motivated them to provide

---

* At the time this is being written, the DCE RPC Application Environment Specification (AES) is in the final stages of review as an X/Open standard. The AESs for other portions of DCE are in earlier stages of the same process.

many features and options that can be used or not, in many different combinations.

Part 4 attempts to address this problem by proposing a small number of specific models for the development of distributed applications. The goal is not theoretical completeness but rather to propose some designs most likely to be useful in practical situations. A small number of possible designs are discussed and four in particular are fully developed.

Chapter 17 discusses two categories of distributed application structure. First, several models of application structure are presented based on their processing flow. Next, a set of distributed application classifications are presented based on how server state is managed.

The next four chapters present in some detail implementations of each of the four main processing flow models. These are all characterized by the structure of their server and are named the single-threaded server, the multithreaded server, the tiered server, and the peer-to-peer server. Each chapter follows the same pattern. First, the essential characteristics of the model are reviewed. Next, the functionality of the implementation is described. Finally, the source code of the example is presented and described.

Each implementation has been designed to provide the minimum of application-specific functionality necessary to illustrate how it operates. The source code of each example is provided on the floppy disk that accompanies this book. The application designer can choose the model most suitable to his or her application and replace the application-specific portions with his or her own code.

Two of the examples make use of an ACL manager. An ACL manager implementation is presented in Chap. 22, following the chapters on the four models.

The final chapter of the book, Chap. 23, presents some observations on the current state of distributed systems and projects some of their likely future directions.

Categories of Distributed Systems

There are almost an unlimited number of possible designs for distributed systems. There are also a very large number of ways in which we can try to make better sense of these by categorizing them. The categories presented in this chapter are based on two criteria. First, they seem the most likely to be of practical value in real applications. Second, they are relatively easy to understand and therefore should make the successful development of real applications based on them that much easier.

The first part of this chapter classifies distributed applications according to their processing flow pattern. The four main models, presented in order of increasing complexity, are (1) the single-threaded server, (2) the multi-threaded server, (3) the tiered server, and (4) the peer-to-peer server. The situations in which each one is appropriate are described. These are the models for which complete skeletal implementations are described in the chapters that follow. Some other processing flow models are also presented in this chapter to provide a broader perspective on the subject.

The second part of this chapter introduces a classification of distributed applications based on how state information is managed. The five categories are (1) stateless server, (2) state private to each operation, (3) state shared within a server, (4) state shared among local servers, and (5) distributed state. Each category is described and examples of situations in which it might be used are discussed.

These two sets of categories are completely independent of each other and can be paired in any combination to meet the requirements of a particular application. The general rule is to select the simplest model that will solve the problem. Additional unnecessary complexity will only make the task of development more difficult.

17.1   Processing Flow Models

These models are based on the processing flow of the components of the application. They are presented in order of increasing complexity.

17.1.1   Single-threaded server model

The single-threaded server is the simplest model. In it the client makes a call to the server, which returns some result. This model is depicted in Fig. 17.1. The server does not have to worry about data access conflicts since there is only one thread.

The two general cases in which this model applies are when a client calls a remote subroutine and when a server calls a non-thread-safe library. The remote subroutine is used when a client wishes to obtain some data or set an application or system attribute on one or more remote systems. For example, a client might ask the application management server at a remote node how

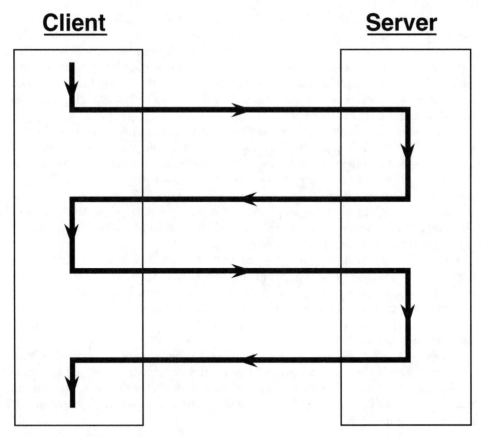

Figure 17.1   Single-threaded server model.

many transactions were performed today. Or it might command the application to begin using a new log file.

In this case, it is often desirable to have the server initiated in response to the RPC, rather than to require that it already be running. This is because such requests or queries are made infrequently and, when they are made, it is not vital to minimize response time. And, it is undesirable to tie up system resources in maintaining a server process that executes only rarely. Unfortunately, there is no provision in DCE to initiate servers when they are invoked. However, several kinds of systems built on top of DCE, soon to become available, will provide this capability. These include both distributed transaction monitors and object request brokers.

The other case in which this model is useful is when a server does most of its work by calling a library that is not thread-safe.* The typical case is when the server calls a database management system that does not support thread-safe access routines. At the present time, most popular commercial database systems do not provide thread-safe libraries.

In order for the routines to be accessed from a multithreaded server, they would have to be provided with jacket routines that would guard them with the global mutex. This means that only one thread could enter any of the routines at any time. Assuming most of the server's work is to access the database, the server would be effectively single-threaded, regardless of the value specified in the call to **rpc_server_listen()**. For that reason, it is simpler to make the server explicitly single-threaded.

In order to provide reasonable response to multiple clients, it would be necessary to run multiple, identical copies of the server. In effect, the application would use processes instead of threads to achieve concurrent execution. This entails some extra overhead, but there is no real alternative. The servers can export separate entries in the namespace or they can all share the same one. In either case, the endpoint mapper will complete the client's partial binding, distributing the requests at random to different servers.

It might at first appear that running multiple servers gains nothing, because the identical servers will have to contend with each other for access to the same database. However, database products are well equipped to handle this kind of concurrency. It is only concurrency within a process that they were not designed for. Although most of the database vendors will provide thread-safe access routines in the near future, the need to use other vendor libraries that are not thread-safe will probably continue to exist for years to come.

---

* Larry Poleshuck drew my attention to this important application of this model.

17.1.2 Multithreaded server model

The multithreaded server is the bread-and-butter design. It is the dominant design among servers that exist today, including disk servers, file servers, database servers, print servers, communications servers, and fax servers. In this model, the server can service several clients concurrently. This model is shown in Fig. 17.2. The multithreaded server typically supports multiple operations and is designed to allow for concurrent access by multiple clients. It does its work by executing instructions, making system calls, and utilizing vendor libraries. The resources it manages are local to the node on which it executes.

If the multithreaded server is well designed, there should be no need to run more than one copy on a node; well-designed multithreading will be more efficient than multiple concurrent processes. For reasons of reliability or performance, it may be desirable to run redundant servers on different nodes. Of course, if the server controls a unique resource, this may not be feasible. And if redundant servers need to share state information, providing for them to keep up to date with each other will add considerable complexity to the programming.

17.1.3 Tiered server model

In the tiered server model, the client calls a server that in turn calls another server to do part of the work. Figure 17.3 illustrates this model. This process can, in principle, involve any number of additional servers. If more than a couple are involved, however, response back to the client is likely to be delayed too

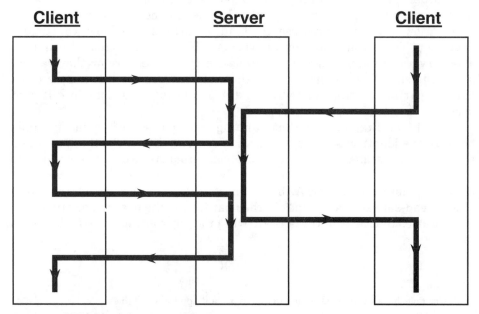

Figure 17.2 Multithreaded server model.

Client	Server	Server

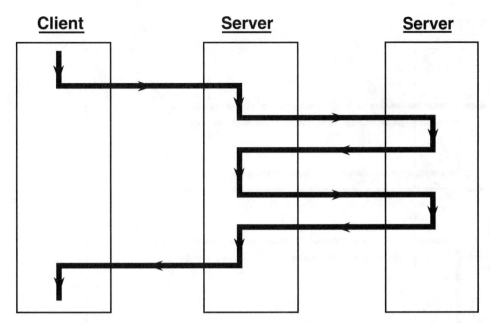

Figure 17.3 Tiered server model.

long. At each step in the chain, the caller blocks until a return is received. Therefore, the response time the client sees is the sum of all the calls. Notice that the intermediate server acts as both client and server.

This model is most often used as a means of layering more-complicated behavior over simpler behavior. For example, a server that does a complex record-keeping task might call a simple database server to store the data on disk. One advantage to this approach is that the simpler server can be used by multiple applications, because its services are more generic. Another benefit is the ability to reuse servers that have already been implemented.

The main problem with implementing this model using DCE is that DCE security currently does not provide for controlled delegation. As was discussed in Chap. 14, planned enhancements to DCE will remedy this. Today, it is necessary to give the required privileges to the intermediate server or to omit security checking in the other server.

17.1.4 Peer-to-peer server model

The fourth of our flow models is the peer-to-peer server. The term *peer-to-peer* means different things in different contexts. In this case it means that every server is also a client. Each program has independent threads to take the client role and to execute the server operations. This is illustrated in Fig. 17.4. By means of shared data, protected by mutexes, the client and server threads can communicate.

Peer   **Peer**

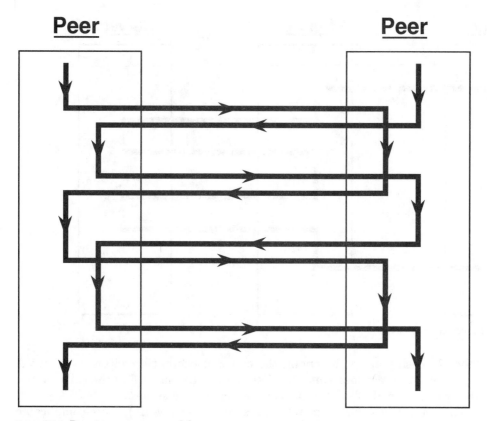

Figure 17.4   Peer-to-peer server model.

It is difficult to think of a realistic application for which this model would be chosen. In most cases of independent processes reading and writing a shared database, the job can be done more efficiently with a simpler design. The popular peer-to-peer notion of everyone accessing data physically stored on everyone else's system is somewhat suspect. In very small configurations, this saves the cost of buying a dedicated server, but the concept does not scale up very well.

In larger configurations, problems begin to occur. First, there is the question of where the "real" data is located. Reliability, performance, and security issues also arise. A dedicated server can be a powerful, fault-tolerant machine kept physically secure. As we have seen, DCE considers single-user systems to be inherently insecure. A dedicated server will be up all the time and can have administrative functions like backups performed on it by people who are responsible for it full-time. In short, the whole peer-to-peer idea is overrated.

Nevertheless, the multithreaded, peer-to-peer client and server is an intriguing model. It is provided in the hope that someone may find a use for it. Also, its design is instructive.

17.1.5   Other flow models

The four models described above are by no means the only ones possible. Here are a few others that have been used in real applications.

Generalized queuing.   In this model, processes throughout the network check queues to get work requests. If there is no work the processes just wait. Once there is some work to do, processes perform it and then may generate one or more messages that are queued to other processes. I have seen this design used for business applications ranging from a system controlling a manufacturing plant to a system for obtaining retail credit information. It can be made to work, but since there is no explicit correlation between requests and responses, there is plenty of scope for bugs.

Distributed computation.   In this model, the client breaks the work to be performed into pieces and gives them out to many different servers running on different nodes. By arranging for these servers to execute simultaneously, the total time to complete the work can be greatly reduced.* This model has great promise. Today, many organizations have PCs and workstations that are underutilized and in theory represent a vast, untapped computing resource. As the deployment of DCE increases, it may be possible to spread certain types of application over many existing systems without any additional investment in hardware.

Unfortunately, several factors limit the usefulness of this model in practice. In the first place, the work to be done must be suitable to this kind of subdivision. Generally, this means that it is highly compute-intensive and that there is a known algorithm for it to be computed in pieces without any necessity of communicating the intermediate results between the nodes. It also means that the time saved must be great enough to compensate for the additional overhead of breaking up the work, transmitting the necessary data across the network, transmitting the results back, and combining the results.

This implies that the required data cannot be excessively bulky; a calculation requiring millions of data points would probably not be suitable. Also, the pieces of the calculation should be relatively equal in size or at least one piece should not require a much larger amount of time to complete than the others. This is because the time to complete the work will depend on the length of the longest piece. Because of all of these restrictions, this model is unlikely to be applicable to the vast majority of applications. When it can be used, however, the benefits can be very significant. One well-known problem to which this model has been applied is shading a 3-D picture.

---

* The book *Power Programming with RPC* by John Bloomer is entirely devoted to describing the use of this model. (See "Recommended Reading" on p. 551.)

Full-duplex communication.   This is how lower-level communication protocols operate. Two processes send messages to each other at any time. Each has to be prepared to receive data at all times. This model can be made to work very well, but most people find it difficult to grasp all the implications and all of the possible states.

Batch file transfer.   This is a popular way of moving data from one system to another, particularly if they are dissimilar. A process on node A transfers a file to node B. A process on node B waits for a file to appear. It seems simple, but plenty can go wrong. For one thing, if nothing appears, what does B do? For another, suppose we send a file every day. Now we need a protocol for identifying the files. What do we do if we skip a day and want to send two files the next? When does B delete the file?

There are many other models, but this is enough to give a feel for the range of alternatives.

17.2   Server State Management Models

Another way of classifying distributed applications is according to how servers manage their state. Remember that server state is information, affecting operation of the server, that is subject to modification. The models below are arranged in order of increasing complexity.

17.2.1   Stateless server

The simplest scheme is not to maintain any state in the server. Each server operation performs its work based on input arguments and, once it has done its work, maintains no information about the request. This has much to recommend it in terms of simplicity. It is easier to get the design right. Stateless servers can easily share a workload because no server knows any more about past requests than any other server. Stateless servers can recover from failures simply by restarting.

A well-known example of a stateless server implementation is the NFS server. It is also an instructive example of how an operation which might otherwise require the server to maintain state can be implemented by a stateless server. For example, a common file operation is to read the next block of a file. Obviously, to do this, a server needs to know what the previous block was. NFS does this by passing this information back to the client. The client is required to remember the value and tell the server what to read next. Notice that in this scheme, from the server's point of view, there is no difference between sequential and random-access reads.

Unfortunately, not everything can be handled this way. For example, the NFS scheme plays havoc with optimization. A more important drawback is that a stateless server cannot coordinate concurrent access of the same file (resource) by more than one client. The stateless model has definite limitations.

17.2.2   State private to each operation

Next in complexity is a server that maintains state, but the state is accessible only within each operation. This model is most suitable when the operations are largely unrelated to each other.

For example, imagine a server that implements a number of operations that report different kinds of status information. Each operation might maintain and report its own state independent of any other operation.

17.2.3   State shared within a server

This is the most common case and is reasonably easy to implement. The state maintained can be about the server as a whole or can be related to each client context. The usual precautions must be taken to guard against concurrent access by multiple threads. If it can be assumed that a client can never make two concurrent calls (perhaps because it is single-threaded), then there will be no need to protect client context with mutexes.

If the server needs to be able to recover its context in the event of a system failure, then it will have to write its context to disk periodically. More commonly, it will simply start afresh after a crash.

17.2.4   State shared among local servers

If several servers must act interchangeably for each other, they must communicate their state to each other periodically. If the servers are on the same system, the means for doing so include using disk files, interprocess communications, and shared memory, among others. The choice will depend on the frequency of state change, performance requirements, and the means available.

A variety of algorithms can be used to maintain consistent state. For example, each server could broadcast every change to all the other servers. Alternatively, one server could act as the master, updating all of the others periodically.

17.2.5   Distributed state

When multiple servers on different nodes must communicate their states to each other, the same considerations apply as in the last case, but the communications options are more limited. Communications links must be employed, and with DCE that means using RPC.

The same choices for update strategies exist as for the local case, but here the relatively low speed of the communications links must be taken into consideration. The coordination of updates of simultaneous changes to the same state must also be considered. In general, this case is so complex that it should not be considered unless the need for it is fundamental to an application.

17.3 Chapter Summary

Distributed applications can be classified according to their processing flow or by how their servers manage state information.

- The single-threaded server is useful for remote subroutines or using non-thread-safe libraries.

- The multithreaded server is the most commonly used model, useful for many types of applications.

- The tiered server is a good way to implement a layered design or to reuse existing servers.

- The peer-to-peer model is appealing, but of uncertain practical value.

Server state strategies range from maintaining no state at all to sharing state dynamically among distributed servers. The application designer can select any of the flow models in conjunction with any of the state models. In both cases, the simplest design that will meet application requirements should be used.

Overview of the Program Examples

The next four chapters describe four complete example DCE applications. The applications correspond to the four main processing flow models described in the previous chapter: single-threaded server, multithreaded server, tiered server, and peer-to-peer server. The applications are complete working programs that have been tested on Gradient Technology's SysV-DCE product. The examples are printed in their entirety in the appendix and provided on the floppy disk that accompanies this book.

Each of the next four chapters has the same format. First, the general description of the model is reviewed and situations where it might be applied are discussed. Next, a functional description of the sample application is given. The sample application is then analyzed from four points of view: its processing flow model, its state model, its naming model, and its security model.

Then, in the largest section of each chapter, the source code of the program is presented and commented upon. Generally, routine DCE functions (which have been thoroughly described in prior chapters) are discussed only briefly; the most time is spent on features that were not extensively discussed previously or that are used in new ways. Any special assumptions or restrictions are noted. Each chapter concludes with some discussion of possible extensions or variations to the sample application.

These sample applications are complete in the sense that they can be compiled and executed on a DCE cell without modification. They are also complete in the sense that they contain the DCE features and coding logic required of production applications. On the other hand, the application functionality provided in each sample is completely trivial. The human interfaces are the absolute minimum necessary to allow the applications to function.

No apology is made for this. The purpose is to illustrate the use of DCE, and elaborate functionality or a GUI interface would distract attention from the DCE issues. It is also intended that the DCE-specific components of these samples be reusable. To build your own DCE application, select the simplest model sufficient for your requirements, remove the sample application logic, and insert your own. In some cases, it may also be possible to combine elements from two or more examples.

These models follow the same philosophy as does the rest of the book, namely, that the goal of the reader is to develop distributed applications and that DCE is being used to accomplish it. Therefore, the examples are the models that are most likely to be of use in common distributed applications. The applications make no effort to illustrate the many specialized capabilities of DCE. Where a DCE feature is useful for implementing one of these models, it has been used; however, no special features are used for their own sake.

The second and third examples illustrate the use of DCE security. They provide the minimum features necessary to implement authenticated RPC. To my knowledge, they are the first examples to be published anywhere that provide all the capabilities necessary to a secure DCE application. One essential component of a secure application is an ACL manager that implements both the local and remote ACL manager interface and maintains its ACL in nonvolatile storage. The ACL manager used by both of these applications is shown and described in Chap. 23.

Example 1: The Single-Threaded Server

This chapter describes the first and simplest of the four distributed application sample programs.

18.1 Review of the Model

In this model, a server implements one or more operations that are processed independently of any other request. In pure form, the model runs only one server thread. In DCE terms, this means that the argument to **rpc_server_listen()** is one. Actually, this is not strictly necessary.

As long as the operations are thread-reentrant with respect to themselves and each other, the server can run with multiple threads. This means that operations must not share any static data that involves a multistep update. If an operation updates a data structure, such as a queue, requiring two operations (e.g., updating two pointers), then a potential race condition exists. This can be overcome either by limiting the server to a single thread or by protecting the data with a mutex.

This model is useful in several types of real applications. One is the utility function. The example in this chapter is based on this type of application. A server providing a utility function is intended to have instances located on multiple nodes of the network and to provide some service to any client that requests it. For example, it might report some information about the node or the network, or it might perform some generic action such as setting a system or application parameter.

Another kind of application for which this model is useful is one in which the server mainly provides its functionality by calling a library that is not thread-safe. This is illustrated in Fig. 18.1. In this case, each remote procedure call must wait its turn to execute serially; thus, there is no advantage to having a multithreaded server.

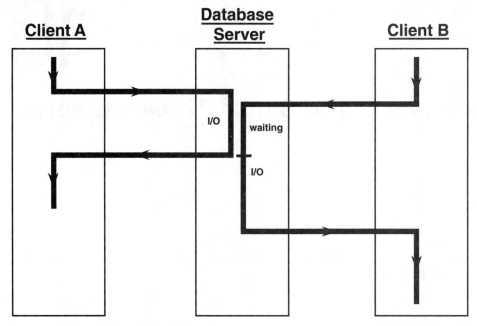

Figure 18.1 Not possible to achieve I/O overlap.

The common case of this type of application is in the use of a database system. Typically, programs access a database server by linking to a library of access routines that are not reentrant. It is frequently desirable to build a server that provides an interface to a business-oriented function in this way. This makes it possible to later change the database or its structure without affecting the operation of clients that use the interface. In such a situation, it is usual to run multiple instances of the same server. This provides the benefits of processor and I/O overlap via multitasking rather than multithreading.

18.2 Functional Description

The sample application is called the Information Server. The interface name is "infpls" (for "information please"). The server implements a single operation: "get_system_info()". This operation returns the information provided by the local operating system in the **uname()** call, which is defined in POSIX.1.

The client calls every server that is a member of the Information Server group. Any server failing to respond is ignored. When an answer is received, the client prints it out, along with the name of the server's directory entry.

A separate installation program is provided, which exports the server's bindings to the namespace and adds the server to the Information Server group. The idea is that the installation program is run only when the program is installed or under unusual circumstances. The server itself will be restarted whenever the system it is on reboots, or even more often. The installation program also has a command for removing the server entry from the directory.

18.3   Processing Flow Model

The processing flow model of this example is very simple. It is shown in Fig. 18.2. The client loops through every entry that is defined in the server group, calling each in turn and waiting for a response. When the call returns, the client prints the result and continues to the next entry. If an error occurs, the client simply goes on.

The server implements a single operation, which retrieves the information and returns it. Since the operation is read-only, any number of server threads can be specified without causing any problems.

18.4   State Model

The Information Server maintains no state.

18.5   Naming Model

Since the Information Server returns information applying to its node, there is no reason for more than one per node. Even if multiple servers were run on the same node for some reason, they would be interchangeable and could share the same directory entry. Therefore, the naming model is based on the name of the local node (host). The server is given a name such as "/.:/applications/info_server/julie", where julie is the name of the node it is running on.

Actually, the server entry name is not that important, because it is intended that the entries will be found using the Information Server group entry. Including server entry names, however, ensures that they are unique and allows nodes to be selected by name if that is desired.

18.6   Security Model

This sample application does not employ security. This omission makes sense if the service provided is intended as a general one available to any client that wishes to use it. It also makes sense if the server is calling a database system that has its own security mechanisms—for example, access control to the record or field level.

18.7   Example Source Code

The Information Server has four components: the IDL file, the server, the client, and the installation program.

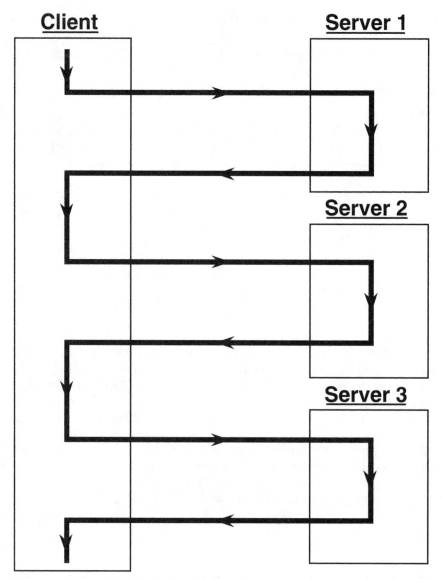

Figure 18.2 Flow model of single-threaded example.

18.7.1   The IDL file

The IDL file "infpls.idl" is shown in Fig. 18.3. The main point of interest is the **typedef** "sys_info_t". This corresponds to the **utsname** structure which is returned by the **uname()** system call. The length of the strings returned by **uname()** is constant on any given system, but is allowed to vary from one conforming POSIX.1 environment to the next.

```
/* INFPLS.IDL Information Server */

[
uuid (00602161-7C3F-1C90-B0AE-0000C07C3610),
version(1.0)
]
interface infpls
{
typedef handle_t RPC_BINDING_HANDLE_T;
typedef struct
    {
    [ptr, string] char *sysname_p;
    [ptr, string] char *nodename_p;
    [ptr, string] char *release_p;
    [ptr, string] char *version_p;
    [ptr, string] char *machine_p;
    } sys_info_t;

error_status_t get_system_info( [in]   RPC_BINDING_HANDLE_T   binding,
                                [ref, out] sys_info_t
*system_info_p);
```

Figure 18.3 Single-threaded server example: IDL file.

Making "sys_info_t" a series of string pointers (instead of character arrays) allows a single client to interoperate with multiple servers that may use different lengths. This is typical of the kind of consideration required when building applications to be portable and interoperable in heterogeneous environments.

The single operation "get_system_info()" has two parameters. The first is a binding handle, which allows the client to step through each server in the group. In other words, the client uses explicit binding. The other parameter is the structure of string pointers in which the result is returned. The operation returns an error-status value that indicates success or failure. The client is built with an ACF file that declares the **comm_status** and **fault_status** attributes. This means that all errors, whether detected by DCE or the application, are reported in the same way.

18.7.2   The server

The name of the server is "infpls_s.c". Note that it uses the header file "infpls.h", which is generated from "infpls.idl". It also uses its own header file, "infpls_s.h", containing various parameters and macro definitions.

The server takes an argument of the number of threads to use for server operations. This is specified because the optimum number may differ from system to system. If the number is not specified, the DCE default is used. Normally, the server would start automatically when the node is booted.

```
/* INFPLS_S.C */

#include <stdio.h>
#include <sys/utsname.h>
#include <sys/errno.h>
#include <dce/rpc.h>
#include <dce/pthread_exc.h>
#include "infpls.h"
#include "errmac.h"

/***** Server Control *****/

main( int argc, char *argv[] )
{
unsigned32            max_threads;
error_status_t        status;
rpc_binding_vector_t  *bindings;
idl_char              annotation[]="Information Please Program";


if (argc > 2 )
    {
    fprintf(stderr, "Usage: %s maximum_threads\n", argv[0] );
    exit(1);
    }

if (argc < 2 )
    {
    max_threads = rpc_c_listen_max_calls_default;
    }
else
    max_threads = atol(argv[1]);

rpc_server_register_if( infpls_v1_0_s_ifspec,              /* (1)
*/
                        NULL,
                        NULL,
                        &status);
ERR_CHK(status,"Could not register interface");

rpc_server_use_protseq( (idl_char *) "ncadg_ip_udp",       /* (2)
*/
                        max_threads,
                        &status);
ERR_CHK(status,"Could not use UDP protocol");

rpc_server_inq_bindings( &bindings,                        /* (3)
*/
                         &status);
```

Figure 18.4 Single-threaded server example: server control.

```
rpc_ep_register( infpls_v1_0_s_ifspec,                          /* (4)
*/
                bindings,
                NULL,
                annotation,
                &status);
ERR_CHK(status,"Could not register endpoint");

printf("Information Server is now available\n");

TRY {

rpc_server_listen( max_threads,                                 /* (5)
*/
                &status);
    }
FINALLY {
    rpc_ep_unregister( infpls_v1_0_s_ifspec,                    /* (6)
*/
                bindings,
                NULL,
                &status);
```

Figure 18.4   (*Continued*)

The server control, or main program, is shown in Fig. 18.4. It performs the usual initialization steps, except for exporting the bindings to the namespace. This has already been done by the installation program.

1. Register the interface with the runtime. The **NULL** object id means that object binding is not used. The **NULL** entry point vector means that the entry point vector generated by the IDL compiler is used. This can always be done when there is just one set of server operations and their names are the same as those specified in the IDL file.

2. The UDP protocol will be used. The maximum threads parameter is specified as determined above, even though DCE currently uses only the default value.

3. Obtain a vector of bindings from the runtime.

4. Register the interface with the endpoint mapper. The **NULL** indicates that object binding is not being used. The annotation is a text string identifying the server, which can be printed out by management programs.

5. After printing a message, the server begins waiting for calls. The number of threads used was determined above. Normally this routine will not return.

6. If the listen routine exits or an exception is received, the server removes its interface from the endpoint map. This could occur as a result of the **kill**

```
/************************ Server Operations ************************/

error_status_t get_system_info(
    rpc_binding_handle_t binding,        /* binding handle is not used
*/
    sys_info_t          *system_info_p)

{
struct utsname *info_p;
info_p=rpc_ss_allocate (sizeof (struct utsname));
if (info_p==NULL)
    {
    return (-1);
    }

if (uname (info_p) < 0)
    {
    return (errno);
    }
else
    {
    system_info_p->sysname_p  = (idl_char *) &info_p->sysname;
    system_info_p->nodename_p = (idl_char *) &info_p->nodename;
    system_info_p->release_p  = (idl_char *) &info_p->release;
    system_info_p->version_p  = (idl_char *) &info_p->version;
    system_info_p->machine_p  = (idl_char *) &info_p->machine;
    return (rpc_s_ok);
    }
```

Figure 18.5 Single-threaded server example: server operation.

command or as a result of some program calling the **rpc_mgmt_stop_ server_listening**() routine.

The next part of the server, shown in Fig. 18.5, implements the operation. This routine is invoked when a client makes a remote procedure call. The routine simply calls **uname**(). If an error occurs, the value of the **errno** variable is returned. If the call is successful, the pointers in the "sys_info_t" structure are set to point to the strings returned by **uname**(). The RPC marshaling routines will determine the actual length of the strings and transmit just that much over the network. The operation returns **rpc_s_ok** to indicate success.

18.7.3   The client

The client is called "infpls_c.c". It is shown in Fig. 18.6. It calls each available server in turn and prints the results received, along with the server directory entry name.

```
/* INFPLS_C.C */

#include <stdio.h>
#include <dce/rpc.h>
#include "infpls.h"
#include "errmac.h"

/* This client calls each server which is a member of the Infopls Group */
/* getting the usname information from each one and printing it out */


static idl_char *  ptr_check          (idl_char *inp_p);
static void        non_null_free      (void *inp_p);

static idl_char unknown_string[]="-Unknown-";



main(int argc, char *argv[])
{

error_status_t        status;
rpc_ns_handle_t       binding_context;
rpc_binding_handle_t  binding;
sys_info_t            system_info;
unsigned_char_t       *server_name_p;



rpc_ns_binding_import_begin( rpc_c_ns_syntax_default,              /* (1) */
                             NULL,
                             infpls_v1_0_c_ifspec,
                             NULL,
                             &binding_context,
                             &status);
ERR_CHK(status,"Could not import binding context");

status=rpc_s_ok;
while (status==rpc_s_ok)
    {
    rpc_ns_binding_import_next( binding_context,                   /* (2) */
                               &binding,
                               &status);
    if (status == rpc_s_ok)
        {
        if (get_system_info(binding, &system_info) == rpc_s_ok)  /* (3) */
            {
            rpc_ns_binding_inq_entry_name( binding,               /* (4) */
                                          rpc_c_ns_syntax_default,
                                          &server_name_p,
```

Figure 18.6 Single-threaded server example: client.

```
            printf("Directory Service Name = %s\n"
                "System Name = %s\n"
                "Node Name = %s\n"
                "Release = %s\n"
                "Version  = %s\n"
                "Machine Type = %s\n",

                ptr_check (server_name_p),
                ptr_check (system_info.sysname_p),
                ptr_check (system_info.nodename_p),
                ptr_check (system_info.release_p),
                ptr_check (system_info.version_p),
                ptr_check (system_info.machine_p));

            rpc_string_free( &server_name_p,                    /* (5) */
                            &status);
            non_null_free (system_info.sysname_p);
            non_null_free (system_info.nodename_p);
            non_null_free (system_info.release_p);
            non_null_free (system_info.version_p);
            non_null_free (system_info.machine_p);

            /* Ignore errors */

            }   /* Don't report binding errors */
        }       /* Don't report RPC errors either */

    }           /* End of while(1) */

rpc_ns_binding_import_done( &binding_context,                   /* (6) */
                            &status);
WRN_CHK(status,"Error releasing binding context");

return(1);
}


idl_char * ptr_check (idl_char * inp_p)
{
return (inp_p !=NULL ? inp_p : unknown_string);
}




void non_null_free (void * inp_p)
{
if (inp_p!=NULL)
    {
    free (inp_p);
    }
```

Figure 18.6 (*Continued*)

1. Initialize a context to begin looking up entries. The first **NULL** argument specifies that the starting point of the search will be taken from the environment variable **RPC_DEFAULT_ENTRY**. The intention is that this would contain the Information Server Group or a profile that in turn contains the Information Server Group. Alternatively, the name of the group could have been specified. The second **NULL** specifies that object binding is not being done.

2. Compatible bindings are obtained one after another until no more are available.

3. Make the remote procedure call.

4. If the call is successful, obtain the directory name associated with the binding used. (This is something of a frill, but it illustrates the use of this call.)

5. After printing the results, deallocate the string that was allocated by the call to **rpc_ns_binding_inq_entry_name()**. Obviously, this step makes little difference in a trivial client like this one, but is good practice to make sure that dynamically allocated storage gets properly freed up, especially when the allocation sits in a loop, as in this case.

6. Once all entries have been tried, release the lookup context. Again, this is mostly a matter of good practice, since the program is about to exit anyway.

18.7.4   The installation program

The installation program, "infpls_i.c", is shown in Fig. 18.7. It takes two commands: "i" (install) and "r" (remove). Both commands take an optional name to identify the server. This allows the installation program to be run on a node other than the one on which the server runs. If no name is specified, the local host name is used.

1. Ask DCE for the name of the local node (host). The name will be a directory name ending "/hosts/<hostname>". We scan off the last part.

2. Use the UDP protocol. It must match the server's. The number of threads specified is not significant because we do not call **rpc_server_listen()**.

3. Get the binding vector.

4. Export the bindings to the namespace. The **NULL** argument indicates that we are not using object binding.

5. Add the server entry to the Information Server group.

6. If the remove command is given, do the opposite. Remove the entry from the namespace.

7. Remove the entry from the Information Server group.

```
/* INFPLS_I.C */

#include <stdio.h>
#include <string.h>
#include <dce/rpc.h>
#include <dce/dce_cf.h>
#include "infpls.h"
#include "errmac.h"


/**** dummy operation entry point since declared in stub ******/

error_status_t get_system_info(
    rpc_binding_handle_t binding,
    sys_info_t          *system_info_p)
{
return rpc_s_ok;
}



/***** Information Server Installation Program *****/

main( int argc, char *argv[] )
{

error_status_t       status;
rpc_binding_vector_t *bindings;
unsigned_char_t      name[100];
unsigned_char_t      group_name[] = "/.:/applications/info_server_group";
char                 *hostname_p, *cp;

if (argc < 2)
    {
    printf("Usage: %s -i [ host name ] or %s -r [ host name ]\n",
            argv[0], argv[0]);
    exit(1);
    }

/*
***** Construct server entry name from the host name typed by the user *****
***** If none was typed use the local hostname as reported by DCE       *****
*/

if (argc = 2)
    {
    dce_cf_get_host_name(&hostname_p, &status);                  /* (1) */
    ERR_CHK(status,"Could not get host name");
    cp = strstr (hostname_p, "hosts/");
    if (cp==NULL)
```

Figure 18.7 Single-threaded server example: installation program.

```
            printf ("Can't interpret local host name format");
            exit (1);
            }
        cp = strchr (cp, '/')+1;
        }
else
        {
        cp = argv[2];
        }
sprintf ((char *)name, "/.:/applications/info_server_%s", cp);

if (strcmp(argv[1], "-i") == 0)
        {
        rpc_server_use_protseq((idl_char *) "ncadg_ip_udp",           /* (2) */
                            rpc_c_protseq_max_reqs_default,
                                &status);
        ERR_CHK(status,"Could not use UDP protocol");

        rpc_server_inq_bindings( &bindings,                           /* (3) */
                                &status);
        ERR_CHK(status,"Could not get binding vector");

        rpc_ns_binding_export( rpc_c_ns_syntax_default,               /* (4) */
                            name,
                            infpls_v1_0_s_ifspec,
                            bindings,
                            NULL,
                            &status);
        ERR_CHK(status,"Could not export server bindings");

        rpc_ns_group_mbr_add( rpc_c_ns_syntax_default,                /* (5) */
                            group_name,
                            rpc_c_ns_syntax_default,
                            name,
                            &status);
        ERR_CHK(status,"Could not add server entry to group");

/* Add code here for additional de-installation tasks */


        }


else if (strcmp(argv[1], "-r") == 0)
            {
            rpc_ns_binding_unexport( rpc_c_ns_syntax_default,         /* (6) */
                                name,
                                infpls_v1_0_s_ifspec,
                                NULL,
                                &status);
            ERR_CHK(status,"Could not remove server bindings");
```

Figure 18.7 (*Continued*)

```
        rpc_ns_group_mbr_remove( rpc_c_ns_syntax_default,          /* (7) */
                                 group_name,
                                 rpc_c_ns_syntax_default,
                                 name,
                                 &status);
        ERR_CHK(status,"Could not remove server entry from group");

/* Add code here for additional de-installation tasks */

        }

else
        {
        printf("Usage: %s -i [ host name ] or %s -r [ host name ]\n",
               argv[0], argv[0]);
        exit(1);
        }
}
```

Figure 18.7 (*Continued*)

18.8 Variations and Extensions

A potentially beneficial change to this application would be to make the client multithreaded. That would allow the client to call all of the servers concurrently, most likely reducing the total amount of time needed to gather all of the information. This flow model was identified in Chap. 17 as the distributed computation model.

In order to make this change, the client would have to make each call in a separate thread. One simple design would be to have a master thread create all of the other threads. The master thread would step through each entry and then create a worker thread to do the RPC. A minor problem would be to avoid having all the output jumbled together on the screen. A mutex could be used to prevent more than one thread from accessing the screen simultaneously. Alternatively, the worker threads could queue up the results and the master thread could print them one at a time.

Another change would be to make the client try harder to reach the server. If an RPC fails, it could be because the client's directory cache is out of date. This might happen if the server directory entry had been recently changed. The client could respond to a communications error by calling **rpc_ns_mgmt_set_exp_age()** with an argument of zero and retrying the call. This forces an immediate update of the cache. Afterward, it is important to set the expiration age back to the default or the cache will not be used.

The "infpls" client does not do this, because server directory entries are not expected to change. The negative aspect of retrying an operation is that the process takes much longer when the server in question is simply unavailable.

18.9   Chapter Summary

The Information Server application is a simple, stateless server that returns information in a structure of string pointers. It uses no security. An installation program exports the server bindings to the namespace. The client program calls every server in the Information Server group in the Directory Service and prints out the result received from each, ignoring errors.

19

Example 2: The Multithreaded Server

This chapter describes the second of the four sample distributed applications. This is the workhorse design, the one most likely to be used in real applications.

19.1 Review of the Model

In the multithreaded server model, client programs make requests of a server that typically offers a number of operations. The server executes multiple requests concurrently, each of which runs in its own thread. Since the threads share writable data, the server must use mutexes or other concurrency-control mechanisms to prevent race conditions. By allowing client requests to execute concurrently, the server achieves an overlap of processor and I/O (and on a multiprocessor system, overlap between processors) that generally reduces the average time required to satisfy requests.

Figure 19.1 illustrates this model. Typically, the client programs have a simple linear flow. Having called the server, the client blocks until it receives a response. In this respect, the server calls behave similarly to library or operating-system calls or ordinary application subroutine calls. The use of RPC, which has the same syntax as local procedure calls, adds to the similarity. All this greatly simplifies design of client programs because the developer uses facilities that behave in familiar ways.

The server design is a little more complex. Except for the initialization code, however, the server consists mainly of independent routines implementing each of the server operations. Using DCE eliminates the need to explicitly create the threads used by the server. The remaining complexity stems from the need to protect against the harmful effects caused by sharing data between threads. Curiously, the difficulty is not so much dealing with the problems as recognizing that they exist. This can be done by observing a few rules of thumb; with a little practice it is not too difficult.

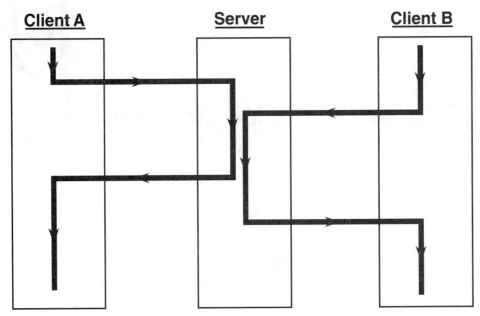

Figure 19.1 Multithreaded server flow model.

Servers of this type typically maintain client context over a series of calls from the same client. DCE provides specialized mechanisms for managing client context. It ensures that once client context is established, later requests are directed to the same server. It provides for context deallocation and cleanup in the event of failures.

This server model typifies most servers in production today—most file servers, print servers, and database servers. That it is easy to understand has contributed to its popularity. No doubt it will continue to be the most popular in the future.

The model is applicable to any environment in which there is a shared resource that can be most easily managed by a server. Concentrating certain capabilities in a single location has a number of advantages. Physical security is easier to maintain. Certain administrative tasks, such as backup, can be performed more efficiently and reliably. Maintenance and repair of hardware is easier to arrange. This application model offers these advantages without sacrificing the benefits of inexpensive processing power at the user's desk.

19.2 Functional Description

This sample application is called the Lookup Table Server. The server provides a rectangular table of data in main memory that can be selectively read and written a row at a time. The server implements eight operations: open, close, set filter criteria, read current, read next, write current, add record, and delete record. Open initiates a client session by allocating client context. Close terminates a session by deallocating context.

Set filter criteria establishes a range of values that must be satisfied by a specified field within any record returned by the read next operation. Read current reads the current record without changing the location pointer. Read next reads the next record satisfying the filter criteria, thereby advancing the current record pointer. Write current writes the current record. Add record allocates a new, blank record. Delete record deletes the current record.

The Lookup Table Server makes use of DCE security mechanisms, mutexes for concurrency control, and client context handles. All of these would normally be features of a production server.

The client is a very simple program that provides access to each of the server operations. It begins by binding to the server and calling the open operation. It then accepts six commands, corresponding to the six operations: set filter, read next, read current, write current, add, and delete. (The filter and write operations take additional arguments.) Then the indicated remote procedure is called. On return, the result is reported. In the case of the reads, it includes the data returned.

After processing each command, the program loops back for another. On the "X" command, the program calls the close operation and exits.

19.3   Processing Flow Model

The processing flow of this application is typical of multithreaded servers. The server control (main) routine starts up and, after performing all necessary initializations, calls **rpc_server_listen()**, which does not return until the server shuts down. Each of the server operations runs in a distinct thread on each invocation. Thus, any number of threads may be executing simultaneously up to the limit set at start-up.

The client also has a typical processing flow pattern. The client starts up and, after initializing, runs in a loop, collecting a command from the user, processing it, and waiting for the next command. Upon receiving a command to exit, it performs an orderly shutdown.

19.4   State Model

The Lookup Table Server maintains several kinds of state within itself while it runs. The most interesting of these states is the per-client context maintained from the time a client calls "look_open()" to the time it calls "look_close()". In this sample application the client context is used to maintain the current state of I/O operations.

The context blocks are allocated from an array protected by a mutex. This illustrates the use of concurrent access to data by multiple threads. Finally, of course, the lookup table itself is shared among all the threads executing the server operations.

19.5   Naming Model

The naming model is rather simple. It is assumed that in such an application there would be only one server. Or, if there were multiple servers, clients would want to bind to a particular one, identifying it by name. The name of the server is exported to the namespace by an installation program.

The client searches the namespace starting from the server's entry or perhaps by means of a profile entry containing one or more entries of servers that export the lookup table interface. The client attempts to bind to each in turn until it is successful or runs out of entries.

19.6   Security Model

The Lookup Table Server makes full use of DCE security features. The assumption is that it will start automatically, probably when the node comes up. Therefore, it can be assumed that the server will be logged into the local operating system, but may not be logged into DCE. The server establishes its principal identity, obtaining a login key (password) from a local key table.

The client uses authenticated RPC to establish its identity to the satisfaction of the server, by means of the DCE Kerberos-based secret key protocol. All messages transmitted between the client and the server are protected against modification, by means of a key used for the life of the session.

The server uses an ACL, stored in a local disk file, to control client access to the lookup table. Only one ACL is maintained for the entire server. In effect, the lookup table is considered a single object. The server determines the principal it is running under and considers it to be its "owner" for the purpose of evaluating the **user_obj** ACL entry. It does not support the use of the **group_obj** ACL entry.

Six permissions are implemented. The open (test) permission controls the open operation. The read permission controls the set filter, read next, and read current operations. The write, add (insert), and delete permissions control the corresponding operations. The owner, (**c**) permission, controls the ability to change (replace) the ACL itself. Other operations on the ACL, such as reading it or checking access, are not controlled.

19.7   Example Source Code

This sample application consists of seven major components: an IDL file, an ACF file, a server control routine, security routines, server operations, a single-threaded client, and an installation program. The server is also linked with

ACL manager routines, which are described in Chap. 22. There are three executables: the server, the client, and the installation program.

19.7.1   The IDL file

The IDL file for the lookup table server is called "lookup.idl". It is shown in Fig. 19.2.

The constant "LOOK_REC_SIZE" is the length of each table row in bytes. The constant "LOOK_FIELD_MAX" effectively controls the size of a key (filter). Defining them in the IDL file makes their values accessible to both the client and server. The **typedef** "filter_t" defines a filter for selecting records to read. The **typedef** "ctx_h" defines the context handle used by this application.

Notice that the eight operations are designed to have a consistent style and syntax. Each begins with a binding handle. Similar parameters appear in similar places in the calls. The input parameters precede the output parameters. The names of the operations suggest their functions, but the "look_" prefix ensures that they will not conflict with other symbols. This kind of regularity makes the operations easy to remember and helps to prevent simple mistakes.

As with all the sample programs, errors are reported as the routine value. The ACF file, shown in Fig. 19.3, declares **comm_status** and **fault_status**; thus, all errors are reported the same way. Because the routines call the ACL manager, which uses **rpc_ss_allocate**(), they also have the **enable_allocate** attribute specified in the ACF file.

The "look_open()" operation returns a context handle that is used in the subsequent calls. The "look_close()" operation deallocates the context handle. It is declared as out as well as in, so that, when the call returns, the client stub will know to deallocate local storage associated with the context handle.

The "look_filter" operation uses a "filter_t" data structure to establish the filter criteria. The fields describe where in the record the filter should be applied—offset and length and what range of values to accept—minimum and maximum. The "look_next()" operation finds the next record meeting the current filter and returns the portion specified by the offset and length parameters. The "look_read()" operation returns the specified portion of the current record.

Similarly, the "look_write()" operation writes the specified portion of the current record. The "look_add()" operation allocates a new, blank record and makes it the current record. The "look_delete()" operation deletes the current record, unless it is the current record of another client.

19.7.2   The server

The server control is called "lookup_s.c" and is shown in Fig. 19.4. Note that it uses the header file "lookup.h", generated from "lookup.idl". It also uses its own header file, "lookup_s.h", containing various parameters and macro definitions.

```
/* LOOKUP.IDL Table Lookup Server */

[
uuid (004C4B41-E7C5-1CB9-94E7-0000C07C3610),
version(1.0)
]
interface lookup

{
const short LOOK_REC_SIZE = 50;
const short LOOK_FIELD_MAX = 30;

typedef handle_t BIND_HDL_T;

typedef enum {
   LOOK_OK,
   LOOK_END_SEARCH,
   LOOK_NO_CURRENT,
   LOOK_FILE_FULL,
   LOOK_OTHERS,
   LOOK_NO_FILTER}
look_sts_t;


typedef struct
   {
   long ofs;
   long len;
   char min[LOOK_FIELD_MAX];
   char max[LOOK_FIELD_MAX];
   }
filter_t;

typedef [context_handle] void *ctx_h;

error_status_t look_open (
     [in]       BIND_HDL_T   bind_h,
     [out]      ctx_h        *ctx_p);

error_status_t look_close (
     [in]       BIND_HDL_T   bind_h,
     [in, out]  ctx_h        *ctx_p);

error_status_t look_filter (
     [in]       BIND_HDL_T   bind_h,
     [in]       ctx_h        ctx_p,
```

Figure 19.2 Multithreaded server example: IDL file.

```
error_status_t look_next (
     [in]         BIND_HDL_T    bind_h,
     [in]         ctx_h         ctx_p,
     [in]         long          start,
     [in]         long          len,
     [out,
     first_is (start),
     length_is (len)]
                  byte          buf[LOOK_REC_SIZE],
     [out]        look_sts_t    *result);

error_status_t look_read (
     [in]         BIND_HDL_T    bind_h,
     [in]         ctx_h         ctx_p,
     [in]         long          start,
     [in]         long          len,
     [out,
     first_is (start),
     length_is (len)]
                  byte          buf[LOOK_REC_SIZE],
     [out]        look_sts_t    *result);

error_status_t look_write (
     [in]         BIND_HDL_T    bind_h,
     [in]         ctx_h         ctx_p,
     [in]         long          start,
     [in]         long          len,
     [in,
     first_is (start),
     length_is (len)]
                  byte          buf[LOOK_REC_SIZE],
     [out]        look_sts_t    *result);

error_status_t look_add (
     [in]         BIND_HDL_T    bind_h,
     [in]         ctx_h         ctx_p,
     [out]        look_sts_t    *result);

error_status_t look_delete (
     [in]         BIND_HDL_T    bind_h,
     [in]         ctx_h         ctx_p,
     [out]        look_sts_t    *result);
```

Figure 19.2 *(Continued)*

The server takes an argument of the number of threads to use for server operations. This is specified because the optimum number may differ from system to system. If the number is not specified, the DCE default is used. Normally, the server would be started automatically when the node is first brought up. The server also accepts the option "-c," which indicates that the ACL data file is to be created.

```
/* LOOKUP.ACF */

interface lookup

{

[comm_status, fault_status, enable_allocate ] look_open ();

[comm_status, fault_status, enable_allocate ] look_close ();

[comm_status, fault_status, enable_allocate ] look_filter ();

[comm_status, fault_status, enable_allocate ] look_next ();

[comm_status, fault_status, enable_allocate ] look_read ();

[comm_status, fault_status, enable_allocate ] look_write ();

[comm_status, fault_status, enable_allocate ] look_add ();

[comm_status, fault_status, enable_allocate ] look_delete ();
```

Figure 19.3 Multithreaded server example: declarations.

The initialization code is similar to the previous example, with two additions. It calls the routine "look_setup_auth()", which initializes security, and "look_ctx_init()" to initialize client contexts and the mutexes. As in the previous example, it does not export its bindings to the namespace; that is done by the installation program.

1. If the "-c" option was specified, set a flag to indicate that the ACL data file is to be created and normal access control checking on the **rdacl_replace()** operation is to be suppressed, since there is no ACL to check.

2. Register the interface with the runtime. The **NULL** object id means that object binding is not used. The **NULL** EPV (entry point vector) means that the EPV generated by the IDL compiler is used. This can always be done when there is just one set of server operations and their names are the same as those specified in the IDL file.

3. All available protocol sequences will be used. The maximum threads parameter is specified as described above, even though DCE currently uses only the default.

4. Obtain a vector of bindings from the runtime.

5. Call the routine to do security initialization. Note that the binding vector and the created ACL database flag are passed.

6. Call the routine to initialize various in-memory data.

```
/* LOOKUP_S.C Lookup Table Server Main Routine */

#include <stdio.h>
#include <sys/types.h>
#include <sys/stat.h>
#include <fcntl.h>

#include <pthread.h>
#include <dce/rpc.h>
#include <dce/daclif.h>
#include <dce/daclmgr.h>

#include "errmac.h"
#include "lookup.h"
#include "lookup_s.h"


/***** Server Control *****/

main (int argc, char *argv[])
{
unsigned32            max_threads;
error_status_t        status;
rpc_binding_vector_t  *bindings;
boolean32             create_db_flag = FALSE;

if (argc > 3 )
    {
    fprintf(stderr, "Usage: %s maximum_threads [-c ]\n", argv[0] );
    exit(1);
    }

if (argc < 2 )
    {
    max_threads = rpc_c_listen_max_calls_default;
    }
else
   max_threads = atol(argv[1]);

if (argc = 3 && (strcmp(argv[2],"-c") == 0))
    {
    create_db_flag = sec_acl_mgr_config_create;              /* (1) */
    }


rpc_server_register_if( lookup_v1_0_s_ifspec,                /* (2) */
                        NULL,
                        NULL,
                        &status);
```

Figure 19.4 Multithreaded server example: server control.

```
rpc_server_use_all_protseqs( max_threads,                          /* (3)
*/
                                &status);
ERR_CHK(status,"Could not use all protocols");


rpc_server_inq_bindings( &bindings,                                /* (4)
*/
                         &status);
ERR_CHK(status,"Could not get binding vector");


look_setup_auth ( bindings, create_db_flag );                      /* (5)
*/

look_ctx_init   ();                                                /* (6)
*/


/* Bindings are exported to the namespace by the install program. */
/* Therefore we do not do it here */

rpc_ep_register( lookup_v1_0_s_ifspec,                             /* (7)
*/
                bindings,
                NULL,
                (idl_char *) "Lookup Table Server",
                &status);
ERR_CHK(status,"Could not register endpoint");

TRY {

printf("Lookup Table Server is now available\n");

rpc_server_listen( max_threads,                                    /* (8)
*/
                   &status);
    }
FINALLY
    {
    rpc_ep_unregister( lookup_v1_0_s_ifspec,                       /* (9)
```

Figure 19.4 (*Continued*)

7. After calling the routine to initialize security, register the interface with the endpoint mapper. The **NULL** indicates that object binding is not being used. The annotation is a text string identifying the server, which can be printed out by management programs.

8. After printing a message, the server begins waiting for calls. The number of threads used was determined above. Normally, this routine will not return.

9. If the listen routine exits or an exception is received, the server removes its interface from the endpoint map. This could occur as a result of the **kill** command or because some program called the **rpc_mgmt_stop_server_listening()** routine.

The security initialization routine "look_setup_auth()" is shown in Fig. 19.5.

1. Declare our security information to the runtime. The principal name is defined in the header file and, for convenience, is the same as the name exported to the name service. DCE secret key authentication is specified. The **NULL** argument indicates that we will use the default routine for acquiring encryption keys. The keytab argument contains the name of the local key file used by this server.

2. Obtain a blank security (login) context. This triggers an RPC to the Security Service to obtain a TGT (ticket-granting ticket). No flags are specified. The only flag defined is one to prevent the credentials from being inherited by any subprocesses we happen to create. The routine returns an opaque handle to a security context.

3. Get a key from the key table. For an interactive user, the key is obtained by encrypting the password. For a server, there is no need for a password; the key is randomly generated and stored in the registry and local key table. The local key table is specified in keytab. The 0 argument means that the most recent version of the key will be used if there is more than one. Note that the routine allocates the space for the key. Therefore, the argument is the address of a pointer.

4. Cause the previously allocated security context to be validated, using the key that we just obtained. One subtle point is that the second argument to this routine can be either a password or a key. The structure containing the item contains a type field that says which it is. As a side effect, this routine destroys the key. The routine returns an indication if the password has expired and if the context was validated by the network. The context must be validated by the network or we will not be able to do anything useful. We can ignore password expiration for now, because the key management routine will take care of it.

5. Now we declare the context that was just validated to be the "default" context. In other words, it will be the one that the runtime uses from now on.

6. Initialize the ACL manager. The first argument specifies that the ACL manager is responsible for maintaining the nonvolatile representation of the server. If the "-c" option was specified at start-up, the database create flag is also set. The second argument specifies the name of the file that contains the ACL. The ACL manager returns a handle to be used in subsequent calls. (This particular manager does not actually make use of the handle.)

```
/*-------------------- Initialize Security --------------------*/

void look_setup_auth( rpc_binding_vector_t *bindings,
                      boolean32 create_db_flag )
{
error_status_t status;
sec_login_handle_t login_context;
void *key_ptr;
boolean32 expired;
sec_login_auth_src_t auth_src;
uuid_vector_t mgr_uuid_vec;
pthread_t thread_hdl;
pthread_attr_t attr;
unsigned_char_t site_name[50] = "";
sec_rgy_handle_t rgy_hdl;
char *cell_name_p;


rpc_server_register_auth_info( princ_name,                      /* (1) */
                               rpc_c_authn_dce_secret,
                               NULL,
                               keytab,
                               &status);
ERR_CHK (status,"Could not register security information");

sec_login_setup_identity( princ_name,                          /* (2) */
                          sec_login_no_flags,
                          &login_context,
                          &status);
ERR_CHK (status,"Could not obtain login context");

sec_key_mgmt_get_key( rpc_c_authn_dce_secret,                   /* (3) */
                      keytab,
                      princ_name,
                      (unsigned32)0,
                      &key_ptr,
                      &status);
ERR_CHK (status,"Could not obtain password");

sec_login_validate_identity( login_context,                    /* (4) */
                             (sec_passwd_rec_t *) key_ptr,
                             &expired,
                             &auth_src,
                             &status);
ERR_CHK (status,"Could not validate identity");
CND_CHK (auth_src != sec_login_auth_src_network,
         "Network identity not available");

sec_login_set_context( login_context,                          /* (5) */
                       &status);
ERR_CHK (status,"Error setting default login context");
```

Figure 19.5 Multithreaded server example: security initialization, part 1.

```
sec_acl_mgr_configure( sec_acl_mgr_config_stable|create_db_flag,   /* (6) */
                       acl_db_name,
                       &mgr_hdl,
                       &status);
ERR_CHK (status,"Error initializing ACL Manager");

rpc_server_register_if( rdaclif_v0_0_s_ifspec,                      /* (7) */
                        NULL,
                        NULL,
                        &status);
ERR_CHK (status,"Error registering ACL Manager interface");

mgr_uuid_vec.count = 1;
mgr_uuid_vec.uuid[0] = &mgr_uuid;

rpc_ep_register( rdaclif_v0_0_s_ifspec,                             /* (8) */
                 bindings,
                 &mgr_uuid_vec,
                 (idl_char *) "ACL Manager for Lookup Server",
                 &status);
ERR_CHK (status,"Error registering ACL Manager with Endpoint Mapper");

/* Install program will export to namespace. No need to do it here */

if ( (pthread_attr_create(&attr) != 0) ||                          /* (9) */
     pthread_attr_setsched(&attr, SCHED_BG_NP) != 0)
   {
   attr = pthread_attr_default;
   }

if (pthread_create( &thread_hdl,                                   /* (10) */
                    attr,
                    (pthread_startroutine_t) manage_key,
                    (pthread_addr_t) 0) != 0)
   {
   WARN ("Could not create thread for key management");
   }
```

Figure 19.5 *(Continued)*

7. Register the **rdaclif** interface with the runtime. Since there is only one set of operations implemented (and hence only one EPV), it is not necessary to register the object UUID with the runtime. Calls specifying the object UUID of the ACL manager will dispatch correctly.

8. Register the **rdaclif** interface with the endpoint mapper. The **sec_acl_bind()** routine, which is used by **acl_edit**, expects to see the ACL manager UUID exported as an object id. This is the same UUID returned by the **rdacl_get_manager_types()** and **rdacl_get_manager_types_semantics()** routines.

9. Create a thread attribute with the scheduling policy of background. When the key expires, this will prevent the thread that updates the key from competing with other, more important, threads. If this call fails, we use the default policy.

10. Create a thread that will update the key before it expires. Use the thread attribute just created to set the scheduling policy. The thread will execute "manage_key()" with a **NULL** argument.

Figure 19.6 shows the second portion of the "look_setup_auth()" routine.

11. Open a connection to the registry. We do not care if it is a read-only site, since we plan only to read.

12. Obtain the UUID of our principal. The second argument specifies that the principal is a person as opposed to a group or organization. If this fails, set the **user_obj** UUID to **NULL**, which tells the ACL manager not to use the **user_obj** ACL entry.

13. End the connection with the registry.

14. This server does not use the **group_obj** ACL entry.

15. This routine runs in its own thread, because it will never return. This routine sleeps until the key is about to expire. Then it generates a random key, updates the registry and the local key table, and calls the garbage collection routine as needed.

The next section of the program contains the server operations that implement the remote procedure calls.

Routine "look_open()", shown in Fig. 19.7, allocates a free context. First, call the security-check routine to see if this operation is permitted. The binding handle is used to get the client's security information. Next, lock the context mutex while we obtain a free context. This prevents a race condition with other threads. The pointer to the context entry is the context handle passed back to the client. The block is marked busy and the record and filter states are initialized. (Note that this could have been allocated by calling **malloc()**, since DCE provides a jacket routine that makes it thread-safe. Our purpose, however, was to illustrate the use of a mutex.) Finish by unlocking the mutex.

Routine "look_close()", shown in Fig. 19.8, releases the context. The context mutex is locked, the context is marked as available and the mutex is unlocked. Setting the context handle to **NULL** will cause the client and server stubs to deallocate resources associated with it. No access permissions are required to close, since a client could obtain the same effect by closing the connection.

Routine "look_filter()", shown in Fig. 19.9, establishes a filter that will be used in the "lookup_next()" operation. The read permission is checked; then the read mutex is locked. The filter structure is copied into the client's context and the filter state is updated. Then the mutex is released.

Routine "look_next()", shown in Fig. 19.10, returns the specified portion of the next record that meets the filter criteria. Read permission is checked. The

```
sec_rgy_site_open( site_name,                              /* (11)
*/
                   &rgy_hdl,
                   &status);
if (status != error_status_ok)
   {
   user_obj = NULL;
   }
   else
   {
   user_obj = malloc( sizeof( sec_id_t));
   user_obj->name = princ_name;
   sec_rgy_pgo_name_to_id( rgy_hdl,                        /* (12)
*/
                           sec_rgy_domain_person,
                           princ_name,
                           &user_obj->uuid,
                           &status);
   if (status != error_status_ok)
      {
      free(user_obj);
      user_obj = NULL;
      }

   }

sec_rgy_site_close( rgy_hdl,                               /* (13)
*/
                    &status);
/* Ignore error on close */

group_obj = NULL;                                          /* (14)
*/

dce_cf_get_cell_name( &cell_name_p,                        /* (15)
*/
                      &status);
ERR_CHK (status,"Could not Obtain Cell Name");

sprintf((char *) full_princ_name, "%s/%s", cell_name_p,
                                  (char *) princ_name);
free((void *) cell_name_p);

}


/*** Routine to do key management - runs in its own thread */

pthread_startroutine_t manage_key(pthread_addr_t arg)
{
error_status_t status;
```

Figure 19.6 Multithreaded server example: security initialization, part 2.

```
/* --------- look_open() - start session --------- */

error_status_t look_open (
      handle_t       bind_h,
      ctx_h          *ctx_p)
{
int i;
client_ctx_t *clt_p;
clt_p=NULL;
*ctx_p=NULL;

if (!look_check_access (bind_h, sec_acl_perm_test))
   return ACCESS_ERROR;
lock (lock_ctx);

for (i=0; i<CLIENT_MAX && clt_p==NULL; i++)
   {
   if (client_table[i].ctx_state==AVAIL)
      clt_p=&client_table[i];
   }

if (clt_p!=NULL)
   {
   *ctx_p=(void *)clt_p;
   clt_p->ctx_state=BUSY;
   clt_p->rec_state=NO_RECORD;
   clt_p->flt_state=NO_FILTER;
   }
unlock (lock_ctx);
return rpc_s_ok;
```

Figure 19.7 Multithreaded server example: the routine "look_open()".

```
/* --------- look_close() - end session --------- */

error_status_t look_close (
      handle_t       bind_h,
      ctx_h          *ctx_p)
{
client_ctx_t *clt_p;

lock (lock_ctx);
clt_p=(client_ctx_t *) *ctx_p;
clt_p->ctx_state=AVAIL;
unlock (lock_ctx);
*ctx_p=NULL;
return rpc_s_ok;
}
```

Figure 19.8 Multithreaded server example: the routine "look_close()".

```
/* --------- look_filter() ----------------
 * Establish a filter criteria to use in subsequent look_next calls
 */


error_status_t look_filter (
      handle_t       bind_h,
      ctx_h          ctx_p,
      filter_t       *filter_p)
{
client_ctx_t *clt_p;

if (!look_check_access (bind_h, sec_acl_perm_read))
   return ACCESS_ERROR;

lock(lock_read);
clt_p=(client_ctx_t *) ctx_p;

clt_p->filter=*filter_p;   /* deposit and use it later */
clt_p->flt_state=BEGIN;    /* doesn't affect client's curr_rec */
                           /* until look_next */
unlock(lock_read);
return rpc_s_ok;
}
```

Figure 19.9 Multithreaded server example: the routine "look_filter()".

read mutex is locked. It is an error if no filter has been established. The filter is applied and a record selected. The specified portion is copied to the input parameter and the record and filter states are updated. The mutex is unlocked.

Routine "look_read()", shown in Fig. 19.11, returns a specified portion of the current record. Obviously, this is a subset of "look_next()".

Routine "look_write", shown in Fig. 19.12, writes the specified portion of the current record. The write permission is required and the write mutex is locked. Otherwise, the code is the same as "look_read()", except the **memcpy()** goes the opposite direction.

Routine "look_add()", shown in Fig. 19.13, adds a new blank record and makes it current. It requires the insert (add) permission. It locks the write mutex and calls a utility routine to allocate a free record. The record is set to current and filled with blanks. Then the mutex is unlocked.

Routine "look_delete()", shown in Fig. 19.14, deletes the current record. It checks for the delete permission. It locks the context mutex, checks that the record in question is not current for some other client, and calls a routine to return it to the free list. Then it unlocks the mutex.

The routine "look_check_access()" is called from the server operations. It is shown in Fig. 19.15. Its arguments are the client's binding handle and the requested permissions. It returns TRUE if security checks out and the ACL manager says that the client is authorized for all of the specified permissions.

```
/*
/* -------------------------- look_next() --------------------------
Find a record satisfying the filter criteria. Requires previous call to
look_filter. If this is the first look_next since look_filter was
called,
we start the search from the beginning of the file, otherwise from
the record after that returned by the previous successful look_next.
*/

error_status_t look_next (
      handle_t      bind_h,
      ctx_h         ctx_p,
      idl_long_int  start,
      idl_long_int  len,
      idl_byte      buf[LOOK_REC_SIZE],
      look_sts_t    *result)
{
client_ctx_t    *clt_p;
look_sts_t      flag;
int             next;

if (!look_check_access (bind_h, sec_acl_perm_read))
   return ACCESS_ERROR;

lock (lock_read);
clt_p=(client_ctx_t *)ctx_p;

next=clt_p->curr_rec+1;        /* Assume filter state is NEXT */
switch (clt_p->flt_state)
   {
   case NO_FILTER:
     *result=LOOK_NO_FILTER;  /* check that a filter exists */
     break;
   case BEGIN:                    /* New filter (or no good look_next yet) */
     next=0;                      /* Drop through into search */
   case NEXT:
     flag=LOOK_END_SEARCH;   /* Assume not found */
     while ( flag == LOOK_END_SEARCH && next < FILE_MAX )
        {
        if (test_used(next) && match(next, &clt_p->filter))
           {                                    /* HERE WHEN RECORD FOUND
*/
           memcpy (&buf[start], &data_file[next].data[start], len);
           clt_p->curr_rec=next;           /* update internal status */
           clt_p->rec_state=HAS_RECORD;
           clt_p->flt_state=NEXT;
           flag=LOOK_OK;                    /* remote call success */
           }
        next++;
        }
     *result=flag;
   }
```

Figure 19.10 Multithreaded server example: the routine "look_next()".

```
/* ----------- look_read() ----------------
 * Return the data from the current record
 */

error_status_t look_read (
      handle_t      bind_h,
      ctx_h         ctx_p,
      idl_long_int start,
      idl_long_int len,
      idl_byte      buf[LOOK_REC_SIZE],
      look_sts_t    *result)
{
client_ctx_t *clt_p;

if (!look_check_access (bind_h, sec_acl_perm_read))
   return ACCESS_ERROR;

lock (lock_read);
clt_p=(client_ctx_t *)ctx_p;
if (clt_p->rec_state==HAS_RECORD)
   {
   memcpy (&buf[start], &data_file [clt_p->curr_rec].data[start], len);
   *result=LOOK_OK;
   }
else
   *result=LOOK_NO_CURRENT;
unlock (lock_read);
return rpc_s_ok;
}
```

Figure 19.11 Multithreaded server example: the routine "look_read()".

1. Get the security information associated with the client's binding handle. It returns the PAC (privilege attribute certificate), the server principal name as specified by the client, protection level, authentication, and authorization service. Each of these values is tested to see if everything is as it should be. Any deviation causes the routine to indicate a security failure.

2. Finally, we call the ACL manager to see if the permissions are authorized. The **NULL** argument is the ACL key. Since this manager supports only one ACL, there is no need for a key. If, for example, the server provided a bunch of objects, the key might be the UUID of the object in question. Note that "mgr_uuid", "user_obj", and "group_obj" are global (within the server). This is fine, because they are essentially constants.

The routine "look_ctx_init()" is called to initialize the mutexes, client context array, and lookup table. It is shown in Fig. 19.16.

```
/* --------- look_write() ---------
 * Update the current record
 */

error_status_t look_write (
      handle_t       bind_h,
      ctx_h          ctx_p,
      idl_long_int   start,
      idl_long_int   len,
      idl_byte       buf[LOOK_REC_SIZE],
      look_sts_t     *result)
{
client_ctx_t *clt_p;

if (!look_check_access (bind_h, sec_acl_perm_write))
   return ACCESS_ERROR;

lock (lock_write);
clt_p=(client_ctx_t *)ctx_p;

if (clt_p->rec_state==HAS_RECORD)
   {
   memcpy (&data_file [clt_p->curr_rec].data[start], &buf[start], len);
   *result=LOOK_OK;
   }
else
   *result=LOOK_NO_CURRENT;

unlock (lock_write);
return rpc_s_ok;
}
```

Figure 19.12 Multithreaded server example: the routine "look_write()".

1. Initialize the three mutexes used by this server.

2. Mark the client context entries as free and initialize the lookup table pointers.

3. When a context handle is used, a context rundown routine should be provided. The context rundown routine is called if communication with a client that has an active context handle is lost. The context rundown routine always has a name beginning with the name of the context handle data type, followed by **_rundown**. In this case, the context handle **typedef** is "ctx_h" so the routine name is "ctx_h_rundown()". The routine takes one parameter—the context handle of the client in question. The job of the rundown routine is to deallocate the resources associated with the context handle. In this case, we simply mark the context as available. The runtime automatically deallocates the context handle on exit.

```
/*------------ look_add() --------------
 * Add a new record, initialized to blanks, make it current
 */

error_status_t look_add (
     handle_t      bind_h,
     ctx_h         ctx_p,
     look_sts_t    *result)
{
client_ctx_t *clt_p;
int i;

if (!look_check_access (bind_h, sec_acl_perm_insert))
   return ACCESS_ERROR;

lock (lock_write);
clt_p=(client_ctx_t *)ctx_p;

if ( (i = pop_free()) >= 0 )
   {
   set_used (i);
   clt_p->curr_rec=i;
   clt_p->rec_state=HAS_RECORD;
   memset (&data_file [clt_p->curr_rec].data[0], ' ', LOOK_REC_SIZE);
   *result=LOOK_OK;
   }
else
   *result=LOOK_FILE_FULL;

unlock (lock_write);
return rpc_s_ok;
```

Figure 19.13 Multithreaded server example: the routine "look_add()".

19.7.3 The client

The client program is called "lookup_c.c". It starts by parsing a schema file, which provides symbolic names for the fields. Then it initializes security. Next, it locates a compatible server by calling "look_open()", obtaining a context handle. Then it enters a while loop, which takes a command, performs the indicated operation, and repeats. This continues until the user types "X". At that point, the program calls "look_close()" and exits. The client is shown in Fig. 19.17.

1. Get a handle to the current default security context.

2. Initialize a context to begin looking up entries. The first **NULL** argument specifies that the starting point of the search will be taken from the environment variable **RPC_DEFAULT_ENTRY**. The intention is that this

```
/* --------- look_delete() ---------
 * Delete the current record, unless someone else is using it
 */

error_status_t look_delete (
      handle_t      bind_h,
      ctx_h         ctx_p,
      look_sts_t    *result)
{
client_ctx_t *clt_p, *peer_p;
idl_long_int i;

if (!look_check_access (bind_h, sec_acl_perm_delete))
   return ACCESS_ERROR;
clt_p=(client_ctx_t *)ctx_p;


if (clt_p->rec_state==HAS_RECORD)
   {
   lock (lock_ctx);
   for (i=0; i<CLIENT_MAX; i++)   /* Check that no other client */
      {                           /* threads are using this record */
      peer_p=&client_table[i];
      if (peer_p->ctx_state==BUSY
      &&  peer_p->rec_state==HAS_RECORD
      &&  peer_p->curr_rec==clt_p->curr_rec
      &&  i != clt_p->my_index)
         break;
      }
   if (i<CLIENT_MAX)              /* if others using record, tell client */
      *result=LOOK_OTHERS;        /* he cant delete it */
   else
      {
      push_free (clt_p->curr_rec);   /* do the deletion: put on free list */
      clt_p->rec_state=NO_RECORD;    /* Note that curr_rec doesnt change */
      *result=LOOK_OK;
      }
   unlock (lock_ctx);
   }
else
  *result=LOOK_NO_CURRENT;

return rpc_s_ok;
```

Figure 19.14 Multithreaded server example: the routine "look_delete()".

```
/*---------- Check access (Reference Monitor) ---------------*/

boolean32 look_check_access (
    rpc_binding_handle_t binding,
    sec_acl_permset_t permissions)
{
unsigned_char_t *server_name;
sec_id_pac_t *pac;
unsigned32 protect_level, authn_svc, authz_svc;
error_status_t status;


rpc_binding_inq_auth_client( binding,                            /* (1)
*/
                             (rpc_authz_handle_t) &pac,
                             &server_name,
                             &protect_level,
                             &authn_svc,
                             &authz_svc,
                             &status);
if (status != rpc_s_ok) return (FALSE);


if (strcmp ((char *) server_name, (char *) full_princ_name) != 0)
    {
    rpc_string_free (&server_name, &status);
    return (FALSE);
    }
else
   rpc_string_free (&server_name, &status);

if (protect_level != rpc_c_protect_level_pkt_integ
    || authn_svc != rpc_c_authn_dce_secret
    || authz_svc != rpc_c_authz_dce)
   return (FALSE);

return (sec_acl_mgr_is_authorized( mgr_hdl,                      /* (2)
*/
                                   permissions,
                                   pac,
                                   NULL,
                                   &mgr_uuid,
                                   user_obj,
```

Figure 19.15 Multithreaded server example: security-check routine.

```
/* ---------- Mutex and Context Initialization --------------- */

void look_ctx_init (void)
{
int i;

if (pthread_mutex_init( &lock_read,                              /* (1)
*/
                        pthread_mutexattr_default) !=0)
    {
    ERROR("Could not initialize read mutex");
    }

if (pthread_mutex_init( &lock_write,
                        pthread_mutexattr_default) !=0)
    {
    ERROR("Could not initialize write mutex");
    }

if (pthread_mutex_init( &lock_ctx,
                        pthread_mutexattr_default) !=0)
    {
    ERROR("Could not initialize context mutex");
    }

lock (lock_write);
free_head=LIST_END;
for ( i = FILE_MAX-1; i >= 0; i-- ) push_free(i);
unlock (lock_write);

lock (lock_ctx);
for (i=0; i<CLIENT_MAX; i++)                                     /* (2)
*/
    {
    client_table[i].ctx_state = AVAIL;
    client_table[i].my_index = i;
    }
unlock (lock_ctx);
}


/*** Context Rundown Routine ***/

void ctx_h_rundown( ctx_h ctx_p )
{
client_ctx_t *clt_p;

if (ctx_p == NULL) return;                                       /* (3)
*/

lock (lock_ctx);
```

Figure 19.16 Multithreaded server example: mutex initialization.

```
int  main (int argc, char *argv[])
{
int i;
error_status_t status;
look_sts_t    result;
idl_long_int  start, length;
cmd_t         cmd;
void          *ctx_p;
char          schema [30];
idl_char      buffer [LOOK_REC_SIZE];
filter_t      filter;
rpc_ns_handle_t binding_context;
rpc_binding_handle_t bind_h;
sec_login_handle_t login_context;

/* Get Command Arguments */
if (!parse_params (schema, argc, argv))
   return -1;

/* Read in Schema File */
if (!read_schema (schema))
   return -2;


sec_login_get_current_context( &login_context,                    /* (1) */
                               &status);
ERR_CHK(status,"Could not get current security context");

rpc_ns_binding_import_begin( rpc_c_ns_syntax_default,             /* (2) */
                             NULL,
                             lookup_v1_0_c_ifspec,
                             NULL,
                             &binding_context,
                             &status);
ERR_CHK(status,"Could not import binding context");

do
    {
    rpc_ns_binding_import_next( binding_context,                  /* (3) */
                                &bind_h,
                                &status);
    ERR_CHK(status,"Could not find any servers to bind to");

    rpc_binding_set_auth_info( bind_h,                            /* (4) */
                               (idl_char *) &princ_name,
                               rpc_c_protect_level_pkt_integ,
                               rpc_c_authn_dce_secret,
                               (rpc_auth_identity_handle_t) login_context,
                               rpc_c_authz_dce,
                               &status);
    ERR_CHK(status,"Could not associate security information with binding");
```

Figure 19.17 Multithreaded server example: client.

```
        status=look_open (bind_h, &ctx_p);                          /* (5) */

        if (ctx_p == NULL) WARN("Server was unable to allocate context");
        }
        while(status != rpc_s_ok);

rpc_ns_binding_import_done(&binding_context,                         /* (6) */
                          &status);
ERR_CHK(status,"Error releasing binding context");

display_help ();

/* Main Command Loop */
cmd.action='\0';
while (cmd.action != 'X')                                            /* (7) */
    {
    get_command (&cmd);
    if (cmd.field == -1) continue;
    start=field_tbl[cmd.field].start;
    length=field_tbl[cmd.field].length;
    pad_field (cmd.value_1, length);
    pad_field (cmd.value_2, length);
    switch (cmd.action)  {
        case 'A':          /* Add an empty record */
           status=look_add (bind_h, ctx_p, &result);
           ERR_CHK (status, "Error calling look_add");
           break;
         case 'C':         /*  Change the current record */
           memcpy (&buffer[start], &cmd.value_1, length);
           status=look_write (bind_h, ctx_p, start, length, buffer, &result);
           ERR_CHK (status, "Error calling look_write");
           break;
        case 'D':          /* Delete the current record */
           look_delete (bind_h, ctx_p, &result);
           ERR_CHK (status, "Error calling look_delete");
           break;
        case 'F':            /* Set filter */
           make_filter (&cmd, &filter);
           status=look_filter (bind_h, ctx_p, &filter);
           ERR_CHK (status, "Error calling look_filter");
           break;
        case 'N':          /* Display the next matching record */
           status=look_next (bind_h, ctx_p, 0, LOOK_REC_SIZE, buffer, &result);
           ERR_CHK (status, "Error calling look_next");
           if (result == LOOK_OK)
              {
              display_field((char *) &buffer[0], LOOK_REC_SIZE);
              printf ("\n");
              }
           break;
```

Figure 19.17   (*Continued*)

```
    case 'S':        /* Display current record */
        status=look_read (bind_h, ctx_p, 0, LOOK_REC_SIZE, buffer, &result);
        ERR_CHK (status, "Error calling look_read");
        if (result==LOOK_OK)
            {
            display_field ((char *) &buffer[0], LOOK_REC_SIZE);
            printf ("\n");
            }
        break;
    case 'X':
        break;
    default:
        display_help();
        break;
    }
}

status=look_close (bind_h, &ctx_p);
ERR_CHK (status, "Error calling look_close");
return 0;
```

Figure 19.17 (*Continued*)

would contain a profile. The second **NULL** specifies that object binding is not being used.

3. Get a binding handle to a compatible server.

4. Associate security information with the binding handle. The client specifies the name of the server's principal, the protection level, the authorization type, and the authentication type.

5. Call the server to get a context handle. If the call fails, try another server.

6. Once a server is found, release the binding context.

7. Loop until the "X" command is seen. Read each command and call the appropriate remote procedure. The "F" command takes a field name and low and high values to set the filter to. The "C" command takes a field name and a new value to set the field to. The other commands take no arguments. Before exiting, "look_close()" is called.

19.7.4 The installation program

The Lookup Table Server installation program is called "lookup_i.c". It is shown in Fig. 19.18. It is even simpler than the installation program of the previous example in that it exports only the server bindings. It does not add the server entry to a group. Like the previous example, it takes two commands: "i" (install) and "r" (remove).

```
/***** Lookup Table Installation Program *****/

main( int argc, char *argv[] )
{

error_status_t        status;
rpc_binding_vector_t  *bindings;
uuid_vector_t mgr_uuid_vec;

if (argc < 2)
    {
    printf("Usage: %s -i or %s -r\n",argv[0], argv[0]);
    exit(1);
    }

if (strcmp(argv[1], "-i") == 0)
    {
    rpc_server_use_all_protseqs( rpc_c_protseq_max_reqs_default,    /* (1) */
                                 &status);
    ERR_CHK(status,"Could not use all protocols");

    rpc_server_inq_bindings( &bindings,                            /* (2) */
                             &status);
    ERR_CHK(status,"Could not get binding vector");

    rpc_ns_binding_export( rpc_c_ns_syntax_default,                /* (3) */
                           name,
                           lookup_v1_0_s_ifspec,
                           bindings,
                           NULL,
                           &status);
    ERR_CHK(status,"Could not export server bindings");

    mgr_uuid_vec.count = 1;
    mgr_uuid_vec.uuid[0] = &mgr_uuid;

    rpc_ns_binding_export( rpc_c_ns_syntax_default,                /* (4) */
                           name,
                           rdaclif_v0_0_s_ifspec,
                           bindings,
                           &mgr_uuid_vec,
                           &status);
    ERR_CHK(status,"Could not export server bindings");

/* Add code here for additional de-installation tasks */

    }
    else if (strcmp(argv[1], "-r") == 0)
```

Figure 19.18 Multithreaded server example: installation program.

```
          rpc_ns_binding_unexport( rpc_c_ns_syntax_default,          /* (5) */
                                   name,
                                   lookup_v1_0_s_ifspec,
                                   NULL,
                                   &status);
          ERR_CHK(status,"Could not remove server bindings");

          rpc_ns_binding_unexport( rpc_c_ns_syntax_default,          /* (6) */
                                   name,
                                   rdaclif_v0_0_s_ifspec,
                                   NULL,
                                   &status);
          ERR_CHK(status,"Could not remove ACL Manager bindings");

/* Add code here for additional de-installation tasks */

          }
          else
          {
          printf("Usage: %s -i or %s -r\n", argv[0], argv[0]);
          exit(1);
          }
}
```

Figure 19.18   *(Continued)*

1. Use all protocol sequences. They must match those of the server. The number of threads specified does not matter, because we do not call **rpc_server_listen()**.

2. Get the binding vector.

3. Export the bindings to the namespace. The **NULL** argument indicates that we are not using object binding.

4. Export the **rdaclif** interface. Note that the ACL manager UUID must be specified as the binding object. This is required by **sec_acl_bind()**.

5. If the remove command is given, do the opposite. Remove the entry from the namespace.

6. Also remove the **rdaclif** entry.

19.8   Variations and Extensions

Many variations are possible. For example, the server concurrency control could be made more fine-grained. For example, we could protect each row in the table individually. If done via mutexes, it would be sensible to allocate them dynamically, as they are needed, instead of at initialization. Alternatively, a table of booleans could be used to protect the rows. That table would then have to be protected by a mutex.

The client could be modified to use automatic binding instead of explicit binding. The steps to do this would be to specify the **auto_handle** interface attribute in the ACF file; to eliminate the calls to **rpc_ns_binding_import_begin()**, **rpc_ns_binding_import_next()**, and **rpc_ns_binding_import_done()**; and to use **rpc_if_register_auth_info()** instead of **rpc_binding_set_auth_info()**.

Instead of using error-status variables, all RPC errors could be reported as exceptions.

19.9   Chapter Summary

This example is the one likely to be most useful in applications. The Lookup Table Server provides eight different operations allowing clients to read and write data maintained in a table in memory. The server uses the full set of DCE security features, including secret key authentication, data-integrity checking, PAC-based authentication, and access control via ACLs. The server uses mutexes to guard against race conditions. A context handle is employed to maintain state on a per-client basis.

The example client is a simple program designed to exercise each of the operations implemented by the server. An installation program is provided to export the server's bindings to the namespace.

20

Example 3: The Tiered Server

This chapter describes the third of the four sample distributed applications. This design allows a new application to build on the capabilities provided by an existing server. The use of this design will become more practical in the future, once DCE supports security delegation.

20.1 Review of the Model

In the tiered server model, there are at least three processes involved: a client, an intermediary, and a server. This design is illustrated in Fig. 20.1. The client

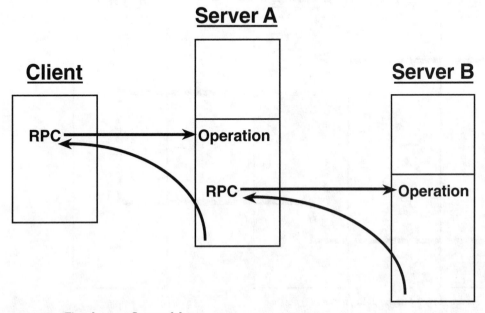

Figure 20.1 Tiered server flow model.

sees only the services provided by the intermediary. From the point of view of the client, this case does not appear to be any different from the previous two models. The client issues a remote procedure call to the intermediary and receives a result.

The difference lies in the way the intermediary works. It implements its operations, in part, by calling one or more other servers. When it receives a remote procedure call, it turns around and uses other servers to do part of the work.

This technique has a number of potential benefits. For one thing, it can reduce the work and therefore the costs involved in developing a new application by making use of servers that have already been implemented. It can also be advantageous when all of the components are being developed for the first time. In addition to creating the possibility of future reuse, it can be a convenient way to create a more modular design in which the components are not closely dependent on each other. It is one way of implementing the layering concept discussed in Chap. 16.

In the simplest version of this model, the flow among the several processes is completely synchronous. This is shown in Fig. 20.2. The initial remote procedure does not return to the client until all of the intermediary's subsequent calls to other servers have been made and returned. This has great advantages of simplicity, but it means that the total time required to satisfy the client's request is the sum of all the steps. This is because there is no overlap in any of the steps. This can be disadvantageous, particularly if large data structures are passed from program to program.

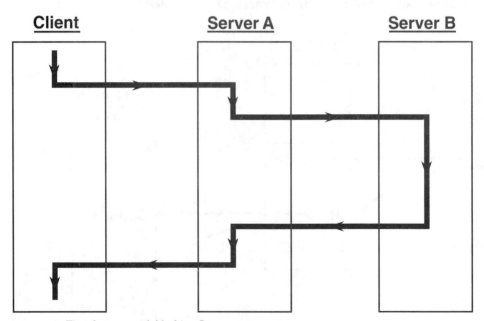

Client **Server A** **Server B**

Figure 20.2 Tiered server with blocking flow.

Many variations on this basic flow are possible. For example, the nature of some applications may make it possible for the initial remote procedure call to return immediately, before the other calls have been completed. This might be because the client does not care if the subsequent calls are successful, or the client might issue another call later to check on the results. Alternatively, the server might use transactional-logging techniques to ensure that an operation is retried until it succeeds.

A variation on the completely synchronous flow is to have the intermediary call several other servers concurrently. Fig. 20.3 illustrates this flow. This can be done by running each of the server-client's calls in its own thread. Obviously, this is not applicable when only a single call is made. Note that the total time required is now the time taken by the longest procedure rather than the sum of the times. One convenient feature of this design is that additional complexity is not visible to the client. It can still have an easy-to-understand synchronous flow model.

The tiered model can be useful in many applications. Probably the most common are those in which the intermediary calls a server that provides a utility function, such as a file server, print server, or database server. Or, the intermediary might be built as a gateway to some existing system or database that does not directly support DCE. This is shown in Fig. 20.4. Such a gateway

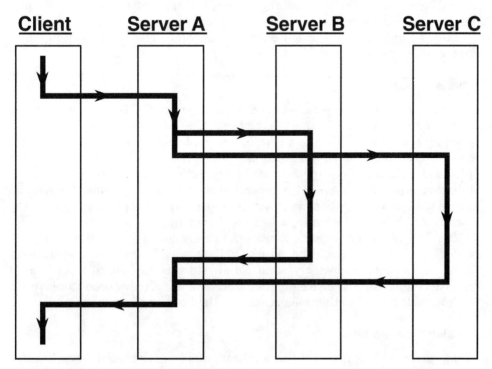

Figure 20.3 Tiered server with nonblocking flow.

Client   # Wrapper System   # Legacy System

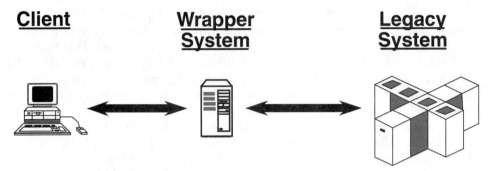

Figure 20.4 A tiered server as a wrapper.

server is often called a wrapper, because it gives the underlying service a different appearance without fundamentally changing how it works.

There are also reasons why the tiered server architecture might be used in totally new development situations. In one common situation, the application is partitioned into different components to take advantage of different hardware capabilities. For example, imagine an application that performs complex mathematical analysis on data obtained from a database. A possible design would be to run the computational portion of the application on a powerful processor, perhaps one equipped with vector processing hardware, and to run the back-end server on a dedicated database machine. The client portion might run on PCs or workstations.

20.2 Functional Description

The sample application is called the Sort List Server. The server portion of the application is the Lookup Table Server from the previous example. The intermediary component of the Sort List Server implements four operations: open, close, begin, and next. The open and close operations are similar to those of the previous example, allocating and deallocating client context. The begin operation retrieves all the available records from the Lookup Table Server and stores them in its own memory in sorted order. The next operation returns the next record in order, indicating when none are left.

The Sort List client expects command-line arguments indicating what portion of each record should be returned. It then calls the server operations: open, begin, next (repeatedly), and close. It prints the sorted records as it receives them. There is an assumption that data has already been stored in the lookup table by some other means, e.g., by the Lookup client.

20.3 Processing Flow Model

The processing flow model of this application follows the simple, synchronous pattern described above. This is depicted in Fig. 20.5. Each of the programs

`srtlst_c`   `srtlst_s`   `lookup_s`

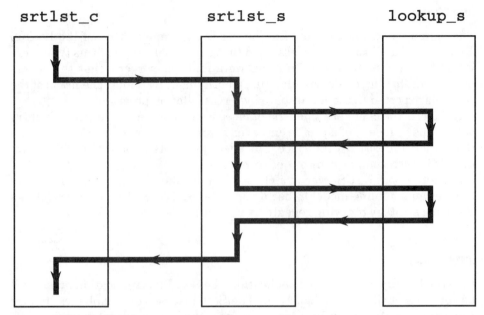

Figure 20.5 Sort list application processing flow.

executes in turn. There is no overlap in execution with respect to a single client. The client calls the Sort List Server "sort_begin()" operation and waits. The Sort List Server in turn calls the Lookup Table Server a number of times, waiting each time for the operation to complete. Finally, the original call returns to the client, which resumes execution. When the client calls the "sort_next()" operation, the records are returned from the list in the Sort List Server's memory. The Lookup Table Server is not called.

Since both of the servers are multithreaded, however, there can be considerable concurrency with respect to distinct clients. The clients' remote procedure calls will invoke separate "sort_begin()" operation threads, which can run concurrently. Similarly, each call to a Lookup Table Server operation can overlap with others of that or any of the other operations.

20.4 State Model

The Sort List Server maintains state on a per-client basis. In addition to various I/O state flags and the context handle associated with the session on the Lookup Table Server, the entire list of sorted records is maintained on a per-client basis. About the only state maintained globally by the Sort List Server is the binding handle to the Lookup Table Server.

The Lookup Table Server maintains a number of types of state, which were described in the previous chapter.

20.5   Naming Model

The naming model of the Sort List Server is the same as that of the Lookup Table Server application. It is assumed that in an application of this type there would be only one server, or, if there were multiple servers, that the clients would want to bind to a particular one, identifying it by name. The name of the server is exported to the namespace by an installation program.

As before, the client searches the namespace starting from the server's entry or perhaps by means of a profile entry containing one or more entries of servers that export the sort list interface. The client attempts to bind to each in turn, until it is successful or runs out of entries.

Since the Sort List Server is a client of the Lookup Table Server, it follows that server's naming model to use its operations. The Sort List Server follows the same strategy of trying repeatedly until it binds successfully.

20.6   Security Model

Like the Lookup Table Server application, the Sort List Application makes full use of the security features of DCE. The Sort List Server establishes its own principal identity, obtaining a login key (password) from a local key table.

The client uses authenticated RPC to establish its identity to the satisfaction of the server by means of the DCE secret key protocol (based on Kerberos). All messages transmitted between the client and the server are protected against modification by means of a key used for the life of the session.

The Sort List Server uses the same ACL manager used by the Lookup Table Server. By storing the ACL in its own file, the Sort List Server can independently control access to its operations. As before, one ACL is maintained for the entire server. The server determines which principal it is running under and considers it to be its "owner" for the purpose of evaluating the **user_obj** ACL entry. It does not support the use of the **group_obj** ACL entry.

The Sort List Server makes use of the open (test) and read permissions only, so it should have its own ACL manager. But the ACL manager, which is described in Chap. 22, is complicated enough that there seems no reason to present two versions with minor differences. As noted in the previous chapter, the owner (**c**) permission controls the ability to change (replace) the ACL itself. Other operations on the ACL, such as reading it or checking access, are not controlled.

This example points up a deficiency in the currently available implementations of DCE. For this application model, the ideal situation would be to provide security delegation. What this means in this case is that when the Sort List Server calls the Lookup Table Server, it really ought to be able to pass along the PAC of the original client and say, "Do this on behalf of this client (principal)." It cannot do this today, for the very good reason that the authentication service goes to considerable trouble to ensure that principals cannot pretend to be other principals; therefore, simply passing on the client's PAC will not work.

What are needed are extensions to the authentication protocols to support delegation. In addition, since there should be means of controlling the extent of delegation, the syntax and semantics of the ACL file must also be extended. Support for security delegation is planned for a future version of DCE. At the current time, the best we can do is have the Lookup Table Server check the credentials of the Sort List Server instead of the true client's.

20.7   Example Source Code

The Sort List Server consists of four executable programs: a client, an intermediary, a server, and an installation program. The server is the Lookup Table Server. Its description is the same as in the previous chapter and is omitted here. The server and the intermediary are both linked with the ACL manager routines described in Chap. 22.

20.7.1   The IDL file

The IDL file for the Sort List Server is called "srtlst.idl". It is shown in Fig. 20.6. The interface it defines is also called "srtlst". The Sort List Server also makes use of "lookup.idl", since it is a client of the lookup interface as well as being a server of the "srtlst" interface.

The "srtlst.idl" file imports the record size and filter definition from the "lookup.idl" file. The "sort_open()" and "sort_close()" operations are similar to those of the previous example. The "sort_begin()" operation takes a filter structure as an argument. Only records satisfying the filter will be sorted. The "sort_next()" operation has exactly the same parameters as the "look_next()" operation.

As with all the sample programs, errors are reported as the routine value. The ACF file, shown in Fig. 20.7, declares **comm_status** and **fault_status**; thus, all errors are reported the same way. Because the routines call the ACL manager, which uses **rpc_ss_allocate()**, they also have the **enable_allocate** attribute specified in the ACF file.

20.7.2   The intermediary

The server control routine of the intermediary is called "srtlst_s.c". It is shown in Fig. 20.8. Note that it uses the header file "lookup.h" generated from "lookup.idl", in addition to "srtlst.h" generated from "srtlst.idl". It also uses its own header file, "srtlst_s.h", containing various parameters and macro definitions.

As in the Lookup Table Server, this program takes an argument of the number of threads to use for server operations. This is specified, because the optimum number may differ from system to system. If the number is not specified, the DCE default is used. Normally, the server would start automatically when the node is first brought up. The server also accepts the option "-c", which indicates that the ACL data file is to be created.

```
/* SRTLST.IDL Tiered Server for sorting */
[
uuid (004c4b41-e7c5-1cb9-94e6-0000c07c3610),
version(1.0)
]
interface srtlst


{

import "lookup.idl";

typedef enum {
   SORT_OK,
   SORT_WRONG_STATE,
   SORT_END}
sort_sts_t;

error_status_t sort_open (
      [in]        BIND_HDL_T   bind_h,
      [out]       ctx_h        *ctx_p);

error_status_t sort_close (
      [in]        BIND_HDL_T   bind_h,
      [in, out]   ctx_h        *ctx_p);

error_status_t sort_begin (
      [in]        BIND_HDL_T   bind_h,
      [in]        ctx_h        ctx_p,
      [in]        filter_t     *filter_p);

error_status_t sort_next (
      [in]        BIND_HDL_T   bind_h,
      [in]        ctx_h        ctx_p,
      [in]        long         start,
      [in]        long         len,
      [out,
      first_is (start),
      length_is (len)]
                  byte         buf[LOOK_REC_SIZE],
      [out]       sort_sts_t   *result);


```

Figure 20.6   Tiered server example: IDL file.

```
/* SRTLST.ACF Tiered Server for sorting */

interface srtlst

{

[comm_status, fault_status, enable_allocate] sort_open ();

[comm_status, fault_status, enable_allocate] sort_close ();

[comm_status, fault_status, enable_allocate] sort_begin ();

[comm_status, fault_status, enable_allocate] sort_next ();

}
```

Figure 20.7 Tiered server example: declarations.

```
/* SRTLST_S.C Sort List Server Control */

#include <stdio.h>
#include <pthread_exc.h>
#include <dce/rpc.h>
#include <dce/daclmgr.h>
#include "errmac.h"
#include "srtlst.h"
#include "srtlst_s.h"

extern void sort_ctx_init ();

main (int argc, char *argv[])
{
unsigned32          max_threads;
error_status_t      status;
rpc_binding_vector_t *bindings;
boolean32           create_db_flag = FALSE;

if (argc > 3 )
    {
    fprintf(stderr, "Usage: %s maximum_threads\n", argv[0] );
    exit(1);
    }

if (argc < 2 )
    {
    max_threads = rpc_c_listen_max_calls_default;
    }
else
```

Figure 20.8 Tiered server example: server control.

```
if (argc = 3 && (strcmp(argv[2],"-c") == 0))
    {
    create_db_flag = sec_acl_mgr_config_create;              /* (1)
*/
    }

rpc_server_register_if( srtlst_v1_0_s_ifspec,               /* (2)
*/
                        NULL,
                        NULL,
                        &status);
ERR_CHK (status, "Could not register interface");

rpc_server_use_all_protseqs( max_threads,                   /* (3)
*/
                             &status);
ERR_CHK (status, "Could not use all protocols");

rpc_server_inq_bindings( &bindings,                         /* (4)
*/
                         &status);
ERR_CHK (status, "Could not get binding vector");

sort_setup_auth( bindings, create_db_flag );               /* (5)
*/

sort_ctx_init();                                           /* (6)
*/

/* Bindings are exported to the namespace by the install program. */
/* Therefore we do not do it here */

rpc_ep_register( srtlst_v1_0_s_ifspec,                     /* (7)
*/
                 bindings,
                 NULL,
                 (unsigned_char_t *) "Sort List Server",
                 &status);
ERR_CHK (status, "Could not register endpoint");

TRY {

printf ("Sort List Server is now available\n");

rpc_server_listen( max_threads,                           /* (8)
*/
                   &status);
    }
FINALLY
```

Figure 20.8   *(Continued)*

The main routine is essentially identical to the previous example. Like the previous example, it does not export its bindings to the namespace; this is done by the installation program.

1. If the "-c" option was specified, set a flag to indicate that the ACL data file is to be created and normal access-control checking on the **rdacl_replace()** operation is to be suppressed, since there is no ACL to check.

2. Register the interface with the runtime. The **NULL** object id means that object binding is not used. The **NULL** EPV (entry point vector) means that the EPV generated by the IDL compiler is used. This can always be done when there is just one set of server operations and their names are the same as those specified in the IDL file.

3. All available protocol sequences will be used. The maximum threads parameter is specified as described above, even though DCE currently uses only the default.

4. Obtain a vector of bindings from the runtime.

5. Call the routine to do security initialization. Note that the binding vector and the created ACL database flag are passed.

6. Call the routine to initialize various in-memory data.

7. After calling the routine to initialize security, register the interface with the endpoint mapper. The **NULL** indicates that object binding is not being used. The annotation is a text string identifying the server, which can be printed out by management programs.

8. After printing a message, the server begins waiting for calls. The number of threads used was determined above. Normally, this routine will not return.

9. If the listen routine exits or an exception is received, the server removes its interface from the endpoint map. This could occur as a result of the **kill** command or some program called the **rpc_mgmt_stop_server_listening()** routine.

The security initialization routine "sort_setup_auth()" is shown in Fig. 20.9.

1. Declare our security information to the runtime. The principal name is defined in the header file and, for convenience, is the same as the name exported to the name service. DCE secret key authentication is specified. The **NULL** argument indicates that we will use the default routine for acquiring encryption keys. The keytab argument contains the name of the local key file used by this server.

2. Obtain a blank security (login) context. This triggers an RPC to the Security Service to obtain a TGT (ticket-granting ticket). No flags are specified. The only flag defined is one to prevent the credentials from being inherited by any subprocesses we happen to create. The routine returns an opaque handle to a security context.

```
/*------------------- Initialize Security -------------------*/

void sort_setup_auth( rpc_binding_vector_t *bindings,
                      boolean32 create_db_flag )
{
error_status_t status;
sec_login_handle_t login_context;
void *key_ptr;
boolean32 expired;
sec_login_auth_src_t auth_src;
uuid_vector_t mgr_uuid_vec;
pthread_t thread_hdl;
pthread_attr_t attr;
unsigned_char_t site_name[50] = "";
sec_rgy_handle_t rgy_hdl;
char *cell_name_p;

rpc_server_register_auth_info( princ_name,                        /* (1) */
                               rpc_c_authn_dce_secret,
                               NULL,
                               keytab,
                               &status);
ERR_CHK (status,"Could not register security information");

sec_login_setup_identity( princ_name,                            /* (2) */
                          sec_login_no_flags,
                          &login_context,
                          &status);
ERR_CHK (status,"Could not obtain login context");

sec_key_mgmt_get_key( rpc_c_authn_dce_secret,                    /* (3) */
                      keytab,
                      princ_name,
                      (unsigned32)0,
                      &key_ptr,
                      &status);
ERR_CHK (status,"Could not obtain password");

sec_login_validate_identity( login_context,                     /* (4) */
                             (sec_passwd_rec_t *) key_ptr,
                             &expired,
                             &auth_src,
                             &status);
ERR_CHK (status,"Could not validate identity");
CND_CHK (auth_src != sec_login_auth_src_network,
         "Network identity not available");

sec_login_set_context( login_context,                           /* (5) */
                       &status);
```

Figure 20.9 Tiered server example: security initialization.

```
sec_acl_mgr_configure( sec_acl_mgr_config_stable|create_db_flag,      /* (6) */
                       acl_db_name,
                       &mgr_hdl,
                       &status);
ERR_CHK (status,"Error initializing ACL Manager");

rpc_server_register_if( rdaclif_v0_0_s_ifspec,                        /* (7) */
                        NULL,
                        NULL,
                        &status);
ERR_CHK (status,"Error registering ACL Manager interface");

mgr_uuid_vec.count = 1;
mgr_uuid_vec.uuid[0] = &mgr_uuid;

rpc_ep_register( rdaclif_v0_0_s_ifspec,                               /* (8) */
                 bindings,
                 &mgr_uuid_vec,
                 (unsigned_char_t *) "ACL Manager for Sort List Server",
                 &status);
ERR_CHK (status,"Error registering ACL Manager with Endpoint Mapper");

/* Install program will export to namespace. No need to do it here */

if ( (pthread_attr_create(&attr) != 0) ||                            /* (9) */
     pthread_attr_setsched(&attr, SCHED_BG_NP) != 0)
   {
   attr = pthread_attr_default;
   }

if (pthread_create( &thread_hdl,                                     /* (10) */
                    attr,
                    (pthread_startroutine_t) manage_key,
                    (pthread_addr_t) 0) != 0)
   {
   WARN ("Could not create thread for key management");
```

Figure 20.9 *(Continued)*

3. Get a key from the key table. For an interactive user, the key is obtained by encrypting the password. For a server, there is no need for a password; the key is randomly generated and stored in the registry and local key table. The local key table is specified in keytab. The zero argument means that the most recent version of the key will be used if there is more than one. Note that the routine allocates the space for the key. Therefore the argument is the address of a pointer.

4. Cause the previously allocated security context to be validated, using the key that we just obtained. One subtle point is that the second argument to this routine can be either a password or a key. The structure containing the item contains a type field that says which it is. As a side effect, this routine destroys the key. The routine returns an indication if the password has expired and if the context was validated by the network. The context must be validated by the network or we will not be able to do anything useful. We can ignore password expiration for now, because the key management routine will take care of it.

5. Now we declare the context that was just validated to be the "default" context. In other words, it will be the one that the runtime uses from now on.

6. Initialize the ACL manager. The first argument specifies that the ACL manager is responsible for maintaining the nonvolatile representation of the server. If the "-c" option was specified at start-up, the database create flag is also set. The second argument specifies the name of the file that contains the ACL. The ACL manager returns a handle to be used in subsequent calls. (This particular manager does not actually make use of the handle.)

7. Register the **rdaclif** interface with the runtime. Since there is only one set of operations implemented (and hence only one entry point vector), it is not necessary to register the object UUID with the runtime. Calls specifying the object UUID of the ACL manager will dispatch correctly.

8. Register the **rdaclif** interface with the endpoint mapper. The **sec_acl_bind()** routine, which is used by **acl_edit**, expects to see the ACL manager UUID exported as an object id. This is the same UUID returned by the **rdacl_get_manager_types()** and **rdacl_get_manager_types_semantics()** routines.

9. Create a thread attribute with the scheduling policy of background. When the key expires, this will prevent the thread that updates the key from competing with other more important threads. If this call fails, we use the default policy.

10. Create a thread that will update the key before it expires. Use the thread attribute just created to set the scheduling policy. The thread will execute "manage_key()" with a **NULL** argument.

Figure 20.10 shows the second portion of the "sort_setup_auth()" routine.

11. Open a connection to the registry. We do not care if it is a read-only site, since we only plan to read.

12. Obtain the UUID of our principal. The second argument specifies that the principal is a person as opposed to a group or organization. If this fails, set the **user_obj** UUID to **NULL**, which tells the ACL manager not to use the **user_obj** ACL entry.

```
sec_rgy_site_open( site_name,                                    /* (11) */
                   &rgy_hdl,
                   &status);
if (status != error_status_ok)
    {
    user_obj = NULL;
    }
    else
    {
    user_obj = malloc( sizeof( sec_id_t));
    user_obj->name = princ_name;
    sec_rgy_pgo_name_to_id( rgy_hdl,                             /* (12) */
                            sec_rgy_domain_person,
                            princ_name,
                            &user_obj->uuid,
                            &status);
    if (status != error_status_ok)
        {
        free(user_obj);
        user_obj = NULL;
        }

    }

sec_rgy_site_close( rgy_hdl,                                     /* (13) */
                    &status);
/* Ignore error on close */

group_obj = NULL;                                               /* (14) */

dce_cf_get_cell_name( &cell_name_p,                             /* (15) */
                      &status);
ERR_CHK (status,"Could not Obtain Cell Name");

sprintf((char *) full_princ_name, "%s/%s", cell_name_p,
                                  (char *) princ_name);
free((void *) cell_name_p);

}


/*** Routine to do key management - runs in its own thread */

pthread_startroutine_t manage_key(pthread_addr_t arg)
{
error_status_t status;

sec_key_mgmt_manage_key( rpc_c_authn_dce_secret,               /* (16) */
                         keytab,
                         princ_name,
                         &status);
WARN ("Key management routine exited");
```

Figure 20.10 Tiered server example: security initialization.

13. End the connection with the registry.

14. This server does not use the **group_obj** ACL entry.

15. This routine runs in its own thread, because it will never return. This routine sleeps until the key is about to expire. Then it generates a random key, updates the registry and the local key table, and calls the garbage collection routine as needed.

The next section of the program contains the server operation that implements the remote procedure call. Note that since the program is both a client and a server, there are two binding handles being manipulated. The first, "bind_h", refers to the connection to the client calling the operation. The second, "tier_bind_h", refers to the connection to the Lookup Table Server.

The "sort_open()" operation is shown in Fig. 20.11. It first checks to see if the client has the open (test) permission. Then it allocates a local context entry. It then calls "look_open()" to allocate a context on the Lookup Table Server. (The binding handle to the lookup server was set up during initialization.) The lookup table context handle is saved in the local context entry for later use.

Figure 20.12 shows the "sort_close()" operation. No access checking is done. It calls "look_close()" to provide a graceful shutdown. Then it cleans up any sorted records in memory and deallocates the context. By assigning **NULL** to the context handle, it tells the client and server stubs to clean up the resources associated with it.

The "sort_begin()" operation is shown in Fig. 20.13. It checks for the open (test) permission. It then updates the local context and deletes any sorted records that might be present from a previous call. Next, it calls "look_filter()" to establish the filter for subsequent "look_next()" calls. Finally, it calls "retrieve_recs()", which in turn does repeated remote procedure calls to "look_next()", inserting the returned records into the sorted tree structure.

Figure 20.14 shows "sort_next()". It first checks for the read permission. This routine does not call the Lookup Table Server. It simply returns records stored in its memory.

The routine "sort_check_access()" is called from the server operations. It is shown in Fig. 20.15 and is the same as in the Lookup Table Server. Its arguments are the client's binding handle and the requested permissions. It returns **TRUE** if security checks out and the ACL manager says that the client is authorized for all of the specified permissions.

1. Get the security information associated with the client's binding handle. It returns the PAC (privilege attribute certificate), server principal name as specified by the client, protection level, authentication, and authorization service. Each of these values is tested to see if everything is as it should be. Any deviation causes the routine to indicate a security failure.

2. Finally, we call the ACL manager to see if the permissions are authorized. The **NULL** argument is the ACL key. Since this manager supports only one

```c
/* sort_open - get context & call look_open */

error_status_t sort_open(
              BIND_HDL_T    bind_h,
              ctx_h         *ctx_p)
{
int i;
client_ctx_t *clt_p;
error_status_t status;
ctx_h         tx_h;

clt_p = NULL;
*ctx_p = NULL;
if (!sort_check_access(bind_h, sec_acl_perm_test))
   return ACCESS_ERROR;
lock (lock_ctx);

for (i=0; (i < CLIENT_MAX) && (clt_p == NULL); i++)
   {
   if (client_table[i].ctx_state == AVAIL)
      clt_p = &client_table[i];
   }

if (clt_p != NULL)
   {
   clt_p->ctx_state = BUSY;
   clt_p->tree = NULL;
   unlock (lock_ctx);

   status = look_open(tier_bind_h, &tx_h);

   lock(lock_read);
   clt_p->tier_ctx_h = tx_h;
   if (status == rpc_s_ok)
       {
       clt_p->sort_state = SORT_NONE;
       *ctx_p = (void *) clt_p;
       unlock(lock_read);
       }
   else
       {
       unlock(lock_read);
       lock(lock_ctx);
       clt_p->ctx_state = AVAIL;
       unlock(lock_ctx);
       }
   }
else
   unlock(lock_ctx);
return status;
}
```

Figure 20.11 Tiered server example: the routine "sort_open()".

```
/* sort_close - cleanup data - deallocate context - call look_close */

error_status_t sort_close(
  BIND_HDL_T    bind_h,
  ctx_h         *ctx_p)
{
client_ctx_t *clt_p;
look_sts_t    result;
error_status_t status;
ctx_h         tx_h;

clt_p = (client_ctx_t *) *ctx_p;

status=look_close(tier_bind_h, &tx_h);

lock(lock_read);
clt_p->tier_ctx_h = tx_h;

destroy_tree(clt_p->tree);
unlock(lock_read);

lock(lock_ctx);
clt_p->ctx_state = AVAIL;

unlock(lock_ctx);
*ctx_p = NULL;
return rpc_s_ok;
}
```

Figure 20.12   Tiered server example: the routine "sort_close()".

ACL, there is no need for a key. If, for example, the server provided a bunch of objects, the key might be the UUID of the object in question. Note that "mgr_uuid", "user_obj", and "group_obj" are global (within the server). This is fine, because they are essentially constants.

The routine "look_ctx_init()" is called to initialize the mutexes and client context array, and to establish a binding to the Lookup Table Server. It is shown in Fig. 20.16.

1. Initialize the two mutexes used by this server.

2. Mark the client context entries as free.

3. Get a handle to the current default security context.

4. Initialize a context to begin looking up entries. The first **NULL** argument specifies that the starting point of the search will be taken from the environment variable **RPC_DEFAULT_ENTRY**. The intention is that this would contain a profile. The second **NULL** specifies that object binding is not being used.

```
/* sort_begin - set lookup filter to read qualified records */

error_status_t sort_begin(
              BIND_HDL_T    bind_h,
              ctx_h         ctx_p,
              filter_t      *filter_p)
{
client_ctx_t *clt_p;
error_status_t status;

if (!sort_check_access(bind_h, sec_acl_perm_test))
   return ACCESS_ERROR;

lock(lock_read);
clt_p = (client_ctx_t *) ctx_p;
clt_p->sort_state = SORT_BEGIN;
clt_p->filter = *filter_p;
destroy_tree(clt_p->tree);
unlock(lock_read);

status=look_filter(tier_bind_h, clt_p->tier_ctx_h, filter_p);

if (status == rpc_s_ok)
   status=retrieve_recs(tier_bind_h, clt_p->tier_ctx_h, &clt_p->tree);

return status;
}
```

Figure 20.13 Tiered server example: the routine "sort_begin()".

5. Get a binding handle to a compatible server.

6. Associate security information with the binding handle. The client specifies the name of the server's principal, the protection level, the authorization type, and the authentication type.

7. Call "look_open()" to get a context handle. If the call fails, try another server.

8. Once a server is found, release the binding context.

9. Call "look_close()" to deallocate the context handle. The "sort_open()" operation will call "look_open()" on behalf of clients.

10. When a context handle is used, a context rundown routine should be provided. The context rundown routine is called if communication with a client that has an active context handle is lost. The context rundown routine always has a name beginning with the name of the context handle data type, followed by **_rundown**. In this case, the context handle **typedef** is "ctx_h", so the routine name is "ctx_h_rundown()". The routine takes one parameter, the context handle of the client in question. The job of the

```
/* sort_next - return next sorted record */

error_status_t sort_next(
            BIND_HDL_T   bind_h,
            ctx_h        ctx_p,
            idl_long_int start,
            idl_long_int len,
            idl_byte     buf[LOOK_REC_SIZE],
            sort_sts_t   *result)

{
client_ctx_t *clt_p;
char * rec_p;


clt_p = (client_ctx_t *) ctx_p;

if (!sort_check_access(bind_h, sec_acl_perm_read))
   return ACCESS_ERROR;
lock(lock_read);

switch (clt_p->sort_state) {
   case SORT_NONE:
      *result = SORT_WRONG_STATE;
      break;
   case SORT_BEGIN:
      init_inorder(clt_p->tree, &clt_p->traverse);
      clt_p->sort_state = SORT_NEXT;
   case SORT_NEXT:
      rec_p = next_inorder(&clt_p->traverse);
      if (rec_p == NULL)
         {
         *result = SORT_END;
         }
      else
         {
         memcpy((char *) &buf[start], rec_p, len);
         *result = SORT_OK;
         }
      break;
   }

unlock(lock_read);
return rpc_s_ok;
```

Figure 20.14   Tiered server example: the routine "sort_next()".

```
/*---------- Check access (Reference Monitor) --------------*/

boolean32 sort_check_access (
    rpc_binding_handle_t binding,
    sec_acl_permset_t permissions)
{
unsigned_char_t *server_name;
sec_id_pac_t *pac;
unsigned32 protect_level, authn_svc, authz_svc;
error_status_t status;

rpc_binding_inq_auth_client( binding,                              /* (1) */
                             (rpc_authz_handle_t) &pac,
                             &server_name,
                             &protect_level,
                             &authn_svc,
                             &authz_svc,
                             &status);
if (status != rpc_s_ok) return (FALSE);


if (strcmp ((char *)server_name, (char *)full_princ_name) != 0)
    {
    rpc_string_free (&server_name, &status);
    return (FALSE);
    }
else
   rpc_string_free (&server_name, &status);

if (protect_level != rpc_c_protect_level_pkt_integ
    || authn_svc != rpc_c_authn_dce_secret
    || authz_svc != rpc_c_authz_dce)
   return (FALSE);

return (sec_acl_mgr_is_authorized( mgr_hdl,                        /* (2) */
                                   permissions,
                                   pac,
                                   NULL,
                                   &mgr_uuid,
                                   user_obj,
                                   group_obj,
                                   &status));
}
```

Figure 20.15   Tiered server example: security-check routine.

```
/* ---------- Mutex and Context Initialization ---------- */

void sort_ctx_init (void)
{
int i;
error_status_t status;
rpc_ns_handle_t binding_context;
sec_login_handle_t login_context;
ctx_h        ctx_p;

if (pthread_mutex_init( &lock_read,                              /* (1) */
                        pthread_mutexattr_default) != 0)
    {
    ERROR("Could not initialize read mutex");
    }

if (pthread_mutex_init( &lock_ctx,
                        pthread_mutexattr_default) != 0)
    {
    ERROR("Could not initialize context mutex");
    }

lock(lock_ctx);

for (i=0; i<CLIENT_MAX; i++)                                     /* (2) */
    {
    client_table[i].ctx_state = AVAIL;
    }
unlock(lock_ctx);

sec_login_get_current_context( &login_context,                  /* (3) */
                               &status);
ERR_CHK(status,"Could not get current security context");

rpc_ns_binding_import_begin( rpc_c_ns_syntax_default,           /* (4) */
                             NULL,
                             lookup_v1_0_c_ifspec,
                             NULL,
                             &binding_context,
                             &status);
ERR_CHK(status,"Could not import binding context");

do
    {
    rpc_ns_binding_import_next( binding_context,                /* (5) */
                                &tier_bind_h,
                                &status);
```

Figure 20.16 Tiered server example: mutex initialization.

```
        rpc_binding_set_auth_info( tier_bind_h,                            /* (6) */
                              (unsigned_char_t *) look_princ_name,
                              rpc_c_protect_level_pkt_integ,
                              rpc_c_authn_dce_secret,
                              (rpc_auth_identity_handle_t) login_context,
                              rpc_c_authz_dce,
                              &status);
        ERR_CHK(status,"Could not associate security information with binding");

        status=look_open ( tier_bind_h, &ctx_p);                          /* (7) */

        }
        while(status != rpc_s_ok);  /* If this fails, try the next one */

rpc_ns_binding_import_done(&binding_context,                              /* (8) */
                              &status);
ERR_CHK(status,"Error releasing binding context");

status=look_close(tier_bind_h, &ctx_p);                                  /* (9) */
        /* ignore error */
}

/*** Context Rundown Routine ***/

void ctx_h_rundown( ctx_h ctx_p )
{
client_ctx_t *clt_p;

if (ctx_p == NULL) return;                                               /* (10) */
clt_p = (client_ctx_t *) ctx_p;

lock(lock_read);
destroy_tree(clt_p->tree);
unlock(lock_read);

lock (lock_ctx);
clt_p->ctx_state = AVAIL;
unlock (lock_ctx);
```

Figure 20.16 *(Continued)*

rundown routine is to deallocate the resources associated with the context handle. In this case, we mark the context as available and deallocate any sorted records in memory. The runtime automatically deallocates the context handle on exit.

20.7.3 The client

The Sort List client is called "srtlst_c.c". It is a very simple program, given here merely to demonstrate the operation of the Sort List Server. It takes the start and length as command-line arguments. It calls the Sort List Server and prints out the records returned.

Figure 20.17 shows the client. Note that it uses "srtlst.h", which was created by the IDL compiler from "srtlst.idl".

1. Get a handle to the current default security context.

2. Initialize a context to begin looking up entries. The first **NULL** argument specifies that the starting point of the search will be taken from the environment variable **RPC_DEFAULT_ENTRY**. The intention is that this would contain a profile. The second **NULL** specifies that object binding is not being used.

3. Get a binding handle to a compatible server.

4. Associate security information with the binding handle. The client specifies the name of the server's principal, the protection level, the authorization type, and the authentication type.

5. Call the server to get a context handle. If the call fails, try another server.

6. Once a server is found, release the binding context.

7. The server specifies a filter which matches all records. It calls "sort_begin()", then it calls "sort_next()" repeatedly, displaying each record returned. When there are no more left, it calls "sort_close()" to clean up.

20.7.4   The installation program

The Sort List installation program is called "srtlst_i.c". It is essentially identical to the one in the previous example. It is shown in Fig. 20.18. Like the previous example, it takes two commands: "i" (install) and "r" (remove).

1. Use all protocol sequences. They must match those of the server. The number of threads specified does not matter, because we do not call **rpc_server_listen()**.

2. Get the binding vector.

3. Export the bindings to the namespace. The **NULL** argument indicates that we are not using object binding.

4. Export the **rdaclif** interface. Note that the ACL manager UUID must be specified as the binding object. This is required by **sec_acl_bind()**.

5. If the remove command is given, do the opposite. Remove the entry from the namespace.

6. Also remove the **rdaclif** entry.

```
/* SRTLST_C.C Sort List Client */

#include <dce/sec_login.h>
#include <stdio.h>
#include "errmac.h"
#include "srtlst.h"
#include "srtlst_s.h"

void display_rec(char *buf);

int main (int argc, char *argv[])
{
void               *ctx_p;
BIND_HDL_T         bind_h;
error_status_t     status;
sort_sts_t         result;
filter_t           filter;
char               buf[LOOK_REC_SIZE];
rpc_ns_handle_t    binding_context;
sec_login_handle_t login_context;

/* Get a pointer to the security credentials */
sec_login_get_current_context( &login_context,                        /* (1) */
                               &status);
ERR_CHK(status,"Could not get current security context");

/* Initialize the search for a server */
rpc_ns_binding_import_begin( rpc_c_ns_syntax_default,                 /* (2) */
                             NULL,
                             srtlst_v1_0_c_ifspec,
                             NULL,
                             &binding_context,
                             &status);
ERR_CHK(status,"Could not import binding context");

do
    {
    rpc_ns_binding_import_next( binding_context,                      /* (3) */
                                &bind_h,
                                &status);
    ERR_CHK(status,"Could not find any servers to bind to");

    rpc_binding_set_auth_info( bind_h,                               /* (4) */
                               (unsigned_char_t *) princ_name,
                               rpc_c_protect_level_pkt_integ,
                               rpc_c_authn_dce_secret,
                               (rpc_auth_identity_handle_t) login_context,
                               rpc_c_authz_dce,
                               &status);
```

Figure 20.17 Tiered server example: client.

```
       status=sort_open(bind_h, &ctx_p);                        /* (5) */

       if (ctx_p == NULL) WARN("Server was unable to allocate context");
       }
       while(status != rpc_s_ok);  /* If this fails, try the next one */

rpc_ns_binding_import_done( &binding_context,                   /* (6) */
                            &status);
ERR_CHK(status,"Error releasing binding context");

filter.ofs = 0;
filter.len = 1;
filter.min[0] = '\x01';
filter.max[0] = '\x7f';

status=sort_begin(bind_h, ctx_p, &filter);                     /* (7) */
ERR_CHK (status, "Sort Begin failed");

result = SORT_OK;
while (result == SORT_OK)
   {
   status=sort_next( bind_h,
                     ctx_p,
                     (idl_long_int) 0,
                     LOOK_REC_SIZE,
                     (unsigned_char_t *) buf,
                     &result);
   ERR_CHK (status, "Sort next failed");

   if (result == SORT_OK) display_rec (buf);
   }
status=sort_close(bind_h, &ctx_p);
ERR_CHK (status, "Sort Close failed");
}

void  display_rec( char *rec )
{
printf("Result=\"%*s\"\n", LOOK_REC_SIZE, rec);
```

Figure 20.17 *(Continued)*

20.8 Variations and Extensions

The Sort List client could be modified to make use of the filter specified in the "sort_begin()" call. The client could also parse a schema, as the lookup table client does.

Other extensions, which would apply to both the client and the intermediary, would be to use automatic binding or to look for another server if the first one were unavailable. Another variation would be to convert to using exceptions instead of error-status variables.

```
/***** Sort List Server Installation Program *****/

main( int argc, char *argv[] )
{

error_status_t          status;
rpc_binding_vector_t    *bindings;
uuid_vector_t mgr_uuid_vec;

if (argc < 2)
    {
    printf("Usage: %s -i or %s -r\n",argv[0], argv[0]);
    exit(1);
    }

if (strcmp(argv[1], "-i") == 0)
    {
    rpc_server_use_all_protseqs( rpc_c_protseq_max_reqs_default,        /* (1) */
                                &status);
    ERR_CHK(status,"Could not use all protocols");

    rpc_server_inq_bindings( &bindings,                                 /* (2) */
                            &status);
    ERR_CHK(status,"Could not get binding vector");

    rpc_ns_binding_export( rpc_c_ns_syntax_default,                     /* (3) */
                           name,
                           srtlst_v1_0_s_ifspec,
                           bindings,
                           NULL,
                           &status);
    ERR_CHK(status,"Could not export server bindings");

    mgr_uuid_vec.count = 1;
    mgr_uuid_vec.uuid[0] = &mgr_uuid;

    rpc_ns_binding_export( rpc_c_ns_syntax_default,                     /* (4) */
                           name,
                           rdaclif_v0_0_s_ifspec,
                           bindings,
                           &mgr_uuid_vec,
                           &status);
    ERR_CHK(status,"Could not export server bindings");
```

Figure 20.18 Tiered server example: installation program.

```
    }
    else if (strcmp(argv[1], "-r") == 0)
        {
        rpc_ns_binding_unexport( rpc_c_ns_syntax_default,          /* (5) */
                                 name,
                                 srtlst_v1_0_s_ifspec,
                                 NULL,
                                 &status);
        ERR_CHK(status,"Could not remove server bindings");

        rpc_ns_binding_unexport( rpc_c_ns_syntax_default,          /* (6) */
                                 name,
                                 rdaclif_v0_0_s_ifspec,
                                 NULL,
                                 &status);
        ERR_CHK(status,"Could not remove ACL Manager bindings");

/* Place additional de-installation tasks here */

        }
        else
        {
        printf("Usage: %s -i or %s -r\n", argv[0], argv[0]);
        exit(1);
        }
}
```

Figure 20.18 *(Continued)*

20.9   Chapter Summary

This example illustrates the basic mechanisms involved in building a tiered server. The key point is that the intermediary component acts as the server to one interface and as the client to another.

Both the servers use the full set of DCE security features, including secret key authentication, data-integrity checking, PAC-based authentication, and access control via ACLs. A future version of DCE will support security delegation, which would allow the Sort List Server to request operations on behalf of the original client principal.

The example client is a simple program designed to demonstrate the functionality of the application. An installation program is provided to export the server's bindings to the namespace.

Example 4: The Peer-to-Peer Server

This chapter describes the last of our four sample distributed applications. This design is useful in situations where the same program needs both to provide and to use the same distributed services.

21.1 Review of the Model

In the peer-to-peer model, a single program acts as both the client and server of the same interface. This flow model is illustrated in Fig. 21.1. In its simplest form, there is only one program, which executes on multiple nodes in the network. It is also possible to conceive of an application in which there might be multiple different programs, each of which acts as both a client and server but performs a different task. There might also be programs that are pure clients or pure servers of the same interface.

Although there has been considerable discussion of peer-to-peer design, it turns out to be difficult to think of real-world applications that require it. Many applications that might use this design can be implemented more simply using another approach.

Figure 21.2 illustrates a hypothetical design for a messaging server. One interface is defined to allow clients to send and receive messages. A different interface is used to communicate between servers. This is similar to the architecture used by systems conforming to the X.400 international messaging standard.

In this design, the server programs are servers on the client interface and they are both clients and servers on the server-to-server interface. The servers store both inbound and outbound messages in a local file. The trouble with this design is that there is little advantage to combining all of these functions into a single server. For example, the clients could just as well write messages directly into the local file or use a dedicated server to do it for them.

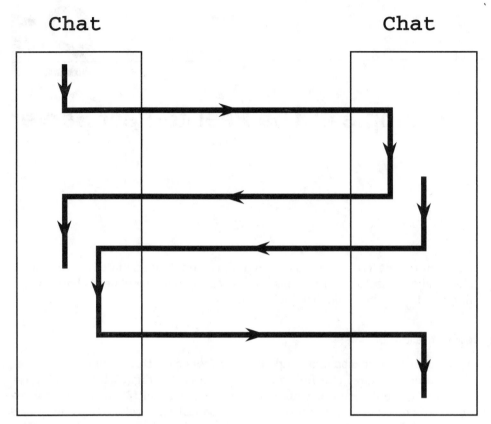

Figure 21.1 The peer-to-peer flow model.

In addition, the sending and receiving functions in the server could be split into two programs, each of which would be simpler to implement. Our general conclusion is that unless the client and server portions of the program need to share data held in main memory, there is little need to use this flow model.

21.2 Functional Description

This sample application is called the Chat Program. It allows a number of users on different nodes to have an unstructured discussion in which everybody can see what everybody else types.

It consists of a single program that acts as both a client and server. The Chat Program takes text typed by a user and broadcasts it to all the other users running the Chat Program. The server side of the program takes incoming messages and displays them on the screen, identifying the user who typed the message.

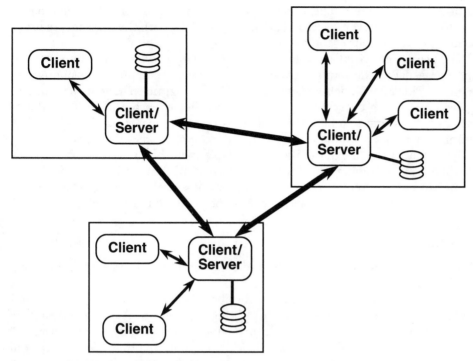

Figure 21.2 Possible design of messaging application.

21.3 Processing Flow Model

The Chat Program consists of a thread that runs the client and a number of server threads. The server threads are generated in the usual way by the run-time as a consequence of calling **rpc_server_listen**() with an argument greater than one. These threads are used to run instances of the server operation, which displays the received messages on the screen.

The client thread is created explicitly by a call to **pthread_create**(). It collects input lines from the user and broadcasts the messages to all the chat instances. The client and server threads operate independently. No attempt is made to synchronize their activities.

21.4 State Model

The Chat Program maintains no state.

21.5 Naming Model

Users are expected to type their name on the command line when they run the Chat Program. If the name is not found, the program does a system call to obtain the user's name. This name is passed as an argument to the remote procedure call. The server operation prints it out, along with the message, in order to identify the sender of the message.

The user's name is also used to create a name for the server binding entry in the namespace. The name created is of the form "/.:/applications/chat/<user name>". This allows each instance of the Chat Program to have its own namespace entry. Each entry has one object identifier exported in it. This allows other chat instances to identify duplicates when broadcasting. The Chat Program adds itself as a member of the group "/.:/applications/chat/group".

The Chat Program exports its namespace entry when it starts and removes it when it exits. It determines what other copies of chat are running by means of the bindings currently in the namespace. It does not use an installation program to export its bindings, because it is not expected to run continuously.

21.6   Security Model

The Chat Program does not use DCE security features. The idea is that anyone is allowed to join the conversation.

In a real peer-to-peer application, a number of possible security models could be used, depending on the nature of the application. All of the program instances could run as the same principal. Alternatively, every program instance could run under a different principal, perhaps that of the user who ran it. Another possibility is that some of the instances might be grouped together in some way.

21.7   Example Source Code

The Chat Program consists of just three files: the IDL file, the ACF, and the Chat Program, which acts as both client and server.

21.7.1   The IDL file

The IDL file for the Chat Program is shown in Fig. 21.3. It is named "chat.idl".

As the comment says, the **no_mepv** option should be specified when running the IDL compiler against "chat.idl". Using this option causes the compiler to suppress the automatic generation of an EPV (entry point vector). Recall that the EPV contains the addresses of the operation routines in the server. It is used by the server runtime to dispatch to the correct routine when a remote procedure call is received.

By default, IDL generates an EPV containing symbolic names of the server operations that are the same as the names specified in the IDL file. Normally, this is very convenient. However, in this case, since the client and server are in the same program, it would cause problems. The stub routines that the client call uses and the actual server operation will both define the same global sym-

```
/* CHAT.IDL Chat Program   */

/* NOTE: run IDL with the no_mepv option */
[
uuid(00602161-7C3F-1C90-9982-0000C07C3610),
version(1.0)
]
interface chat
{

const long CHAT_NAME_SIZE = 20;
const long CHAT_TEXT_SIZE = 100;

error_status_t send_msg( [in] handle_t            bind_hdl,
                         [in, string] char   name[CHAT_NAME_SIZE],
                         [in, string] char   text[CHAT_TEXT_SIZE]);

}
```

Figure 21.3 Peer-to-peer server example: IDL file.

bol. The cure is simple. Suppress the EPV generated by IDL, use a different name for the actual server operation routine, and generate the EPV explicitly.

The interface defines just one operation, "send_msg()". In addition to the binding handle, it takes two input-only arguments: the user's name and the message. Both are defined as arrays with the **string** attribute, which means that the length transmitted will be determined when marshaling is done.

21.7.2 The Chat Program

The Chat Program is called "chat.c". The server control portion of it is shown in Fig. 21.4. Notice that the EPV is declared at the top. The **typedef** name is always constructed from the interface name and version number, followed by "_epv_t". The name declared can be anything. Each entry is the name of a server operation routine. They must be in the order in which they appear in the IDL file. Note that in this case the server operation routine is called "send_msg_op" to avoid conflict with the client call to "send_msg".

1. Get the user name typed on the command line or, if not found, get the user's login name. Concatenate this to the directory entry string.

2. Create a UUID to identify this instance of the program.

3. Register the interface with the runtime. The **NULL** is used because, although we are exporting an object to the namespace, there is only one EPV, which all calls will use. Note that the address of the EPV, "chat_epv", which was declared above, is specified in this call.

4. Get all available protocol sequences.

```
/* CHAT.C */

#include <stdio.h>
#include <string.h>
#include <dce/rpc.h>
#include <pthread.h>
#include "chat.h"
#include "errmac.h"

idl_char chat_dir_name[50] = "/.:/applications/chat/";
idl_char chat_group_name[] = "/.:/applications/chat/group";
idl_char user_name[CHAT_NAME_SIZE];

uuid_t          my_obj;
uuid_vector_t obj_vec;

        /* Number of other chat programs we can talk to */
#define OBJ_TBL_MAX 20

error_status_t send_msg_op( rpc_binding_handle_t bind_h,
                            idl_char              name[],
                            idl_char              text[]);
void client_thread();

chat_v1_0_epv_t chat_epv = { send_msg_op };




/***** Server Control *****/

main( int argc, char *argv[] )
{
error_status_t        status;
rpc_binding_vector_t *bindings;
pthread_t             thread_hdl;

if (argc > 2 )
    {
    fprintf(stderr, "Usage: %s name\n", argv[0] );
    exit(1);
    }

if (argc < 2 )                                                      /* (1) */
    {
    strcpy((char *) user_name, getlogin());
    }
    else
    {
    strcpy((char *) user_name, argv[1]);
    }
```

Figure 21.4 Peer-to-peer server example: server control.

```
uuid_create(&my_obj,&status);                                          /* (2) */
ERR_CHK(status,"Error creating object UUID");

obj_vec.count = 1;
obj_vec.uuid[0] = &my_obj;

rpc_server_register_if( chat_v1_0_s_ifspec,                            /* (3) */
                        NULL,
                        (rpc_mgr_epv_t) &chat_epv,
                        &status);
ERR_CHK(status,"Could not register interface");

rpc_server_use_all_protseqs( rpc_c_listen_max_calls_default,          /* (4) */
                             &status);
ERR_CHK(status,"Could not use all protocols");

rpc_server_inq_bindings( &bindings,                                    /* (5) */
                         &status);
ERR_CHK(status,"Could not get binding vector");

rpc_ns_binding_export( rpc_c_ns_syntax_default,                        /* (6) */
                       chat_dir_name,
                       chat_v1_0_s_ifspec,
                       bindings,
                       &obj_vec,
                       &status);
ERR_CHK(status,"Could not export server bindings");

rpc_ns_group_mbr_add( rpc_c_ns_syntax_default,                        /* (7) */
                      chat_group_name,
                      rpc_c_ns_syntax_default,
                      chat_dir_name,
                      &status);
ERR_CHK(status,"Could not add server entry to group");

rpc_ep_register( chat_v1_0_s_ifspec,                                  /* (8) */
                 bindings,
                 &obj_vec,
                 (idl_char *) "Chat Program",
                 &status);
ERR_CHK(status,"Could not register endpoint");

if (pthread_create( &thread_hdl,                                      /* (9) */
                    pthread_attr_default,
                    (pthread_startroutine_t) client_thread,
                    (pthread_addr_t) 0) != 0)
   {
   ERROR("Could not create client thread");
```

Figure 21.4 *(Continued)*

```
rpc_server_listen( rpc_c_listen_max_calls_default,                     /* (10) */
                   &status);

rpc_ns_binding_unexport( rpc_c_ns_syntax_default,                      /* (11) */
                         chat_dir_name,
                         chat_v1_0_s_ifspec,
                         &obj_vec,
                         &status);
ERR_CHK(status,"Could not remove server bindings");

rpc_ns_group_mbr_remove( rpc_c_ns_syntax_default,                     /* (12) */
                         chat_group_name,
                         rpc_c_ns_syntax_default,
                         chat_dir_name,
                         &status);
ERR_CHK(status,"Could not add server entry to group");

rpc_ep_unregister( chat_v1_0_s_ifspec,                               /* (13) */
                   bindings,
                   &obj_vec,
                   &status);
```

Figure 21.4 *(Continued)*

5. Get the binding vector.

6. Export the binding to the namespace. The entry name is the one constructed above. The object UUID created earlier is exported to identify this instance of the program.

7. Add our entry to the chat group, so others can find us.

8. Export the binding to the endpoint mapper. The object UUID created earlier is exported to identify this instance of the program. The annotation string identifies the endpoint mapping to administrative programs.

9. Create a thread to run the client routine.

10. Wait for calls. In this example, the default number of threads is used.

11. On shutdown, remove our entry from the namespace.

12. Remove this instance from the chat group entry.

13. Also remove our entry from the endpoint map.

The server operation routine is shown in Fig. 21.5. Notice that it is named "send_msg_op()" to avoid name conflict. It simply prints out the arguments on the user's screen.

```
/************************* Server Operations **************************/

error_status_t send_msg_op( rpc_binding_handle_t  bind_h,
                            idl_char               name[],
                            idl_char               text[])
{

printf("\n%s - %s\n\n", name, text);

return(rpc_s_ok);

}
```

Figure 21.5 Peer-to-peer server example: server operation.

Figure 21.6 shows the client routine. It runs in its own thread, which was created near the beginning of the program.

1. Prompt the user, read the message.

2. Initialize a context to begin looking up entries. The first **NULL** argument specifies that the starting point of the search will be taken from the environment variable **RPC_DEFAULT_ENTRY**. The intention is that this would contain the chat group name. The second **NULL** means that we will see all entries, whatever objects they have exported.

3. Get a binding handle to a compatible server.

4. Get the object associated with this binding handle. Check if we have already sent this message to this instance (object UUID). Note that our UUID is always the first entry in the table. If the UUID is a new one, add it to the table.

5. Send the message.

6. Release the binding context.

7. After falling out of the loop above, request an orderly shutdown of the server. This will allow any pending calls to complete and then cause the main routine to return from **rpc_server_listen**(). The server will then remove its binding from the namespace and the endpoint map.

21.8 Variations and Extensions

The best variation would be to think of a real-life application for this model.

Given the Chat Program, a number of improvements are possible. It would be good to synchronize the client and server threads in some way. The simplest change would be to use a mutex to prevent the client from starting before the server-control routine finished initializing.

```
/************************* Client Thread *************************/

void client_thread()
{
error_status_t status;
idl_char *cp, msg_txt[CHAT_TEXT_SIZE];
int i, num_ids;
uuid_t obj_tbl[OBJ_TBL_MAX];
uuid_t curr_obj;
rpc_ns_handle_t binding_context;
rpc_binding_handle_t bind_h;

obj_tbl[0] = my_obj;
num_ids=1;

printf("Type your message. Control D to exit\n\n");

while(1)                                                          /* (1) */
    {
    printf("MSG: ");
    cp = (idl_char *) gets( (char *) msg_txt );
    if (cp == NULL) break;

    rpc_ns_binding_import_begin( rpc_c_ns_syntax_default,         /* (2) */
                                 NULL,
                                 chat_v1_0_c_ifspec,
                                 NULL,
                                 &binding_context,
                                 &status);
    ERR_CHK(status,"Could not import binding context");

    num_ids = 1;
    while (1)  /* Try every binding */
        {
        rpc_ns_binding_import_next( binding_context,             /* (3) */
                                    &bind_h,
                                    &status);
        if (status != rpc_s_ok) break;

        rpc_binding_inq_object( bind_h,                          /* (4) */
                                &curr_obj,
                                &status);
        if (status != rpc_s_ok) continue;

        i = 0;
        while (i < num_ids)
            {
            if ( uuid_equal(&obj_tbl[i], &curr_obj, &status) ) break;
            i++;
            }
```

Figure 21.6 Peer-to-peer server example: client thread.

```
        if (num_ids >= OBJ_TBL_MAX )
            ERROR("Too many chat programs running");

        obj_tbl[num_ids++] = curr_obj;

        status = send_msg( bind_h, user_name, msg_txt);              /* (5) */
            /* ignore error */

        }   /* end of trying bindings */

rpc_ns_binding_import_done(&binding_context,                         /* (6) */
                            &status);
ERR_CHK(status,"Error releasing binding context");

    } /* end of message loop */

rpc_mgmt_stop_server_listening( NULL, &status);                     /* (7) */

}
```

Figure 21.6   (*Continued*)

Another idea would be to interlock the threads, so that the output does not get jumbled together on the screen. It would be easy to interlock the server operation threads by using a mutex, but it is harder to see what to do about the client thread, since the user could be typing at any time. Obviously, a windowing interface would eliminate the problem.

Since we are depending on the namespace to tell us who is running, it might be nice to avoid using out-of-date namespace entries. The cache could be disabled by calling **rpc_ns_mgmt_set_exp_age()** with an argument of zero. This would force the bindings to be taken from the CDS server every time.

A good extension would be to think of some state that could be shared between the client and server threads, with a mutex to protect it.

21.9   Chapter Summary

This example illustrates the use of a peer-to-peer program, defined as a program acting as both a client and a server of the same interface.

Several features are essential to this design. The server operations must be given names different from those declared in the IDL file, and an EPV must be generated explicitly rather than by the IDL compiler. A separate thread must be created explicitly to run the client routine.

22

ACL Manager Example

This chapter presents a sample implementation of an Access Control List (ACL) manager. This ACL manager is used by the second and third example distributed applications, which were presented in Chap. 19 and 20. Normally, every server would use a distinct ACL manager implementation tailored to its requirements. In this case, it would be redundant to present two of them that have only minor differences.

22.1 ACL Manager General Description

The general characteristics of an ACL manager were described in Chap. 11. This section reviews them briefly.

Every secure server must provide an ACL manager, which implements the ACLs associated with the resources that the server provides. The ACL manager does basically four things. It stores and retrieves the ACLs from non-volatile storage (disk); allows them to be created, read, and modified; determines the permissions that should be granted; and provides assorted utility functions.

The standard way to implement an ACL manager is to link it into the server as part of the same program. There are three sets of program interfaces associated with an ACL manager. Figure 22.1 shows the relationship of these interfaces to each other.

The routines that have names beginning with **sec_acl_mgr_** are used locally within the server. Typically, the server calls **sec_acl_mgr_configure()** during initialization and calls **sec_acl_mgr_is_authorized()** from an operation routine to see if the operation should be permitted.

The routines that have names that begin with **sec_acl_** are used by any other program that wishes to access or manipulate the ACLs. The most common use of these routines is by an editor or browser, such as the **acl_edit** program.

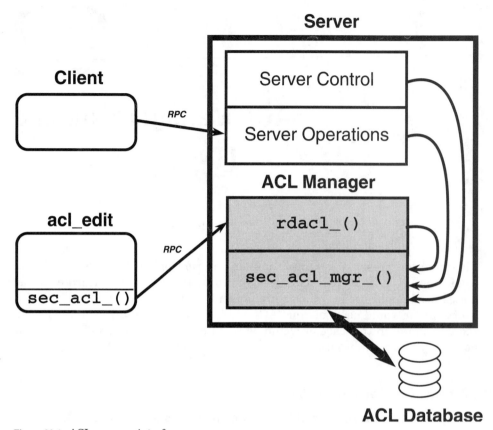

Figure 22.1 ACL manager interfaces.

For example, a program of this kind would call **sec_acl_lookup()**, **sec_acl_get_printstring()**, and **sec_acl_replace()** to display and edit an ACL.

It is not necessary, however, for the ACL manager to implement the **sec_acl_** interface. DCE provides the implementation of these routines. They all work by making remote procedure calls to an interface called **rdaclif**, which declares operations with names beginning with **rdacl_**. The ACL manager must implement these routines.

22.2 Functional Description of the Example ACL Manager

The behavior provided by the **sec_acl_mgr** and **rdacl_** interfaces is specified by DCE. However, the implementor of an ACL manager must make a number of decisions based on the needs of the particular server that will use the ACL manager. The most basic decision is what the ACLs correspond to. In this example, there is just one ACL. In effect, it protects the server as a whole.

Servers that implement container objects must provide an ACL manager that implements all three kinds of ACL: Object ACLs, Initial Object Creation ACLs, and Initial Container Creation ACLs. Since the servers in question do not use container objects, the ACL manager does not implement Initial Object Creation ACLs or Initial Container Creation ACLs.

This ACL manager implements six permissions: read, write, open, add, delete, and control. The first five are used to protect the operations the server performs. The control permission is required of any principal that performs the **rdacl_replace()** operation. No permissions are required to perform any of the other **rdacl_** operations. In order to prevent the possibility of creating an ACL that cannot be modified by any principal, the **rdacl_replace()** routine checks to ensure that at least one of the ACL entries contains the control permission.

The single ACL is stored in a disk file, the name of which is specified in the call to **sec_acl_mgr_configure()**. When **rdacl_replace()** is called, the ACL is written out and the file is closed. When any operation that reads the ACL, such as **rdacl_lookup()** or **rdacl_is_authorized()**, is called, the ACL is read in from disk.*

The **sec_acl_mgr_configure()** routine is supposed to return a pointer to a manager handle, which is then provided as an argument to all of the other **sec_acl_mgr_** routines. In this example, the ACL manager does not make any use of this handle.

The ACL manager is supposed to implement one or more actual manager types, each of which is identified by a UUID. This manager implements just one. Its UUID is a compiled-in constant generated by using the **s** option to **uuidgen**.

An ACL manager is responsible for determining which principal is referred to by the **user_obj** and **group_obj** entries. In other words, it specifies each object's individual owner and group owner. This ACL manager determines the principal under which it is executing and considers that to be the **user_obj** principal. It does not assign any meaning to the **group_obj** entry.

22.3 The ACL Data Structure

The key to understanding the example ACL manager is to become familiar with the data structure that represents an ACL. Although some of the code in the ACL manager looks quite formidable, a careful study of this data structure will make it relatively easy to understand what is going on.

First, let us review the important components of an ACL. The ACL contains some information that applies to the ACL as a whole. For example, the home cell of the ACL. In an ACL, principals, groups, and cells are unambiguously identified by their UUIDs. As a convenience, their names are also stored as a string.

---

* This does not appear to be terribly efficient but, in most cases, the data will remain in the file system's cache, so no physical disk I/O will occur.

Most of the information in the ACL is contained in one or more ACL entries. There are nine types of entries that refer to categories of principals and two types of mask entries. There is also an entry type called *extended*. It is not interpreted by the ACL manager, but is provided for future enhancement.

In theory, the total number of entries in an ACL is unlimited. All entry types contain a 32-bit field of permissions. There are six types of entries, such as **user_obj**, that do not contain any other information. These are also the entry types that can appear at most once in any ACL. There are three other types of entries, for example **user**, that have one additional identifier, again consisting of a UUID and a string. There are two other types (for example, **foreign_user**) that carry two identifiers. The extended entry contains a pointer to a still more complex structure.

The IDL declarations defining the components of an ACL are shown in Fig. 22.2. They were assembled from several different IDL files. The base structure is a **sec_acl_t**, which contains the general information, a count of the number of entries, and a pointer to the table of entries. For historical reasons, the term *realm* is used in place of cell. The actual entries are defined as a permission set, followed by a tagged union on the entry type. It contains zero, one, or two identifiers, or a pointer to extended data as just described.

Notice the **sec_acl_id_t** declaration, which is used all over the place. It contains a UUID and a pointer to a string. It is used whenever a principal, group, or cell needs to be identified.

The corresponding C declarations generated by the IDL compiler are shown in Fig. 22.3. They were extracted from several header files and reformatted for readability. Notice the deeply nested structures in the ACL entries, particularly in those entry types containing a foreign ID.

Figure 22.4 represents the ACL graphically. These are the key features. The base structure, **sec_acl_t**, is of fixed size and contains a count of the number of entries and a pointer to an array of entries. Each entry is of fixed size because, in addition to the permission set, it contains a tagged union. Throughout, identifiers are stored as an inline UUID and a pointer to a string, which is allocated separately.

22.4   ACL Manager Source Code

As previously stated, the ACL manager implements two different sets of routines. The routines that may be called internally within the server are: **sec_acl_mgr_configure()**, **sec_acl_mgr_is_authorized()**, **sec_acl_mgr_replace()**, **sec_acl_mgr_lookup()**, and **sec_acl_mgr_get_access()**.

The routines that are accessible via remote procedure call are: **rdacl_lookup()**, **rdacl_replace()**, **rdacl_test_access()**, **rdacl_test_access_on_behalf()**, **rdacl_get_manager_types()**, **rdacl_get_manager_types_semantics()**, **rdacl_get_printstring()**, **rdacl_get_referral()**, and **rdacl_get_access()**.

Each of these routines is shown and described in the following sections.

```
/* IDL file definitions for the ACL data structure */

/**** TYPEDEF sec_acl_t and sec_acl_p_t ****/

    typedef struct {
        sec_acl_id_t              default_realm;
        uuid_t                    sec_acl_manager_type;
        unsigned32                num_entries;
        [ptr, size_is(num_entries)]
            sec_acl_entry_t       *sec_acl_entries;
    } sec_acl_t;

    typedef [ptr] sec_acl_t *sec_acl_p_t;

/**** TYPEDEF sec_acl_entry_t ****/

    typedef struct {
        sec_acl_permset_t         perms;
        union sec_acl_entry_u
                switch (sec_acl_entry_type_t entry_type) tagged_union {

            case sec_acl_e_type_mask_obj:
            case sec_acl_e_type_user_obj:
            case sec_acl_e_type_group_obj:
            case sec_acl_e_type_other_obj:
            case sec_acl_e_type_unauthenticated:
            case sec_acl_e_type_any_other:
                /* ... just the permset_t ... */;

            case sec_acl_e_type_user:
            case sec_acl_e_type_group:
            case sec_acl_e_type_foreign_other:
                sec_id_t        id;

            case sec_acl_e_type_foreign_user:
            case sec_acl_e_type_foreign_group:
                sec_id_foreign_t foreign_id;

            case sec_acl_e_type_extended:
            default:
                [ptr] sec_acl_extend_info_t *extended_info;
        } entry_info;
    } sec_acl_entry_t;

/**** TYPEDEF sec_acl_permset_t ****/

    typedef unsigned32 sec_acl_permset_t;
```

Figure 22.2 ACL data structures: IDL declarations.

```
    typedef enum {
        sec_acl_e_type_user_obj,
        sec_acl_e_type_group_obj,
        sec_acl_e_type_other_obj,
        sec_acl_e_type_user,
        sec_acl_e_type_group,
        sec_acl_e_type_mask_obj,
        sec_acl_e_type_foreign_user,
        sec_acl_e_type_foreign_group,
        sec_acl_e_type_foreign_other,
        sec_acl_e_type_unauthenticated,
        sec_acl_e_type_extended,
        sec_acl_e_type_any_other
    } sec_acl_entry_type_t;

/**** TYPEDEF sec_id_t and sec_acl_id_t ****/

    typedef struct {
        uuid_t              uuid;
        [ string,ptr ] char *name;
    } sec_id_t;

    typedef sec_id_t sec_acl_id_t;

/**** TYPEDEF sec_id_foreign_t ****/

    typedef struct {
        sec_id_t            id;
        sec_id_t            realm;
    } sec_id_foreign_t;


/**** TYPEDEF sec_acl_extend_info_t ****/

    typedef struct {
        uuid_t          extension_type;
        ndr_format_t    format_label;
        unsigned32      num_bytes;
        [size_is(num_bytes)]
            byte        pickled_data[];
```

Figure 22.2   *(Continued)*

```
/* C Header file definitions for the ACL data structure */


/**** TYPEDEF sec_acl_t and sec_acl_p_t ****/

typedef struct
    {
    sec_acl_id_t default_realm;
    uuid_t sec_acl_manager_type;
    unsigned32 num_entries;
    sec_acl_entry_t *sec_acl_entries;
    }
sec_acl_t;

typedef sec_acl_t *sec_acl_p_t;

/**** TYPEDEF sec_acl_entry_t ****/

typedef struct
    {
    sec_acl_permset_t perms;
    struct sec_acl_entry_u
        {
        sec_acl_entry_type_t entry_type;
        union
            {
            /* case(s): 5, 0, 1, 2, 9, 11 */
            /* Empty arm */
            /* case(s): 3, 4, 8 */
            sec_id_t id;
            /* case(s): 6, 7 */
            sec_id_foreign_t foreign_id;
            /* case(s): 10, default */
            sec_acl_extend_info_t *extended_info;
            }
        tagged_union;
        }
    entry_info;
    }
sec_acl_entry_t;

/**** TYPEDEF sec_acl_permset_t ****/

typedef unsigned32 sec_acl_permset_t;

/**** TYPEDEF sec_acl_entry_type_t ****/
```

Figure 22.3 ACL data structures: C header files.

```
typedef enum
    {
    sec_acl_e_type_user_obj,
    sec_acl_e_type_group_obj,
    sec_acl_e_type_other_obj,
    sec_acl_e_type_user,
    sec_acl_e_type_group,
    sec_acl_e_type_mask_obj,
    sec_acl_e_type_foreign_user,
    sec_acl_e_type_foreign_group,
    sec_acl_e_type_foreign_other,
    sec_acl_e_type_unauthenticated,
    sec_acl_e_type_extended,
    sec_acl_e_type_any_other
    }
sec_acl_entry_type_t;

/**** TYPEDEF sec_id_t and sec_acl_id_t ****/

typedef struct
    {
    uuid_t uuid;
    idl_char *name;
    }
sec_id_t;

typedef sec_id_t sec_acl_id_t;

/**** TYPEDEF sec_id_foreign_t ****/

typedef struct
    {
    sec_id_t id;
    sec_id_t realm;
    }
sec_id_foreign_t;

/**** TYPEDEF sec_acl_extend_info_t ****/

typedef struct
    {
    uuid_t extension_type;
    ndr_format_t format_label;
    unsigned32 num_bytes;
    idl_byte pickled_data[1];
    }
```

Figure 22.3   *(Continued)*

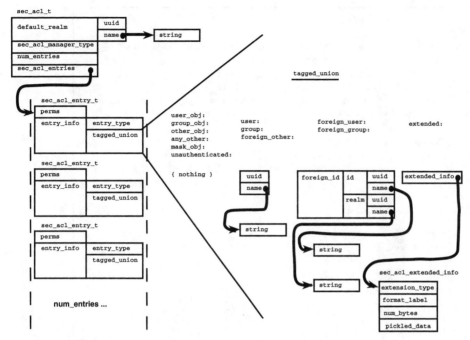

Figure 22.4 ACL data structures: diagram.

22.4.1   Source code
for sec_acl_mgr_configure()

This is the initialization routine for the ACL manager. It is the only internal call for which there is no corresponding remote procedure call operation. The server is expected to call this routine at start-up. Figure 22.5 shows this routine.

The inputs are some flags and the name of the ACL database. In this case, it is simply the name of an ordinary file containing the ACL. The routine requires that the stable storage flag be set. If the create flag is set, the routine makes sure that the file does not already exist. Otherwise, it opens it, ignoring whether it exists or not, and returns success unless a file error occurs. It does not leave the file open. It returns **NULL** for the manager handle.

22.4.2   Source code
for sec_acl_mgr_is_authorized()

This is the basic routine to check if a given principal should be granted a certain set of permissions. The most important arguments are the PAC and the desired permissions. The routine returns TRUE only if all of the permissions should be granted.

The ACL key argument is used to specify which ACL is referred to. The meaning of this argument is something that the server and the ACL manager

```
/* s e c _ a c l _ m g r _ c o n f i g u r e
 *
 *  Configure the dacl manager.  This operation provides a handle that
 *  refers to the particular acl database in use and is necessary for all
 *  other sec_acl manager operations.  The db_name identifies which acl
 *  database to use (and generally refers to the file system object that
 *  represents the persistent storage for the database).  The config_info
 *  provides information on how to configure this database.
 */
void sec_acl_mgr_configure( sec_acl_mgr_config_t    config_info,
                            unsigned_char_p_t       db_name,
                            sec_acl_mgr_handle_t    *sec_acl_mgr,
                            error_status_t          *st_p )
{
int fd, oflag;

/* This ACL manager requires that sec_acl_mgr_config_stable be set */
if ( !(config_info & sec_acl_mgr_config_stable) )
    {
    *st_p = sec_acl_not_implemented;
    return;
    }

/* save database name for later */
strcpy((char *)acl_file_name, (char *) db_name);

/* Set up ACL File header for sec_acl_mgr_replace and sec_acl_mgr_lookup */
strcpy((char *)&acl_file_header.acl_text, file_text);
acl_file_header.major_ver = ACL_FILE_MAJ_VER;
acl_file_header.minor_ver = ACL_FILE_MIN_VER;
memcpy( &acl_file_header.mgr_id, &mgr_uuid, sizeof(uuid_t));

/* Make sure we can read and write the file.  If sec_acl_mgr_config_create
 * is set insure that the file does not exist. Also set global flag for the
 * use of radcl_replace()
 */
oflag = O_RDWR;
if (config_info & sec_acl_mgr_config_create)
    {
    oflag = O_WRONLY|O_CREAT|O_EXCL;
    new_db = TRUE;
    }

/* When creating the file set the mode to user read and write */
fd = open((char *) db_name, oflag, S_IRUSR|S_IWUSR );
if (fd == -1)
    {
    *st_p = sec_acl_mgr_file_open_error;
    return;
```

Figure 22.5 The routine "sec_acl_mgr_configure()".

```
close(fd);

/* Don't bother with a real handle, since the server only
        implements one type of acl storage */
*sec_acl_mgr = NULL;

*st_p = error_status_ok;
```

Figure 22.5 *(Continued)*

must agree upon. It could be an object UUID, a numeric index, a text string, or anything else that uniquely identifies the object in question and therefore its ACL. As this ACL manager uses only one ACL, the key is ignored.

The first part of the routine is shown in Fig. 22.6. First, **sec_acl_mgr_lookup()** is called to get the ACL. Although, in theory, **sec_acl_mgr_lookup()** returns a list of ACLs, this routine takes advantage of the fact that there is only one and always uses the first one in the list.

The next part of the code makes a pass through all of the ACL entries, noting the location of entries of certain types. This is because the entries can appear in any order, but the actual checking algorithm requires that entry types be considered in a certain order. This pass also ensures that every entry that identifies a particular principal will not be considered unless it matches the principal in question.

Figure 22.7 shows the remainder of the **sec_acl_mgr_is_authorized()** routine. The code looks complex, but a little study will show that it implements the algorithm described in Chap. 10. Because of the preprocessing step, checking all the entries except for group type entries is straightforward. The variable associated with each entry type either has the value ENTRY_NOT_FOUND or the index of the entry. Note that as soon as an applicable entry is found, the search ends with success or failure.

The processing of group entries is a little more complex, but the basic idea is to loop through all the group type entries and combine all those that apply. If at least one applicable entry is found, then the search ends with success or failure.

If the routine hasn't returned failure somewhere along the way, it finally ends up at the code that processes the unauthenticated mask. If the PAC is unauthenticated, the unauthenticated mask is applied to the permissions.

22.4.3 Source code
for sec_acl_mgr_replace()

This routine is the means by which ACLs are created and modified. The current interface makes the update an atomic operation. The only way to modify an ACL is to call **sec_acl_mgr_lookup()** and then **sec_acl_mgr_replace()**.

```
/* s e c _ a c l _ m g r _ i s _ a u t h o r i z e d
 *
 *  The basic operation in the authorization package, this function will
 *  yield true if the principal (as described in the privilege attribute
 *  certificate referred to by "accessor_info") is authorized to perform
 *  the requested operation.  The dacl controlling this decision is
 *  not passed directly to this function, but is referred to via the
 *  sec_acl_key and the manager_type_p parameters.
 */

boolean32 sec_acl_mgr_is_authorized( sec_acl_mgr_handle_t    sec_acl_mgr,
                                     sec_acl_permset_t       desired_access,
                                     sec_id_pac_t            *accessor_info,
                                     sec_acl_key_t           sec_acl_key,
                                     uuid_t                  *manager_type_p,
                                     sec_id_t                *user_obj,
                                     sec_id_t                *group_obj,
                                     error_status_t          *st_p)
{
sec_acl_list_t      *sec_acl_list;
sec_acl_t           *sec_acl_p;
int                 i;              /* For traversing entry list. */
unsigned int        j;              /* For traversing entry list. */
int                 mask,          /* For keeping track of entries... */
                    user_obj_entry,
                    user_entry,
                    foreign_user_entry,
                    other_obj_entry,
                    foreign_other_entry,
                    any_other_entry,
                    unauth_entry;
sec_id_t            *group_id, *realm_id;
error_status_t      st;
sec_acl_permset_t   mask_perms, granted, group_access;
boolean32           chk_loc_groups = FALSE, one_group_found = FALSE;
boolean32           access = FALSE;     /* Keep running tab on access */

/* Retrieve the sec_acl for this key */

sec_acl_mgr_lookup( sec_acl_mgr,
                    sec_acl_key,
                    manager_type_p,
                    sec_acl_type_object,
                    &sec_acl_list,
                    st_p);
if (*st_p != error_status_ok) return FALSE;

/* At this point, st_p must be error_status_ok, and will remain that
 * unless explicitly set otherwise.  Thus we can return prematurely without
 * having to explicitly set the status.
```

Figure 22.6 The routine "sec_acl_mgr_is_authorized()": part 1.

```
/* Take advantage of the fact that there can only be one ACL */
sec_acl_p = sec_acl_list->sec_acls[0];

/* No masks found to start with */
mask = ENTRY_NOT_FOUND;

/* Only 1 of each type of entry could possibly match this
 *  principal id, so keep a running tab on if/where each
 *  type of entry is found in the list
 */
user_entry = user_obj_entry = foreign_user_entry =
other_obj_entry = foreign_other_entry = unauth_entry = any_other_entry =
    ENTRY_NOT_FOUND;

/* If masks isn't explicitly set, then it should have no effect
    when masking, so turn all perm bits on by default */
mask_perms = MAX_PERMISSIONS;

/* PRE-PROCESS the acl entries so we only have to loop
 * through once looking for specific types of entries
 *
 * Note, the accessor may be a member of multiple {foreign_}groups.
 * Therefore, the *group checks must be done below, in a separate
 * pass through the entry list.
 */
for (i = 0; i < sec_acl_p->num_entries; i++)
    {

    /* Check for existence of each type of entry, and keep track
     * of where each type was found in the entry list.
     * Don't mark type as found if the associated realm id's
     * are not the same
     */
    switch(sec_acl_p->sec_acl_entries[i].entry_info.entry_type)
        {
        case sec_acl_e_type_mask_obj:
            mask = i;
            mask_perms = sec_acl_p->sec_acl_entries[i].perms;
            break;
        case sec_acl_e_type_user_obj:
            if (default_realm_eq(i)) user_obj_entry = i;
            break;
        case sec_acl_e_type_user:
            if ((uuid_equal(&accessor_info->principal.uuid,
&sec_acl_p->sec_acl_entries[i].entry_info.tagged_union.id.uuid,
                        &st)) && (default_realm_eq(i)))
                user_entry = i;
            break;
        case sec_acl_e_type_foreign_user:
```

Figure 22.6 (*Continued*)

```
&sec_acl_p-> sec_acl_entries[i].entry_info.tagged_union.foreign_id.id.uuid,
          &st)) && (foreign_realm_eq(i))) foreign_user_entry = i;
        break;
    case sec_acl_e_type_other_obj:
        if (default_realm_eq(i)) other_obj_entry = i;
        break;
    case sec_acl_e_type_foreign_other:
        if ( uuid_equal( &accessor_info->realm.uuid,
&sec_acl_p->sec_acl_entries[i].entry_info.tagged_union.id.uuid,
                        &st)) foreign_other_entry = i;
        break;
    case sec_acl_e_type_any_other:
        any_other_entry = i;
        break;
    case sec_acl_e_type_unauthenticated:
        unauth_entry = i;
        break;
    default:
        break;
    } /* end switch */
```

Figure 22.6 (*Continued*)

```
/* Now that we know which entries match the user described in the PAC,
 * check the permissions corresponding to each entry until access is
 * granted by one of them.
 */

/* USER_OBJ check */
if (user_obj_entry != ENTRY_NOT_FOUND)
    {

    /* If e_type_user_obj entry exists, then user_obj can't be NULL */
    if (user_obj == NULL)
        {
        *st_p = sec_acl_expected_user_obj;
        return FALSE;
        }

    /* If the id assoc w/ user_obj matches the principal id */
    if (uuid_equal(&accessor_info->principal.uuid, &user_obj->uuid, &st))
        {
        /* then check the permsets to see if access is granted */
        if (access_granted(sec_acl_p->sec_acl_entries[user_obj_entry],
```

Figure 22.7 The routine "sec_acl_mgr_is_authorized()": part 2.

```
              {
              access = TRUE;
              }
              else
              {
              return FALSE;        /* implied denial rights */
              }
          } /* end if uuid_equal */
      } /* end if user_obj_entry */

/* USER check */
if ((! access) && (user_entry != ENTRY_NOT_FOUND))
    {
    /* check the permsets to see if access is granted */
    if (access_granted(sec_acl_p->sec_acl_entries[user_entry],
                     mask_perms, desired_access, &granted))
        {
        access = TRUE;
        }
        else
        {
        return FALSE;              /* implied denial rights */
        }
    }

/* FOREIGN_USER check */
if ((! access) && (foreign_user_entry != ENTRY_NOT_FOUND))
    {
    /* check the permsets to see if access is granted */
    if (access_granted(sec_acl_p->sec_acl_entries[foreign_user_entry],
                     mask_perms, desired_access, &granted))
        {
        access = TRUE;
        }
        else
        {
        return FALSE;              /* implied denial rights */
        }
    }

/* GROUP checks */
group_access = (sec_acl_permset_t) 0;
for (i = 0;((! access) && (i < sec_acl_p->num_entries)); i++)
    {
    switch(sec_acl_p->sec_acl_entries[i].entry_info.entry_type) {
    case sec_acl_e_type_group_obj:
    case sec_acl_e_type_group:
    case sec_acl_e_type_foreign_group:
        if (sec_acl_p->sec_acl_entries[i].entry_info.entry_type
                                == sec_acl_e_type_group_obj)
```

Figure 22.7 (*Continued*)

```
      {  /* If group_obj entry exists then group_obj cant be NULL */
      if (group_obj == NULL)
        {
        *st_p = sec_acl_expected_group_obj;
        return FALSE;
        }
      group_id = group_obj;   /* check against group_obj param */
      realm_id = &sec_acl_p->default_realm;
      chk_loc_groups = default_realm_eq(i);
      }
  else if (sec_acl_p->sec_acl_entries[i].entry_info.entry_type
                                        == sec_acl_e_type_group)
    {
    chk_loc_groups = default_realm_eq(i);
    group_id =
       &sec_acl_p->sec_acl_entries[i].entry_info.tagged_union.id;
          realm_id = &sec_acl_p->default_realm;
    }
  else
    {
    chk_loc_groups = foreign_realm_eq(i);
    group_id = &sec_acl_p->
       sec_acl_entries[i].entry_info.tagged_union.foreign_id.id;
    realm_id = &sec_acl_p->
       sec_acl_entries[i].entry_info.tagged_union.foreign_id.realm;
    }
/* Check either the local groups or the foreign groups */
if (chk_loc_groups)
   { /* CHECK PAC GROUP */
   if (uuid_equal(&accessor_info->group.uuid,
                          &group_id->uuid, &st) )
     {
     one_group_found = TRUE;
               /* then check the perms to see if access is granted */
     if (access_granted(sec_acl_p->sec_acl_entries[i],
        mask_perms, desired_access, &granted))
        {
        access = TRUE;
        }
     else
        {
        group_access = (group_access | granted);
        }
```

Figure 22.7   (*Continued*)

```
          /* CHECK LOCAL GROUPS */
          for (j = 0;
            ((! access) && (j < accessor_info->num_groups)); j++)
              {
            if (uuid_equal(&accessor_info->groups[j].uuid,
               &group_id->uuid, &st) )
                {
               one_group_found = TRUE;
               /* check the perms to see if access granted */
               if (access_granted(sec_acl_p->sec_acl_entries[i],
                  mask_perms, desired_access, &granted))
                   {
                  access = TRUE;
                   }
               else
                   {
                  group_access = (group_access | granted);
                   }
                } /* end if uuid_equal */
              } /* end for */
            } /* end if chk_loc_groups */
        else
            {
          /* CHECK FOREIGN GROUPS */
          for (j = 0;
             (! access) && (j < accessor_info->num_foreign_groups);
             j++)
              {
            if ((uuid_equal( &accessor_info->foreign_groups[j].id.uuid,
               &group_id->uuid, &st))
               && (uuid_equal(&accessor_info->foreign_groups[j].realm.uuid,
                  &realm_id->uuid, &st)) )
                {
               one_group_found = TRUE;
               /* check the perms to see if access granted */
               if (access_granted(sec_acl_p->sec_acl_entries[i],
                  mask_perms, desired_access, &granted))
                   {
                  access = TRUE;
                   }
               else
                   {
                  group_access = (group_access | granted);
                   }
                } /* end if uuid_equal */
              } /* end for */
            } /* end else */
        break;
    default:
        break;
      } /* end switch (entry type) */
```

Figure 22.7   *(Continued)*

```
    /* See if the union of multiple group entries granted access */
    if ((group_access & desired_access) == desired_access) access = TRUE;

    } /* end GROUP check */

/* If at least 1 group found and !access, then deny any access */
if (!access && one_group_found) return FALSE;

/* OTHER_OBJ check */
if ((! access) && (other_obj_entry != ENTRY_NOT_FOUND))
    {
    /* check the permsets to see if access is granted */
    if (access_granted(sec_acl_p->sec_acl_entries[other_obj_entry],
                       mask_perms, desired_access, &granted))
        {
        access = TRUE;
        }
        else
        {
        return FALSE;              /* implied denial rights */
        }
    }

/* FOREIGN_OTHER check */
if ((! access) && (foreign_other_entry != ENTRY_NOT_FOUND))
    {
    /* check the permsets to see if access is granted */
    if (access_granted(sec_acl_p->sec_acl_entries[foreign_other_entry],
                       mask_perms, desired_access, &granted))
        {
        access = TRUE;
        }
        else
        {
        return FALSE;              /* implied denial rights */
        }
    }

/* ANY_OTHER check */
if ((! access) && (any_other_entry != ENTRY_NOT_FOUND))
    {
    /* check the permsets to see if access is granted */
    if (access_granted(sec_acl_p->sec_acl_entries[any_other_entry],
                       mask_perms, desired_access, &granted))
        {
        access = TRUE;
        }
        else
        {
        return FALSE;              /* implied denial rights */
        }
```

Figure 22.7 *(Continued)*

```
/* UNAUTHENTICATED check
* If pac isn't authenticated and access was granted by one of the above
* checks, then desired_access must be masked by unauthenticated entry.
*/
if ((access) && (! accessor_info->authenticated))
    {
    if (unauth_entry == ENTRY_NOT_FOUND)
        {
        access = FALSE;
        }
    else if (! access_granted(sec_acl_p->sec_acl_entries[unauth_entry],
                            mask_perms, desired_access, &granted))
        {
        access = FALSE;
        }
    }

return access;
```

Figure 22.7 (*Continued*)

A side effect of this is that it is perfectly possible for two different processes to create a race condition when modifying an ACL. Fortunately, this is rare in practice. First of all, ACLs usually are not modified very frequently. A particular ACL might be modified once a week or once a day, but certainly not once a minute or once a second. Second, the number of different principals who can modify the same ACL should be small, typically one. This means that there will not be a lot of different users modifying the same ACL.

The basic algorithm of this particular ACL manager copies all the pieces of the ACL into contiguous memory and writes them out into a file. Because, when it is read back in later on by the lookup routine, it will not be at the same memory location; all of the pointers are adjusted to be the offset relative to the beginning of the structure. The routine also performs a few consistency checks on the ACL and returns without writing out the ACL if any error is found.

This scheme of fixing up the pointers is somewhat messy. A future version of DCE will support a feature called *pickled data*. This allows data to be converted locally to the NDR format used to transmit it across the network. This would be a convenient way to handle the ACL. We could let the stub routines pack it and unpack it for us. Another advantage is that the file we wrote out would be portable. If we wanted to move it to another type of computer, the stub routines on that machine would be able to unpack it correctly.

The first part of **sec_acl_mgr_replace()** is shown in Fig. 22.8. The most important input argument is a pointer to an ACL the caller wants written out. As before, the routine assumes that the one and only ACL is the first in the list.

```
/* s e c _ a c l _ m g r _ r e p l a c e
 *
 *   Replace the dacl associated with the key.  This package treats dacls as
 *   immutable objects - the old dacl is thrown away and the new one created
 *   Some implementations of this interface may choose to optimize storage
 *   and share dacl representation for many objects - in which case the real
 *   dacl storage must be reference counted, but that is of no concern to
 *   the consumer of the interface.
 *
 *   This ACL manager implements a single ACL which is stored in a disk file.
 *   The ACL is stored in the file in the same format as in memory except that
 *   the pointers are relocated to be offsets relative to the start of the ACL.
 *   This routine does not check permissions, but rdacl_replace, which calls
 *   it requires that the called have the sec_acl_perm_owner ("c") permission.
 *   Therefore, this routine checks to make sure that at least one entry in the
 *   ACL has the sec_acl_perm_owner permission set.
 */

void sec_acl_mgr_replace( sec_acl_mgr_handle_t    sec_acl_mgr,
                          sec_acl_key_t           sec_acl_key,
                          uuid_t                  *manager_type_p,
                          sec_acl_type_t          sec_acl_type,
                          sec_acl_list_t          *sec_acl_list_p,
                          error_status_t          *st_p)
{
int               index, i, j, num_bytes, fd;
sec_acl_t         *nacl_p, *sec_acl_p;
acl_file_header_t *hdr_p;
sec_acl_entry_t   *new_e, *my_e;
boolean32         seen_c_perm = FALSE,        /* Syntax check flags */
                  seen_user_obj = FALSE,
                  seen_group_obj = FALSE,
                  seen_other_obj = FALSE,
                  seen_any_other = FALSE,
                  seen_mask_obj = FALSE,
                  seen_unauthenticated = FALSE;
char              *acl_buf_p;                 /* Pointer to ACL buffer */
int               buf_size;                   /* Number of bytes in buffer */

/* We know that there's only one acl in the list */
sec_acl_p = sec_acl_list_p->sec_acls[0];

/* This manager does not support container object ACLs. */
if (sec_acl_type != sec_acl_type_object)
    {
    *st_p = sec_acl_not_implemented;
    return;
    }

/* Initialize buffer */
```

Figure 22.8   The routine "sec_acl_mgr_replace()": part 1.

```
/* Set up the file header */
hdr_p = (acl_file_header_t *) BUFFER_ALLOC(sizeof(acl_file_header_t));

memcpy( hdr_p, &acl_file_header, sizeof(acl_file_header_t));

/* Allocate space for the base data structure */
nacl_p = (sec_acl_t *) BUFFER_ALLOC(sizeof(sec_acl_t));


/* Copy the acl information into the new sec_acl */
nacl_p->default_realm.uuid = sec_acl_p->default_realm.uuid;
nacl_p->default_realm.name = (unsigned_char_p_t) BUFFER_ALLOC(
            (strlen((char *) sec_acl_p->default_realm.name)+1) * sizeof(char));
strcpy((char *) nacl_p->default_realm.name,
                (char *) sec_acl_p->default_realm.name);
nacl_p->sec_acl_manager_type = sec_acl_p->sec_acl_manager_type;
nacl_p->num_entries = sec_acl_p->num_entries;

/* Copy the ACL entries into the buffer */
nacl_p->sec_acl_entries = (sec_acl_entry_t *) BUFFER_ALLOC(
                            sec_acl_p->num_entries * sizeof(sec_acl_entry_t));
for (i = 0; i < sec_acl_p->num_entries; i++)
    {
    /* Copy the pointers to the storage entry and the incoming
     * entry, to make this more readable (ie: <= 80 columns)
     */
    my_e = &(nacl_p->sec_acl_entries[i]);
    new_e = &(sec_acl_p->sec_acl_entries[i]);

    /* Copy the permissions and entry type from old to new */
    my_e->perms = new_e->perms;
    my_e->entry_info.entry_type = new_e->entry_info.entry_type;

    /* Make sure entry does not contain unsupported permissions */
    if (my_e->perms & (~SUPPORTED_PERMS))
        {
        *st_p = sec_acl_bad_acl_syntax;
        return;
        }

    /* Check each entry to see if it has the sec_acl_perm_owner permission */
    if (my_e->perms & sec_acl_perm_owner) seen_c_perm = TRUE;

    switch (new_e->entry_info.entry_type)
    {
    case sec_acl_e_type_user:
    case sec_acl_e_type_group:
    case sec_acl_e_type_foreign_other: /* Copy the id's uuid */
        my_e->entry_info.tagged_union.id.uuid =
            new_e->entry_info.tagged_union.id.uuid;
```

Figure 22.8 (*Continued*)

```
      /* Make room for the name, and copy it */
      my_e->entry_info.tagged_union.id.name = (unsigned_char_p_t)
        BUFFER_ALLOC(sizeof(unsigned_char_t) *
        (1 + strlen((char *) new_e->entry_info.tagged_union.id.name)));

      strcpy((char *) my_e->entry_info.tagged_union.id.name,
          (char *) new_e->entry_info.tagged_union.id.name);
          break;

      case sec_acl_e_type_foreign_user:
      case sec_acl_e_type_foreign_group:
          /* Copy the foreign id's uuids */
          my_e->entry_info.tagged_union.foreign_id.id.uuid =
                     new_e->entry_info.tagged_union.foreign_id.id.uuid;
          my_e->entry_info.tagged_union.foreign_id.realm.uuid =
                     new_e->entry_info.tagged_union.foreign_id.realm.uuid;

          /* Make room for the names, and copy them */
          my_e->entry_info.tagged_union.foreign_id.id.name =
              (unsigned_char_p_t) BUFFER_ALLOC(sizeof(unsigned_char_t) *
                  (1 + strlen((char *)
                  new_e->entry_info.tagged_union.foreign_id.id.name)) );
          strcpy( (char *) my_e->entry_info.tagged_union.foreign_id.id.name,
              (char *) new_e->entry_info.tagged_union.foreign_id.id.name );

          my_e->entry_info.tagged_union.foreign_id.realm.name =
              (unsigned_char_p_t) BUFFER_ALLOC(sizeof(unsigned_char_t) *
              (1 + strlen((char *)
              new_e->entry_info.tagged_union.foreign_id.realm.name)) );
          strcpy((char *) my_e->entry_info.tagged_union.foreign_id.realm.name,
              (char *) new_e->entry_info.tagged_union.foreign_id.realm.name);
          break;

      case sec_acl_e_type_extended:
          num_bytes = new_e->entry_info.tagged_union.extended_info->num_bytes;
          my_e->entry_info.tagged_union.extended_info =
              (sec_acl_extend_info_t *) BUFFER_ALLOC(
              sizeof(uuid_t) + sizeof(ndr_format_t) +
              sizeof(unsigned32) + (num_bytes * sizeof(ndr_byte)) );

          my_e->entry_info.tagged_union.extended_info->extension_type =
              new_e->entry_info.tagged_union.extended_info->extension_type;

          my_e->entry_info.tagged_union.extended_info->format_label =
              new_e->entry_info.tagged_union.extended_info->format_label;

          my_e->entry_info.tagged_union.extended_info->num_bytes =
```

Figure 22.8   *(Continued)*

```
        for (j = 0; j < num_bytes; j++)
            my_e->entry_info.tagged_union.extended_info->pickled_data[j] =
            new_e->entry_info.tagged_union.extended_info->pickled_data[j];

        break;

        /* No data associated with these entries.
         * Check that each appears at most once
         */
    case sec_acl_e_type_user_obj:
        CHK_IF_SEEN(seen_user_obj);
        break;
    case sec_acl_e_type_group_obj:
        CHK_IF_SEEN(seen_group_obj);
        break;
    case sec_acl_e_type_other_obj:
        CHK_IF_SEEN(seen_other_obj);
        break;
    case sec_acl_e_type_any_other:
        CHK_IF_SEEN(seen_any_other);
        break;
    case sec_acl_e_type_mask_obj:
        CHK_IF_SEEN(seen_mask_obj);
        break;
    case sec_acl_e_type_unauthenticated:
        CHK_IF_SEEN(seen_unauthenticated);
        break;

    default: break;} /* end switch entry_type */
    } /* end for num_entries */

/* If no entry contains the "c" permission, don't allow the update */
if(!seen_c_perm)
    {
    *st_p = sec_acl_bad_acl_syntax;
    return;
```

Figure 22.8 *(Continued)*

The routine checks to ensure that the ACL is an object ACL rather than one of the container types. Then each of the components is copied into the buffer.

The allocation routine ensures that the pieces will be contiguous. The allocation routine also keeps track of the end of the buffer, so that the amount to write out can be determined. A large fixed-size buffer is used as a simplification. If a dynamic buffer were used, it would be necessary to make a preliminary pass over the ACL to calculate the space needed.

While this is going on, two other checks are performed. Each entry is checked to see if it contains the **c** permission. If none do, the ACL is rejected.

Likewise, the entries that should appear only once are checked. If there are any duplicates, the ACL is rejected.

Figure 22.9 shows the second part of the routine. Every pointer is adjusted so that it represents an offset from the start of the data structure. The order in which the pointers are fixed is chosen so that we adjust pointers only after we are finished using them.

Finally, the buffer is written out in a single operation and the file is closed.

22.4.4 Source code
for sec_acl_mgr_lookup()

This is the routine that reads the ACL out of the file in which it is stored. In principle, it returns a list of pointers to the ACLs. In this case there is just one.

This routine will be called by a server operation thread that is either running some application-defined operation or is executing one of the **rdacl_** routines. For this reason, the ACL is stored in space allocated by **rpc_ss_allocate**(). This means that when the server operation thread completes, the space will automatically be deallocated.

The routine is shown in Fig. 22.10. It begins by opening the file containing the ACL and allocating a buffer big enough to hold it. It then reads it into the buffer and closes the file.

Next it reverses the process performed by **sec_acl_mgr_replace**(). It adjusts each of the pointers, converting them from a relative offset to an absolute memory address. Here again, it is important that the pointers are done in the right order.

The final step is to fix up the list so it points to the ACL and indicates that it has one entry.

22.4.5 Source code
for sec_acl_mgr_get_access()

This routine is similar to **sec_acl_mgr_is_authorized**(), except that instead of deciding if a given set of permissions should be granted, it computes the actual permissions that should be granted. This is intended primarily for use by a program that wants to display the effective permissions for a particular principal.

This routine is shown in Fig. 22.11. The logic is quite similar to that of **sec_acl_mgr_is_authorized**(). First, a preprocessing pass is made to locate the entries of particular types and to eliminate ones that do not apply. Next, each entry type is checked, as described in Chap. 10. The checking of groups is more complicated, because it is necessary to loop through all of the groups and accumulate all of the permissions from any groups that the principal is a member of.

At the very end of the routine the unauthorized mask is applied, if appropriate.

```
/* In preparation for writing out the buffer, relocate all of the pointers
 * to represent the offset from the start of the buffer
 */


for (i = 0; i < sec_acl_p->num_entries; i++)
    {
    /* Use the same trick as before */
    my_e = &(nacl_p->sec_acl_entries[i]);
    switch (my_e->entry_info.entry_type)
        {
        case sec_acl_e_type_user:
        case sec_acl_e_type_group:
        case sec_acl_e_type_foreign_other:
            PtrToOfs (EITU(id.name), (char *) nacl_p);
            break;

        case sec_acl_e_type_foreign_user:
        case sec_acl_e_type_foreign_group:
            PtrToOfs (EITU(foreign_id.id.name), (char *) nacl_p);
            PtrToOfs (EITU(foreign_id.realm.name), (char *) nacl_p);
            break;

        case sec_acl_e_type_extended:
            PtrToOfs (EITU(extended_info), (char *) nacl_p);
            break;
        } /* end switch entry type */
    } /* end for num entries */
PtrToOfs ((char **) &nacl_p->default_realm.name, (char *) nacl_p);
PtrToOfs ((char **) &nacl_p->sec_acl_entries, (char *) nacl_p);

/* Now write out the buffer */
fd = open((char *) acl_file_name, O_WRONLY);

if (fd == -1)
    {
    *st_p = sec_acl_mgr_file_open_error;
    return;
    }

if (write(fd, acl_buf_p, buf_size) == -1)
    {
    *st_p = sec_acl_mgr_file_io_error;
    close(fd);
    return;
    }

close(fd);

*st_p = error_status_ok;

}
```

Figure 22.9 The routine "sec_acl_mgr_replace()": part 2.

```
/* s e c _ a c l _ m g r _ l o o k u p
 *
 *   Extract the dacl associated with the key.
 *   In this version there is only one ACL so the key is ignored.
 */
void sec_acl_mgr_lookup( sec_acl_mgr_handle_t    sec_acl_mgr,
                         sec_acl_key_t           sec_acl_key,
                         uuid_t                  *manager_type_p,
                         sec_acl_type_t          sec_acl_type,
                         sec_acl_list_t          **sec_acl_list_p,
                         error_status_t          *st_p)
{
int             i, fd, sts;
struct stat     st_buf;
char            *acl_buf_p;    /* Pointer to ACL buffer */
int             buf_size;      /* Number of bytes in buffer */
sec_acl_t       *nacl_p;
sec_acl_entry_t *my_e;
acl_file_header_t *hdr_p;
error_status_t  st;

/* Allocate the ACL list.
 * NOTE: this use of sizeof depends on the fact that only 1 ACL is returned
 */
*sec_acl_list_p = (sec_acl_list_t *)
   rpc_ss_allocate((idl_size_t)sizeof(sec_acl_list_t));

/* Read in the ACL */
fd = open((char *) acl_file_name, O_RDONLY);
if (fd == -1)
    {
    *st_p = sec_acl_mgr_file_open_error;
    return;
    }

sts = fstat(fd, &st_buf);
if (sts  == -1)
    {
    *st_p = sec_acl_mgr_file_io_error;
    close(fd);
    return;
    }

/* If the file is zero length, return a NULL pointer */
if (st_buf.st_size == 0)
    {
    (*sec_acl_list_p)->num_acls = 1;
    (*sec_acl_list_p)->sec_acls[0] = NULL;
    *st_p = sec_acl_no_acl_found;
    close(fd);
    return;
    }
```

Figure 22.10 The routine "sec_acl_mgr_lookup()".

```
/* Use rpc_ss_allocate so the stub will deallocate it for us */
acl_buf_p = (char *) rpc_ss_allocate(st_buf.st_size);

buf_size = read(fd, acl_buf_p, st_buf.st_size);
if (buf_size  == -1)
    {
    *st_p = sec_acl_mgr_file_io_error;
    close(fd);
    return;
    }

close(fd);

/* Check to be sure that this is a valid ACL file and that we know how to
 * interpret it. The constant text string must match, the manager uuid must be
 * the same as ours and the major version must match.  A minor version number
 * change indicates a compatible change, so it is not checked.
 */
hdr_p = (acl_file_header_t *) acl_buf_p;

if ((strcmp( (char *)&hdr_p->acl_text, (char *)&acl_file_header.acl_text)
    != 0) ||
    (!uuid_equal( &hdr_p->mgr_id, &acl_file_header.mgr_id, &st)) ||
    ( hdr_p->major_ver != acl_file_header.major_ver) )
    {
    *st_p = sec_acl_bad_acl_syntax;
    return;
    }


/* The pointers stored in the file are all relative to start of the structure
relocate them to reflect their current location in memory.
*/

nacl_p = (sec_acl_t *) (sizeof (acl_file_header_t));
OfsToPtr ((char **) &nacl_p, (char *) acl_buf_p);
OfsToPtr ((char **) &nacl_p->default_realm.name, (char *) nacl_p);
OfsToPtr ((char **) &nacl_p->sec_acl_entries, (char *) nacl_p);

for (i = 0; i < nacl_p->num_entries; i++)
    {
    /* Use the same trick as before */
    my_e = &(nacl_p->sec_acl_entries[i]);

    switch (my_e->entry_info.entry_type)
        {
        case sec_acl_e_type_user:
        case sec_acl_e_type_group:
        case sec_acl_e_type_foreign_other:
            OfsToPtr (EITU (id.name), (char *) nacl_p);
```

Figure 22.10 *(Continued)*

```
        case sec_acl_e_type_foreign_user:
        case sec_acl_e_type_foreign_group:
            OfsToPtr (EITU (foreign_id.id.name), (char *) nacl_p);
            OfsToPtr (EITU (foreign_id.realm.name), (char *) nacl_p);
            break;

        case sec_acl_e_type_extended:
            OfsToPtr (EITU (extended_info), (char *) nacl_p);
            break;
        } /* end switch entry type */
    } /* end for num entries */

/* Return the results */

(*sec_acl_list_p) -> num_acls = 1;
(*sec_acl_list_p) -> sec_acls[0] = nacl_p;

*st_p = error_status_ok;
```

Figure 22.10   *(Continued)*

```
/*  s e c _ a c l _ m g r _ g e t _ a c c e s s
 *
 * Look through all the ACL entries and gather up all the permissions that
 * can be granted to the client.  Return this list of effective permissions.
 *
 * NOTE: This implementation of sec_acl_mgr_get_access implements
 * GROUP_OBJ and EXTENDED types *only* to provide a complete reference.
 * These types are not used by this sec_acl manager.  A real sec_acl_mgr
 * implementation should return the error sec_acl_invalid_entry_type,
 * for any one of these types passed in, that is not supported by the mgr.
 * (ie: if there's no user or group owner stored with an object, then
 *  it does not make sense to support user_obj and group_obj types)
 */

void sec_acl_mgr_get_access( sec_acl_mgr_handle_t    sec_acl_mgr,
                             sec_id_pac_t            *accessor_info,
                             sec_acl_key_t           sec_acl_key,
                             uuid_t                  *manager_type_p,
                             sec_id_t                *user_obj,
                             sec_id_t                *group_obj,
                             sec_acl_permset_t       *net_rights,
                             error_status_t          *st_p )
{
sec_acl_list_t      *sec_acl_list;              /* list of object acls */
```

Figure 22.11   The routine "sec_acl_mgr_get_access()".

```
int               i;              /* For traversing entry list. */
int               j;

error_status_t    st;

int               user_entry, user_obj_entry, foreign_user_entry;
int               other_obj_entry, foreign_other_entry, any_other_entry;

sec_acl_permset_t mask_obj_perms;
sec_acl_permset_t unauthenticated_perms;


boolean32         match = FALSE;   /* set when match ACL entry is found */

sec_id_t          *group_id, *realm_id;
boolean32         chk_loc_groups = FALSE;

/* Assume this principal has no permissions until proven otherwise */
*net_rights = NO_PERMISSIONS;

/* Retrieve the sec_acl for this key */

sec_acl_mgr_lookup( sec_acl_mgr,
                    sec_acl_key,
                    manager_type_p,
                    sec_acl_type_object,
                    &sec_acl_list,
                    st_p);
if (st_p != error_status_ok) return;

/* At this point, st_p must be error_status_ok, and will remain that
 * unless explicitly set otherwise.  Thus we can return prematurely without
 * having to explicitly set the status.
 */

/* Take advantage of the fact that there can only be one ACL */
sec_acl_p = sec_acl_list->sec_acls[0];

/* Have not seen any ACL entries yet */
user_entry = user_obj_entry = foreign_user_entry =
other_obj_entry = foreign_other_entry = any_other_entry =
    ENTRY_NOT_FOUND;

/* If masks aren't explicitly set, then it should have no effect
 * when masking, so turn all perm bits on by default
 */
mask_obj_perms = MAX_PERMISSIONS;
```

Figure 22.11   (*Continued*)

```
/* PRE-PROCESS the ACL entries so we only have to loop
 * through once looking for specific types of entries
 *
 * Only 1 of each type of entry could possibly match this
 *  principal id, so keep a running tab on if/where each
 *  type of entry is found in the list
 *
 * Note, the accessor may be a member of multiple {foreign_}groups.
 * Therefore, the *group checks must be done below, in a separate
 * pass through the entry list.
 */
for (i = 0; i < sec_acl_p->num_entries; i++)
    {

    /* Check for existence of each type of entry, and keep track
     * of where each type was found in the entry list.
     * Don't mark type as found if the associated realm id's
     * are not the same
     */
    switch(sec_acl_p->sec_acl_entries[i].entry_info.entry_type)
        {
        case sec_acl_e_type_mask_obj:
            mask_obj_perms = sec_acl_p->sec_acl_entries[i].perms;
            break;
        case sec_acl_e_type_user_obj:
            if (default_realm_eq(i)) user_obj_entry = i;
            break;
            case sec_acl_e_type_user:
                if ((uuid_equal(&accessor_info->principal.uuid,
&sec_acl_p->sec_acl_entries[i].entry_info.tagged_union.id.uuid,
                        &st)) && (default_realm_eq(i)))
                    user_entry = i;
            break;
        case sec_acl_e_type_foreign_user:
            if ((uuid_equal(&accessor_info->principal.uuid,
&sec_acl_p->sec_acl_entries[i].entry_info.tagged_union.foreign_id.id.uuid,
                        &st)) && (foreign_realm_eq(i)))
                foreign_user_entry = i;
            break;
        case sec_acl_e_type_other_obj:
            if (default_realm_eq(i)) other_obj_entry = i;
            break;
        case sec_acl_e_type_foreign_other:
            if ( uuid_equal( &accessor_info->realm.uuid,
&sec_acl_p->sec_acl_entries[i].entry_info.tagged_union.id.uuid,
                        &st)) foreign_other_entry = i;
```

Figure 22.11 *(Continued)*

```
                break;
          case sec_acl_e_type_any_other:
                any_other_entry = i;
                break;
          case sec_acl_e_type_unauthenticated:
                unauthenticated_perms = sec_acl_p->sec_acl_entries[i].perms;
                break;
          default:
                break;
          } /* end switch */
      } /* end for */

/* Now that we know which entries match the user described in the PAC,
 * check the permissions corresponding to each entry until access is
 * granted by one of them.
 */

/* USER_OBJ check */
if (user_obj_entry != ENTRY_NOT_FOUND)
      {

      /* If e_type_user_obj entry exists, then user_obj can't be NULL */
      if (user_obj == NULL)
          {
          *st_p = sec_acl_expected_user_obj;
          return;
          }

      /* If the id assoc w/ user_obj matches the principal id */
      if (uuid_equal(&accessor_info->principal.uuid, &user_obj->uuid, &st))
          {

          match = TRUE;
          *net_rights = sec_acl_p->sec_acl_entries[user_obj_entry].perms;
          }
      } /* end if user_obj_entry */

/* USER check */
if ((! match) && (user_entry != ENTRY_NOT_FOUND))
      {
      /* get the permsets */
      match = TRUE;
      *net_rights =
        sec_acl_p->sec_acl_entries[user_entry].perms & mask_obj_perms;
      }

/* FOREIGN_USER check */
if ((! match) && (foreign_user_entry != ENTRY_NOT_FOUND))
      {
```

Figure 22.11 (*Continued*)

```
        match = TRUE;
        *net_rights = sec_acl_p->sec_acl_entries[foreign_user_entry].perms
                    & mask_obj_perms;
        }

/* GROUP checks */
if (! match)
    {
    for (i = 0; i < sec_acl_p->num_entries; i++)
        {
        switch(sec_acl_p->sec_acl_entries[i].entry_info.entry_type)
            {
            case sec_acl_e_type_group_obj:
            case sec_acl_e_type_group:
            case sec_acl_e_type_foreign_group:
                if ((sec_acl_p->sec_acl_entries[i].entry_info.entry_type
                     == sec_acl_e_type_group_obj) && (group_obj != NULL))
                    {
                    /* check against group_obj param */
                    group_id = group_obj;
                    realm_id = &sec_acl_p->default_realm;
                    chk_loc_groups = default_realm_eq(i);
                    }
                else if (sec_acl_p->sec_acl_entries[i].entry_info.entry_type
                                                == sec_acl_e_type_group)
                    {
                    chk_loc_groups = default_realm_eq(i);
                    group_id =
                    &sec_acl_p->sec_acl_entries[i].entry_info.tagged_union.id;
                    realm_id = &sec_acl_p->default_realm;
                    }
                else
                    {
                    chk_loc_groups = foreign_realm_eq(i);
                    group_id =
&sec_acl_p->sec_acl_entries[i].entry_info.tagged_union.foreign_id.id;
                    realm_id =
&sec_acl_p->sec_acl_entries[i].entry_info.tagged_union.foreign_id.realm;
                    }
                    /* Check either the local groups or the foreign groups */
                if (chk_loc_groups)
                    {
                    /* CHECK PAC GROUP */
                if (uuid_equal(&accessor_info->group.uuid,&group_id->uuid,&st))
                        {
                        /* get the perms associated with this ACL entry */
                        match = TRUE;
                        *net_rights |= sec_acl_p->sec_acl_entries[i].perms;
```

Figure 22.11 *(Continued)*

```
                        /* CHECK LOCAL GROUPS */
                        for (j = 0; j < (int) accessor_info->num_groups; j++)
                            {
                            if (uuid_equal(&accessor_info->groups[j].uuid,
                                           &group_id->uuid, &st) )
                                {
                             /* get the perms associated with this group entry */
                                match = TRUE;
                                *net_rights |= sec_acl_p->sec_acl_entries[i].perms;
                                }
                            } /* end for j */
                        } /* end if check_loc */
                    else
                        {
                        /* CHECK FOREIGN GROUPS */
                        for (j = 0; j <(int) accessor_info->num_foreign_groups;
                                 j++)
                            {
                            if ((uuid_equal(
                                 &accessor_info->foreign_groups[j].id.uuid,
                                 &group_id->uuid, &st))
                            && (uuid_equal(
                                 &accessor_info->foreign_groups[j].realm.uuid,
                                 &realm_id->uuid, &st)) )
                                {
                                /* check the perms to see if access granted */
                                match = TRUE;
                                *net_rights |= sec_acl_p->sec_acl_entries[i].perms;
                                } /* end if uuid_equal */
                            } /* end for j */
                        } /* end else */
                    break;
                default:
                    break;
                } /* switch (entry type) */
            } /* end for i */
        *net_rights &= mask_obj_perms;      /* group permissions are masked */
        } /* end if !match */

/* OTHER_OBJ check */
if ((! match) && (other_obj_entry != ENTRY_NOT_FOUND))
    {
    /* get the permsets */
    match = TRUE;
    *net_rights = sec_acl_p->sec_acl_entries[other_obj_entry].perms;
```

Figure 22.11 (*Continued*)

```
/* FOREIGN_OTHER check */
if ((! match) && (foreign_other_entry != ENTRY_NOT_FOUND))
    {
    /* get the permsets */
    match = TRUE;
    *net_rights = sec_acl_p->sec_acl_entries[foreign_other_entry].perms
                & mask_obj_perms;
    }

/* ANY_OTHER check */
if ((! match) && (any_other_entry != ENTRY_NOT_FOUND))
    {
    /* get the permsets to see if access is granted */
    match = TRUE;
    *net_rights = sec_acl_p->sec_acl_entries[any_other_entry].perms
                & mask_obj_perms;
    }

/* UNAUTHENTICATED check
 * If pac isn't authenticated and access was granted by one of the above
 * checks, then desired_access must be masked by unauthenticated entry.
 */
if (!accessor_info-> authenticated)
    *net_rights = *net_rights & unauthenticated_perms;

return;
```

Figure 22.11 (*Continued*)

22.4.6 Source code for rdacl_lookup()

Most of the routines that make up the **rdaclif** interface are implemented partially or completely by calling one or more of the **sec_acl_mgr_**routines. As can be seen in Fig. 22.12, **rdacl_lookup()** simply calls **sec_acl_mgr_lookup()** to do the work.

22.4.7 Source code for rdacl_replace()

Figure 22.13 shows **rdacl_replace()**. It begins by checking the caller's security credentials. Then it calls **sec_acl_mgr_is_authorized()** to ensure that the caller has the "c" permission (**sec_acl_perm_owner**).

Finally, it calls **sec_acl_mgr_replace()** to do the work.

22.4.8 Source code for rdacl_test_access()

This routine is shown in Fig. 22.14. First it determines that the correct manager UUID has been specified. Then it uses the handle to obtain the caller's PAC. Finally, it calls **sec_acl_mgr_is_authorized()** to do the actual work.

```
/*  r d a c l _ l o o k u p
 *
 *  retrieve an acl associated with the object referred to in the handle
 *  parameter.  The component_name argument is used to further identify
 *  the entity being protected by the sec_acl.
 *
 *  Comparable to POSIX acl_read()
 */

void rdacl_lookup( handle_t                    h,
                   sec_acl_component_name_t    component_name,
                   uuid_t                      *manager_type_p,
                   sec_acl_type_t              sec_acl_type,
                   sec_acl_result_t            *sec_acl_result_p)
{
error_status_t  st;

sec_acl_mgr_lookup(sec_acl_mgr, (sec_acl_key_t) component_name,
                   manager_type_p, sec_acl_type,
                   &sec_acl_result_p->tagged_union.sec_acl_list, &st);

sec_acl_result_p->st = st;
```

Figure 22.12 The routine "rdacl_lookup()".

```
/*  r d a c l _ r e p l a c e
 *
 * Replace the acl associated with the object referred to in the handle.
 * ACLs are immutable, the replace operation takes the new acl and throws
 * away the old acl associated with the object.  The component_name
 * argument is used to further identify the entity being protected by the
 * acl.
 *
 * Comparable to POSIX acl_write()
 */

void rdacl_replace( handle_t                    h,
                    sec_acl_component_name_t    component_name,
                    uuid_t                      *manager_type_p,
                    sec_acl_type_t              sec_acl_type,
                    sec_acl_list_t              *sec_acl_list_p,
                    error_status_t              *st_p)
{
unsigned_char_t *server_name;
sec_id_pac_t *pac;
unsigned32 protect_level, authn_svc, authz_svc;
```

Figure 22.13 The routine "rdacl_replace()".

```
if (new_db)              /* If creating a new ACL db don't check permissions */
    {
    new_db = FALSE;      /* One shot only */
    }
else
    {
    rpc_binding_inq_auth_client( h,
                                 (rpc_authz_handle_t) &pac,
                                 &server_name,
                                 &protect_level,
                                 &authn_svc,
                                 &authz_svc,
                                 st_p);
    if (*st_p != rpc_s_ok) return;

    rpc_string_free(&server_name, st_p);

    if ((authn_svc !=
        rpc_c_authn_dce_secret) || (authz_svc != rpc_c_authz_dce))
        {
        *st_p = sec_acl_not_authorized;
        return;
        }

    if (!sec_acl_mgr_is_authorized( sec_acl_mgr,
                                    sec_acl_perm_owner,
                                    pac,
                                    NULL,
                                    manager_type_p,
                                    user_obj,
                                    group_obj,
                                    st_p) )
        {
        *st_p = sec_acl_not_authorized;
        return;
        }
    }      /* End else */

sec_acl_mgr_replace( sec_acl_mgr,
                     (sec_acl_key_t) component_name,
                     manager_type_p,
                     sec_acl_type,
                     sec_acl_list_p,
                     st_p);
}
```

Figure 22.13   (*Continued*)

```
/* r d a c l _ t e s t _ a c c e s s
 *
 * Determine if the caller has the requested access.
 */

boolean32 rdacl_test_access( handle_t                    h,
                             sec_acl_component_name_t    component_name,
                             uuid_t
*manager_type_p,
                             sec_acl_permset_t
desired_permset,
                             error_status_t              *st_p)
{
error_status_t        st;
rpc_authz_handle_t    privs;
unsigned_char_p_t     server_princ_name;
unsigned32            authn_level;
unsigned32            authn_svc;
unsigned32            authz_svc;

if (! uuid_equal(&mgr_uuid, manager_type_p, &st))
    {
    *st_p = sec_acl_unknown_manager_type;
    return FALSE;
    }
    else
    {
    *st_p = error_status_ok;
    }

/* inquire the runtime as to who called us */
rpc_binding_inq_auth_client(h, &privs, &server_princ_name, &authn_level,
                        &authn_svc, &authz_svc, st_p);
if (st_p != error_status_ok) return FALSE;

/* Must use DCE authorization */
if (authz_svc != rpc_c_authz_dce) return FALSE;

return(sec_acl_mgr_is_authorized( sec_acl_mgr,
                                  desired_permset,
                                  (sec_id_pac_t *) privs,
                                  (sec_acl_key_t) component_name,
                                  manager_type_p,
                                  user_obj,
```

Figure 22.14 The routine "rdacl_test_access()".

22.4.9   Source code
for rdacl_test_access_on_behalf()

Figure 22.15 shows this routine. It is very similar to the previous one. The only difference is that it calls **sec_acl_mgr_is_authorized**() twice, first with the caller's PAC and then with the PAC that was provided as an argument. Only if both tests succeed does the routine return **TRUE**.

22.4.10   Source code
for rdacl_get_manager_types()

This routine and the next one return information about the types of managers implemented. They are intended primarily to allow browsing programs to display this information. This routine is shown in Fig. 22.16. This sample returns hard-coded values.

22.4.11   Source code
for rdacl_get_manager_types_semantics()

This routine is intended to eventually obsolete the previous one. As can be seen in Fig. 22.17, it returns the same information as **rdacl_get_manager_types**(). In addition, it indicates what POSIX semantics are supported.

Once again, this sample returns hard-coded values.

22.4.12   Source code
for rdacl_get_printstring()

This routine, shown in Fig. 22.18, returns information useful for displaying the ACL. The information includes the name and helpstring for the server, permissions supported, and the strings used to represent them. This sample returns hard-coded values.

22.4.13   Source code
for rdacl_get_referral()

Figure 22.19 shows this routine. It is intended for implementations that support replicated ACL managers, some of which are read-only; the routine allows a caller to locate a manager that is not read-only.

As this sample ACL manager does not support any kind of replication, this operation is not implemented.

22.4.14   Source code for rdacl_get_access()

This routine is analogous to **rdacl_test_access**(). It is shown in Fig. 22.20. It first ensures that the proper manager type was called. Next, it uses the handle to obtain the caller's PAC. Finally, it calls **sec_acl_mgr_get_access**() to do the work.

```
/* r d a c l _ t e s t _ a c c e s s _ o n _ b e h a l f
 *
 * Determine if the subject has the requested access.  This function
 * returns true if the access is available to both the caller and
 * the subject identified in the call
 */

boolean32 rdacl_test_access_on_behalf(
    handle_t                h,
    sec_acl_component_name_t  component_name,
    uuid_t                  *manager_type_p,
    sec_id_pac_t            *subject_p,
    sec_acl_permset_t       desired_permset,
    error_status_t          *st_p)
{
error_status_t      st;
rpc_authz_handle_t  privs;
unsigned_char_p_t   server_princ_name;
unsigned32          authn_level;
unsigned32          authn_svc;
unsigned32          authz_svc;

if (! uuid_equal(&mgr_uuid, manager_type_p, &st))
    {
    *st_p = sec_acl_unknown_manager_type;
    return FALSE;
    }
    else
    {
    *st_p = error_status_ok;
    }

/* inquire the runtime as to who called us */
rpc_binding_inq_auth_client(h, &privs, &server_princ_name, &authn_level,
                            &authn_svc, &authz_svc, st_p);

/* Must use DCE authorization */
if (authz_svc != rpc_c_authz_dce) return FALSE;

return( (sec_acl_mgr_is_authorized( sec_acl_mgr,
                                    desired_permset,
                                    (sec_id_pac_t *) privs,
                                    (sec_acl_key_t) component_name,
                                    manager_type_p,
                                    user_obj,
                                    group_obj,
                                    st_p))
        &&
        (sec_acl_mgr_is_authorized( sec_acl_mgr,
                                    desired_permset,
                                    (sec_id_pac_t *) subject_p,
                                    (sec_acl_key_t) component_name,
                                    manager_type_p,
                                    user_obj,
                                    group_obj,
                                    st_p)) );
```

Figure 22.15 The routine "rdacl_test_access_on_behalf()".

```
/* r d a c l _ g e t _ m a n a g e r _ t y p e s
 *
 * Determine the types of acls protecting an object.  ACL editors/browsers
 * use this operation to determine the acl manager types that a particular
 * reference monitor is using to protect a selected entity.
 */

/* In this version, there is 1 manager type and it has been hardcoded.
 */

void rdacl_get_manager_types( handle_t                 h,
                              sec_acl_component_name_t component_name,
                              sec_acl_type_t           acl_type,
                              unsigned32               size_avail,
                              unsigned32               *size_used_p,
                              unsigned32               *num_types_p,
                              uuid_t                   *manager_types,
                              error_status_t           *st_p)
{

*num_types_p = 1;

if (size_avail < 1)
    {
    *size_used_p = 0;
    }
    else
    {
    *size_used_p = 1;
    *manager_types = mgr_uuid;
    }

*st_p = error_status_ok;
```

Figure 22.16 The routine "rdacl_get_manager_types()".

```
/* r d a c l _ g e t _ m g r _ t y p e s _ s e m a n t i c s
 *
 * Determine the types of acls protecting an object.  ACL editors/browsers
 * use this operation to determine the acl manager types that a particular
 * reference monitor is using to protect a selected entity.
 */
/* In this version, there is 1 manager type and it has been hardcoded.
 */

void rdacl_get_mgr_types_semantics(
    handle_t                    h,
    sec_acl_component_name_t    component_name,
    sec_acl_type_t              acl_type,
    unsigned32                  size_avail,
    unsigned32                  *size_used_p,
    unsigned32                  *num_types_p,
    uuid_t                      manager_types[],
    sec_acl_posix_semantics_t   posix_semantics[],
    error_status_t              *st_p)
{
*num_types_p = 1;

if (size_avail < 1)
    {
    *size_used_p = 0;
    }
    else
    {
    *size_used_p = 1;
    manager_types[0]    = mgr_uuid;
    posix_semantics[0] = sec_acl_posix_mask_obj;
    }

*st_p = error_status_ok;
}
```

Figure 22.17 The routine "rdacl_get_manager_types_semantics()".

```
/*   r d a c l _ g e t _ p r i n t s t r i n g
 *
 *   Retrieve printable representations for each permission bit that
 *   the acl manager will support.  There may be aliases for common
 *   permission combinations - by convention simple entries should appear
 *   at the beginning of the array, and combinations should appear at the
 *   end.  When false the tokenize flag indicates that permission
 *   printstrings are unambiguous and therefore printstrings for various
 *   permissions can be concatenated.  When true, however,  this property
 *   does not hold and the strings should be tokenized before input or output.
 */


void rdacl_get_printstring(
    handle_t                h,
    uuid_t                  *manager_type_p,
    unsigned32              size_avail,
    uuid_t                  *manager_type_chain,
    sec_acl_printstring_t   *manager_info,
    boolean32               *tokenize_p,
    unsigned32              *total_num_printstrings_p,
    unsigned32              *size_used_p,
    sec_acl_printstring_t   printstrings[],
    error_status_t          *st_p)
{
error_status_t  st;
int             i;

*total_num_printstrings_p = NUM_PSTRS;
*size_used_p = (size_avail < NUM_PSTRS) ? size_avail : NUM_PSTRS;
*manager_info = hardcoded_manager_info;
uuid_create_nil(manager_type_chain, &st);

if (! uuid_equal(&mgr_uuid, manager_type_p, &st))
    {
    *st_p = sec_acl_unknown_manager_type;
    }
    else
    {
    *st_p = error_status_ok;
    *tokenize_p = FALSE;
    for (i = 0; i < *size_used_p; i++)
        printstrings[i] = hardcoded_printstrings[i];
    }
```

Figure 22.18 The routine "rdacl_get_printstring()".

```
/*  r d a c l _ g e t _ r e f e r r a l
 *
 * Obtain a referral to an acl update site.  This function is used when
 * the current acl site yields a sec_acl_site_readonly error.  Some
 * replication managers will require all updates for a given object to
 * be directed to a given replica.  Clients of the generic acl interface
 * may know they are dealing with an object that is replicated in this way.
 * This function allows them to recover from this problem and rebind to
 * the proper update site.
 */


void rdacl_get_referral( handle_t                    h,
                         sec_acl_component_name_t    component_name,
                         uuid_t                      *manager_type_p,
                         sec_acl_type_t              sec_acl_type,
                         sec_acl_tower_set_t         *towers_p,
                         error_status_t              *st_p)
{

*st_p = sec_acl_not_implemented;

}
```

Figure 22.19 The routine "rdacl_get_referral()".

```
/*  r d a c l _ g e t _ a c c e s s
 *
 *  Determine the caller's access to the specified object.  This is
 *  useful for implementing operations like the conventional UNIX access
 *  function.
 */
void rdacl_get_access( handle_t                    h,
                       sec_acl_component_name_t    component_name,
                       uuid_t                      *manager_type,
                       sec_acl_permset_t           *net_rights,
                       error_status_t              *st_p)
{

    error_status_t        st;

    rpc_authz_handle_t    privs;
    unsigned_char_p_t     server_princ_name;
    unsigned32            authn_level;
    unsigned32            authn_svc;
    unsigned32            authz_svc;
```

Figure 22.20 The routine "rdacl_get_access()".

```
    *net_rights = NULL;

if (! uuid_equal(&mgr_uuid, manager_type, &st))
    {
    *st_p = sec_acl_unknown_manager_type;
    return;
    }
    else
    {
    *st_p = error_status_ok;
    }

/* inquire the runtime as to who called us */
rpc_binding_inq_auth_client(h, &privs, &server_princ_name, &authn_level,
                            &authn_svc, &authz_svc, st_p);
if (st_p != error_status_ok) return;

/* Must use DCE authorization */
if (authz_svc != rpc_c_authz_dce) return;

sec_acl_mgr_get_access ( sec_acl_mgr,
                         (sec_id_pac_t *) privs,
                         (sec_acl_key_t) component_name,
                         manager_type,
                         user_obj,
                         group_obj,
                         net_rights,
                         st_p );
```

Figure 22.20   *(Continued)*

22.5   Chapter Summary

This chapter describes a sample ACL manager that can be used as the basis for building your own. It manages a single ACL that supports six permissions. The ACL manager writes the ACL whenever it is changed and reads it back whenever it is used.

Any ACL manager must support two sets of interfaces. One set of routines, which begins with **sec_acl_mgr_**, is intended to be called locally within the server. The other set of routines includes operations on the **rdaclif** interface, and all begin with **rdacl_**. They are accessed via remote procedure call. Generally, the **rdacl_** routines are implemented by calling the **sec_acl_mgr_** routines.

Although some of the ACL manager code appears quite complex, it can be understood with a little study. Two things are key to understanding it. The first is to grasp the data structure that represents an ACL. The second is to review the ACL-checking algorithm, which is presented in Chap. 10.

23

Future Challenges

This book is intended for those who wish to build "industrial strength" distributed systems. The increasing availability of the ingredients of affordable distributed systems over the last decade—LANs, internetworks, PCs, RISC computers—has given us a vision of what is possible. The tools and techniques described in this book are intended as another element in making it happen.

In spite of the advances, many more challenges lie ahead. It will be necessary for every organization to translate the generic capabilities available in DCE and other technologies into specific solutions that meet their needs. The use of DCE will also give rise to new operational issues that must be addressed before large-scale distributed systems can become practical. New tools are entering the market, based on the distributed object paradigm. This approach promises enormous benefits in the development of distributed systems. Because of the immaturity of this field, however, many questions remain unanswered.

This chapter discusses some of these important issues that will confront distributed system developers in the immediate and longer-term future. There are no simple roadmaps laying out resolution of these issues, but this chapter presents some practical suggestions about how to proceed.

23.1 Interaction Analysis

In the past, development of distributed systems was limited by the scarcity of tools available. In most situations there were few technologies (and few options associated with them) from which to choose. The design problem devolved to finding some way to meet the minimum requirements of an application with the limited capabilities available.

As more complex and sophisticated technologies such as DCE become widely available, the range of choices increases. We can confidently expect that technology will be at hand to meet most, if not all, of our needs. This creates new dilemmas, however. The range of choices seems bewildering. How does one decide whether to use DCE, X.400, APPC, OSI, ORB, X.25, NetWare, MQI, ONC, ATM, TxRPC, or SQL, to name just a few of the options?

In such a situation it is common for individuals to fall back on semireligious beliefs (e.g., connectionless is better, RPC is better). Usually this results in trying to apply the technology one is most familiar with to every new problem. This is only natural and has some merits. If two approaches both will provide an adequate solution, using what is familiar can lower the overall risk of a project.

A better approach is to try to separate out and focus on the essential properties an application requires from distributed system technology, apart from all the possible capabilities distributed system technology offers. Most vendor products address a combination, bound together. Database management system vendors, for example, bury remote procedure call mechanisms within their product. By analyzing the interactions between an application and the required distributed system technology support it will require, the system designer will be better guided in selecting both technology and product, and in choosing which of their features to make use of.

In the past, technology limitations made it impossible to hide the existence and specific characteristics of network configuration from distributed applications. Limitations in interoperability, naming, security, data formats, and a hundred other factors have made most distributed applications a fragile patchwork. Any change to the environment threatened to collapse the whole house of cards. Because of this, for a decade or more, theorists and practitioners have sought technology that would render all the characteristics of the network transparent. Making distributed systems look like nondistributed systems was the goal.

Now that technologies like DCE are beginning to make this goal attainable, it becomes clear that transparency is not desirable in every case. In some situations it is desirable for applications to exercise some control over the characteristics of the services available to them. If I print a memo, I want it to come out on the printer down the hall, not on the other side of the planet. If a bank transfers $100 million via an interbank network, it is more important that it not be lost or altered than that it arrive 10 milliseconds faster.

With analysis of the interactions taking place in distributed applications, it is possible to look past the details of particular products and technologies and understand the distributed properties that are important. This will help the system designer both in selecting and in applying new technology. It will also help vendors to understand the capabilities their products must provide.

A few properties of different kinds of distributed system applications that require the designer's attention in this regard are reviewed below. Some represent engineering compromises. If unlimited network and processing bandwidth were available at little or no cost, one option would always be preferable. For example, if transactional semantics were free, we would do everything in a transaction. In a sense, this particular consideration may be seen as temporary. Universal availability of unlimited communications bandwidth, however, is not likely to happen any time soon.

In most cases, technology is unlikely to erase the necessity to choose alternatives. The need to sometimes defer processing to a later time seems beyond any technological solution. If nothing else, the fact of human beings scheduling events around the demands of daily life argues that this capability will continue to be required. For example, people in the Orient sleep while those in the West are awake, and vice versa.

23.1.1 Synchronous versus asynchronous

A synchronous interaction is characterized by the fact that the result of any interaction is known before any further processing occurs. In asynchronous processing the result may not be known until later. Synchronous processing is often associated with using a remote procedure call, but several methods of providing asynchronous interactions via the RPC have been discussed in this book. These include the use of threads or simply implementing the operation so that it returns immediately.

Generally, synchronous interactions are easier to understand and implement correctly. Asynchronous interactions, however, provide greater flexibility and, in particular, enable deferred interactions.

23.1.2 Deferred versus nondeferred

Deferred interactions use some kind of storage or queuing mechanism to allow interactions to occur even if both parties are never simultaneously active. Nondeferred interactions require both parties to be active at the same time and, further, require that a communications path be available between them.

Deferred interactions are frequently associated with messaging systems, but can be implemented in a variety of other ways as well.

23.1.3 Context versus no context

Whether or not the parties to a distributed interaction are to maintain state, or context, about the interaction, is another choice for the designer. In network terminology, the alternatives are referred to as connection-oriented versus connectionless communication. The tradeoffs have been discussed in earlier chapters. Basically, context-free interactions can be simpler to implement, in particular in the area of error recovery. On the other hand, maintaining context is a powerful technique useful in many situations.

Mechanisms for maintaining context in DCE are described in the chapters on the RPC and in the second example application. It is perfectly possible to maintain context in a deferred interaction.

23.1.4 Transactional versus nontransactional

Transactional semantics mean that either all of some set of changes will take effect or none of them will. Transaction integrity is often referred to by the abbreviation ACID—Atomicity, Consistency, Isolation, and Durability. Nontransactional interactions may produce partial results.

The technology exists to make every interaction transactional, but does not come free. Extra processing and more messages are required, along with more complex tools and techniques such as locking. All of these can increase the time it takes to complete execution, and they add cost because of the need for additional hardware and software. The trend toward ever-lower-cost communications and processing bandwidth will tend to make the choice of transaction semantics more common in the future.

23.1.5 Idempotent versus not idempotent

Idempotent operations can be performed repeatedly without harmful effects. This concept is discussed in Chap. 6. Like context-free interactions, idempotent operations are simpler to implement, particularly when error recovery is performed. Many times, however, the requirements of the application do not permit operations to be idempotent.

23.1.6 Data conversion issues

Data conversion is not a binary property, but a range of options. The DCE RPC provides very strong support for data conversion by means of its marshaling routines, which present data to applications in their native format. At the other extreme are facilities which present data to a receiver in exactly the form it was provided by the sender, with some differences. Some transmission services (e.g., X.25) at least preserve the original boundaries of the data as presented. Others (e.g., TCP/IP) consider data to be a continuous stream, presenting it in the order received, but not necessarily with the same record boundaries.

Other interaction properties exist. This is only a sample of some most commonly encountered. The main point is to begin with analysis of the fundamental requirements of the application and use that to drive technology decisions, rather than some predetermined allegiance to a favorite product or technology.

23.2 New Issues Created by the Use of DCE

The existence of standardized facilities such as those for naming, security, and distributed transaction management, coupled with the proliferation of distributed applications that will certainly follow, will present totally new operational challenges as well. Operational issues that never existed in nondistributed environments will require new techniques and new organizational approaches.

In some cases, new solutions will be required because new dynamic facilities have replaced old static ones. Where there used to be nothing to do, suddenly there are operational decisions to be made. An example of this is name-based binding. In monolithic applications, binding is over and done with at compile time. There are no operational issues at all. When clients bind to servers via a distributed name service, however, suddenly there are. If the directory server is not running, if the namespace is misconfigured, the application cannot function.

A second issue presenting new operational challenges is that the distributed equivalent of a function found in nondistributed systems often represents a quantum leap in complexity. An example is access control. In a typical time-sharing system, the main resource to be protected is files, most files belong to an individual user who controls access to them, and the access options are quite limited (e.g., owner, group, world). Compare this to a DCE environment of the future in which there will be a wide variety of resources to be protected, affiliations among resources that fall along many dimensions (e.g., individual, application, location, organization), and much richer access control primitives provided by ACLs.

Other challenges derive from inherent differences of distributed systems from monolithic systems. These are sometimes a two-edged sword. Replication is an example. Distributed systems provide the opportunity to replicate resources, increasing their availability. At the same time, they often require use of replication, because their greater complexity makes failures more likely. And replication presents a host of operational issues. They include policy issues (e.g., how many replicas, where located, which is master), routine operational issues (e.g., the master replica system needs to be shut down for hardware maintenance), and troubleshooting issues (e.g., two replicas both think they are the master).

Most computing environments today can be roughly characterized as either "big system" environments or "LAN" environments. A major difference between the two is the way management and administrative responsibilities are assigned. In big system environments, separate organizations usually have responsibility for network management and system management. In LAN environments, the same people do both.

The reason for the difference is partly historical. Big systems mean big infrastructure and a long heritage of independent (and perhaps rival) computer and telecommunications groups. LANs evolved from stand-alone PCs (which evolved from word processors and electric typewriters) and, at first, nobody realized that there was anything to manage. It was often the most enthusiastic power user who installed the LAN and, when managing it proved boring, fobbed off the responsibility on some beleaguered secretary.

But this is not the whole story. For most organizations, LANs represented the first true distributed systems. Those who had to make them work quickly discovered the basic fact that, at least when it comes to troubleshooting, there are no clear boundaries of responsibility for a distributed system. A nonfunctioning printer might be caused by a cable break, bad adapter card, incompatible driver version, invalid user ID, incorrectly configured parameter file, or buggy TSR. Clearly, different individuals will have expertise in these separate areas, but a large amount of overlap in their efforts is required to keep heterogeneous distributed systems running.

The OSF Distributed Management Environment (DME) is the first major management architecture to throw down the gauntlet and say that management and administration of networks and systems are not separable. Management systems that address one and not the other are obsolete today and will be more obsolete tomorrow.

The new challenge is to take the still incomplete synthesis of the disciplines and add to it the concept of application management and administration. Only by holding all the strings will it be possible for those with operational responsibilities to provide the kind of service that distributed systems are capable of. Just as today's user doesn't want to hear "The network is up, but the TCP/IP versions are incompatible," tomorrow's user won't want to hear "The server is up, but the namespace is misconfigured."

Of course, it is possible to ignore these issues. Operational organizations can wait until problems occur and try to deal with them then. Software development organizations can deal with issues in the context of each application and address them on an ad hoc basis. The fact that this lack of consistency drives up the cost of operations and support will probably not be visible to them, at least at first.

A real case from a large financial institution illustrates the point very nicely. Ten years ago, in order to support the needs of a variety of applications, this organization developed a name-based transport service we will call NBT. NBT succeeded beyond anyone's expectation. It was used for many needs that were unanticipated in the original design. The naming service in particular was extended many times, both to support connection establishment (binding) and to meet a variety of other application requirements. As a result, however, the service ended up posing significant operational problems as well as real development constraints.

This is not to say that 10 years ago operations personnel would have been able to foresee the outcome any more than the developers did. But the example illustrates that everyone has a stake in the game and that only by establishing an ongoing process to work together can everyone succeed. For operations, the goal is to be able to do the management job they have been chartered to do. For development, the goal is to produce applications that will be operationally successful without having to use precious (and expensive) development resources to backstop operations.

An ongoing process should be established that includes participants from both disciplines. This team should be chartered to identify the areas of joint interest in planning for application of technologies and to create specifications for it, evolving these standards over time as technology and application requirements change.

The NBT experience illustrates three principles that should guide such a group. First, once an interface (API) is established, applications will depend on it; therefore, upward compatibility is mandatory. (Backward compatibility is not.) Second, as new capabilities will trigger new uses, facilities should be designed with more generality than is absolutely required by current needs, as long as there are no unacceptable short-term penalties (e.g., excessive complexity, inadequate performance). Third, both an operational view and a development view are required for the process to succeed, and both organizations have a stake in its success.

Here is a list of some of the issues that should be considered in this process.

- DCE cell configuration guidelines

  Size range and other boundary considerations

  Number and disposition of replicated servers (CDS, security, time)

  Cell naming

- Namespace usage

  Conventions for binding entries

  Use of UUIDs

  Conventions for other namespace entries

  Guidelines for profiles and groups

- Security administration conventions

  Guidelines for principals/accounts

  Guidelines for security groups (organizations)

  Conventions for ACL usage

  Intercell authorization guidelines

- Application operations considerations

  Guidelines for location and replication of application servers

  Conventions for application installation and start-up

- Guidelines for use of vendor software products

  Namespace guidelines

  Operational considerations

  Transaction management

- Development principles for reuse

  Allocating interface names to avoid conflicts

  DCE portability considerations

Different organizations will want to address these issues in different ways. Some will assign responsibility for them to existing groups. Others will reorganize to reflect the new ways of working. The objective is not to create additional bureaucracy, but to attain a higher level of coordination. The key points are clear. These issues require input from both development and operations; neither can achieve success alone.

23.3   Distributed Object Computing

Issues relating to the development of distributed objects are one of the most significant challenges for the future of distributed systems. The object-oriented paradigm is having an increasing impact on the software industry. Even former skeptics see potential for significant benefits from producing software using object-oriented techniques. It seems possible that object-oriented approaches will reduce the time and cost associated with implementing software systems while improving their overall quality and suitability to their intended purpose.

At the same time, it must be recognized that both the theory and practice of object-oriented techniques are in their infancy. Major authorities disagree about which object-oriented features should be mandatory and whether some of them are even desirable. Users have already learned to proceed cautiously, and take exaggerated claims with a grain of salt. The best approach is to examine the individual features that comprise object-oriented systems and use those that provide benefits to a given application.

It seems certain that distributed object systems will be a major tool in the future. The most influential model so far is the Object Management Group's Common Object Request Broker Architecture (CORBA). This has been embraced by many major vendors and will be the focus of continuing standardization efforts.

As of this writing, the CORBA addresses portability very well, but does not specify the network protocols necessary to ensure interoperability between different vendors' products. A sound approach would be to use DCE as the foundation for interoperability. As this is being written, some vendors are actively following this path, but there is no certainty of its codification as a standard.

To illustrate the role DCE might play in distributed object systems, following are some of the key features of the object paradigm and how they relate to DCE.

The fundamental idea is that of an *object,* which is a software construct consisting of both data (attributes) and procedures (methods) and usually representing something that is meaningful in the problem domain. For example, a system might contain an automobile object, a credit-rating object, or an inventory-restocking object.

Objects come in different *types*. The set of all object instances of a given type is a *class*. All members of a class share the same methods, but each instance has distinct attribute values. For example, if you and I own the same model car, the way of starting the engine is the same, but your car may be a different color than mine. DCE does not directly support this concept of an object, but it provides several mechanisms that are useful in implementing distributed object systems.

Objects have *identity*. In other words, it is possible to distinguish between two objects even if they belong to the same class and have identical attribute values. In a local object system, an object is typically identified by a pointer. In distributed object systems, a mechanism is needed for allowing objects to be given unique labels.

The DCE UUID is an excellent tool for this purpose. As UUIDs are guaranteed to be unique for all time, we can create an object and label it with a UUID that will distinguish it from any other object. (How others can discover the UUID of the object is a separate issue.)

Object-oriented systems provide four key features: *encapsulation, inheritance, late binding,* and *polymorphism.*

Encapsulation means that objects are like black boxes. Only those aspects of objects that have been explicitly specified are accessible from outside the object. Generally, objects can have methods or operations that can be invoked externally, and attributes whose values may be read or written or both. Other than that, nothing about the object is known to the rest of the system. This means that the object can be changed, to use a B tree instead of a hash table, for example, without having any effect on the rest of the system.

DCE has no objects or classes per se. However, a remote procedure naturally encapsulates its data and is accessible only through well-defined operations. By means of suitably defined read and write operations, it is possible to simulate attributes as well. In fact, encapsulation has been recognized as an important principle of good distributed system design for a long time.

Inheritance means that classes can have subclasses that inherit all the attributes and methods that are not explicitly defined for the subclass. An insurance company might have an insurance policy class with life insurance and automobile insurance subclasses. Abstract classes are classes with no instances (objects). Their only purpose is to provide a framework for other classes to inherit. The insurance policy class might be an abstract class. A major activity in object-oriented design is determining the structure of the inheritance hierarchy.

DCE does not support inheritance. A distributed object system built on DCE must implement inheritance itself.

Late binding means that the association between a caller and a callee is established at runtime rather than at compile or link time. Like encapsulation, this is a concept integral to distributed systems. In traditional monolithic applications, all of the libraries are linked with the application during development. In a client/server architecture, the client must establish a connection to the server at runtime because the connection crosses the network. DCE provides many flexible capabilities for dynamic, runtime binding.

Polymorphism means the ability to invoke a generic operation which is defined for a variety of objects. The actual method used is determined at runtime, depending on the object type. A standard example is the operation to "print" an object. The actual processing involved in "printing" the object depends on whether it is a text file, a picture, a spreadsheet, or a directory. Polymorphism depends on late binding to establish the necessary association only after the type of object has been determined at runtime.

DCE supports polymorphism via its object model of binding. Although there are some restrictions associated with DCE object binding (see the discussion of the object binding model in Chap. 8), it provides the essential functionality necessary for polymorphism. DCE therefore provides an excellent foundation for polymorphism in a distributed object system.

Even assuming that existing CORBA-compliant systems converge on interoperability standards based on DCE or some related technology, this will by no means exhaust the issues related to distributed object systems. Following are some of the open questions.

Should multiple inheritance be supported? Multiple inheritance means that an object inherits attributes from more than one class. For example, a Ford convertible shares some properties with all Fords and some properties with all convertibles. Some languages, such as C++, support multiple inheritance, but not all authorities are convinced it is a good idea.

Should dynamic inheritance be supported? Dynamic inheritance means that when a class definition changes, it affects not only objects created in the future but all existing objects. Aside from the difficulties implementing this, it is not clear whether it is a good idea.

Should it be permissible for an object instance to have multiple, physical implementations (other than replicated copies)? In other words, should it be possible for there to be two independent, noncooperating implementations of the "same" object instance?

Should it be possible to move object instances around the network and, if so, why and how? Should it be possible to pass objects themselves as an argument when invoking an object method, or just object references?

Should it be possible for an object's implementation to be split among several nodes or does this violate encapsulation? Should this be attacked by means of strong support of the "contains" relationship (i.e., an object contains multiple components that are distributed)?

Should binding for operations on classes be different from operations on instances and, if so, in what ways? The most common case is supporting the "new" operation. The "right" place for the implementation of a new object may be very different from that of a preexisting object.

Although many of these issues will not be settled for years, it would seem that real progress toward open distributed object systems hinges on beginning the discussions that will achieve consensus about what is desirable and what is not. The rapid evolution of technology in the recent past shows us that it is not safe to ignore such issues just because implementation is not currently feasible.

There is an important role here to be played by the readers of this book. You are the ones who have to try to meet the real needs of distributed applications. You are in the best position to judge whether specific capabilities will make real systems more robust and cost-effective or whether they are merely a flight of fancy. Only by joining the debate can you help to ensure that the next generation of distributed system technology will meet your needs.

23.4 Chapter Summary

The availability of open, distributed computing technology such as DCE provides great benefits, but presents new challenges as well. The first challenge is the selection and use of the technology most appropriate to the application problem. This can be approached by analyzing the fundamental properties of the distributed interactions that should be visible in the application programs. Some of these properties include: synchronous versus asynchronous, deferred versus nondeferred, context versus no context, transactional versus nontransactional, idempotent versus not idempotent, and the extent of data conversion.

A second challenge arises from the need to manage and control the use of DCE technology. The development and operation of DCE-based systems requires organizations and processes to deal with issues that did not exist previously. Only cooperation between individuals responsible for development and for operations can result in the necessary integration of network management, systems management, and applications management.

The third challenge is to take part in shaping the future. As practical distributed object environments emerge, they will likely make use of DCE as a foundation for interoperability. This will require DCE to evolve, but the potential benefits to distributed application development are great. Many unanswered questions exist as to how distributed object systems ought to behave. Open distributed object environments will only come into being as consensus emerges on these issues. Developers of distributed systems have a strong stake in the results of this debate.

IDL Summary

```
[header_attrib,…] interface interface_name
{
declaration…
}

header_attrib::
        <<uuid (xxxxxxxx-xxxx-xxxx-xxxx-xxxxxxxxxxxx) | local >>
        version (major_number) | (major_number.minor_number)
        endpoint ("ncacn_ip_tcp | ncadg_ud_udp : [endpoint_name]",…)
        pointer_default (ref | ptr)

declaration::
        import "file_name",…;
        const constant_type constant_ident = constant_expression;
        typedef [type_attrib,…]        type_spec augmented_ident;
        typedef pipe              type_spec pipe_ident;
        [operation_attrib,…]    simple_type_spec function_ident
==>     ( void |<[param_attrib,…]        type_spec augmented_ident>,…);

type_attrib::
        ref | ptr | string | handle | context_handle |
==>     v1_array | v1_string | v1_struct | v1_enum
        transmit_as (type_name)
        switch_type (switch_type)

parameter_attrib::
        <<in | out | in, out>>
        ignore
        field_attrib

field_attrib::
        ref | ptr | context_handle | string | v1_string | v1_array
        array_attrib (<*>variable_name)
        switch_type (switch_type)
```

```
operation_attrib::
        idempotent | broadcast | maybe
        ptr | context_handle | string | v1_string

type_spec::
        simple_type_spec
        struct    tag_name
        struct    <tag_ident> {<<[field_attrib,…] type_spec augmented_ident,…;>>…}
        union     tag_name
        union     <tag_ident>switch (switch_type discriminator_name) <C_struct_ident>
==>     {union_case … <default:<union_arm> >}
        enum      <tag_ident> {ident,…}

simple_type_spec::
        integer_h_type | float | double | char | boolean | byte | void | handle_t |
==>     error_status_t | ISO_LATIN_1 | ISO_MULTI_LINGUAL | ISO_UCS
integer_h_type::    <unsigned> small | short | long | hyper <int>
integer_type::      <unsigned> small | short | long <int>
union_case::        <<case constant_expression :>>… union_arm…
union_arm::         [union_attrib,…] type_spec augmented_ident;
union_attrib::      ptr | string | v1_array | v1_string
switch_type::       integer_type | <unsigned > char | boolean | enum_tag_name
constant_type::     integer_type | boolean | char | char* | void*
augmented_ident::   *… ident <[array_bound_first] [array_bound]…>

array_attrib::
    first_is
    size_is | max_is
    last_is | length_is

array_bound_first::
    lower_zero_constant..upper_constant
    lower_zero_constant..*
    size_constant
    nothing

array_bound::
    lower_zero_constant..upper_constant
    size_constant
```

Notation

Meaning	Format
literal value	**bold**
composite element	*italics*
alternatives	choice_1 | choice_2 | choice_k

optional group	<items>
repeated 0 or more times	...
repeated group	<items>
once per repeated list	<<items>>
at least once per list	<<items>>
continuation	==> in first column

Note: The <<>> are used only in composite definitions.

- Multiple lines under a composite definition imply alternative choices.

- When a composite is repeated (by an ellipsis) the same noncomposite line from the definition may be used only once within the list.

- A comma before an ellipsis means the comma is placed in the source to separate the repeated items and is omitted if the list contains only one item.

- Square brackets around a repeated list are omitted if the list is null.

ACF Syntax Summary

```
[header_attrib,…] interface interface_name
{
declaration…
}

declaration::
    include "file_name",…;
    typedef [type_attrib,…] type_name;
    [operation_attrib,…] operation_name (<[parameter_attrib,…] parameter_name>,…);

header_attrib::
    code | nocode
    in_line | out_of_line
    auto_handle | explicit_handle | implicit_handle (handle_type handle_name)

type_attrib::
    represent_as (local_type_name)
    in_line | out_of_line
    heap

operation_attrib::
    explicit_handle
    enable_allocate
    nocode
    comm_status | fault_status

parameter_attrib::
    comm_status | fault_status
    heap
```

Notation

Meaning	*Format*
literal value	**bold**
composite element	*italics*
alternatives	choice_1 | choice_2 | choice_k
optional group	\<items\>
repeated 0 or more times	...
repeated group	\<items\>
once per repeated list	\<\<items\>\>
at least once per list	\<\<items\>\>
continuation	==\> in first column

Note: The \<\<\>\> are used only in composite definitions.

- Multiple lines under a composite definition imply alternative choices.
- When a composite is repeated (by an ellipsis) the same noncomposite line from the definition may be used only once within the list.
- A comma before an ellipsis means the comma is placed in the source to separate the repeated items and is omitted if the list contains only one item.
- Square brackets around a repeated list are omitted if the list is null.

DCE Library Calls Used in This Book

General

dce_cf_get_host_name   Returns the local node name.

dce_error_inq_inq_text   Translates an error code into text.

Threads

pthread_attr_create   Creates a thread attributes object.

pthread_attr_setsched   Sets the scheduling policy attribute.

pthread_cancel   Requests that a thread be canceled.

pthread_cond_broadcast   Wakes all of the threads waiting on a condition variable.

pthread_cond_destroy   Deletes a condition variable.

pthread_cond_init   Creates a condition variable.

pthread_cond_signal   Wakes one thread that is waiting on a condition variable.

pthread_cond_wait   Causes a thread to wait on a condition variable.

pthread_create   Creates a thread.

pthread_detach   Requests deletion of a thread.

pthread_exit   Causes the calling thread to terminate.

pthread_getspecific   Reads thread-specific static data.

pthread_join   Causes the calling thread to wait for a specified thread to terminate.

pthread_keycreate   Creates a key that identifies thread-specific static data.

pthread_lock_global_np   Locks the global mutex.

pthread_mutex_destroy	Deletes a mutex.
pthread_mutex_init	Creates a mutex.
pthread_mutex_lock	Waits until a mutex is unlocked and returns with it locked.
pthread_mutex_trylock	Tests if a mutex is unlocked and, if it is, returns with it locked.
pthread_mutex_unlock	Unlocks a mutex.
pthread_once	Calls a specified routine unless it has been called previously.
pthread_setspecific	Writes thread-specific static data.
pthread_testcancel	Allows the current thread to be canceled, if a cancel has been requested previously.
pthread_unlock_global_np	Unlocks the global mutex.

ACL Manager Remote Interface

rdacl_get_access	Returns the caller's permissions.
rdacl_get_manager_types	Returns all supported manager UUIDs.
rdacl_get_manager_types_semantics	Returns all supported manager UUIDs and their POSIX semantics.
rdacl_get_printstring	Returns printable representation of supported permissions.
rdacl_get_referral	Returns reference to manager instance that can perform updates.
rdacl_lookup	Returns an ACL.
rdacl_replace	Updates an ACL.
rdacl_test_access	Determines if the caller is allowed specified permissions.
rdacl_test_access_on_behalf	Determines if the caller and another specified principal are both allowed specified permissions.

RPC

rpc_binding_inq_auth_client	Returns security information associated with a client (server).
rpc_binding_inq_object	Returns object UUID associated with a binding.
rpc_binding_set_auth_info	Associates security information with a binding handle (client).
rpc_ep_register	Provides server information to the endpoint mapper (server).

rpc_ep_register_no_replace
Provides additional server information to the endpoint mapper (server).

rpc_ep_unregister
Removes server information from the endpoint mapper (server).

rpc_if_register_auth_info
Associates security information with an interface (client).

rpc_mgmt_stop_server_listening
Requests that a server shut down.

rpc_network_inq_protseqs
Returns all protocol sequences supported by the runtime.

rpc_network_is_protseq_valid
Indicates if a specified protocol sequence is supported by the runtime.

rpc_ns_binding_export
Provides server binding information to the namespace (server).

rpc_ns_binding_import_begin
Initiates obtaining individual binding handles (client).

rpc_ns_binding_import_done
Completes obtaining individual binding handles (client).

rpc_ns_binding_import_next
Obtains a binding handle (client).

rpc_ns_binding_inq_entry_name
Returns the server name associated with a binding handle (client).

rpc_ns_binding_lookup_begin
Initiates obtaining lists of binding handles (client).

rpc_ns_binding_lookup_done
Completes obtaining lists of binding handles (client).

rpc_ns_binding_lookup_next
Obtains a list of binding handles (client).

rpc_ns_binding_unexport
Removes server binding information from the namespace (server).

rpc_ns_group_mgr_add
Adds a namespace entry to a group, creating it if it does not exist.

rpc_ns_group_mgr_remove
Removes an entry from a group.

rpc_ns_mgmt_set_exp_age
Controls the expiration of data in the directory cache.

rpc_object_set_type
Associates a type UUID with an object UUID (server).

rpc_server_inq_bindings
Returns the server bindings created by the runtime (server).

rpc_server_listen
Causes the server to begin waiting for remote procedure calls (server).

rpc_server_register_auth_info
Specifies the security options used by the server (server).

rpc_server_register_if	Registers an interface with the runtime (server).
rpc_server_use_all_protseqs	Tells the runtime to use all supported protocols (server).
rpc_server_use_all_protseqs_if	Tells the runtime to use all supported protocols and the well-known endpoints specified in the IDL file (server).
rpc_server_use_protseq	Tells the runtime to use a specified protocol sequence (server).
rpc_server_use_protseq_ep	Tells the runtime to use all supported protocols and the specified, well-known endpoints (server).
rpc_server_use_protseq_if	Tells the runtime to use a specified protocol and the well-known endpoints specified in the IDL file (server).
rpc_ss_allocate	Allocates memory which will be freed automatically after marshaling, upon remote procedure call return (server).
rpc_ss_free	Deallocates memory that was allocated by rpc_ss_allocate (server).
rpc_string_free	Frees a character string allocated by the runtime.

ACL Manager Client Interface

sec_acl_bind	Returns a handle to an ACL.
sec_acl_get_manager_types	Returns all supported manager UUIDs.
sec_acl_get_manager_types_semantics	Returns all supported manager UUIDs and their POSIX semantics.
sec_acl_get_printstring	Returns printable representation of supported permissions.
sec_acl_lookup	Returns an ACL.
sec_acl_replace	Updates an ACL.
sec_acl_test_access_on_behalf	Determines if the caller and another specified principal are both allowed specified permissions.

ACL Manager Internal Interface

sec_acl_mgr_configure	Initializes the ACL manager.
sec_acl_mgr_get_access	Returns the permissions available to a principal with the specified PAC.

sec_acl_mgr_is_authorized	Determines if the specified permissions are available to a principal with the specified PAC.
sec_acl_mgr_lookup	Returns an ACL.
sec_acl_mgr_replace	Updates an ACL.

Security Service

sec_key_mgmt_get_key	Returns a server key from a keytable.
sec_key_mgmt_manage_key	Periodically changes server key before it expires. Never returns.
sec_login_get_current_context	Returns a handle to the current login context.
sec_login_set_context	Makes a specified security context the current login context.
sec_login_setup_identity	Returns a handle to a new, unvalidated security context.
sec_login_validate_identity	Validates the specified security context.
sec_rgy_pgo_name_to_id	Returns the UUID identifying a specified principal, group, or organization.
sec_rgy_site_close	Ends a session with a registry server.
sec_rgy_site_open	Begins a session with a registry server.

Distributed Time Service

utc_abstime	Computes the absolute value of a relative binary timestamp.
utc_addtime	Adds two binary timestamps.
utc_anytime	Converts a timestamp to a tm structure.
utc_anyzone	Gets the time zone and GMT offset from a binary timestamp.
utc_ascanytime	Converts a timestamp to an ASCII string, deriving the time zone from the TDF.
utc_ascgmtime	Converts a timestamp to an ASCII string, using the GMT time zone.
utc_asclocaltime	Converts a timestamp to an ASCII string, using the local time zone.
utc_ascreltime	Converts a relative binary timestamp to an ASCII string.

utc_binreltime	Converts a relative binary time-stamp to two timespec structures.
utc_bintime	Converts a binary timestamp to a timespec structure.
utc_boundtime	Returns a UTC which encompasses two specified UTCs.
utc_cmpintervaltime	Compares two binary timestamps or two relative binary timestamps.
utc_cmpmidtime	Compares two binary timestamps or two relative binary timestamps, ignoring their inaccuracies.
utc_gettime	Returns the current time as a binary timestamp.
utc_getusertime	Returns the current time as a binary timestamp, using the user's time zone.
utc_gmtime	Converts a binary timestamp to a tm structure using the GMT time zone.
utc_gmtzone	Returns the time zone label for GMT.
utc_local_time	Converts a binary timestamp to a tm structure using the local time zone.
utc_localzone	Returns the local time zone label and offset from GMT of a specified UTC.
utc_mkanytime	Converts a tm structure and a specified TDF to a binary timestamp.
utc_mkascreltime	Converts an ASCII relative time to a binary relative timestamp.
utc_mkasctime	Converts an ASCII absolute time to a binary timestamp.
utc_mkbinreltime	Converts a timespec structure to a relative binary timestamp.
utc_mkbintime	Converts a timespec structure to a binary timestamp.
utc_mkgmtime	Converts a tm structure to a binary timestamp, using the GMT time zone.
utc_mklocaltime	Converts a tm structure to a binary timestamp, using the local time zone.
utc_mkreltime	Converts a tm structure to a relative binary timestamp.

utc_mulftime	Multiplies a relative binary time-stamp by a floating-point number.
utc_multime	Multiplies a relative binary time-stamp by an integer.
utc_pointtime	Converts a binary timestamp to three timestamps representing the earliest, most likely, and latest time it represents.
utc_reltime	Converts a relative binary time-stamp to a tm structure.
utc_spantime	Returns a UTC which encompasses two specified UTCs.
utc_subtime	Subtracts one binary timestamp from another.

UUID

uuid_create	Returns a new UUID.
uuid_equal	Tests if two specified UUIDs are equal.

The Single-Threaded Server

The IDL File

```
/* INFPLS.IDL Information Server */


[
uuid (00602161-7C3F-1C90-B0AE-0000C07C3610),
version(1.0)
]
interface infpls
{
typedef handle_t RPC_BINDING_HANDLE_T;
typedef struct
    {
    [ptr, string] char *sysname_p;
    [ptr, string] char *nodename_p;
    [ptr, string] char *release_p;
    [ptr, string] char *version_p;
    [ptr, string] char *machine_p;
    } sys_info_t;

error_status_t get_system_info( [in]  RPC_BINDING_HANDLE_T   binding,
                                [ref, out] sys_info_t    *system_info_p);
    }
```

The ACL File

```
/* INFOPLS.ACF Information Server */

interface infpls
{

[comm_status, fault_status] get_system_info();

}
```

The Error Macro File

```
#include <dce/dce_error.h>

#define ERROR(msg)\
   {fprintf (stderr, "Error: %s in file: %s at line %d.\n", \
       msg, __FILE__, __LINE__);\
   exit (1);}

#define WARN(msg)\
   {fprintf (stderr, "Warning: %s in file: %s at line %d.\n", \
       msg, __FILE__, __LINE__);}

#define ERR_CHK(stat, msg) if (stat !=rpc_s_ok)\
   {dce_error_string_t _dcemsg_; int _st_;\
    dce_error_inq_text( stat, _dcemsg_, &_st_ );\
    fprintf (stderr, "Error: %s in file: %s at line %d.\nDCE Error: %s\n", \
       msg, __FILE__, __LINE__, _dcemsg_);\
   exit (1);}

#define WRN_CHK(stat, msg) if (stat != rpc_s_ok)\
   {dce_error_string_t _dcemsg_; int _st_;\
    dce_error_inq_text( stat, _dcemsg_, &_st_ );\
    fprintf (stderr, "Warning: %s in file: %s at line %d.\nDCE Error: %s\n", \
       msg, __FILE__, __LINE__,_dcemsg_);}

#define CND_CHK(cond, msg) if ((cond))\
   {fprintf (stderr, "Error: %s in file: %s at line %d.\n", \
       msg, __FILE__, __LINE__);\
   exit (1);}
```

The Server File

```
/* INFPLS_S.C */

#include <stdio.h>
#include <sys/utsname.h>
#include <sys/errno.h>
#include <dce/rpc.h>
#include <dce/pthread_exc.h>
#include "infpls.h"
#include "errmac.h"

/***** Server Control *****/

main( int argc, char *argv[] )
{
unsigned32          max_threads;
error_status_t      status;
rpc_binding_vector_t *bindings;
idl_char          annotation[]="Information Please Program";
```

```
if (argc > 2 )
    {
    fprintf(stderr, "Usage: %s maximum_threads\n", argv[0] );
    exit(1);
    }

if (argc < 2 )
    {
    max_threads = rpc_c_listen_max_calls_default;
    }
else
    max_threads = atol(argv[1]);

rpc_server_register_if( infpls_v1_0_s_ifspec,                    /* (1) */
                        NULL,
                        NULL,
                        &status);
ERR_CHK(status,"Could not register interface");

rpc_server_use_protseq( (idl_char *) "ncadg_ip_udp",            /* (2) */
                        max_threads,
                        &status);
ERR_CHK(status,"Could not use UDP protocol");

rpc_server_inq_bindings( &bindings,                            /* (3) */
                         &status);
ERR_CHK(status,"Could not get binding vector");

/* Bindings are exported to the namespace by the install program. */

/* Therefore we do not do it here */

rpc_ep_register( infpls_v1_0_s_ifspec,                         /* (4) */
                 bindings,
                 NULL,
                 annotation,
                 &status);
ERR_CHK(status,"Could not register endpoint");

printf("Information Server is now available\n");

TRY {

rpc_server_listen( max_threads,                               /* (5) */
                   &status);
    }
FINALLY {
    rpc_ep_unregister( infpls_v1_0_s_ifspec,                  /* (6) */
                       bindings,
                       NULL,
                       &status);
    } ENDTRY;

}  /* End of Server Control Routine */
```

```
/*********************** Server Operations **********************/

error_status_t get_system_info(
    rpc_binding_handle_t binding,     /* binding handle is not used */
    sys_info_t           *system_info_p)

{
struct utsname *info_p;
info_p=rpc_ss_allocate (sizeof (struct utsname));
if (info_p==NULL)
    {
    return (-1);
    }

if (uname (info_p) < 0)
    {
    return (errno);
    }
else
    {
    system_info_p->sysname_p  = (idl_char *) &info_p->sysname;
    system_info_p->nodename_p = (idl_char *) &info_p->nodename;
    system_info_p->release_p  = (idl_char *) &info_p->release;
    system_info_p->version_p  = (idl_char *) &info_p->version;
    system_info_p->machine_p  = (idl_char *) &info_p->machine;
    return (rpc_s_ok);
    }
}
```

The Client File

```
/* INFPLS_C.C */

#include <stdio.h>
#include <dce/rpc.h>
#include "infpls.h"
#include "errmac.h"

/* This client calls each server which is a member of the Infopls */
/* Group getting the usname information from each one and printing */
/* it out */


static idl_char *  ptr_check          (idl_char *inp_p);
static void        non_null_free      (void *inp_p);

static idl_char unknown_string[]="-Unknown-";




main(int argc, char *argv[])
{
```

```
error_status_t          status;
rpc_ns_handle_t         binding_context;
rpc_binding_handle_t binding;
sys_info_t              system_info;
unsigned_char_t         *server_name_p;




rpc_ns_binding_import_begin( rpc_c_ns_syntax_defaut          /* (1) */
                             NULL,
                             infpls_v1_0_c_ifspec,
                             NULL,
                             &binding_context,
                             &status);
ERR_CHK(status,"Could not import binding context");

status=rpc_s_ok;
while (status==rpc_s_ok)
    {
    rpc_ns_binding_import_next( binding_context,              /* (2) */
                               &binding,
                               &status);
    if (status == rpc_s_ok)
        {
        if (get_system_info(binding, &system_info)           /* (3) */
            == rpc_s_ok)
            {
            rpc_ns_binding_inq_entry_name( binding,          /* (4) */
                                          rpc_c_ns_syntax_default,
                                          &server_name_p,
                                          &status);

            printf("Directory Service Name = %s\n"
                "System Name = %s\n"
                "Node Name = %s\n"
                "Release = %s\n"
                "Version  = %s\n"
                "Machine Type = %s\n",

                ptr_check (server_name_p),
                ptr_check (system_info.sysname_p),
                ptr_check (system_info.nodename_p),
                ptr_check (system_info.release_p),
                ptr_check (system_info.version_p),
                ptr_check (system_info.machine_p));

            rpc_string_free( &server_name_p,                 /* (5) */
                            &status);
            non_null_free (system_info.sysname_p);
            non_null_free (system_info.nodename_p);
            non_null_free (system_info.release_p);
            non_null_free (system_info.version_p);
            non_null_free (system_info.machine_p);
```

```
                          /* Ignore errors */

                    }   /* Don't report binding errors */
              }          /* Don't report RPC errors either */

          }              /* End of while(1) */

    rpc_ns_binding_import_done( &binding_context,                    /* (6) */
                                &status);
    WRN_CHK(status,"Error releasing binding context");

    return(1);
    }


    idl_char * ptr_check (idl_char * inp_p)
    {
    return (inp_p !=NULL ? inp_p : unknown_string);
    }



    void non_null_free (void * inp_p)
    {
    if (inp_p!=NULL)
      {
      free (inp_p);
      }
    }
```

The Installation File

```
    /* INFPLS_I.C */

    #include <stdio.h>
    #include <string.h>
    #include <dce/rpc.h>
    #include <dce/dce_cf.h>
    #include "infpls.h"
    #include "errmac.h"


    /**** dummy operation entry point since declared in stub ******/

    error_status_t get_system_info(
        rpc_binding_handle_t binding,
        sys_info_t           *system_info_p)
    {
    return rpc_s_ok;
    }
```

```
/***** Information Server Installation Program *****/

main( int argc, char *argv[] )
{

error_status_t        status;
rpc_binding_vector_t  *bindings;
unsigned_char_t       name[100];
unsigned_char_t       group_name[] = "/.:/applications/info_server_group";
char                  *hostname_p, *cp;

if (argc < 2)
    {
    printf("Usage: %s -i [ host name ] or %s -r [ host name ]\n",
           argv[0], argv[0]);
    exit(1);
    }

/*
***** Construct server entry name from the host name typed by *****
***** the user. If none was typed use the local hostname as   *****
***** reported by DCE                                         *****
*/

if (argc = 2)
    {
    dce_cf_get_host_name(&hostname_p, &status);              /* (1) */
    ERR_CHK(status,"Could not get host name");
    cp = strstr (hostname_p, "hosts/");
    if (cp==NULL)
        {
        printf ("Can't interpret local host name format");
        exit (1);
        }
    cp = strchr (cp, '/')+1;
    }
else
    {
    cp = argv[2];
    }
sprintf ((char *)name, "/.:/applications/info_server_%s", cp);

if (strcmp(argv[1], "-i") == 0)
    {
    rpc_server_use_protseq((idl_char *) "ncadg_ip_udp",      /* (2) */
                           rpc_c_protseq_max_reqs_default,
                               &status);
    ERR_CHK(status,"Could not use UDP protocol");

    rpc_server_inq_bindings( &bindings,                      /* (3) */
                             &status);
    ERR_CHK(status,"Could not get binding vector");
```

```
            rpc_ns_binding_export( rpc_c_ns_syntax_default,              /* (4) */
                                   name,
                                   infpls_v1_0_s_ifspec,
                                   bindings,
                                   NULL,
                                   &status);
        ERR_CHK(status,"Could not export server bindings");

            rpc_ns_group_mbr_add( rpc_c_ns_syntax_default,               /* (5) */
                                  group_name,
                                  rpc_c_ns_syntax_default,
                                  name,
                                  &status);
        ERR_CHK(status,"Could not add server entry to group");

    /* Add code here for additional de-installation tasks */

        }


    else if (strcmp(argv[1], "-r") == 0)
        {
        rpc_ns_binding_unexport( rpc_c_ns_syntax_default,               /* (6) */
                                 name,
                                 infpls_v1_0_s_ifspec,
                                 NULL,
                                 &status);
        ERR_CHK(status,"Could not remove server bindings");

        rpc_ns_group_mbr_remove( rpc_c_ns_syntax_default,              /* (7) */
                                 group_name,
                                 rpc_c_ns_syntax_default,
                                 name,
                                 &status);
        ERR_CHK(status,"Could not remove server entry from group");

    /* Add code here for additional de-installation tasks */

        }

    else
        {
        printf("Usage: %s -i [ host name ] or %s -r [ host name ]\n",
               argv[0], argv[0]);
        exit(1);
        }
    }
```

The Build File

```
PGM=infpls
DCE=/opt/dcelocal
```

```
DCELIB=-L $(DCE)/lib
LIBS=$(DCELIB) -l dce
IDL=/opt/dcelocal/bin/idl
LIBS=$(DCELIB) -l dce -l dcedes -l seccrypt -l socket  -l nsl
CC=/usr/bin/cc -g


default: $(PGM)_c.out $(PGM)_s.out  $(PGM)_i.out

$(PGM)_c.out: $(PGM)_c.c errmac.h $(PGM).h $(PGM)_cstub.o
        $(CC) -o $(PGM)_c.out $(LIBS) $(PGM)_cstub.o $(PGM)_c.c

$(PGM)_s.out: $(PGM)_s.c errmac.h $(PGM).h $(PGM)_sstub.o
        $(CC) -o $(PGM)_s.out $(LIBS) $(PGM)_sstub.o $(PGM)_s.c

$(PGM)_i.out: $(PGM)_i.c errmac.h $(PGM).h $(PGM)_sstub.o
        $(CC) -o $(PGM)_i.out $(LIBS) $(PGM)_sstub.o $(PGM)_i.c

$(PGM)_cstub.o $(PGM)_sstub.o $(PGM).h: $(PGM).idl $(PGM).acf
        $(IDL) $(PGM).idl
```

The Multithreaded Server

The IDL File

```
/* LOOKUP.IDL Table Lookup Server */

[
uuid (004C4B41-E7C5-1CB9-94E7-0000C07C3610,
version(1.0)
]
interface lookup

{
const short LOOK_REC_SIZE = 50;
const short LOOK_FIELD_MAX = 30;

typedef handle_t BIND_HDL_T;

typedef enum {
    LOOK_OK,
    LOOK_END_SEARCH,
    LOOK_NO_CURRENT,
    LOOK_FILE_FULL,
    LOOK_OTHERS,
    LOOK_NO_FILTER}
look_sts_t;


typedef struct
    {
    long ofs;
    long len;
    char min[LOOK_FIELD_MAX];
    char max[LOOK_FIELD_MAX];
    }
filter_t;
```

```
typedef [context_handle] void *ctx_h;

error_status_t look_open (
        [in]        BIND_HDL_T    bind_h,
        [out]       ctx_h         *ctx_p);

error_status_t look_close (
        [in]        BIND_HDL_T    bind_h,
        [in, out]   ctx_h         *ctx_p);

error_status_t look_filter (
        [in]        BIND_HDL_T    bind_h,
        [in]        ctx_h         ctx_p,
        [in]        filter_t      *filter_p);

error_status_t look_next (
        [in]        BIND_HDL_T    bind_h,
        [in]        ctx_h         ctx_p,
        [in]        long          start,
        [in]        long          len,
        [out,
        first_is (start),
        length_is (len)]
                    byte          buf[LOOK_REC_SIZE],
        [out]       look_sts_t    *result);

error_status_t look_read (
        [in]        BIND_HDL_T    bind_h,
        [in]        ctx_h         ctx_p,
        [in]        long          start,
        [in]        long          len,
        [out,
        first_is (start),
        length_is (len)]
                    byte          buf[LOOK_REC_SIZE],
        [out]       look_sts_t    *result);

error_status_t look_write (
        [in]        BIND_HDL_T    bind_h,
        [in]        ctx_h         ctx_p,
        [in]        long          start,
        [in]        long          len,
        [in,
        first_is (start),
        length_is (len)]
                    byte          buf[LOOK_REC_SIZE],
        [out]       look_sts_t    *result);

error_status_t look_add (
        [in]        BIND_HDL_T    bind_h,
        [in]        ctx_h         ctx_p,
        [out]       look_sts_t    *result);
```

```
error_status_t look_delete (
     [in]        BIND_HDL_T   bind_h,
     [in]        ctx_h        ctx_p,
     [out]       look_sts_t   *result);
}
```

The ACF File

```
/* LOOKUP.ACF */

interface lookup

{

[comm_status, fault_status, enable_allocate ] look_open ();

[comm_status, fault_status, enable_allocate ] look_close ();

[comm_status, fault_status, enable_allocate ] look_filter ();

[comm_status, fault_status, enable_allocate ] look_next ();

[comm_status, fault_status, enable_allocate ] look_read ();

[comm_status, fault_status, enable_allocate ] look_write ();

[comm_status, fault_status, enable_allocate ] look_add ();

[comm_status, fault_status, enable_allocate ] look_delete ();
}
```

The ACL Manager ACF File

```
/*
 * **** RDACLIF.ACF ****
 * sec_acl_mgr_lookup() and sec_acl_mgr_replace call rpc_ss_allocate()
 * therefore the operations that call them must be declared to have the
 * enable_allocate attribute
 */

interface rdaclif {

    [enable_allocate] rdacl_lookup ();

    [enable_allocate] rdacl_replace ();

    [enable_allocate] rdacl_get_access();

    [enable_allocate] rdacl_test_access ();

    [enable_allocate] rdacl_test_access_on_behalf ();

}
```

The Error Macro File

```
#include <dce/dce_error.h>

#define ERROR(msg)\
   {fprintf (stderr, "Error: %s in file: %s at line %d.\n", \
       msg, __FILE__, __LINE__);\
   exit (1);}

#define WARN(msg)\
   {fprintf (stderr, "Warning: %s in file: %s at line %d.\n", \
       msg, __FILE__, __LINE__);}

#define ERR_CHK(stat, msg) if (stat !=rpc_s_ok)\
   {dce_error_string_t _dcemsg_; int _st_;\
    dce_error_inq_text( stat, _dcemsg_, &_st_ );\
    fprintf (stderr, "Error: %s in file: %s at line %d.\nDCE Error: %s\n", \
     msg, __FILE__, __LINE__, _dcemsg_);\
   exit (1);}

#define WRN_CHK(stat, msg) if (stat != rpc_s_ok)\
   {dce_error_string_t _dcemsg_; int _st_;\
    dce_error_inq_text( stat, _dcemsg_, &_st_ );\
    fprintf (stderr, "Warning: %s in file: %s at line %d.\nDCE Error: %s\n", \
    msg, __FILE__, __LINE__,_dcemsg_);}

#define CND_CHK(cond, msg) if ((cond))\
   {fprintf (stderr, "Error: %s in file: %s at line %d.\n", \
       msg, __FILE__, __LINE__);\
   exit (1);}
```

The Server Definitions File

```
/* LOOKUP_S.H Lookup Server Definitions */

/* We only have one ACL manager, therefore one manager uuid */

static uuid_t  mgr_uuid = { /* 0050DF20-927B-1C53-AF86-0000C07C3610 */
       0x0050df20,
       0x927b,
       0x1c53,
       0xaf,
       0x86,
       {0x00, 0x00, 0xc0, 0x7c, 0x36, 0x10}
      };

static unsigned_char_t  name[]     = "/.:/applications/lookup_server";
static unsigned_char_t  princ_name[] = "lookup_server";
static unsigned_char_t  keytab[]     = "lookup_keytab";
static unsigned_char_t  acl_db_name[] = "lookup_acl";
```

The Server Control File

```
/* LOOKUP_S.C Lookup Table Server Main Routine */

#include <stdio.h>
#include <sys/types.h>
#include <sys/stat.h>
#include <fcntl.h>

#include <pthread.h>
#include <dce/rpc.h>
#include <dce/daclif.h>
#include <dce/daclmgr.h>

#include "errmac.h"
#include "lookup.h"
#include "lookup_s.h"


/***** Server Control *****/

main (int argc, char *argv[])
{
unsigned32          max_threads;
error_status_t      status;
rpc_binding_vector_t *bindings;
boolean32           create_db_flag = FALSE;

if (argc > 3 )
    {
    fprintf(stderr, "Usage: %s maximum_threads [-c ]\n", argv[0] );
    exit(1);
    }

if (argc < 2 )
    {
    max_threads = rpc_c_listen_max_calls_default;
    }
else
   max_threads = atol(argv[1]);

if (argc = 3 && (strcmp(argv[2],"-c") == 0))
    {
    create_db_flag = sec_acl_mgr_config_create;                    /* (1) */
    }


rpc_server_register_if( lookup_v1_0_s_ifspec,                      /* (2) */
                        NULL,
                        NULL,
                        &status);
ERR_CHK(status,"Could not register interface");
```

```
    rpc_server_use_all_protseqs( max_threads,                    /* (3) */
                        &status);
    ERR_CHK(status,"Could not use all protocols");

    rpc_server_inq_bindings( &bindings,                          /* (4) */
                        &status);
    ERR_CHK(status,"Could not get binding vector");


    look_setup_auth ( bindings, create_db_flag );                /* (5) */

    look_ctx_init   ();                                          /* (6) */


    /* Bindings are exported to the namespace by the install program. */
    /* Therefore we do not do it here */

    rpc_ep_register( lookup_v1_0_s_ifspec,                       /* (7) */
                    bindings,
                    NULL,
                    (idl_char *) "Lookup Table Server",
                    &status);
    ERR_CHK(status,"Could not register endpoint");

    TRY {

    printf("Lookup Table Server is now available\n");

    rpc_server_listen( max_threads,                             /* (8) */
                    &status);
        }
    FINALLY
        {
        rpc_ep_unregister( lookup_v1_0_s_ifspec,               /* (9) */
                            bindings,
                            NULL,
                            &status);

        } ENDTRY;

    }
```

The Server Security File

```
    /* LOOKUP_A.C Access Control Routines */

    #include <sys/types.h>
    #include <stdio.h>
    #include <string.h>
    #include <pthread.h>
    #include <dce/rpc.h>
    #include <dce/binding.h>
    #include <dce/pgo.h>
```

```
#include <dce/rdaclif.h>
#include <dce/daclmgr.h>
#include <dce/daclif.h>
#include <dce/sec_login.h>
#include <dce/keymgmt.h>
#include <dce/dce_cf.h>
#include "lookup.h"
#include "errmac.h"
#include "lookup_s.h"


/* Internal Routines */

pthread_startroutine_t manage_key(pthread_addr_t arg);

/* Internal Variables */

sec_id_t *user_obj, *group_obj;
sec_acl_mgr_handle_t mgr_hdl;
unsigned_char_t full_princ_name[50];

/*---------- Check access (Reference Monitor) --------------*/

boolean32 look_check_access (
    rpc_binding_handle_t binding,
    sec_acl_permset_t permissions)
{
unsigned_char_t *server_name;
sec_id_pac_t *pac;
unsigned32 protect_level, authn_svc, authz_svc;
error_status_t status;


rpc_binding_inq_auth_client( binding,                          /* (1) */
                             (rpc_authz_handle_t) &pac,
                             &server_name,
                             &protect_level,
                             &authn_svc,
                             &authz_svc,
                             &status);
if (status != rpc_s_ok) return (FALSE);


if (strcmp ((char *) server_name, (char *) full_princ_name) != 0)
    {
    rpc_string_free (&server_name, &status);
    return (FALSE);
    }
else
    rpc_string_free (&server_name, &status);

if (protect_level != rpc_c_protect_level_pkt_integ
    || authn_svc != rpc_c_authn_dce_secret
```

```
                || authz_svc != rpc_c_authz_dce)
              return (FALSE);


         return (sec_acl_mgr_is_authorized( mgr_hdl,                    /* (2) */
                                            permissions,
                                            pac,
                                            NULL,
                                            &mgr_uuid,
                                            user_obj,
                                            group_obj,
                                            &status));
         }


         /*------------------- Initialize Security -------------------*/

         void look_setup_auth( rpc_binding_vector_t *bindings,
                               boolean32 create_db_flag )
         {
         error_status_t status;
         sec_login_handle_t login_context;
         void *key_ptr;
         boolean32 expired;
         sec_login_auth_src_t auth_src;
         uuid_vector_t mgr_uuid_vec;
         pthread_t thread_hdl;
         pthread_attr_t attr;
         unsigned_char_t site_name[50] = "";
         sec_rgy_handle_t rgy_hdl;
         char *cell_name_p;



         rpc_server_register_auth_info( princ_name,                    /* (1) */
                                        rpc_c_authn_dce_secret,
                                        NULL,
                                        keytab,
                                        &status);
         ERR_CHK (status,"Could not register security information");


         sec_login_setup_identity( princ_name,                         /* (2) */
                                   sec_login_no_flags,
                                   &login_context,
                                   &status);
         ERR_CHK (status,"Could not obtain login context");


         sec_key_mgmt_get_key( rpc_c_authn_dce_secret,                 /* (3) */
                               keytab,
                               princ_name,
                               (unsigned32)0,
                               &key_ptr,
                               &status);
         ERR_CHK (status,"Could not obtain password");
```

```
sec_login_validate_identity( login_context,                            /* (4) */
                             (sec_passwd_rec_t *) key_ptr,
                             &expired,
                             &auth_src,
                             &status);
ERR_CHK (status,"Could not validate identity");
CND_CHK (auth_src != sec_login_auth_src_network,
         "Network identity not available");


sec_login_set_context( login_context,                                  /* (5) */
                       &status);
ERR_CHK (status,"Error setting default login context");


sec_acl_mgr_configure( sec_acl_mgr_config_stable|                      /* (6) */
                       create_db_flag,
                       acl_db_name,
                       &mgr_hdl,
                       &status);
ERR_CHK (status,"Error initializing ACL Manager");


rpc_server_register_if( rdaclif_v0_0_s_ifspec,                         /* (7) */
                        NULL,
                        NULL,
                        &status);
ERR_CHK (status,"Error registering ACL Manager interface");


mgr_uuid_vec.count = 1;
mgr_uuid_vec.uuid[0] = &mgr_uuid;


rpc_ep_register( rdaclif_v0_0_s_ifspec,                                /* (8) */
                 bindings,
                 &mgr_uuid_vec,
                 (idl_char *) "ACL Manager for Lookup Server",
                 &status);
ERR_CHK (status,"Error registering ACL Manager with Endpoint Mapper");


/* Install program will export to namespace. No need to do it here */

if ( (pthread_attr_create(&attr) != 0) ||                              /* (9) */
     pthread_attr_setsched(&attr, SCHED_BG_NP) != 0)
   {
   attr = pthread_attr_default;
   }


if (pthread_create( &thread_hdl,                                      /* (10) */
                    attr,
                    (pthread_startroutine_t) manage_key,
                    (pthread_addr_t) 0) != 0)
   {
   WARN ("Could not create thread for key management");
   }
```

```
            sec_rgy_site_open( site_name,                          /* (11) */
                        &rgy_hdl,
                        &status);
        if (status != error_status_ok)
            {
            user_obj = NULL;
            }
            else
            {
            user_obj = malloc( sizeof( sec_id_t));
            user_obj->name = princ_name;
            sec_rgy_pgo_name_to_id( rgy_hdl,                       /* (12) */
                            sec_rgy_domain_person,
                            princ_name,
                            &user_obj->uuid,
                            &status);
            if (status != error_status_ok)
                {
                free(user_obj);
                user_obj = NULL;
                }


            }

        sec_rgy_site_close( rgy_hdl,                               /* (13) */
                        &status);
        /* Ignore error on close */

        group_obj = NULL;                                         /* (14) */

        dce_cf_get_cell_name( &cell_name_p,                       /* (15) */
                            &status);
        ERR_CHK (status,"Could not Obtain Cell Name");

        sprintf((char *) full_princ_name, "%s/%s", cell_name_p,
                                    (char *) princ_name);
        free((void *) cell_name_p);


        }



        /*** Routine to do key management - runs in its own thread */

        pthread_startroutine_t manage_key(pthread_addr_t arg)
        {
        error_status_t status;
```

```
sec_key_mgmt_manage_key( rpc_c_authn_dce_secret,              /* (16) */
                         keytab,
                         princ_name,
                         &status);
WARN ("Key management routine exited");
}
```

The Server Operations File

```
/* LOOKUP_E.C Server Operations */

#include <pthread.h>
#include <dce/daclmgr.h>
#include <stdio.h>
#include <string.h>
#include "errmac.h"
#include "lookup.h"


typedef enum {AVAIL, BUSY}              ctx_state_t;
typedef enum {NO_RECORD, HAS_RECORD}    rec_state_t;
typedef enum {NO_FILTER, BEGIN, NEXT}   filter_state_t;



typedef struct
    {
    idl_long_int        curr_rec;
    ctx_state_t         ctx_state;
    rec_state_t         rec_state;
    filter_state_t      flt_state;
    filter_t            filter;
    idl_long_int  my_index;
    }
client_ctx_t;

#define CLIENT_MAX      30
#define FILE_MAX        50

#define LIST_END -1
#define IN_USE -2

#define ACCESS_ERROR    sec_acl_not_authorized

static pthread_mutex_t lock_read, lock_write, lock_ctx;
static client_ctx_t    client_table [CLIENT_MAX];

static struct
    {
```

```
        idl_long_int              link;
        idl_byte          data[LOOK_REC_SIZE];
        }
data_file[FILE_MAX];

static idl_long_int    free_head;


/* --------- externals -------------- */

int     look_check_access   ( rpc_binding_handle_t bind_h,
                                sec_acl_permset_t access);
void    look_ctx_init       (void);




/* --------- subroutines ----------- */

static int          match      (idl_long_int rec, filter_t *filter);
static int          test_used  (idl_long_int rec);
static void         set_used   (idl_long_int rec);
static void         push_free  (idl_long_int rec);
static idl_long_int pop_free   (void);
static void         lock       (pthread_mutex_t lock_type);
static void         unlock     (pthread_mutex_t lock_type);
static idl_long_int get_next   (idl_long_int rec);


/* --------- look_open() - start session --------- */

error_status_t look_open (
     handle_t      bind_h,
     ctx_h         *ctx_p)
{
int i;
client_ctx_t *clt_p;
clt_p=NULL;
*ctx_p=NULL;

if (!look_check_access (bind_h, sec_acl_perm_test))
   return ACCESS_ERROR;
lock (lock_ctx);

for (i=0; i<CLIENT_MAX && clt_p==NULL; i++)
   {
   if (client_table[i].ctx_state==AVAIL)
     clt_p=&client_table[i];
   }

if (clt_p!=NULL)
  {
```

```
  *ctx_p=(void *)clt_p;
  clt_p->ctx_state=BUSY;
  clt_p->rec_state=NO_RECORD;
  clt_p->flt_state=NO_FILTER;
  }
unlock (lock_ctx);
return rpc_s_ok;
}



/* --------- look_close() - end session --------- */

error_status_t look_close (
    handle_t      bind_h,
    ctx_h         *ctx_p)
{
client_ctx_t *clt_p;

lock (lock_ctx);
clt_p=(client_ctx_t *) *ctx_p;
clt_p->ctx_state=AVAIL;
unlock (lock_ctx);
*ctx_p=NULL;
return rpc_s_ok;
}



/* --------- look_filter() ----------------
 * Establish a filter criteria to use in subsequent look_next calls
 */

error_status_t look_filter (
    handle_t      bind_h,
    ctx_h         ctx_p,
    filter_t      *filter_p)
{
client_ctx_t *clt_p;

if (!look_check_access (bind_h, sec_acl_perm_read))
   return ACCESS_ERROR;

lock(lock_read);
clt_p=(client_ctx_t *) ctx_p;

clt_p->filter=*filter_p;  /* deposit and use it later */
clt_p->flt_state=BEGIN;   /* doesn't affect client's curr_rec */
                          /* until look_next */
unlock(lock_read);
return rpc_s_ok;
}
```

```
/*
/* ------------------------ look_next() --------------------------
Find a record satisfying the filter criteria. Requires previous call
to look_filter. If this is the first look_next since look_filter was
called, we start the search from the beginning of the file,
otherwise from the record after that returned by the previous
successful look_next.
*/

error_status_t look_next (
      handle_t      bind_h,
      ctx_h         ctx_p,
      idl_long_int  start,
      idl_long_int  len,
      idl_byte      buf[LOOK_REC_SIZE],
      look_sts_t    *result)
{
client_ctx_t    *clt_p;
look_sts_t   flag;
int          next;


if (!look_check_access (bind_h, sec_acl_perm_read))
   return ACCESS_ERROR;


lock (lock_read);
clt_p=(client_ctx_t *)ctx_p;

next=clt_p->curr_rec+1;        /* Assume filter state is NEXT */
switch (clt_p->flt_state)
   {
   case NO_FILTER:
     *result=LOOK_NO_FILTER;  /* check that a filter exists */
     break;
   case BEGIN:             /* New filter (or no good look_next yet) */
     next=0;              /* Drop through into search */
   case NEXT:
     flag=LOOK_END_SEARCH;    /* Assume not found */
     while ( flag == LOOK_END_SEARCH && next < FILE_MAX )
        {
        if (test_used(next) && match(next, &clt_p->filter))
           {                              /* HERE WHEN RECORD FOUND */
           memcpy (&buf[start], &data_file[next].data[start], len);
           clt_p->curr_rec=next;          /* update internal status */
           clt_p->rec_state=HAS_RECORD;
           clt_p->flt_state=NEXT;
           flag=LOOK_OK;                  /* remote call success */
           }
        next++;
        }
     *result=flag;
   }
```

```
unlock (lock_read);
return rpc_s_ok;
}

/* ----------- look_read() ----------------
 * Return the data from the current record
 */

error_status_t look_read (
      handle_t      bind_h,
      ctx_h         ctx_p,
      idl_long_int  start,
      idl_long_int  len,
      idl_byte      buf[LOOK_REC_SIZE],
      look_sts_t    *result)
{
client_ctx_t *clt_p;

if (!look_check_access (bind_h, sec_acl_perm_read))
   return ACCESS_ERROR;

lock (lock_read);
clt_p=(client_ctx_t *)ctx_p;
if (clt_p->rec_state==HAS_RECORD)
   {
   memcpy (&buf[start], &data_file [clt_p->curr_rec].data[start], len);
   *result=LOOK_OK;
   }
else
   *result=LOOK_NO_CURRENT;
unlock (lock_read);
return rpc_s_ok;
}

/* --------- look_write() ---------
 * Update the current record
 */

error_status_t look_write (
      handle_t      bind_h,
      ctx_h         ctx_p,
      idl_long_int  start,
      idl_long_int  len,
      idl_byte      buf[LOOK_REC_SIZE],
      look_sts_t    *result)
{
client_ctx_t *clt_p;

if (!look_check_access (bind_h, sec_acl_perm_write))
   return ACCESS_ERROR;

lock (lock_write);
clt_p=(client_ctx_t *)ctx_p;
```

```
if (clt_p->rec_state==HAS_RECORD)
   {
   memcpy (&data_file [clt_p->curr_rec].data[start], &buf[start], len);
   *result=LOOK_OK;
   }
else
   *result=LOOK_NO_CURRENT;

unlock (lock_write);
return rpc_s_ok;
}


/*------------ look_add() --------------
 * Add a new record, initialized to blanks, make it current
 */

error_status_t look_add (
     handle_t      bind_h,
     ctx_h         ctx_p,
     look_sts_t    *result)
{
client_ctx_t *clt_p;
int i;

if (!look_check_access (bind_h, sec_acl_perm_insert))
   return ACCESS_ERROR;

lock (lock_write);
clt_p=(client_ctx_t *)ctx_p;

if ( (i = pop_free()) >= 0 )
   {
   set_used (i);
   clt_p->curr_rec=i;
   clt_p->rec_state=HAS_RECORD;
   memset (&data_file [clt_p->curr_rec].data[0], ' ', LOOK_REC_SIZE);
   *result=LOOK_OK;
   }
else
   *result=LOOK_FILE_FULL;

unlock (lock_write);
return rpc_s_ok;
}

/* --------- look_delete() ---------
 * Delete the current record, unless someone else is using it
 */

error_status_t look_delete (
     handle_t      bind_h,
     ctx_h         ctx_p,
     look_sts_t    *result)
```

```
{
client_ctx_t *clt_p, *peer_p;
idl_long_int i;

if (!look_check_access (bind_h, sec_acl_perm_delete))
    return ACCESS_ERROR;
clt_p=(client_ctx_t *)ctx_p;


if (clt_p->rec_state==HAS_RECORD)
    {
    lock (lock_ctx);
    for (i=0; i<CLIENT_MAX; i++)   /* Check that no other client */
        {                          /* threads are using this record */
        peer_p=&client_table[i];
        if (peer_p->ctx_state==BUSY
        &&  peer_p->rec_state==HAS_RECORD
        &&  peer_p->curr_rec==clt_p->curr_rec
        && i != clt_p->my_index)
            break;
        }
    if (i<CLIENT_MAX)               /* if others using record, tell */
        *result=LOOK_OTHERS;        /* client he cant delete it */
    else
        {
        push_free (clt_p->curr_rec);   /* do the deletion: put on */
                                       /* free list */
        clt_p->rec_state=NO_RECORD;    /* Note that curr_rec doesnt */
                                       /* change */
        *result=LOOK_OK;
        }
    unlock (lock_ctx);
    }
else
   *result=LOOK_NO_CURRENT;

return rpc_s_ok;
}


/* ---------- Mutex and Context Initialization ---------- */

void look_ctx_init (void)
{
int i;

if (pthread_mutex_init( &lock_read,                              /* (1) */
                     pthread_mutexattr_default) !=0)
    {
    ERROR("Could not initialize read mutex");
    }


if (pthread_mutex_init( &lock_write,
                     pthread_mutexattr_default) !=0)
```

```
        {
        ERROR("Could not initialize write mutex");
        }

    if (pthread_mutex_init( &lock_ctx,
                            pthread_mutexattr_default) !=0)
        {
        ERROR("Could not initialize context mutex");
        }

    lock (lock_write);
    free_head=LIST_END;
    for ( i = FILE_MAX-1; i >= 0; i-- ) push_free(i);
    unlock (lock_write);

    lock (lock_ctx);
    for (i=0; i<CLIENT_MAX; i++)                                    /* (2) */
        {
        client_table[i].ctx_state = AVAIL;
        client_table[i].my_index = i;
        }
    unlock (lock_ctx);
    }


/*** Context Rundown Routine ***/

void ctx_h_rundown( ctx_h ctx_p )
{
client_ctx_t *clt_p;

if (ctx_p == NULL) return;                                          /* (3) */

lock (lock_ctx);
clt_p=(client_ctx_t *) ctx_p;
clt_p->ctx_state=AVAIL;
unlock (lock_ctx);
}

/*
Returns non-zero if the specified record matches the filter criteria.
*/

int match (idl_long_int rec, filter_t *filter)
{
idl_byte *p;

p=&data_file[rec].data[filter->ofs];
if (memcmp (p, filter->min, filter->len)>=0
&&  memcmp (p, filter->max, filter->len)<=0)
    return 1;
else
    return 0;
}
```

```
/* ---------- Free record and list manipulation ----------- */


/* returns non-zero if record contains data */

int  test_used (idl_long_int rec)
{
return ( data_file[rec].link == IN_USE );
}


/* mark a record as containing data */

void set_used  (idl_long_int rec)
{
data_file[rec].link = IN_USE;
}


/* push a record onto the free list, marking it as not containing data*/

void push_free  (idl_long_int rec)
{
data_file[rec].link = free_head;
free_head=rec;
}




/* pop a record from the free list (DOESN'T mark it as having data) */

idl_long_int pop_free (void)
{
idl_long_int i;
i=free_head;
if ( i !=  LIST_END )
   free_head=get_next (i);
return i;
}


/* returns free list successor field */

idl_long_int get_next (idl_long_int rec)
{
return ( data_file[rec].link );
}




void    lock        (pthread_mutex_t lock_type)
{
```

```
if (pthread_mutex_lock(&lock_type) != 0)
    {
    ERROR("Error locking mutex")
    }
}

void    unlock      (pthread_mutex_t lock_type)
{
if (pthread_mutex_unlock(&lock_type) != 0)
    {
    ERROR("Error unlocking mutex")
    }
}
```

The Client File

```
/* LOOKUP_C.C Lookup Client Program */

#include <dce/sec_login.h>
#include <stdio.h>
#include <ctype.h>
#include <string.h>
#include "errmac.h"
#include "lookup.h"
#include "lookup_s.h"

#define NAME_MAX    10      /* max length of null-terminated field name */
#define SCHEMA_MAX  10      /* max number of fields in schema */

typedef struct {
    char name[NAME_MAX];
    int start;
    int length;
    } field_t;

typedef struct {
    char action;
    int field;
    char value_1 [LOOK_FIELD_MAX];
    char value_2 [LOOK_FIELD_MAX];
    } cmd_t;


void  get_command   (cmd_t *cmd);
void  make_filter   (cmd_t *cmd, filter_t *filter);
void  display_help  (void);
int   parse_params  (char *schema, int argc, char *argv[]);
int   read_schema   (char *filename);
int   get_field     (char *name);
void  pad_field     (char *text, int length);
void  display_field (char *rec, int len);
int   bind_to_server (void);
```

```
static field_t  field_tbl [SCHEMA_MAX];
static int      field_count;

/* returns 0 for success, -1 for failure */

int  main (int argc, char *argv[])
{
int i;
error_status_t status;
look_sts_t     result;
idl_long_int   start, length;
cmd_t          cmd;
void           *ctx_p;
char           schema [30];
idl_char        buffer [LOOK_REC_SIZE];
filter_t       filter;
rpc_ns_handle_t binding_context;
rpc_binding_handle_t bind_h;
sec_login_handle_t login_context;

/* Get Command Arguments */
if (!parse_params (schema, argc, argv))
   return -1;

/* Read in Schema File */
if (!read_schema (schema))
   return -2;


sec_login_get_current_context( &login_context,                    /* (1) */
                               &status);
ERR_CHK(status,"Could not get current security context");

rpc_ns_binding_import_begin( rpc_c_ns_syntax_default,             /* (2) */
                             NULL,
                             lookup_v1_0_c_ifspec,
                             NULL,
                             &binding_context,
                             &status);
ERR_CHK(status,"Could not import binding context");

do
   {
   rpc_ns_binding_import_next( binding_context,                   /* (3) */
                               &bind_h,
                               &status);
   ERR_CHK(status,"Could not find any servers to bind to");

   rpc_binding_set_auth_info( bind_h,                             /* (4) */
                              (idl_char *) &princ_name,
                              rpc_c_protect_level_pkt_integ,
                              rpc_c_authn_dce_secret,
                              (rpc_auth_identity_handle_t) login_context,
```

```
                                     rpc_c_authz_dce,
                                     &status);
         ERR_CHK(status,"Could not associate security information with binding");


         status=look_open (bind_h, &ctx_p);                              /* (5) */

         if (ctx_p == NULL) WARN("Server was unable to allocate context");
         }
         while(status != rpc_s_ok);

    rpc_ns_binding_import_done(&binding_context,                         /* (6) */
                               &status);
    ERR_CHK(status,"Error releasing binding context");


    display_help ();

    /* Main Command Loop */
    cmd.action='\0';
    while (cmd.action != 'X')
       {
       get_command (&cmd);
       if (cmd.field == -1) continue;
       start=field_tbl[cmd.field].start;
       length=field_tbl[cmd.field].length;
       pad_field (cmd.value_1, length);
       pad_field (cmd.value_2, length);
       switch (cmd.action) {
          case 'A':         /* Add an empty record */
             status=look_add (bind_h, ctx_p, &result);
             ERR_CHK (status, "Error calling look_add");
             break;
           case 'C':        /* Change the current record */
             memcpy (&buffer[start], &cmd.value_1, length);
             status=look_write (bind_h, ctx_p, start, length, buffer, &result);
             ERR_CHK (status, "Error calling look_write");
             break;
          case 'D':         /* Delete the current record */
             look_delete (bind_h, ctx_p, &result);
             ERR_CHK (status, "Error calling look_delete");
             break;
          case 'F':          /* Set filter */
             make_filter (&cmd, &filter);
             status=look_filter (bind_h, ctx_p, &filter);
             ERR_CHK (status, "Error calling look_filter");
             break;
          case 'N':          /* Display the next matching record */
             status=look_next (bind_h, ctx_p, 0, LOOK_REC_SIZE, buffer, &result);
             ERR_CHK (status, "Error calling look_next");
             if (result == LOOK_OK)
```

```
                    {
                    display_field((char *) &buffer[0], LOOK_REC_SIZE);
                    printf ("\n");
                    }
                break;
            case 'S':        /* Display current record */
                status=look_read (bind_h, ctx_p, 0, LOOK_REC_SIZE, buffer, &result);
                ERR_CHK (status, "Error calling look_read");
                if (result==LOOK_OK)
                    {
                    display_field ((char *) &buffer[0], LOOK_REC_SIZE);
                    printf ("\n");
                    }
                break;
            case 'X':
                break;
            default:
                display_help();
                break;
            }
        }

status=look_close (bind_h, &ctx_p);
ERR_CHK (status, "Error calling look_close");
return 0;
}



/* Uses the cmd structure to create a filter */

void  make_filter     (cmd_t *cmd, filter_t *filter)
{
strncpy ((char *) filter->min, cmd->value_1, LOOK_FIELD_MAX);
strncpy ((char *) filter->max, cmd->value_2, LOOK_FIELD_MAX);
filter->ofs=field_tbl [cmd->field].start;
filter->len=field_tbl [cmd->field].length;
}




/* Prompts user for command and parses input. See display_help at
end of file for command syntax. */


void  get_command     (cmd_t *cmd)
{
char line[100], field[100], *cp, inp_act;
int i, j, nr_fields_input;
```

```
          cmd->action='\0';
          while (!cmd->action)
            {
            cmd->field=0;  /* default to first field if none supplied */
            cmd->value_1[0]='\0';
            cmd->value_2[0]='\0';
            printf ("lookup=>");
            cp=gets(line);
            nr_fields_input=0;
            if (cp)
               {
               nr_fields_input=sscanf (line, "%c%30s%30s%30s",
                  &inp_act,
                  field,
                  &cmd->value_1,
                  &cmd->value_2);
               }
            if (nr_fields_input>0)
               {
               inp_act=toupper(inp_act);
               if (nr_fields_input>1)
                  if ( (cmd->field=get_field (field)) == -1 ) return;

               switch (inp_act) {  /* set j to number of fields required */
                  case 'C':    {j=1; break;}
                  case 'F':    {j=2; break;}
                  default: {j=0; break;}
                  }
               if (inp_act=='F' && nr_fields_input==1)    /* dummy args to */
                                                          /* find all */
                  {
                  strcpy (cmd->value_1, " ");
                  strcpy (cmd->value_2, "\x7f");
                  cmd->field=0;
                  }
               if (nr_fields_input>0 || !j)  /* if have field or dont need */
                  {                          /* any, cmd okay */
                  cmd->action=inp_act;
                  }  /* i>=0 */
               }      /* cp */
            }          /* while */
          }            /* get_command */


/* returns non-zero for success, 0 for error,  */

int   parse_params   (char *schema, int argc, char *argv[])
  {
if (argc!=2)
   {
   printf ("Usage: %s <schema file name>\n", argv[0]);
   return 0;
   }
```

```
        strcpy (schema, argv[1]);
        return -1;
        }


        /* returns record length or zero for errors in schema */

        int   read_schema     (char *filename)
        {
        char line[100], *cp;
        FILE *fh;
        int i;

        fh=fopen (filename, "r");
        if (fh==NULL)
            {
            printf ("file %s can't be opened for reading\n", filename);
            return 0;
            }
        printf ("Field \t Start \t Length \n");
        field_count=0;
        cp= fgets (line, sizeof(line), fh); /* skip first line: name, rec len */

        while (field_count<LOOK_FIELD_MAX
        &&    cp!=NULL)
            {
            cp=fgets (line, sizeof(line), fh);
            if (cp!=NULL)
                {
                sscanf (line, "%s %d %d",
                field_tbl  [field_count].name,
                &field_tbl [field_count].start,
                &field_tbl [field_count].length);
                }
            i=field_tbl [field_count].length;
            if (field_tbl [field_count].name[0] != '\0'
            &&  field_tbl [field_count].start+i <= LOOK_REC_SIZE)
                {
                printf ("%s \t %d \t %d\n",
                    field_tbl[field_count].name,
                    field_tbl[field_count].start,
                    field_tbl[field_count].length);
                field_count++;
                }
            }
        printf ("%d Fields\n", field_count);
        fclose (fh);
        return field_count ? LOOK_REC_SIZE : 0;
        }


        void   pad_field      (char *text, int length)
        {
```

```
int i, start, pad;
start=strlen(text);
pad=length-start;
for (i=0; i<pad; i++)
   {
   *(text+start+i)=' ';
   }
}


/* Match as much of field name that was typed against the names
in the table. Return field index for succes, or <0 for failure.
Deposit field length and offset in callers variables.
*/

int   get_field      (char *name)
{
int i, j, field;
i=strlen(name);
for (field=0; field<field_count; field++)
   {
   if (!strncmp (field_tbl[field].name, name, i))
      break;
   }

if (field<field_count)
   return field;
else
   {
   printf("Field name: %s not found in schema\n",name);
   return -1;
   }
}


void display_field    (char *rec, int length)
{
printf ("Result=\"%-50.*s\"", length, rec);
}


void display_help   (void)
{
char *msg[]={
   "Commands are: \n",
   "  A  Add blank record (becomes current)\n",
   "  D  Delete current record\n",
   "  C  Change <field><new value>\n",
   "  F  Set filter to <field><low-value><high-value>  \n",
   "      (use F with no args to allow all records) \n",
   "  N  Display next record satisfying filter\n",
   "  S  Display current record (with any changes) \n",
   "  X  Exit \n",
```

```
    "      A field is a name defined in the schema (case sensitive)\n",
    ""};
int i;

for (i=0; *msg[i]; i++)
   printf ("%s", msg[i]);
}
```

The Client Schema File

```
INVEN   40
PART     0   5
QUANT    5   5
NAME    10  20
VENDOR  30  20
```

The Installation File

```
/* LOOKUP_I.C Lookup Installation Program */

#include <stdio.h>
#include <string.h>
#include <dce/rpc.h>
#include <dce/dce_cf.h>
#include <dce/rdaclif.h>
#include "errmac.h"
#include "lookup.h"
#include "lookup_s.h"


/*** Dummy Context Rundown Routine to satisfy reference in stub ***/

void ctx_h_rundown( ctx_h ctx_p )
{
}

/***** Lookup Table Installation Program *****/

main( int argc, char *argv[] )
{

error_status_t       status;
rpc_binding_vector_t *bindings;
uuid_vector_t mgr_uuid_vec;

if (argc < 2)
    {
    printf("Usage: %s -i or %s -r\n",argv[0], argv[0]);
    exit(1);
    }
```

```
            if (strcmp(argv[1], "-i") == 0)
                {
                rpc_server_use_all_protseqs ( rpc_c_protseq_max_reqs_default,     /* (1) */
                                        &status);
                ERR_CHK(status,"Could not use all protocols");

                rpc_server_inq_bindings( &bindings,                               /* (2) */
                                    &status);
                ERR_CHK(status,"Could not get binding vector");

                rpc_ns_binding_export( rpc_c_ns_syntax_default,                   /* (3) */
                                    name,
                                    lookup_v1_0_s_ifspec,
                                    bindings,
                                    NULL,
                                    &status);
                ERR_CHK(status,"Could not export server bindings");

                mgr_uuid_vec.count = 1;
                mgr_uuid_vec.uuid[0] = &mgr_uuid;

                rpc_ns_binding_export( rpc_c_ns_syntax_default,                   /* (4) */
                                    name,
                                    rdaclif_v0_0_s_ifspec,
                                    bindings,
                                    &mgr_uuid_vec,
                                    &status);
                ERR_CHK(status,"Could not export server bindings");

        /* Add code here for additional de-installation tasks */

                }
            else if (strcmp(argv[1], "-r") == 0)
                {
                rpc_ns_binding_unexport( rpc_c_ns_syntax_default,                 /* (5) */
                                    name,
                                    lookup_v1_0_s_ifspec,
                                    NULL,
                                    &status);
                ERR_CHK(status,"Could not remove server bindings");

                rpc_ns_binding_unexport( rpc_c_ns_syntax_default,                 /* (6) */
                                    name,
                                    rdaclif_v0_0_s_ifspec,
                                    NULL,
                                    &status);
                ERR_CHK(status,"Could not remove ACL Manager bindings");

        /* Add code here for additional de-installation tasks */

                }
            else
```

```
            {
            printf("Usage: %s -i or %s -r\n", argv[0], argv[0]);
            exit(1);
            }
    }
```

The Build File

```
    PGM=lookup
    DCE=/opt/dcelocal
    DCELIB=-L $(DCE)/lib
    LIBS=$(DCELIB) -l dce -l dcedes -l seccrypt -l socket  -l nsl
    IDL=/opt/dcelocal/bin/idl
    CC=/usr/bin/cc -g

    default: $(PGM)_c.out $(PGM)_s.out  $(PGM)_i.out

    $(PGM)_c.out: $(PGM)_c.c $(PGM).h $(PGM)_cstub.o errmac.h $(PGM)_s.h
          $(CC) -o $(PGM)_c.out $(LIBS) $(PGM)_cstub.o $(PGM)_c.c

    $(PGM)_s.out: $(PGM)_s.c $(PGM).h $(PGM)_sstub.o $(PGM)_e.c $(PGM)_a.c \
                acl_mgr.c errmac.h $(PGM)_s.h rdaclif_sstub.o
          $(CC) -o $(PGM)_s.out $(LIBS) $(PGM)_sstub.o $(PGM)_s.c $(PGM)_e.c \
                $(PGM)_a.c acl_mgr.c rdaclif_sstub.o

    $(PGM)_i.out: $(PGM)_i.c $(PGM).h $(PGM)_i_sstub.o errmac.h $(PGM)_s.h \
                          rdaclif_i_sstub.o
          $(CC) -o $(PGM)_i.out $(LIBS) $(PGM)_i_sstub.o $(PGM)_i.c \
                rdaclif_i_sstub.o

    $(PGM)_sstub.o $(PGM)_cstub.o $(PGM).h: $(PGM).idl $(PGM).acf
          $(IDL) $(PGM).idl

    $(PGM)_i_sstub.o: $(PGM).idl $(PGM).acf
          $(IDL) $(PGM).idl -client none -no_mepv -sstub $(PGM)_i_sstub

    rdaclif_sstub.o: /usr/include/dce/rdaclif.idl rdaclif.acf
          $(IDL) /usr/include/dce/rdaclif.idl  -client none

    rdaclif_i_sstub.o: /usr/include/dce/rdaclif.idl rdaclif.acf
          $(IDL) /usr/include/dce/rdaclif.idl  -client none -no_mepv \
                -sstub rdaclif_i_sstub
```

The Tiered Server

The IDL File

```
/* SRTLST.IDL Tiered Server for sorting */
[
uuid (004c4b41-e7c5-1cb9-94e6-0000c07c3610),
version(1.0)
]
interface srtlst

{

import "lookup.idl";

typedef enum {
   SORT_OK,
   SORT_WRONG_STATE,
   SORT_END}
sort_sts_t;

error_status_t sort_open (
      [in]      BIND_HDL_T    bind_h,
      [out]     ctx_h         *ctx_p);

error_status_t sort_close (
      [in]      BIND_HDL_T    bind_h,
      [in, out] ctx_h         *ctx_p);

error_status_t sort_begin (
      [in]      BIND_HDL_T    bind_h,
      [in]      ctx_h         ctx_p,
      [in]      filter_t      *filter_p);

error_status_t sort_next (
      [in]      BIND_HDL_T    bind_h,
```

```
            [in]        ctx_h       ctx_p,
            [in]        long        start,
            [in]        long        len,
            [out,
            first_is (start),
            length_is (len)]
                        byte        buf[LOOK_REC_SIZE],
            [out]       sort_sts_t  *result);

}
```

The ACF File

```
/* SRTLST.ACF Tiered Server for sorting */

interface srtlst

{

[comm_status, fault_status, enable_allocate] sort_open ();

[comm_status, fault_status, enable_allocate] sort_close ();

[comm_status, fault_status, enable_allocate] sort_begin ();

[comm_status, fault_status, enable_allocate] sort_next ();

}
```

The ACL Manager ACF File

```
/*
 * **** RDACLIF.ACF ****
 * sec_acl_mgr_lookup() and sec_acl_mgr_replace call rpc_ss_allocate()
 * therefore the operations that call them must be declared to have the
 * enable_allocate attribute
 */

interface rdaclif {

    [enable_allocate] rdacl_lookup ();

    [enable_allocate] rdacl_replace ();

    [enable_allocate] rdacl_get_access();

    [enable_allocate] rdacl_test_access ();

    [enable_allocate] rdacl_test_access_on_behalf ();

}
```

The Server Definitions File

```
/* SRTLST_S.H Sort List Server Definitions */

/* We only have one ACL manager, therefore one manager uuid */

static uuid_t  mgr_uuid
                      = { /* 0050DF20-927B-1C53-AF86-0000C07C3610 */
        0x0050df20,
        0x927b,
        0x1c53,
        0xaf,
        0x86,
        {0x00, 0x00, 0xc0, 0x7c, 0x36, 0x10}
      };


static unsigned_char_t name[]     = "/.:/applications/srtlst_server";
static unsigned_char_t princ_name[]     = "srtlst_server";
static unsigned_char_t keytab[]         = "srtlst_keytab";
static unsigned_char_t acl_db_name[]    = "srtlst_acl";


static unsigned_char_t look_princ_name[] = "lookup_server";
```

The Server Control File

```
/* SRTLST_S.C Sort List Server Control */

#include <stdio.h>
#include <pthread_exc.h>
#include <dce/rpc.h>
#include <dce/daclmgr.h>
#include "errmac.h"
#include "srtlst.h"
#include "srtlst_s.h"


extern void sort_ctx_init ();


main (int argc, char *argv[])
{
unsigned32            max_threads;
error_status_t        status;
rpc_binding_vector_t  *bindings;
boolean32             create_db_flag = FALSE;

if (argc > 3 )
    {
    fprintf(stderr, "Usage: %s maximum_threads\n", argv[0] );
    exit(1);
    }
```

```
if (argc < 2 )
    {
    max_threads = rpc_c_listen_max_calls_default;
    }
else
    max_threads = atol(argv[1]);

if (argc = 3 && (strcmp(argv[2],"-c") == 0))
    {
    create_db_flag = sec_acl_mgr_config_create;              /* (1) */
    }


rpc_server_register_if( srtlst_v1_0_s_ifspec,               /* (2) */
                        NULL,
                        NULL,
                        &status);
ERR_CHK (status, "Could not register interface");

rpc_server_use_all_protseqs( max_threads,                  /* (3) */
                             &status);
ERR_CHK (status, "Could not use all protocols");

rpc_server_inq_bindings( &bindings,                        /* (4) */
                         &status);
ERR_CHK (status, "Could not get binding vector");


sort_setup_auth( bindings, create_db_flag );               /* (5) */

sort_ctx_init();                                           /* (6) */


/* Bindings are exported to the namespace by the install program. */
/* Therefore we do not do it here */

rpc_ep_register( srtlst_v1_0_s_ifspec,                     /* (7) */
                 bindings,
                 NULL,
                 (unsigned_char_t *) "Sort List Server",
                 &status);
ERR_CHK (status, "Could not register endpoint");

TRY {

printf ("Sort List Server is now available\n");

rpc_server_listen( max_threads,                            /* (8) */
                   &status);
    }
FINALLY
    {
```

```
        rpc_ep_unregister( srtlst_v1_0_s_ifspec,                    /* (9) */
                           bindings,
                           NULL,
                           &status);

    }
ENDTRY;
}
```

The Server Security File

```
/* SRTLST_A.C Access Control Routines */

#include <sys/types.h>
#include <stdio.h>
#include <string.h>
#include <pthread.h>
#include <dce/rpc.h>
#include <dce/binding.h>
#include <dce/pgo.h>
#include <dce/rdaclif.h>
#include <dce/daclmgr.h>
#include <dce/daclif.h>
#include <dce/sec_login.h>
#include <dce/keymgmt.h>
#include <dce/dce_cf.h>
#include "srtlst.h"
#include "errmac.h"
#include "srtlst_s.h"

/* Global Variables */

extern  uuid_t mgr_uuid;

/* Internal Routines */

pthread_startroutine_t manage_key(pthread_addr_t arg);

/* Internal Variables */

sec_id_t *user_obj, *group_obj;
sec_acl_mgr_handle_t mgr_hdl;
unsigned_char_t full_princ_name[50];

/*---------- Check access (Reference Monitor) --------------*/

boolean32 sort_check_access (
    rpc_binding_handle_t binding,
    sec_acl_permset_t permissions)
{
```

```
        unsigned_char_t *server_name;
        sec_id_pac_t *pac;
        unsigned32 protect_level, authn_svc, authz_svc;
        error_status_t status;

        rpc_binding_inq_auth_client( binding,                              /* (1) */
                                     (rpc_authz_handle_t) &pac,
                                     &server_name,
                                     &protect_level,
                                     &authn_svc,
                                     &authz_svc,
                                     &status);
        if (status != rpc_s_ok) return (FALSE);


        if (strcmp ((char *)server_name, (char *)full_princ_name) != 0)
            {
            rpc_string_free (&server_name, &status);
            return (FALSE);
            }
        else
            rpc_string_free (&server_name, &status);

        if (protect_level != rpc_c_protect_level_pkt_integ
            || authn_svc != rpc_c_authn_dce_secret
            || authz_svc != rpc_c_authz_dce)
            return (FALSE);

        return (sec_acl_mgr_is_authorized( mgr_hdl,                        /* (2) */
                                           permissions,
                                           pac,
                                           NULL,
                                           &mgr_uuid,
                                           user_obj,
                                           group_obj,
                                           &status));
        }




        /*------------------- Initialize Security -------------------*/

        void sort_setup_auth( rpc_binding_vector_t *bindings,
                              boolean32 create_db_flag )
        {
        error_status_t status;
        sec_login_handle_t login_context;
        void *key_ptr;
        boolean32 expired;
        sec_login_auth_src_t auth_src;
        uuid_vector_t mgr_uuid_vec;
```

```
pthread_t thread_hdl;
pthread_attr_t attr;
unsigned_char_t site_name[50] = "";
sec_rgy_handle_t rgy_hdl;
char *cell_name_p;

rpc_server_register_auth_info( princ_name,                      /* (1) */
                               rpc_c_authn_dce_secret,
                               NULL,
                               keytab,
                               &status);
ERR_CHK (status,"Could not register security information");

sec_login_setup_identity( princ_name,                          /* (2) */
                          sec_login_no_flags,
                          &login_context,
                          &status);
ERR_CHK (status,"Could not obtain login context");

sec_key_mgmt_get_key( rpc_c_authn_dce_secret,                  /* (3) */
                      keytab,
                      princ_name,
                      (unsigned32)0,
                      &key_ptr,
                      &status);
ERR_CHK (status,"Could not obtain password");

sec_login_validate_identity( login_context,                    /* (4) */
                             (sec_passwd_rec_t *) key_ptr,
                             &expired,
                             &auth_src,
                             &status);
ERR_CHK (status,"Could not validate identity");
CND_CHK (auth_src != sec_login_auth_src_network,
         "Network identity not available");

sec_login_set_context( login_context,                          /* (5) */
                       &status);
ERR_CHK (status,"Error setting default login context");

sec_acl_mgr_configure( sec_acl_mgr_config_stable|create_db_flag,  /* (6) */
                       acl_db_name,
                       &mgr_hdl,
                       &status);
ERR_CHK (status,"Error initializing ACL Manager");

rpc_server_register_if( rdaclif_v0_0_s_ifspec,                 /* (7) */
                        NULL,
                        NULL,
                        &status);
ERR_CHK (status,"Error registering ACL Manager interface");
```

```
            mgr_uuid_vec.count = 1;
            mgr_uuid_vec.uuid[0] = &mgr_uuid;

            rpc_ep_register( rdaclif_v0_0_s_ifspec,                        /* (8) */
                        bindings,
                        &mgr_uuid_vec,
                        (unsigned_char_t *) "ACL Manager for Sort List Server",
                        &status);
            ERR_CHK (status,"Error registering ACL Manager with Endpoint Mapper");

            /* Install program will export to namespace. No need to do it here */

            if ( (pthread_attr_create(&attr) != 0) ||                     /* (9) */
                 pthread_attr_setsched(&attr, SCHED_BG_NP) != 0)
               {
               attr = pthread_attr_default;
               }

            if (pthread_create( &thread_hdl,                              /* (10) */
                            attr,
                            (pthread_startroutine_t) manage_key,
                            (pthread_addr_t) 0) != 0)
               {
               WARN ("Could not create thread for key management");
               }

            sec_rgy_site_open( site_name,                                 /* (11) */
                            &rgy_hdl,
                            &status);
            if (status != error_status_ok)
               {
               user_obj = NULL;
               }
               else
               {
               user_obj = malloc( sizeof( sec_id_t));
               user_obj->name = princ_name;
               sec_rgy_pgo_name_to_id( rgy_hdl,                           /* (12) */
                                    sec_rgy_domain_person,
                                    princ_name,
                                    &user_obj->uuid,
                                    &status);
               if (status != error_status_ok)
                  {
                  free(user_obj);
                  user_obj = NULL;
                  }

               }

            sec_rgy_site_close( rgy_hdl,                                  /* (13) */
                            &status);
            /* Ignore error on close */
```

```
group_obj = NULL;                                            /* (14) */

dce_cf_get_cell_name( &cell_name_p,                          /* (15) */
                      &status);
ERR_CHK (status,"Could not Obtain Cell Name");

sprintf((char *) full_princ_name, "%s/%s", cell_name_p,
                                  (char *) princ_name);
free((void *) cell_name_p);

}


/*** Routine to do key management - runs in its own thread */

pthread_startroutine_t manage_key(pthread_addr_t arg)
{
error_status_t status;

sec_key_mgmt_manage_key( rpc_c_authn_dce_secret,            /* (16) */
                         keytab,
                         princ_name,
                         &status);
WARN ("Key management routine exited");
}
```

The Server Operations File

```
/* SRTLST_E.C Server Operations */


#include <pthread.h>
#include <dce/daclmgr.h>
#include <stdio.h>
#include <stdlib.h>
#include <string.h>
#include <dce/sec_login.h>
#include "lookup.h"
#include "errmac.h"
#include "srtlst.h"
#include "srtlst_s.h"

#define STACK_MAX 50
#define CLIENT_MAX 30

#define ACCESS_ERROR    sec_acl_not_authorized

typedef enum {BUSY, AVAIL} ctx_state_t;
typedef enum {SORT_NONE, SORT_BEGIN, SORT_NEXT}  sort_state_t;

typedef struct node_s *node_t_p;
typedef struct node_s
   {
```

```
            node_t_p left;
            node_t_p right;
            char    *data;
            } node_t;

typedef struct {
   node_t *sub_tree;
   node_t *stack[STACK_MAX];
   node_t **stack_top;
   } traverse_t;

typedef struct {
   node_t        *tree;
   traverse_t    traverse;
   filter_t      filter;
   sort_state_t  sort_state;
   ctx_state_t   ctx_state;
   ctx_h         tier_ctx_h;
   } client_ctx_t;

/* -------------- Data common to all threads ------------------- */

static client_ctx_t   client_table [CLIENT_MAX];
static BIND_HDL_T     tier_bind_h;
static pthread_mutex_t lock_read, lock_ctx;

/* --------- Externals -------------- */

extern int    sort_check_access( rpc_binding_handle_t bind_h,
                                 sec_acl_permset_t access);

/* ----------------- Exported ------------------------------- */

void sort_ctx_init();

/* ---------------- Internal Subroutines ---------------------- */

static error_status_t retrieve_recs(BIND_HDL_T tier_bind_h,
                                    ctx_h tier_ctx_p,
                                    node_t **tree);
static void      insert_tree(node_t **root, char *buf, int length);
static void      init_inorder(node_t *tree, traverse_t *traverse);
static char *    next_inorder(traverse_t *traverse);
static void      destroy_tree(node_t *root);
static void      lock(pthread_mutex_t lock_type );
static void      unlock(pthread_mutex_t lock_type );

/* sort_open - get context & call look_open */

error_status_t sort_open(
            BIND_HDL_T   bind_h,
            ctx_h        *ctx_p)
```

```
{
int i;
client_ctx_t *clt_p;
error_status_t status;
ctx_h          tx_h;

clt_p = NULL;
*ctx_p = NULL;
if (!sort_check_access(bind_h, sec_acl_perm_test))
   return ACCESS_ERROR;
lock (lock_ctx);

for (i=0; (i < CLIENT_MAX) && (clt_p == NULL); i++)
   {
   if (client_table[i].ctx_state == AVAIL)
      clt_p = &client_table[i];
   }

if (clt_p != NULL)
   {
   clt_p->ctx_state = BUSY;
   clt_p->tree = NULL;
   unlock (lock_ctx);

   status = look_open(tier_bind_h, &tx_h);

   lock(lock_read);
   clt_p->tier_ctx_h = tx_h;
   if (status == rpc_s_ok)
      {
      clt_p->sort_state = SORT_NONE;
      *ctx_p = (void *) clt_p;
      unlock(lock_read);
      }
   else
      {
      unlock(lock_read);
      lock(lock_ctx);
      clt_p->ctx_state = AVAIL;
      unlock(lock_ctx);
      }
   }
else
   unlock(lock_ctx);
return status;
}

/* sort_close - cleanup data - deallocate context - call look_close */

error_status_t sort_close(
  BIND_HDL_T    bind_h,
  ctx_h         *ctx_p)
```

```
{
client_ctx_t *clt_p;
look_sts_t   result;
error_status_t status;
ctx_h        tx_h;

clt_p = (client_ctx_t *) *ctx_p;

status=look_close(tier_bind_h, &tx_h);

lock(lock_read);
clt_p->tier_ctx_h = tx_h;

destroy_tree(clt_p->tree);
unlock(lock_read);

lock(lock_ctx);
clt_p->ctx_state = AVAIL;

unlock(lock_ctx);
*ctx_p = NULL;
return rpc_s_ok;
}

/* sort_begin - set lookup filter to read qualified records */

error_status_t sort_begin(
            BIND_HDL_T   bind_h,
            ctx_h        ctx_p,
            filter_t     *filter_p)
{
client_ctx_t *clt_p;
error_status_t status;

if (!sort_check_access(bind_h, sec_acl_perm_test))
   return ACCESS_ERROR;

lock(lock_read);
clt_p = (client_ctx_t *) ctx_p;
clt_p->sort_state = SORT_BEGIN;
clt_p->filter = *filter_p;
destroy_tree(clt_p->tree);
unlock(lock_read);

status=look_filter(tier_bind_h, clt_p->tier_ctx_h, filter_p);

if (status == rpc_s_ok)
   status=retrieve_recs(tier_bind_h, clt_p->tier_ctx_h, &clt_p->tree);

return status;
}
```

```
/* sort_next - return next sorted record */

error_status_t sort_next(
            BIND_HDL_T    bind_h,
            ctx_h         ctx_p,
            idl_long_int  start,
            idl_long_int  len,
            idl_byte      buf[LOOK_REC_SIZE],
            sort_sts_t    *result)

{
client_ctx_t *clt_p;
char * rec_p;


clt_p = (client_ctx_t *) ctx_p;

if (!sort_check_access(bind_h, sec_acl_perm_read))
   return ACCESS_ERROR;
lock(lock_read);

switch (clt_p->sort_state) {
   case SORT_NONE:
      *result = SORT_WRONG_STATE;
      break;
   case SORT_BEGIN:
      init_inorder(clt_p->tree, &clt_p->traverse);
      clt_p->sort_state = SORT_NEXT;
   case SORT_NEXT:
      rec_p = next_inorder(&clt_p->traverse);
      if (rec_p == NULL)
         {
         *result = SORT_END;
         }
      else
         {
         memcpy((char *) &buf[start], rec_p, len);
         *result = SORT_OK;
         }
      break;
   }

unlock(lock_read);
return rpc_s_ok;
}

/* ---------- Mutex and Context Initialization ---------- */

void sort_ctx_init (void)
{
int i;
error_status_t status;
rpc_ns_handle_t binding_context;
```

```
      sec_login_handle_t login_context;
      ctx_h        ctx_p;

      if (pthread_mutex_init( &lock_read,                              /* (1) */
                          pthread_mutexattr_default) != 0)
          {
          ERROR("Could not initialize read mutex");
          }

      if (pthread_mutex_init( &lock_ctx,
                          pthread_mutexattr_default) != 0)
          {
          ERROR("Could not initialize context mutex");
          }

  lock(lock_ctx);

  for (i=0; i<CLIENT_MAX; i++)                                        /* (2) */
      {
      client_table[i].ctx_state = AVAIL;
      }
  unlock(lock_ctx);

  sec_login_get_current_context( &login_context,                     /* (3) */
                                &status);
  ERR_CHK(status,"Could not get current security context");

  rpc_ns_binding_import_begin( rpc_c_ns_syntax_default,              /* (4) */
                              NULL,
                              lookup_v1_0_c_ifspec,
                              NULL,
                              &binding_context,
                              &status);
  ERR_CHK(status,"Could not import binding context");

  do
      {
      rpc_ns_binding_import_next( binding_context,                   /* (5) */
                                  &tier_bind_h,
                                  &status);
      ERR_CHK(status,"Could not find any servers to bind to");

      rpc_binding_set_auth_info( tier_bind_h,                        /* (6) */
                                  (unsigned_char_t *) look_princ_name,
                                  rpc_c_protect_level_pkt_integ,
                                  rpc_c_authn_dce_secret,
                                  (rpc_auth_identity_handle_t) login_context,
                                  rpc_c_authz_dce,
                                  &status);
      ERR_CHK(status,"Could not associate security information with
      binding");

      status=look_open ( tier_bind_h, &ctx_p);                      /* (7) */
```

```
        }
     while(status != rpc_s_ok);   /* If this fails, try the next one */

rpc_ns_binding_import_done(&binding_context,                      /* (8) */
                           &status);
ERR_CHK(status,"Error releasing binding context");

status=look_close(tier_bind_h, &ctx_p);                          /* (9) */
        /* ignore error */
}

/*** Context Rundown Routine ***/

void ctx_h_rundown( ctx_h ctx_p )
{
client_ctx_t *clt_p;

if (ctx_p == NULL) return;                                       /* (10) */
clt_p = (client_ctx_t *) ctx_p;

lock(lock_read);
destroy_tree(clt_p->tree);
unlock(lock_read);

lock (lock_ctx);
clt_p->ctx_state = AVAIL;
unlock (lock_ctx);
}

/* Retrieves records specified by the filter from the LOOKUP server
 * and places them in an ascending search tree.
 */

error_status_t retrieve_recs( BIND_HDL_T tier_bind_h,
                              ctx_h tier_ctx_p,
                              node_t **tree)
{
look_sts_t result;
error_status_t status;
char buf[LOOK_REC_SIZE];

result = LOOK_OK;
while (result == LOOK_OK)
   {
   status=look_next (tier_bind_h, tier_ctx_p, 0, LOOK_REC_SIZE,
                     (unsigned_char_t *) buf, &result);
   if (status != rpc_s_ok) break;
   if (result == LOOK_OK)
      {
      lock(lock_read);
      insert_tree (tree, buf, LOOK_REC_SIZE );
      unlock(lock_read);
      }
```

```
        }
    return status;
    }

void lock(pthread_mutex_t lock_type)
{
if (pthread_mutex_lock(&lock_type) != 0)
    {
    ERROR("Error locking mutex")
    }
}

void unlock(pthread_mutex_t lock_type)
{
if (pthread_mutex_unlock(&lock_type) != 0)
    {
    ERROR("Error unlocking mutex")
    }
}

void insert_tree (node_t **root, char *buf, int length)
{
node_t *child, **owner, *new;
int i;

owner = root;
child = *root;

while (child != NULL)
    {
    i=memcmp (child->data, buf, length);
    if (i >= 0)
        {
        owner = &child->left;
        child = child->left;
        }
    else
        {
        owner = &child->right;
        child = child->right;
        }
    }
new=malloc (sizeof (node_t));
if (new != NULL)
    {
    new->left = NULL;
    new->right = NULL;
    new->data = malloc(length);
    if (new->data)
        {
        *owner = new;
        memcpy(new->data, buf, length);
        }
    }
}
```

```
void       init_inorder(node_t *tree, traverse_t *traverse)
{
traverse->stack_top = &traverse->stack[0];
traverse->stack[0] = (node_t *) NULL;
traverse->sub_tree = tree;
}

char * next_inorder(traverse_t *traverse)
{
node_t *sub;
char *next;

if ((sub = traverse->sub_tree) == NULL)
   {
   if ((sub = *traverse->stack_top--) == NULL)
      return NULL;
   }
else
   {
   while (sub->left != NULL)
      {
      *++traverse->stack_top = sub;
      sub = sub->left;
      }
   }
traverse->sub_tree = sub->right;
return sub->data;
}

void destroy_tree(node_t *root)
{
if (root!=NULL)
   {
   destroy_tree(root->left);
   destroy_tree(root->right);
   free(root->data);
   free(root);
   }
}
```

The Client File

```
/* SRTLST_C.C Sort List Client */

#include <dce/sec_login.h>
#include <stdio.h>
#include "errmac.h"
#include "srtlst.h"
#include "srtlst_s.h"

void display_rec(char *buf);

int main (int argc, char *argv[])
{
```

```
void                *ctx_p;
BIND_HDL_T          bind_h;
error_status_t      status;
sort_sts_t          result;
filter_t            filter;
char                buf[LOOK_REC_SIZE];
rpc_ns_handle_t     binding_context;
sec_login_handle_t  login_context;

/* Get a pointer to the security credentials */
sec_login_get_current_context( &login_context,                    /* (1) */
                               &status);
ERR_CHK(status,"Could not get current security context");

/* Initialize the search for a server */
rpc_ns_binding_import_begin( rpc_c_ns_syntax_default,              /* (2) */
                             NULL,
                             srtlst_v1_0_c_ifspec,
                             NULL,
                             &binding_context,
                             &status);
ERR_CHK(status,"Could not import binding context");

do
    {
    rpc_ns_binding_import_next( binding_context,                  /* (3) */
                                &bind_h,
                                &status);
    ERR_CHK(status,"Could not find any servers to bind to");

    rpc_binding_set_auth_info( bind_h,                            /* (4) */
                               (unsigned_char_t *) princ_name,
                               rpc_c_protect_level_pkt_integ,
                               rpc_c_authn_dce_secret,
                               (rpc_auth_identity_handle_t) login_context,
                               rpc_c_authz_dce,
                               &status);
    ERR_CHK(status,"Could not associate security information with binding");

    status=sort_open(bind_h, &ctx_p);                             /* (5) */

    if (ctx_p == NULL) WARN("Server was unable to allocate context");
    }
    while(status != rpc_s_ok);   /* If this fails, try the next one */

rpc_ns_binding_import_done( &binding_context,                     /* (6) */
                            &status);
ERR_CHK(status,"Error releasing binding context");

filter.ofs = 0;
filter.len = 1;
```

```
filter.min[0] = '\x01';
filter.max[0] = '\x7f';

status=sort_begin(bind_h, ctx_p, &filter);                           /* (7) */
ERR_CHK (status, "Sort Begin failed");

result = SORT_OK;
while (result == SORT_OK)
    {
    status=sort_next( bind_h,
                      ctx_p,
                      (idl_long_int) 0,
                      LOOK_REC_SIZE,
                      (unsigned_char_t *) buf,
                      &result);
    ERR_CHK (status, "Sort next failed");

    if (result == SORT_OK) display_rec (buf);
    }
status=sort_close(bind_h, &ctx_p);
ERR_CHK (status, "Sort Close failed");
}

void  display_rec( char *rec )
{
printf("Result=\"%*s\"\n", LOOK_REC_SIZE, rec);
}
```

The Installation File

```
/* SRTLST_I.C */

#include <stdio.h>
#include <string.h>
#include <dce/rpc.h>
#include <dce/dce_cf.h>
#include <dce/rdaclif.h>
#include "errmac.h"
#include "srtlst.h"
#include "srtlst_s.h"


/*** Dummy Context Rundown Routine to satisfy reference in stub ***/

void ctx_h_rundown( ctx_h ctx_p )
{
}

/***** Sort List Server Installation Program *****/

main( int argc, char *argv[] )
{
```

```
error_status_t        status;
rpc_binding_vector_t  *bindings;
uuid_vector_t mgr_uuid_vec;

if (argc < 2)
    {
    printf("Usage: %s -i or %s -r\n",argv[0], argv[0]);
    exit(1);
    }

if (strcmp(argv[1], "-i") == 0)
    {
    rpc_server_use_all_protseqs( rpc_c_protseq_max_reqs_default,    /* (1) */
                                 &status);
    ERR_CHK(status,"Could not use all protocols");

    rpc_server_inq_bindings( &bindings,                            /* (2) */
                             &status);
    ERR_CHK(status,"Could not get binding vector");

    rpc_ns_binding_export( rpc_c_ns_syntax_default,               /* (3) */
                           name,
                           srtlst_v1_0_s_ifspec,
                           bindings,
                           NULL,
                           &status);
    ERR_CHK(status,"Could not export server bindings");

    mgr_uuid_vec.count = 1;
    mgr_uuid_vec.uuid[0] = &mgr_uuid;

    rpc_ns_binding_export( rpc_c_ns_syntax_default,               /* (4) */
                           name,
                           rdaclif_v0_0_s_ifspec,
                           bindings,
                           &mgr_uuid_vec,
                           &status);
    ERR_CHK(status,"Could not export server bindings");

/* This is the place to add code to perform additional installation tasks */

    }
    else if (strcmp(argv[1], "-r") == 0)
        {
        rpc_ns_binding_unexport( rpc_c_ns_syntax_default,        /* (5) */
                                 name,
                                 srtlst_v1_0_s_ifspec,
                                 NULL,
                                 &status);
        ERR_CHK(status,"Could not remove server bindings");
```

```
                rpc_ns_binding_unexport( rpc_c_ns_syntax_default,          /* (6) */
                                  name,
                                  rdaclif_v0_0_s_ifspec,
                                  NULL,
                                  &status);
            ERR_CHK(status,"Could not remove ACL Manager bindings");

    /* Place additional de-installation tasks here */

        }
        else
        {
        printf("Usage: %s -i or %s -r\n", argv[0], argv[0]);
        exit(1);
        }
    }
```

The Build File

```
PGM=srtlst
DCE=/opt/dcelocal
DCELIB=-L $(DCE)/lib
LIBS=$(DCELIB) -l dce -l seccrypt -l socket  -l nsl
IDL=/opt/dcelocal/bin/idl
CC=/usr/bin/cc -g -I .

default: $(PGM)_c.out $(PGM)_s.out  $(PGM)_i.out

$(PGM)_c.out: $(PGM)_c.c    $(PGM).h $(PGM)_cstub.o errmac.h $(PGM)_s.h
        $(CC) -o $(PGM)_c.out $(LIBS)  $(PGM)_cstub.o $(PGM)_c.c

$(PGM)_s.out: $(PGM)_s.c $(PGM).h $(PGM)_sstub.o $(PGM)_e.c $(PGM)_a.c \
                acl_mgr.c errmac.h $(PGM)_s.h rdaclif_sstub.o
$(CC) -o $(PGM)_s.out $(LIBS) $(PGM)_sstub.o $(PGM)_s.c $(PGM)_e.c \
            $(PGM)_a.c acl_mgr.c rdaclif_sstub.o lookup_cstub.o

$(PGM)_i.out: $(PGM)_i.c $(PGM).h $(PGM)_i_sstub.o errmac.h $(PGM)_s.h \
                rdaclif_i_sstub.o
        $(CC) -o $(PGM)_i.out $(LIBS) $(PGM)_i_sstub.o $(PGM)_i.c \
                rdaclif_i_sstub.o

$(PGM)_sstub.o  $(PGM)_cstub.o  $(PGM).h: $(PGM).idl $(PGM).acf
        $(IDL) $(PGM).idl

$(PGM)_i_sstub.o: $(PGM).idl $(PGM).acf
        $(IDL) $(PGM).idl -client none -no_mepv -sstub $(PGM)_i_sstub

rdaclif_sstub.o: /usr/include/dce/rdaclif.idl rdaclif.acf
        $(IDL) /usr/include/dce/rdaclif.idl  -client none

rdaclif_i_sstub.o: /usr/include/dce/rdaclif.idl rdaclif.acf
        $(IDL) /usr/include/dce/rdaclif.idl  -client none -no_mepv \
            -sstub rdaclif_i_sstub
```

The Peer-to-Peer Server

The IDL File

```
/* CHAT.IDL Chat Program  */

/* NOTE: run IDL with the no_mepv option */
[
uuid(00602161-7C3F-1C90-9982-0000C07C3610),
version(1.0)
]
interface chat
{

const long CHAT_NAME_SIZE = 20;
const long CHAT_TEXT_SIZE = 100;

error_status_t send_msg( [in] handle_t           bind_hdl,
                         [in, string] char    name[CHAT_NAME_SIZE],
                         [in, string] char    text[CHAT_TEXT_SIZE]);
}
```

The ACF File

```
/* CHAT.ACF */

interface chat
{

[comm_status, fault_status] send_msg();

}
```

The Error Macro File

```
#include <dce/dce_error.h>

#define ERROR(msg)\
    {fprintf (stderr, "Error: %s in file: %s at line %d.\n", \
        msg, __FILE__, __LINE__);\
    exit (1);}

#define WARN(msg)\
    {fprintf (stderr, "Warning: %s in file: %s at line %d.\n", \
        msg, __FILE__, __LINE__);}

#define ERR_CHK(stat, msg) if (stat !=rpc_s_ok)\
    {dce_error_string_t _dcemsg_; int _st_;\
     dce_error_inq_text( stat, _dcemsg_, &_st_ );\
     fprintf (stderr, "Error: %s in file: %s at line %d.\nDCE Error: %s\n", \
        msg, __FILE__, __LINE__, _dcemsg_);\
    exit (1);}

#define WRN_CHK(stat, msg) if (stat != rpc_s_ok)\
    {dce_error_string_t _dcemsg_; int _st_;\
     dce_error_inq_text( stat, _dcemsg_, &_st_ );\
     fprintf (stderr, "Warning: %s in file: %s at line %d.\nDCE Error: %s\n", \
        msg, __FILE__, __LINE__,_dcemsg_);}

#define CND_CHK(cond, msg) if ((cond))\
    {fprintf (stderr, "Error: %s in file: %s at line %d.\n", \
        msg, __FILE__, __LINE__);\
    exit (1);}
```

The Program File

```
/* CHAT.C */

#include <stdio.h>
#include <string.h>
#include <dce/rpc.h>
#include <pthread.h>
#include "chat.h"
#include "errmac.h"

idl_char chat_dir_name[50] = "/.:/applications/chat/";
idl_char chat_group_name[] = "/.:/applications/chat/group";
idl_char user_name[CHAT_NAME_SIZE];

uuid_t        my_obj;
uuid_vector_t obj_vec;

        /* Number of other chat programs we can talk to */
#define OBJ_TBL_MAX 20
```

```
error_status_t send_msg_op( rpc_binding_handle_t bind_h,
                            idl_char              name[],
                            idl_char              text[]);
void client_thread();

chat_v1_0_epv_t chat_epv = { send_msg_op };




/***** Server Control *****/

main( int argc, char *argv[] )
{
error_status_t          status;
rpc_binding_vector_t    *bindings;
pthread_t               thread_hdl;

if (argc > 2 )
    {
    fprintf(stderr, "Usage: %s name\n", argv[0] );
    exit(1);
    }

if (argc < 2 )                                              /* (1) */
    {
    strcpy((char *) user_name, getlogin());
    }
    else
    {
    strcpy((char *) user_name, argv[1]);
    }
strcat((char *) chat_dir_name, (char *) user_name);


uuid_create(&my_obj,&status);                               /* (2) */
ERR_CHK(status,"Error creating object UUID");

obj_vec.count = 1;
obj_vec.uuid[0] = &my_obj;

rpc_server_register_if( chat_v1_0_s_ifspec,                 /* (3) */
                        NULL,
                        (rpc_mgr_epv_t) &chat_epv,
                        &status);
ERR_CHK(status,"Could not register interface");

rpc_server_use_all_protseqs( rpc_c_listen_max_calls_default, /* (4) */
                             &status);
ERR_CHK(status,"Could not use all protocols");

rpc_server_inq_bindings( &bindings,                        /* (5) */
                         &status);
ERR_CHK(status,"Could not get binding vector");
```

```
            rpc_ns_binding_export( rpc_c_ns_syntax_default,            /* (6) */
                            chat_dir_name,
                            chat_v1_0_s_ifspec,
                            bindings,
                            &obj_vec,
                            &status);
        ERR_CHK(status,"Could not export server bindings");

            rpc_ns_group_mbr_add( rpc_c_ns_syntax_default,             /* (7) */
                            chat_group_name,
                            rpc_c_ns_syntax_default,
                            chat_dir_name,
                            &status);
        ERR_CHK(status,"Could not add server entry to group");

            rpc_ep_register( chat_v1_0_s_ifspec,                       /* (8) */
                        bindings,
                        &obj_vec,
                        (idl_char *) "Chat Program",
                        &status);
        ERR_CHK(status,"Could not register endpoint");

            if (pthread_create( &thread_hdl,                           /* (9) */
                        pthread_attr_default,
                        (pthread_startroutine_t) client_thread,
                        (pthread_addr_t) 0) != 0)
            {
            ERROR("Could not create client thread");
            }

            rpc_server_listen( rpc_c_listen_max_calls_default,         /* (10) */
                        &status);

            rpc_ns_binding_unexport( rpc_c_ns_syntax_default,          /* (11) */
                            chat_dir_name,
                            chat_v1_0_s_ifspec,
                            &obj_vec,
                            &status);
        ERR_CHK(status,"Could not remove server bindings");

            rpc_ns_group_mbr_remove( rpc_c_ns_syntax_default,          /* (12) */
                            chat_group_name,
                            rpc_c_ns_syntax_default,
                            chat_dir_name,
                            &status);
        ERR_CHK(status,"Could not add server entry to group");

            rpc_ep_unregister( chat_v1_0_s_ifspec,                     /* (13) */
                        bindings,
                        &obj_vec,
                        &status);

        }  /* End of Server Control Routine */
```

```
/*********************** Server Operations ***********************/

error_status_t send_msg_op( rpc_binding_handle_t  bind_h,
                            idl_char               name[],
                            idl_char               text[])
{

printf("\n%s - %s\n\n", name, text);

return(rpc_s_ok);

}

/******************** End of Server Operations ********************/

/************************** Client Thread **************************/

void client_thread()
{
error_status_t status;
idl_char *cp, msg_txt[CHAT_TEXT_SIZE];
int i, num_ids;
uuid_t obj_tbl[OBJ_TBL_MAX];
uuid_t curr_obj;
rpc_ns_handle_t binding_context;
rpc_binding_handle_t bind_h;

obj_tbl[0] = my_obj;
num_ids=1;

printf("Type your message. Control D to exit\n\n");

while(1)                                                        /* (1) */
    {
    printf("MSG: ");
    cp = (idl_char *) gets( (char *) msg_txt );
    if (cp == NULL) break;

    rpc_ns_binding_import_begin( rpc_c_ns_syntax_default,       /* (2) */
                                 NULL,
                                 chat_v1_0_c_ifspec,
                                 NULL,
                                 &binding_context,
                                 &status);
    ERR_CHK(status,"Could not import binding context");

    num_ids = 1;
    while (1)  /* Try every binding */
        {
        rpc_ns_binding_import_next( binding_context,            /* (3) */
                                    &bind_h,
                                    &status);
        if (status != rpc_s_ok) break;
```

```
                    rpc_binding_inq_object( bind_h,                       /* (4) */
                                            &curr_obj,
                                            &status);
                    if (status != rpc_s_ok) continue;

                    i = 0;
                    while (i < num_ids)
                        {
                        if ( uuid_equal(&obj_tbl[i], &curr_obj, &status) ) break;
                        i++;
                        }
                    if ( i != num_ids) continue;

                    if (num_ids >= OBJ_TBL_MAX )
                        ERROR("Too many chat programs running");

                    obj_tbl[num_ids++] = curr_obj;

                    status = send_msg( bind_h, user_name, msg_txt);          /* (5) */
                        /* ignore error */

                    }   /* end of trying bindings */

            rpc_ns_binding_import_done(&binding_context,                     /* (6) */
                                        &status);
            ERR_CHK(status,"Error releasing binding context");

                } /* end of message loop */

            rpc_mgmt_stop_server_listening( NULL, &status);                 /* (7) */

                }
```

The Build File

```
            PGM=chat
            DCE=/opt/dcelocal
            DCELIB=-L $(DCE)/lib
            LIBS=$(DCELIB) -l dce -l dcedes -l seccrypt -l socket  -l nsl
            IDL=/opt/dcelocal/bin/idl -no_mepv
            CC=/usr/bin/cc -g


            default: $(PGM).out

            $(PGM).out: $(PGM).c $(PGM).h errmac.h $(PGM)_cstub.o
                    $(CC) -o $(PGM).out $(LIBS) $(PGM)_cstub.o $(PGM)_sstub.o $(PGM).c

            $(PGM)_cstub.o $(PGM)_sstub.o $(PGM).h: $(PGM).idl $(PGM).acf
                    $(IDL) $(PGM).idl
```

The ACL Manager

```
/* ACL_MGR.C ACL Manager */

/*
 * @OSF_COPYRIGHT@
 * COPYRIGHT NOTICE
 * Copyright (c) 1990, 1991, 1992, 1993 Open Software Foundation, Inc.
 * ALL RIGHTS RESERVED (DCE).
 */
/*
** Copyright (c) Hewlett-Packard Company 1991
** Unpublished work. All Rights Reserved.
*/
/*
 * (c) Copyright 1991, 1992 Siemens-Nixdorf Information Systems,
 *                      Burlington, MA, USA
 * All Rights Reserved
 */
/*
 *      ACL manager - wire and mgr implementation
 *
 * CONTENTS:
 *          Implementation of mgr interface  (daclmgr.idl) at top
 *          Implementation of wire interface (rdaclif.idl) at bottom
 */

#include <dce/uuid.h>
#include <dce/rdaclif.h>
#include <dce/daclmgr.h>

#include <stdio.h>
#include <string.h>
#include <macros.h>
#include <sys/types.h>
#include <sys/stat.h>
```

```c
#include <fcntl.h>
#include "errmac.h"
#include "lookup_s.h"

/* Global Variables */

extern sec_id_t *user_obj, *group_obj;

/* Internal Functions */

boolean32 access_granted( sec_acl_entry_t     entry,
                          sec_acl_permset_t   mask_perms,
                          sec_acl_permset_t   desired,
                          sec_acl_permset_t   *granted);

void acl_buffer_init(char **acl_buf_p, int *buf_size);

char *acl_buffer_alloc( size_t size, char **acl_buf_p, int    *buf_size);

/* Macros *****/

/* Compare default realm with accessor's realm */
#define default_realm_eq(entry) uuid_equal(&accessor_info->realm.uuid, \
                                  &sec_acl_p->default_realm.uuid, \
                                  &st)

/* Compare foreign realm with accessor's realm */
#define foreign_realm_eq(entry) uuid_equal(&accessor_info->realm.uuid, \
&sec_acl_p->sec_acl_entries[entry].entry_info.tagged_union.foreign_id.\
realm.uuid, &st)

/* Need to pass the automatic variables: acl_buf_p and buf_size so as to
 * preserve reentrancy.  This macro makes the calls to allocate look cleaner
 */
#define BUFFER_ALLOC(SIZE) acl_buffer_alloc((SIZE),&acl_buf_p,&buf_size)

#define CHK_IF_SEEN(flag) if (flag) { *st_p = sec_acl_bad_acl_syntax; \
    return; } else flag = TRUE

/* Private definitions, mostly for efficiency of auth checks */
#define ENTRY_NOT_FOUND -1
#define MAX_PERMISSIONS ((sec_acl_permset_t)~0)
#define NO_PERMISSIONS  ((sec_acl_permset_t)0)

#define MAX_ACL_SIZE 1000
#define sec_acl_mgr_file_io_error sec_acl_PADf


/*  NOTE:   This version has hardcoded printstrings. If you modify the number
 *          of printstrings in the hardcoded array, you must change the
 *          hardcoded NUM_PSTRS so the stub will pass the correct number of
 *          printstrings back.
 */
#define NUM_PSTRS 6
```

```
static sec_acl_printstring_t hardcoded_printstrings[] = {
    { "c",  "control",  sec_acl_perm_owner    },
    { "r",  "read",     sec_acl_perm_read     },
    { "w",  "write",    sec_acl_perm_write    },
    { "o",  "open",     sec_acl_perm_test     },
    { "a",  "add",      sec_acl_perm_insert   },
    { "d",  "delete",   sec_acl_perm_delete   },
};

#define SUPPORTED_PERMS  (sec_acl_perm_owner | sec_acl_perm_read | \
                          sec_acl_perm_write | sec_acl_perm_test | \
                          sec_acl_perm_insert| sec_acl_perm_delete)

static sec_acl_printstring_t hardcoded_manager_info = {
    "acl_manager", "Sample ACL manager.", SUPPORTED_PERMS
};

#define ACL_FILE_MAJ_VER 1
#define ACL_FILE_MIN_VER 0

const char file_text[] = "ACL_file";

typedef struct
    {
    char acl_text[9];
    idl_short_int major_ver;
    idl_short_int minor_ver;
    uuid_t mgr_id;
    } acl_file_header_t;

acl_file_header_t acl_file_header;

boolean32 new_db = FALSE;                /* Indicates creating new ACL db */
unsigned_char_t acl_file_name[50];
sec_acl_mgr_handle_t sec_acl_mgr = NULL;    /* Dummy handle */


/******************** SEC_ACL Manager routines ********************/

/* s e c _ a c l _ m g r _ c o n f i g u r e
 *
 * Configure the dacl manager.  This operation provides a handle that
 * refers to the particular acl database in use and is necessary for all
 * other sec_acl manager operations.  The db_name identifies which acl
 * database to use (and generally refers to the file system object that
 * represents the persistent storage for the database).  The config_info
 * provides information on how to configure this database.
 */
void sec_acl_mgr_configure( sec_acl_mgr_config_t    config_info,
                            unsigned_char_p_t       db_name,
                            sec_acl_mgr_handle_t    *sec_acl_mgr,
                            error_status_t          *st_p )
{
int fd, oflag;
```

```
/* This ACL manager requires that sec_acl_mgr_config_stable be set */
if ( !(config_info & sec_acl_mgr_config_stable) )
    {
    *st_p = sec_acl_not_implemented;
    return;
    }

/* save database name for later */
strcpy((char *)acl_file_name, (char *) db_name);

/* Set up ACL File header for sec_acl_mgr_replace and sec_acl_mgr_lookup */
strcpy((char *)&acl_file_header.acl_text, file_text);
acl_file_header.major_ver = ACL_FILE_MAJ_VER;
acl_file_header.minor_ver = ACL_FILE_MIN_VER;
memcpy( &acl_file_header.mgr_id, &mgr_uuid, sizeof(uuid_t));

/* Make sure we can read and write the file.  If sec_acl_mgr_config_create
 * is set insure that the file does not exist. Also set global flag for the
 * use of radcl_replace()
 */
oflag = O_RDWR;
if (config_info & sec_acl_mgr_config_create)
    {
    oflag = O_WRONLY|O_CREAT|O_EXCL;
    new_db = TRUE;
    }

/* When creating the file set the mode to user read and write */
fd = open((char *) db_name, oflag, S_IRUSR|S_IWUSR );
if (fd == -1)
    {
    *st_p = sec_acl_mgr_file_open_error;
    return;
    }

close(fd);

/* Don't bother with a real handle, since the server only
        implements one type of acl storage */
*sec_acl_mgr = NULL;

*st_p = error_status_ok;

}

/* access_granted
 *
 * Private routine to mask entry permset against mask_obj if necessary
 * and compare the result of that operation with the desired_access
 * permset, to determine if access should be granted
 */
```

```
boolean32 access_granted( sec_acl_entry_t     entry,
                          sec_acl_permset_t   mask_perms,
                          sec_acl_permset_t   desired,
                          sec_acl_permset_t   *granted)
{
boolean32 grant_access = false;

switch (entry.entry_info.entry_type)
    {
    case sec_acl_e_type_user_obj:
    case sec_acl_e_type_other_obj:
    case sec_acl_e_type_mask_obj:
    case sec_acl_e_type_unauthenticated:
        *granted = (entry.perms  & desired);
        break;
    case sec_acl_e_type_group_obj:
    case sec_acl_e_type_any_other:
    case sec_acl_e_type_user:
    case sec_acl_e_type_group:
    case sec_acl_e_type_foreign_other:
    case sec_acl_e_type_foreign_user:
    case sec_acl_e_type_foreign_group:
    case sec_acl_e_type_extended:
        *granted = ((entry.perms & mask_perms) & desired);
        break;
    default:
        *granted = (sec_acl_permset_t) 0;
    }
if ( *granted == desired ) grant_access = true;

return (grant_access);
}


/* s e c _ a c l _ m g r _ i s _ a u t h o r i z e d
 *
 * The basic operation in the authorization package, this function will
 * yield true if the principal (as described in the privilege attribute
 * certificate referred to by "accessor_info") is authorized to perform
 * the requested operation.  The dacl controlling this decision is
 * not passed directly to this function, but is referred to via the
 * sec_acl_key and the manager_type_p parameters.
 */


boolean32 sec_acl_mgr_is_authorized( sec_acl_mgr_handle_t   sec_acl_mgr,
                                     sec_acl_permset_t      desired_access,
                                     sec_id_pac_t           *accessor_info,
                                     sec_acl_key_t          sec_acl_key,
                                     uuid_t                 *manager_type_p,
                                     sec_id_t               *user_obj,
                                     sec_id_t               *group_obj,
                                     error_status_t         *st_p)
{
```

```
sec_acl_list_t        *sec_acl_list;
sec_acl_t             *sec_acl_p;
int                   i;              /* For traversing entry list. */
unsigned int          j;              /* For traversing entry list. */
int                   mask,          /* For keeping track of entries... */
                      user_obj_entry,
                      user_entry,
                      foreign_user_entry,
                      other_obj_entry,
                      foreign_other_entry,
                      any_other_entry,
                      unauth_entry;
sec_id_t              *group_id, *realm_id;
error_status_t        st;
sec_acl_permset_t     mask_perms, granted, group_access;
boolean32             chk_loc_groups = FALSE, one_group_found = FALSE;
boolean32             access = FALSE;    /* Keep running tab on access */


/* Retrieve the sec_acl for this key */

sec_acl_mgr_lookup( sec_acl_mgr,
                    sec_acl_key,
                    manager_type_p,
                    sec_acl_type_object,
                    &sec_acl_list,
                    st_p);
if (*st_p != error_status_ok) return FALSE;

/* At this point, st_p must be error_status_ok, and will remain that
 * unless explicitly set otherwise.  Thus we can return prematurely without
 * having to explicitly set the status.
 */

/* Take advantage of the fact that there can only be one ACL */
sec_acl_p = sec_acl_list->sec_acls[0];

/* No masks found to start with */
mask = ENTRY_NOT_FOUND;

/* Only 1 of each type of entry could possibly match this
 *  principal id, so keep a running tab on if/where each
 *  type of entry is found in the list
 */
user_entry = user_obj_entry = foreign_user_entry =
other_obj_entry = foreign_other_entry = unauth_entry = any_other_entry =
    ENTRY_NOT_FOUND;

/* If masks isn't explicitly set, then it should have no effect
    when masking, so turn all perm bits on by default */
mask_perms = MAX_PERMISSIONS;
```

```
/* PRE-PROCESS the acl entries so we only have to loop
 * through once looking for specific types of entries
 *
 * Note, the accessor may be a member of multiple {foreign_}groups.
 * Therefore, the *group checks must be done below, in a separate
 * pass through the entry list.
 */
for (i = 0; i < sec_acl_p->num_entries; i++)
    {

    /* Check for existence of each type of entry, and keep track
     * of where each type was found in the entry list.
     * Don't mark type as found if the associated realm id's
     * are not the same
     */
    switch(sec_acl_p->sec_acl_entries[i].entry_info.entry_type)
        {
        case sec_acl_e_type_mask_obj:
            mask = i;
            mask_perms = sec_acl_p->sec_acl_entries[i].perms;
            break;
        case sec_acl_e_type_user_obj:
            if (default_realm_eq(i)) user_obj_entry = i;
            break;
        case sec_acl_e_type_user:
            if ((uuid_equal(&accessor_info->principal.uuid,
&sec_acl_p->sec_acl_entries[i].entry_info.tagged_union.id.uuid,
                        &st)) && (default_realm_eq(i)))
                user_entry = i;
            break;
        case sec_acl_e_type_foreign_user:
            if ((uuid_equal(&accessor_info->principal.uuid,
&sec_acl_p-> sec_acl_entries[i].entry_info.tagged_union.foreign_id.id.uuid,
                &st)) && (foreign_realm_eq(i))) foreign_user_entry = i;
            break;
        case sec_acl_e_type_other_obj:
            if (default_realm_eq(i)) other_obj_entry = i;
            break;
        case sec_acl_e_type_foreign_other:
            if ( uuid_equal( &accessor_info->realm.uuid,
&sec_acl_p->sec_acl_entries[i].entry_info.tagged_union.id.uuid,
                        &st)) foreign_other_entry = i;
            break;
        case sec_acl_e_type_any_other:
            any_other_entry = i;
            break;
        case sec_acl_e_type_unauthenticated:
            unauth_entry = i;
            break;
        default:
            break;
```

```
            } /* end switch */
        } /* end for */

/* Now that we know which entries match the user described in the PAC,
 * check the permissions corresponding to each entry until access is
 * granted by one of them.
 */

/* USER_OBJ check */
if (user_obj_entry != ENTRY_NOT_FOUND)
    {

    /* If e_type_user_obj entry exists, then user_obj can't be NULL */
    if (user_obj == NULL)
        {
        *st_p = sec_acl_expected_user_obj;
        return FALSE;
        }

    /* If the id assoc w/ user_obj matches the principal id */
    if (uuid_equal(&accessor_info->principal.uuid, &user_obj->uuid, &st))
        {
        /* then check the permsets to see if access is granted */
        if (access_granted(sec_acl_p->sec_acl_entries[user_obj_entry],
                        mask_perms, desired_access, &granted))
            {
            access = TRUE;
            }
            else
            {
            return FALSE;         /* implied denial rights */
            }
        } /* end if uuid_equal */
    } /* end if user_obj_entry */

/* USER check */
if ((! access) && (user_entry != ENTRY_NOT_FOUND))
    {
    /* check the permsets to see if access is granted */
    if (access_granted(sec_acl_p->sec_acl_entries[user_entry],
                    mask_perms, desired_access, &granted))
        {
        access = TRUE;
        }
        else
        {
        return FALSE;             /* implied denial rights */
        }
    }


/* FOREIGN_USER check */
if ((! access) && (foreign_user_entry != ENTRY_NOT_FOUND))
    {
```

```
    /* check the permsets to see if access is granted */
    if (access_granted(sec_acl_p->sec_acl_entries[foreign_user_entry],
                       mask_perms, desired_access, &granted))
        {
        access = TRUE;
        }
        else
        {
        return FALSE;            /* implied denial rights */
        }
    }

/* GROUP checks */
group_access = (sec_acl_permset_t) 0;
for (i = 0;((! access) && (i < sec_acl_p->num_entries)); i++)
    {
    switch(sec_acl_p->sec_acl_entries[i].entry_info.entry_type) {
    case sec_acl_e_type_group_obj:
    case sec_acl_e_type_group:
    case sec_acl_e_type_foreign_group:
        if (sec_acl_p->sec_acl_entries[i].entry_info.entry_type
                              == sec_acl_e_type_group_obj)
            {  /* If group_obj entry exists then group_obj cant be NULL */
            if (group_obj == NULL)
                {
                *st_p = sec_acl_expected_group_obj;
                return FALSE;
                }
            group_id = group_obj;   /* check against group_obj param */
            realm_id = &sec_acl_p->default_realm;
            chk_loc_groups = default_realm_eq(i);
            }
        else if (sec_acl_p->sec_acl_entries[i].entry_info.entry_type
                                            == sec_acl_e_type_group)
            {
            chk_loc_groups = default_realm_eq(i);
            group_id =
                &sec_acl_p->sec_acl_entries[i].entry_info.tagged_union.id;
                    realm_id = &sec_acl_p->default_realm;
            }
        else
            {
            chk_loc_groups = foreign_realm_eq(i);
            group_id = &sec_acl_p->
                sec_acl_entries[i].entry_info.tagged_union.foreign_id.id;
            realm_id = &sec_acl_p->
                sec_acl_entries[i].entry_info.tagged_union.foreign_id.realm;
            }
        /* Check either the local groups or the foreign groups */
        if (chk_loc_groups)
            { /* CHECK PAC GROUP */
            if (uuid_equal(&accessor_info->group.uuid,
                              &group_id->uuid, &st) )
```

```
                      {
            one_group_found = TRUE;
                      /* then check the perms to see if access is granted */
            if (access_granted(sec_acl_p->sec_acl_entries[i],
               mask_perms, desired_access, &granted))
               {
               access = TRUE;
               }
            else
               {
               group_access = (group_access | granted);
               }
            }

         /* CHECK LOCAL GROUPS */
         for (j = 0;
            ((! access) && (j < accessor_info->num_groups)); j++)
            {
            if (uuid_equal(&accessor_info->groups[j].uuid,
               &group_id->uuid, &st) )
               {
               one_group_found = TRUE;
               /* check the perms to see if access granted */
               if (access_granted(sec_acl_p->sec_acl_entries[i],
                  mask_perms, desired_access, &granted))
                  {
                  access = TRUE;
                  }
               else
                  {
                  group_access = (group_access | granted);
                  }
               } /* end if uuid_equal */
            } /* end for */
         } /* end if chk_loc_groups */
      else
         {
         /* CHECK FOREIGN GROUPS */
         for (j = 0;
            (! access) && (j < accessor_info->num_foreign_groups);
            j++)
            {
            if ((uuid_equal( &accessor_info->foreign_groups[j].id.uuid,
               &group_id->uuid, &st))
               && (uuid_equal(&accessor_info->foreign_groups[j].realm.uuid,
               &realm_id->uuid, &st)) )
               {
               one_group_found = TRUE;
               /* check the perms to see if access granted */
               if (access_granted(sec_acl_p->sec_acl_entries[i],
                  mask_perms, desired_access, &granted))
                  {
                  access = TRUE;
```

```
                    }
                else
                    {
                    group_access = (group_access | granted);
                    }
                } /* end if uuid_equal */
            } /* end for */
        } /* end else */
    break;
default:
    break;
    } /* end switch (entry type) */

/* See if the union of multiple group entries granted access */
if ((group_access & desired_access) == desired_access) access = TRUE;

} /* end GROUP check */

/* If at least 1 group found and !access, then deny any access */
if (!access && one_group_found) return FALSE;

/* OTHER_OBJ check */
if ((! access) && (other_obj_entry != ENTRY_NOT_FOUND))
    {
    /* check the permsets to see if access is granted */
    if (access_granted(sec_acl_p->sec_acl_entries[other_obj_entry],
                    mask_perms, desired_access, &granted))
        {
        access = TRUE;
        }
        else
        {
        return FALSE;              /* implied denial rights */
        }
    }

/* FOREIGN_OTHER check */
if ((! access) && (foreign_other_entry != ENTRY_NOT_FOUND))
    {
    /* check the permsets to see if access is granted */
    if (access_granted(sec_acl_p->sec_acl_entries[foreign_other_entry],
                    mask_perms, desired_access, &granted))
        {
        access = TRUE;
        }
        else
        {
        return FALSE;              /* implied denial rights */
        }
    }

/* ANY_OTHER check */
if ((! access) && (any_other_entry != ENTRY_NOT_FOUND))
    {
```

```
                    /* check the permsets to see if access is granted */
                    if (access_granted(sec_acl_p->sec_acl_entries[any_other_entry],
                                    mask_perms, desired_access, &granted))
                        {
                        access = TRUE;
                        }
                        else
                        {
                        return FALSE;           /* implied denial rights */
                        }
                    }

        /* UNAUTHENTICATED check
        * If pac isn't authenticated and access was granted by one of the above
        * checks, then desired_access must be masked by unauthenticated entry.
        */
        if ((access) && (! accessor_info->authenticated))
            {
            if (unauth_entry == ENTRY_NOT_FOUND)
                {
                access = FALSE;
                }
            else if (! access_granted(sec_acl_p->sec_acl_entries[unauth_entry],
                                    mask_perms, desired_access, &granted))
                {
                access = FALSE;
                }
            }

        return access;

        }

        /* Utility Routines */

        /* A macro to expand the tagged union name to keep statements on one line */
        #define EITU(A) ((char **) &my_e->entry_info.tagged_union.A)

        void PtrToOfs (char **PtrOfs, char *Base)
        {
        int offset;
        offset= *PtrOfs - Base;        /* Like ptrs can be subtracted */
        *PtrOfs = (char *)offset;      /* Any pointer is large enough to hold an int*/
        }

        void OfsToPtr (char **OfsPtr, char *Base)    /* Inverse of above */
        {
        int offset;
        offset= * (int *)OfsPtr;       /* Get offset value */
        *OfsPtr=Base+offset;           /* Displace from Base by adding an int*/
        }
```

```
void acl_buffer_init(char **acl_buf_p,
                     int *buf_size)
{
/* We use rpc_ss_allocate so that the stub code will free it up for us */
*acl_buf_p = (char *) rpc_ss_allocate(MAX_ACL_SIZE);

*buf_size = 0;
}

char *acl_buffer_alloc( size_t size,
                        char **acl_buf_p,
                        int *buf_size)
{
char *temp;

temp = *acl_buf_p + *buf_size;
if ((*buf_size += size) > MAX_ACL_SIZE ) ERROR("ACL Buffer Overflow");

return(temp);
}


/* s e c _ a c l _ m g r _ r e p l a c e
 *
 * Replace the dacl associated with the key.  This package treats dacls as
 * immutable objects - the old dacl is thrown away and the new one created
 * Some implementations of this interface may choose to optimize storage
 * and share dacl representation for many objects - in which case the real
 * dacl storage must be reference counted, but that is of no concern to
 * the consumer of the interface.
 *
 * This ACL manager implements a single ACL which is stored in a disk file.
 * The ACL is stored in the file in the same format as in memory except that
 * the pointers are relocated to be offsets relative to the start of the ACL.
 * This routine does not check permissions, but rdacl_replace, which calls
 * it requires that the caller have the sec_acl_perm_owner ("c") permission.
 * Therefore, this routine checks to make sure that at least one entry in the
 * ACL has the sec_acl_perm_owner permission set.
 */

void sec_acl_mgr_replace( sec_acl_mgr_handle_t    sec_acl_mgr,
                          sec_acl_key_t           sec_acl_key,
                          uuid_t                  *manager_type_p,
                          sec_acl_type_t          sec_acl_type,
                          sec_acl_list_t          *sec_acl_list_p,
                          error_status_t          *st_p)
{
int               index, i, j, num_bytes, fd;
sec_acl_t         *nacl_p, *sec_acl_p;
acl_file_header_t *hdr_p;
sec_acl_entry_t   *new_e, *my_e;
boolean32         seen_c_perm = FALSE,      /* Syntax check flags */
                  seen_user_obj = FALSE,
                  seen_group_obj = FALSE,
```

```
                        seen_other_obj = FALSE,
                        seen_any_other = FALSE,
                        seen_mask_obj = FALSE,
                        seen_unauthenticated = FALSE;
char            *acl_buf_p;                 /* Pointer to ACL buffer */
int             buf_size;                   /* Number of bytes in buffer */

/* We know that there's only one acl in the list */
sec_acl_p = sec_acl_list_p->sec_acls[0];

/* This manager does not support container object ACLs. */
if (sec_acl_type != sec_acl_type_object)
    {
    *st_p = sec_acl_not_implemented;
    return;
    }

/* Initialize buffer */
acl_buffer_init( &acl_buf_p, &buf_size);

/* Set up the file header */
hdr_p = (acl_file_header_t *) BUFFER_ALLOC(sizeof(acl_file_header_t));

memcpy( hdr_p, &acl_file_header, sizeof(acl_file_header_t));

/* Allocate space for the base data structure */
nacl_p = (sec_acl_t *) BUFFER_ALLOC(sizeof(sec_acl_t));


/* Copy the acl information into the new sec_acl */
nacl_p->default_realm.uuid = sec_acl_p->default_realm.uuid;
nacl_p->default_realm.name = (unsigned_char_p_t) BUFFER_ALLOC(
            (strlen((char *) sec_acl_p->default_realm.name)+1) * sizeof(char));
strcpy((char *) nacl_p->default_realm.name,
                (char *) sec_acl_p->default_realm.name);
nacl_p->sec_acl_manager_type = sec_acl_p->sec_acl_manager_type;
nacl_p->num_entries = sec_acl_p->num_entries;

/* Copy the ACL entries into the buffer */
nacl_p->sec_acl_entries = (sec_acl_entry_t *) BUFFER_ALLOC(
                            sec_acl_p->num_entries * sizeof(sec_acl_entry_t));
for (i = 0; i < sec_acl_p->num_entries; i++)
    {
    /* Copy the pointers to the storage entry and the incoming
     * entry, to make this more readable (ie: <= 80 columns)
     */
    my_e = &(nacl_p->sec_acl_entries[i]);
    new_e = &(sec_acl_p->sec_acl_entries[i]);

    /* Copy the permissions and entry type from old to new */
    my_e->perms = new_e->perms;
    my_e->entry_info.entry_type = new_e->entry_info.entry_type;
```

```
/* Make sure entry does not contain unsupported permissions */
if (my_e->perms & (~SUPPORTED_PERMS))
    {
    *st_p = sec_acl_bad_acl_syntax;
    return;
    }

/* Check each entry to see if it has the sec_acl_perm_owner permission */
if (my_e->perms & sec_acl_perm_owner) seen_c_perm = TRUE;

switch (new_e->entry_info.entry_type)
{
case sec_acl_e_type_user:
case sec_acl_e_type_group:
case sec_acl_e_type_foreign_other: /* Copy the id's uuid */
    my_e->entry_info.tagged_union.id.uuid =
        new_e->entry_info.tagged_union.id.uuid;

/* Make room for the name, and copy it */
my_e->entry_info.tagged_union.id.name = (unsigned_char_p_t)
  BUFFER_ALLOC(sizeof(unsigned_char_t) *
  (1 + strlen((char *) new_e->entry_info.tagged_union.id.name)));

strcpy((char *) my_e->entry_info.tagged_union.id.name,
    (char *) new_e->entry_info.tagged_union.id.name);
    break;

case sec_acl_e_type_foreign_user:
case sec_acl_e_type_foreign_group:
    /* Copy the foreign id's uuids */
    my_e->entry_info.tagged_union.foreign_id.id.uuid =
               new_e->entry_info.tagged_union.foreign_id.id.uuid;
    my_e->entry_info.tagged_union.foreign_id.realm.uuid =
               new_e->entry_info.tagged_union.foreign_id.realm.uuid;

    /* Make room for the names, and copy them */
    my_e->entry_info.tagged_union.foreign_id.id.name =
        (unsigned_char_p_t) BUFFER_ALLOC(sizeof(unsigned_char_t) *
            (1 + strlen((char *)
            new_e->entry_info.tagged_union.foreign_id.id.name)) );
    strcpy( (char *) my_e->entry_info.tagged_union.foreign_id.id.name,
        (char *) new_e->entry_info.tagged_union.foreign_id.id.name );

    my_e->entry_info.tagged_union.foreign_id.realm.name =
        (unsigned_char_p_t) BUFFER_ALLOC(sizeof(unsigned_char_t) *
        (1 + strlen((char *)
        new_e->entry_info.tagged_union.foreign_id.realm.name)) );
    strcpy((char *) my_e->entry_info.tagged_union.foreign_id.realm.name,
        (char *) new_e->entry_info.tagged_union.foreign_id.realm.name);
    break;

case sec_acl_e_type_extended:
    num_bytes = new_e->entry_info.tagged_union.extended_info->num_bytes;
```

```
                my_e->entry_info.tagged_union.extended_info =
                    (sec_acl_extend_info_t *) BUFFER_ALLOC(
                    sizeof(uuid_t) + sizeof(ndr_format_t) +
                    sizeof(unsigned32) + (num_bytes * sizeof(ndr_byte)) );

                my_e->entry_info.tagged_union.extended_info->extension_type =
                    new_e->entry_info.tagged_union.extended_info->extension_type;

                my_e->entry_info.tagged_union.extended_info->format_label =
                    new_e->entry_info.tagged_union.extended_info->format_label;

                my_e->entry_info.tagged_union.extended_info->num_bytes =
                    new_e->entry_info.tagged_union.extended_info->num_bytes;

                for (j = 0; j < num_bytes; j++)
                    my_e->entry_info.tagged_union.extended_info->pickled_data[j] =
                    new_e->entry_info.tagged_union.extended_info->pickled_data[j];

                break;

                /* No data associated with these entries.
                 * Check that each appears at most once
                 */
            case sec_acl_e_type_user_obj:
                CHK_IF_SEEN(seen_user_obj);
                break;
            case sec_acl_e_type_group_obj:
                CHK_IF_SEEN(seen_group_obj);
                break;
            case sec_acl_e_type_other_obj:
                CHK_IF_SEEN(seen_other_obj);
                break;
            case sec_acl_e_type_any_other:
                CHK_IF_SEEN(seen_any_other);
                break;
            case sec_acl_e_type_mask_obj:
                CHK_IF_SEEN(seen_mask_obj);
                break;
            case sec_acl_e_type_unauthenticated:
                CHK_IF_SEEN(seen_unauthenticated);
                break;

            default: break;} /* end switch entry_type */
        } /* end for num_entries */

    /* If no entry contains the "c" permission, don't allow the update */
    if(!seen_c_perm)
        {
        *st_p = sec_acl_bad_acl_syntax;
        return;
        }
```

```
/* In preparation for writing out the buffer, relocate all of the pointers
 * to represent the offset from the start of the buffer
 */


for (i = 0; i < sec_acl_p->num_entries; i++)
    {
    /* Use the same trick as before */
    my_e = &(nacl_p->sec_acl_entries[i]);
    switch (my_e->entry_info.entry_type)
        {
        case sec_acl_e_type_user:
        case sec_acl_e_type_group:
        case sec_acl_e_type_foreign_other:
            PtrToOfs (EITU(id.name), (char *) nacl_p);
            break;

        case sec_acl_e_type_foreign_user:
        case sec_acl_e_type_foreign_group:
            PtrToOfs (EITU(foreign_id.id.name), (char *) nacl_p);
            PtrToOfs (EITU(foreign_id.realm.name), (char *) nacl_p);
            break;

        case sec_acl_e_type_extended:
            PtrToOfs (EITU(extended_info), (char *) nacl_p);
            break;
        } /* end switch entry type */
    } /* end for num entries */

PtrToOfs ((char **) &nacl_p->default_realm.name, (char *) nacl_p);
PtrToOfs ((char **) &nacl_p->sec_acl_entries, (char *) nacl_p);

/* Now write out the buffer */
fd = open((char *) acl_file_name, O_WRONLY);

if (fd == -1)
    {
    *st_p = sec_acl_mgr_file_open_error;
    return;
    }

if (write(fd, acl_buf_p, buf_size) == -1)
    {
    *st_p = sec_acl_mgr_file_io_error;
    close(fd);
    return;
    }

close(fd);

*st_p = error_status_ok;

}
```

```
/* s e c _ a c l _ m g r _ l o o k u p
 *
 *  Extract the dacl associated with the key.
 *  In this version there is only one ACL so the key is ignored.
 */
void sec_acl_mgr_lookup( sec_acl_mgr_handle_t      sec_acl_mgr,
                         sec_acl_key_t             sec_acl_key,
                         uuid_t                    *manager_type_p,
                         sec_acl_type_t            sec_acl_type,
                         sec_acl_list_t            **sec_acl_list_p,
                         error_status_t            *st_p)
{
int                i, fd, sts;
struct stat        st_buf;
char               *acl_buf_p;      /* Pointer to ACL buffer */
int                buf_size;        /* Number of bytes in buffer */
sec_acl_t          *nacl_p;
sec_acl_entry_t    *my_e;
acl_file_header_t  *hdr_p;
error_status_t     st;

/* Allocate the ACL list.
 * NOTE: this use of sizeof depends on the fact that only 1 ACL is returned
 */
*sec_acl_list_p = (sec_acl_list_t *)
    rpc_ss_allocate((idl_size_t)sizeof(sec_acl_list_t));

/* Read in the ACL */
fd = open((char *) acl_file_name, O_RDONLY);
if (fd == -1)
    {
    *st_p = sec_acl_mgr_file_open_error;
    return;
    }

sts = fstat(fd, &st_buf);
if (sts  == -1)
    {
    *st_p = sec_acl_mgr_file_io_error;
    close(fd);
    return;
    }

/* If the file is zero length, return a NULL pointer */
if (st_buf.st_size == 0)
    {
    (*sec_acl_list_p)->num_acls = 1;
    (*sec_acl_list_p)->sec_acls[0] = NULL;
    *st_p = sec_acl_no_acl_found;
    close(fd);
    return;
    }
```

```
/* Use rpc_ss_allocate so the stub will deallocate it for us */
acl_buf_p = (char *) rpc_ss_allocate(st_buf.st_size);

buf_size = read(fd, acl_buf_p, st_buf.st_size);
if (buf_size  == -1)
    {
    *st_p = sec_acl_mgr_file_io_error;
    close(fd);
    return;
    }


close(fd);

/* Check to be sure that this is a valid ACL file and that we know how to
 * interpret it. The constant text string must match, the manager uuid must be
 * the same as ours and the major version must match.  A minor version number
 * change indicates a compatible change, so it is not checked.
 */
hdr_p = (acl_file_header_t *) acl_buf_p;

if ((strcmp( (char *)&hdr_p->acl_text, (char *)&acl_file_header.acl_text)
    != 0) ||
    (!uuid_equal( &hdr_p->mgr_id, &acl_file_header.mgr_id, &st)) ||
    ( hdr_p->major_ver != acl_file_header.major_ver) )
    {
    *st_p = sec_acl_bad_acl_syntax;
    return;
    }


/* The pointers stored in the file are all relative to start of the structure
relocate them to reflect their current location in memory.
*/

nacl_p = (sec_acl_t *) (sizeof (acl_file_header_t));
OfsToPtr ((char **) &nacl_p, (char *) acl_buf_p);
OfsToPtr ((char **) &nacl_p->default_realm.name, (char *) nacl_p);
OfsToPtr ((char **) &nacl_p->sec_acl_entries, (char *) nacl_p);

for (i = 0; i < nacl_p->num_entries; i++)
    {
    /* Use the same trick as before */
    my_e = &(nacl_p->sec_acl_entries[i]);

    switch (my_e->entry_info.entry_type)
        {
        case sec_acl_e_type_user:
        case sec_acl_e_type_group:
        case sec_acl_e_type_foreign_other:
            OfsToPtr (EITU (id.name), (char *) nacl_p);
            break;
```

```
            case sec_acl_e_type_foreign_user:
            case sec_acl_e_type_foreign_group:
                OfsToPtr (EITU (foreign_id.id.name), (char *) nacl_p);
                OfsToPtr (EITU (foreign_id.realm.name), (char *) nacl_p);
                break;

            case sec_acl_e_type_extended:
                OfsToPtr (EITU (extended_info), (char *) nacl_p);
                break;
            } /* end switch entry type */
        } /* end for num entries */


/* Return the results */

(*sec_acl_list_p) -> num_acls = 1;
(*sec_acl_list_p) -> sec_acls[0] = nacl_p;


*st_p = error_status_ok;



}




/* s e c _ a c l _ m g r _ g e t _ a c c e s s
 *
 * Look through all the ACL entries and gather up all the permissions that
 * can be granted to the client.  Return this list of effective permissions.
 *
 * NOTE: This implementation of sec_acl_mgr_get_access implements
 * GROUP_OBJ and EXTENDED types *only* to provide a complete reference.
 * These types are not used by this sec_acl manager.  A real sec_acl_mgr
 * implementation should return the error sec_acl_invalid_entry_type,
 * for any one of these types passed in, that is not supported by the mgr.
 * (ie: if there's no user or group owner stored with an object, then
 *   it does not make sense to support user_obj and group_obj types)
 */

void sec_acl_mgr_get_access( sec_acl_mgr_handle_t     sec_acl_mgr,
                             sec_id_pac_t             *accessor_info,
                             sec_acl_key_t            sec_acl_key,
                             uuid_t                   *manager_type_p,
                             sec_id_t                 *user_obj,
                             sec_id_t                 *group_obj,
                             sec_acl_permset_t        *net_rights,
                             error_status_t           *st_p )
{
sec_acl_list_t    *sec_acl_list;          /* list of object acls */
sec_acl_t         *sec_acl_p;             /* ptr to ACL in use */
```

```
int               i;                /* For traversing entry list. */
int               j;

error_status_t    st;

int               user_entry, user_obj_entry, foreign_user_entry;
int               other_obj_entry, foreign_other_entry, any_other_entry;

sec_acl_permset_t mask_obj_perms;
sec_acl_permset_t unauthenticated_perms;


boolean32         match = FALSE;  /* set when match ACL entry is found */

sec_id_t          *group_id, *realm_id;
boolean32         chk_loc_groups = FALSE;

/* Assume this principal has no permissions until proven otherwise */
*net_rights = NO_PERMISSIONS;

/* Retrieve the sec_acl for this key */

sec_acl_mgr_lookup( sec_acl_mgr,
                    sec_acl_key,
                    manager_type_p,
                    sec_acl_type_object,
                    &sec_acl_list,
                    st_p);
if (st_p != error_status_ok) return;

/* At this point, st_p must be error_status_ok, and will remain that
 * unless explicitly set otherwise.  Thus we can return prematurely without
 * having to explicitly set the status.
 */

/* Take advantage of the fact that there can only be one ACL */
sec_acl_p = sec_acl_list->sec_acls[0];

/* Have not seen any ACL entries yet */
user_entry = user_obj_entry = foreign_user_entry =
other_obj_entry = foreign_other_entry = any_other_entry =
    ENTRY_NOT_FOUND;

/* If masks aren't explicitly set, then it should have no effect
 * when masking, so turn all perm bits on by default
 */
mask_obj_perms = MAX_PERMISSIONS;
unauthenticated_perms = NO_PERMISSIONS;


/* PRE-PROCESS the ACL entries so we only have to loop
 * through once looking for specific types of entries
 *
```

```
                    * Only 1 of each type of entry could possibly match this
                    *  principal id, so keep a running tab on if/where each
                    *  type of entry is found in the list
                    *
                    * Note, the accessor may be a member of multiple {foreign_}groups.
                    * Therefore, the *group checks must be done below, in a separate
                    * pass through the entry list.
                    */
                   for (i = 0; i < sec_acl_p->num_entries; i++)
                       {

                       /* Check for existence of each type of entry, and keep track
                        * of where each type was found in the entry list.
                        * Don't mark type as found if the associated realm id's
                        * are not the same
                        */
                       switch(sec_acl_p->sec_acl_entries[i].entry_info.entry_type)
                          {
                          case sec_acl_e_type_mask_obj:
                              mask_obj_perms = sec_acl_p->sec_acl_entries[i].perms;
                              break;
                          case sec_acl_e_type_user_obj:
                              if (default_realm_eq(i)) user_obj_entry = i;
                              break;
                              case sec_acl_e_type_user:
                                  if ((uuid_equal(&accessor_info->principal.uuid,
              &sec_acl_p->sec_acl_entries[i].entry_info.tagged_union.id.uuid,
                                  &st)) && (default_realm_eq(i)))
                                  user_entry = i;
                              break;
                          case sec_acl_e_type_foreign_user:
                              if ((uuid_equal(&accessor_info->principal.uuid,
              &sec_acl_p->sec_acl_entries[i].entry_info.tagged_union.foreign_id.id.uuid,
                                  &st)) && (foreign_realm_eq(i)))
                                  foreign_user_entry = i;
                              break;
                          case sec_acl_e_type_other_obj:
                              if (default_realm_eq(i)) other_obj_entry = i;
                              break;
                          case sec_acl_e_type_foreign_other:
                              if ( uuid_equal( &accessor_info->realm.uuid,
              &sec_acl_p->sec_acl_entries[i].entry_info.tagged_union.id.uuid,
                                  &st)) foreign_other_entry = i;
                              break;
                          case sec_acl_e_type_any_other:
                              any_other_entry = i;
                              break;
                          case sec_acl_e_type_unauthenticated:
                              unauthenticated_perms = sec_acl_p->sec_acl_entries[i].perms;
                              break;
                          default:
                              break;
                          } /* end switch */
                       } /* end for */
```

```
/* Now that we know which entries match the user described in the PAC,
 * check the permissions corresponding to each entry until access is
 * granted by one of them.
 */

/* USER_OBJ check */
if (user_obj_entry != ENTRY_NOT_FOUND)
    {

    /* If e_type_user_obj entry exists, then user_obj can't be NULL */
    if (user_obj == NULL)
        {
        *st_p = sec_acl_expected_user_obj;
        return;
        }

    /* If the id assoc w/ user_obj matches the principal id */
    if (uuid_equal(&accessor_info->principal.uuid, &user_obj->uuid, &st))
        {

        match = TRUE;
        *net_rights = sec_acl_p->sec_acl_entries[user_obj_entry].perms;
        }
    } /* end if user_obj_entry */

/* USER check */
if ((! match) && (user_entry != ENTRY_NOT_FOUND))
    {
    /* get the permsets */
    match = TRUE;
    *net_rights =
      sec_acl_p->sec_acl_entries[user_entry].perms & mask_obj_perms;
    }

/* FOREIGN_USER check */
if ((! match) && (foreign_user_entry != ENTRY_NOT_FOUND))
    {
    /* get the permsets */
    match = TRUE;
    *net_rights = sec_acl_p->sec_acl_entries[foreign_user_entry].perms
                & mask_obj_perms;
    }

/* GROUP checks */
if (! match)
    {
    for (i = 0; i < sec_acl_p->num_entries; i++)
        {
        switch(sec_acl_p->sec_acl_entries[i].entry_info.entry_type)
            {
            case sec_acl_e_type_group_obj:
            case sec_acl_e_type_group:
            case sec_acl_e_type_foreign_group:
```

```
                              if ((sec_acl_p->sec_acl_entries[i].entry_info.entry_type
                                  == sec_acl_e_type_group_obj) && (group_obj != NULL))
                                  {
                                  /* check against group_obj param */
                                  group_id = group_obj;
                                  realm_id = &sec_acl_p->default_realm;
                                  chk_loc_groups = default_realm_eq(i);
                                  }
                              else if (sec_acl_p->sec_acl_entries[i].entry_info.entry_type
                                                            == sec_acl_e_type_group)
                                  {
                                  chk_loc_groups = default_realm_eq(i);
                                  group_id =
                                  &sec_acl_p->sec_acl_entries[i].entry_info.tagged_union.id;
                                  realm_id = &sec_acl_p->default_realm;
                                  }
                              else
                                  {
                                  chk_loc_groups = foreign_realm_eq(i);
                                  group_id =
&sec_acl_p->sec_acl_entries[i].entry_info.tagged_union.foreign_id.id;
                                      realm_id =
&sec_acl_p->sec_acl_entries[i].entry_info.tagged_union.foreign_id.realm;
                                  }
                                  /* Check either the local groups or the foreign groups */
                              if (chk_loc_groups)
                                  {
                                  /* CHECK PAC GROUP */
                              if (uuid_equal(&accessor_info->group.uuid,&group_id->uuid,&st))
                                      {
                                      /* get the perms associated with this ACL entry */
                                      match = TRUE;
                                      *net_rights |= sec_acl_p->sec_acl_entries[i].perms;
                                      }
                                  /* CHECK LOCAL GROUPS */
                                  for (j = 0; j < (int) accessor_info->num_groups; j++)
                                      {
                                      if (uuid_equal(&accessor_info->groups[j].uuid,
                                                  &group_id->uuid, &st) )
                                          {
                                      /* get the perms associated with this group entry */
                                          match = TRUE;
                                          *net_rights |= sec_acl_p->sec_acl_entries[i].perms;
                                          }
                                      } /* end for j */
                                  } /* end if check_loc */
                              else
                                  {
                                  /* CHECK FOREIGN GROUPS */
                                  for (j = 0; j <(int) accessor_info->num_foreign_groups;
                                          j++)
                                      {
                                      if ((uuid_equal(
                                          &accessor_info->foreign_groups[j].id.uuid,
```

```
                                       &group_id->uuid, &st))
                          && (uuid_equal(
                               &accessor_info->foreign_groups[j].realm.uuid,
                               &realm_id->uuid, &st)) )
                               {
                               /* check the perms to see if access granted */
                               match = TRUE;
                               *net_rights |= sec_acl_p->sec_acl_entries[i].perms;
                               } /* end if uuid_equal */
                          } /* end for j */
                     } /* end else */
                break;
            default:
                break;
          } /* switch (entry type) */
        } /* end for i */
    *net_rights &= mask_obj_perms;      /* group permissions are masked */
    } /* end if !match */

/* OTHER_OBJ check */
if ((! match) && (other_obj_entry != ENTRY_NOT_FOUND))
    {
    /* get the permsets */
    match = TRUE;
    *net_rights = sec_acl_p->sec_acl_entries[other_obj_entry].perms;
    }

/* FOREIGN_OTHER check */
if ((! match) && (foreign_other_entry != ENTRY_NOT_FOUND))
    {
    /* get the permsets */
    match = TRUE;
    *net_rights = sec_acl_p->sec_acl_entries[foreign_other_entry].perms
               & mask_obj_perms;
    }

/* ANY_OTHER check */
if ((! match) && (any_other_entry != ENTRY_NOT_FOUND))
    {
    /* get the permsets to see if access is granted */
    match = TRUE;
    *net_rights = sec_acl_p->sec_acl_entries[any_other_entry].perms
               & mask_obj_perms;
    }

/* UNAUTHENTICATED check
 * If pac isn't authenticated and access was granted by one of the above
 * checks, then desired_access must be masked by unauthenticated entry.
 */
if (!accessor_info-> authenticated)
    *net_rights = *net_rights & unauthenticated_perms;

return;

}
```

```
/*
 *   IMPLEMENTATION OF THE SEC_ACL WIRE INTERFACE ROUTINES
 */

/* r d a c l _ l o o k u p
 *
 * retrieve an acl associated with the object referred to in the handle
 * parameter.  The component_name argument is used to further identify
 * the entity being protected by the sec_acl.
 *
 * Comparable to POSIX acl_read()
 */

void rdacl_lookup( handle_t                    h,
                   sec_acl_component_name_t    component_name,
                   uuid_t                      *manager_type_p,
                   sec_acl_type_t              sec_acl_type,
                   sec_acl_result_t            *sec_acl_result_p)
{
error_status_t  st;

sec_acl_mgr_lookup(sec_acl_mgr, (sec_acl_key_t) component_name,
                   manager_type_p, sec_acl_type,
                   &sec_acl_result_p->tagged_union.sec_acl_list, &st);

sec_acl_result_p->st = st;


}


/* r d a c l _ r e p l a c e
 *
 * Replace the acl associated with the object referred to in the handle.
 * ACLs are immutable, the replace operation takes the new acl and throws
 * away the old acl associated with the object.  The component_name
 * argument is used to further identify the entity being protected by the
 * acl.
 *
 * Comparable to POSIX acl_write()
 */

void rdacl_replace( handle_t                    h,
                    sec_acl_component_name_t    component_name,
                    uuid_t                      *manager_type_p,
                    sec_acl_type_t              sec_acl_type,
                    sec_acl_list_t              *sec_acl_list_p,
                    error_status_t              *st_p)
{
unsigned_char_t *server_name;
sec_id_pac_t *pac;
unsigned32 protect_level, authn_svc, authz_svc;

if (new_db)             /* If creating a new ACL db don't check permissions */
```

```
            {
        new_db = FALSE;        /* One shot only */
            }
    else
            {
        rpc_binding_inq_auth_client( h,
                                    (rpc_authz_handle_t) &pac,
                                    &server_name,
                                    &protect_level,
                                    &authn_svc,
                                    &authz_svc,
                                    st_p);
        if (*st_p != rpc_s_ok) return;

        rpc_string_free(&server_name, st_p);

        if ((authn_svc !=
            rpc_c_authn_dce_secret) || (authz_svc != rpc_c_authz_dce))
                {
            *st_p = sec_acl_not_authorized;
            return;
                }

        if (!sec_acl_mgr_is_authorized( sec_acl_mgr,
                                        sec_acl_perm_owner,
                                        pac,
                                        NULL,
                                        manager_type_p,
                                        user_obj,
                                        group_obj,
                                        st_p) )
                {
            *st_p = sec_acl_not_authorized;
            return;
                }
            }     /* End else */

    sec_acl_mgr_replace( sec_acl_mgr,
                        (sec_acl_key_t) component_name,
                        manager_type_p,
                        sec_acl_type,
                        sec_acl_list_p,
                        st_p);
    }


/* r d a c l _ t e s t _ a c c e s s
 *
 * Determine if the caller has the requested access.
 */

boolean32 rdacl_test_access( handle_t                    h,
                            sec_acl_component_name_t     component_name,
```

```
                                  uuid_t                  *manager_type_p,
                                  sec_acl_permset_t        desired_permset,
                                  error_status_t           *st_p)
{
error_status_t      st;
rpc_authz_handle_t  privs;
unsigned_char_p_t   server_princ_name;
unsigned32          authn_level;
unsigned32          authn_svc;
unsigned32          authz_svc;

if (! uuid_equal(&mgr_uuid, manager_type_p, &st))
    {
    *st_p = sec_acl_unknown_manager_type;
    return FALSE;
    }
    else
    {
    *st_p = error_status_ok;
    }

/* inquire the runtime as to who called us */
rpc_binding_inq_auth_client(h, &privs, &server_princ_name, &authn_level,
                            &authn_svc, &authz_svc, st_p);
if (st_p != error_status_ok) return FALSE;

/* Must use DCE authorization */
if (authz_svc != rpc_c_authz_dce) return FALSE;

return(sec_acl_mgr_is_authorized( sec_acl_mgr,
                                  desired_permset,
                                  (sec_id_pac_t *) privs,
                                  (sec_acl_key_t) component_name,
                                  manager_type_p,
                                  user_obj,
                                  group_obj,
                                  st_p) );
}


/* r d a c l _ t e s t _ a c c e s s _ o n _ b e h a l f
 *
 * Determine if the subject has the requested access.  This function
 * returns true if the access is available to both the caller and
 * the subject identified in the call.
 */

boolean32 rdacl_test_access_on_behalf(
    handle_t                   h,
    sec_acl_component_name_t   component_name,
    uuid_t                     *manager_type_p,
    sec_id_pac_t               *subject_p,
    sec_acl_permset_t          desired_permset,
    error_status_t             *st_p)
```

```
{
error_status_t       st;
rpc_authz_handle_t   privs;
unsigned_char_p_t    server_princ_name;
unsigned32           authn_level;
unsigned32           authn_svc;
unsigned32           authz_svc;

if (! uuid_equal(&mgr_uuid, manager_type_p, &st))
    {
    *st_p = sec_acl_unknown_manager_type;
    return FALSE;
    }
    else
    {
    *st_p = error_status_ok;
    }

/* inquire the runtime as to who called us */
rpc_binding_inq_auth_client(h, &privs, &server_princ_name, &authn_level,
                            &authn_svc, &authz_svc, st_p);

/* Must use DCE authorization */
if (authz_svc != rpc_c_authz_dce) return FALSE;

return( (sec_acl_mgr_is_authorized( sec_acl_mgr,
                                    desired_permset,
                                    (sec_id_pac_t *) privs,
                                    (sec_acl_key_t) component_name,
                                    manager_type_p,
                                    user_obj,
                                    group_obj,
                                    st_p))
        &&
        (sec_acl_mgr_is_authorized( sec_acl_mgr,
                                    desired_permset,
                                    (sec_id_pac_t *) subject_p,
                                    (sec_acl_key_t) component_name,
                                    manager_type_p,
                                    user_obj,
                                    group_obj,
                                    st_p)) );

}


/* r d a c l _ g e t _ m a n a g e r _ t y p e s
 *
 * Determine the types of acls protecting an object.  ACL editors/browsers
 * use this operation to determine the acl manager types that a particular
 * reference monitor is using to protect a selected entity.
 */
```

```
/* In this version, there is 1 manager type and it has been hardcoded.
 */

void rdacl_get_manager_types( handle_t                    h,
                              sec_acl_component_name_t    component_name,
                              sec_acl_type_t              acl_type,
                              unsigned32                  size_avail,
                              unsigned32                  *size_used_p,
                              unsigned32                  *num_types_p,
                              uuid_t                      *manager_types,
                              error_status_t              *st_p)
{

*num_types_p = 1;

if (size_avail < 1)
    {
    *size_used_p = 0;
    }
    else
    {
    *size_used_p = 1;
    *manager_types = mgr_uuid;
    }

*st_p = error_status_ok;
}


/* r d a c l _ g e t _ m g r _ t y p e s _ s e m a n t i c s
 *
 * Determine the types of acls protecting an object.  ACL editors/browsers
 * use this operation to determine the acl manager types that a particular
 * reference monitor is using to protect a selected entity.
 */
/* In this version, there is 1 manager type and it has been hardcoded.
 */

void rdacl_get_mgr_types_semantics(
    handle_t                    h,
    sec_acl_component_name_t    component_name,
    sec_acl_type_t              acl_type,
    unsigned32                  size_avail,
    unsigned32                  *size_used_p,
    unsigned32                  *num_types_p,
    uuid_t                      manager_types[],
    sec_acl_posix_semantics_t   posix_semantics[],
    error_status_t              *st_p)
{
*num_types_p = 1;

if (size_avail < 1)
    {
```

```
        *size_used_p = 0;
        }
    else
        {
        *size_used_p = 1;
        manager_types[0]    = mgr_uuid;
        posix_semantics[0] = sec_acl_posix_mask_obj;
        }

*st_p = error_status_ok;

}



/*  r d a c l _ g e t _ p r i n t s t r i n g
 *
 *  Retrieve printable representations for each permission bit that
 *  the acl manager will support.  There may be aliases for common
 *  permission combinations - by convention simple entries should appear
 *  at the beginning of the array, and combinations should appear at the
 *  end.  When false the tokenize flag indicates that permission
 *  printstrings are unambiguous and therefore printstrings for various
 *  permissions can be concatenated.  When true, however,  this property
 *  does not hold and the strings should be tokenized before input or output.
 */


void rdacl_get_printstring(
    handle_t                h,
    uuid_t                  *manager_type_p,
    unsigned32              size_avail,
    uuid_t                  *manager_type_chain,
    sec_acl_printstring_t   *manager_info,
    boolean32               *tokenize_p,
    unsigned32              *total_num_printstrings_p,
    unsigned32              *size_used_p,
    sec_acl_printstring_t   printstrings[],
    error_status_t          *st_p)
{
error_status_t  st;
int             i;

*total_num_printstrings_p = NUM_PSTRS;
*size_used_p = (size_avail < NUM_PSTRS) ? size_avail : NUM_PSTRS;
*manager_info = hardcoded_manager_info;
uuid_create_nil(manager_type_chain, &st);

if (! uuid_equal(&mgr_uuid, manager_type_p, &st))
    {
    *st_p = sec_acl_unknown_manager_type;
    }
    else
    {
```

```
        *st_p = error_status_ok;
        *tokenize_p = FALSE;
        for (i = 0; i < *size_used_p; i++)
            printstrings[i] = hardcoded_printstrings[i];
        }

}



/*  r d a c l _ g e t _ r e f e r r a l
 *
 * Obtain a referral to an acl update site.  This function is used when
 * the current acl site yields a sec_acl_site_readonly error.  Some
 * replication managers will require all updates for a given object to
 * be directed to a given replica.  Clients of the generic acl interface
 * may know they are dealing with an object that is replicated in this way.
 * This function allows them to recover from this problem and rebind to
 * the proper update site.
 */


void rdacl_get_referral( handle_t                    h,
                         sec_acl_component_name_t    component_name,
                         uuid_t                      *manager_type_p,
                         sec_acl_type_t              sec_acl_type,
                         sec_acl_tower_set_t         *towers_p,
                         error_status_t              *st_p)
{

*st_p = sec_acl_not_implemented;

}

/*  r d a c l _ g e t _ a c c e s s
 *
 * Determine the caller's access to the specified object.  This is
 * useful for implementing operations like the conventional UNIX access
 * function.
 */
void rdacl_get_access( handle_t                    h,
                       sec_acl_component_name_t    component_name,
                       uuid_t                      *manager_type,
                       sec_acl_permset_t           *net_rights,
                       error_status_t              *st_p)
{

    error_status_t      st;

    rpc_authz_handle_t  privs;
    unsigned_char_p_t   server_princ_name;
    unsigned32          authn_level;
```

```
        unsigned32          authn_svc;
        unsigned32          authz_svc;
        boolean32           is_auth;


        *net_rights = NULL;

    if (! uuid_equal(&mgr_uuid, manager_type, &st))
        {
        *st_p = sec_acl_unknown_manager_type;
        return;
        }
        else
        {
        *st_p = error_status_ok;
        }

    /* inquire the runtime as to who called us */
    rpc_binding_inq_auth_client(h, &privs, &server_princ_name, &authn_level,
                            &authn_svc, &authz_svc, st_p);
    if (st_p != error_status_ok) return;

    /* Must use DCE authorization */
    if (authz_svc != rpc_c_authz_dce) return;

    sec_acl_mgr_get_access ( sec_acl_mgr,
                            (sec_id_pac_t *) privs,
                            (sec_acl_key_t) component_name,
                            manager_type,
                            user_obj,
                            group_obj,
                            net_rights,
                            st_p );
    }
```

Glossary

absolute time   A value representing a particular moment in time.

access control   One of the three services of the DCE Security Service. It determines the actions that a principal can perform on a particular distributed system resource.

access control list   A list of the accesses allowed to a particular distributed system resource.

account   One of the entries in which DCE principal authorization information is kept in the DCE Security Service registry database. Accounts may be local and/or network accounts.

ACF   See **attribute configuration file.**

ACL   See **access control list.**

ACL manager   The user-provided software that stores, updates, and evaluates an access control list.

ACL manager type   A particular implementation of an ACL manager, identified by a UUID, supporting the permissions appropriate to an application.

address space   The set of locations in virtual memory that are available to a given process.

alias   In the DCE Security Service, a principal that has the same UUID and account as another principal but a different name and network account. In the DCE Directory Service, an entry pointing to another entry; a soft link.

ANSI   American National Standards Institute. The U.S. coordinating body for standards groups. It is a member of the International Organization for Standardization (ISO).

API   Application programming interface.

ARPA   Advanced Research Projects Agency. U.S. government agency now called the Defense Advanced Research Projects Agency (DARPA).

ARPANET   The packet-switching network developed in the early 1970s for ARPA. It evolved into the Internet.

asymmetrical multiprocessor   A multiprocessor in which one of the processors has a special role.

at-most-once semantics   Behavior in which an RPC will not be retried if an error occurs. The DCE RPC default.

attribute   In the DCE Interface Definition Language (IDL), a special property associated with a declaration. In the DCE Directory Service, data associated with an entry.

Attribute Configuration File   A DCE utility that controls local aspects of an interface particular to a client or server.

authenticated RPC   An RPC that makes use of the DCE security mechanisms, especially authentication.

authentication   One of the three services of the DCE Security Service. It validates a user's identity.

authorization   One of the three services of the DCE Security Service. It determines the categories into which a user falls.

automatic binding   A binding method in which the RPC runtime selects the binding to use. See also **implicit binding** and **explicit binding.**

automatic storage   Memory allocated on the stack. In C, it includes automatic variables, register variables, and function arguments.

bandwidth   The difference between the highest and lowest frequencies available for network signals. By extension, the rated throughput capacity of a given network media or protocol.

binding   The process by which a client locates and establishes a connection to a server. Also, a particular set of information that could be used to perform binding.

binding handle   An opaque data structure that refers to a binding.

binding vector   A list of binding handles created by the RPC server runtime.

broadcast attribute   A DCE RPC operation attribute that causes the RPC to be sent to every node in the local LAN.

broadcast message   A multicast message sent to every node.

capacity   A performance metric that reflects the quantity of simultaneous activity that a system is capable of sustaining.

CCITT   Consultative Committee for International Telegraph and Telephone. An international organization that develops communications standards.

CDS   Cell Directory Service.

cell   A collection of nodes and associated administrative information, administered as a unit and defined as such to the DCE Directory Service and DCE Security Service.

Cell Directory Service   The component of the DCE Directory Service that provides naming within a cell.

ciphertext   A message that has been converted to a form from which its original contents cannot be recovered without the use of a decryption key.

class   In the DCE Directory Service, entries that have the same attributes. In object-oriented terminology, objects that share the same methods.

clearinghouse   A file containing the DCE directory replica on any given node, which the Directory Service reads and writes in response to application requests.

cleartext   In security terminology, the natural form of a message (e.g., letters, numbers, images) prior to encryption.

clerk   A DCE software component that requests services of a server for the purpose of carrying out maintenance functions for a DCE service.

client   An application program that requests services.

client application code   The user-provided code within a DCE client program.

client runtime   Code within a DCE client program that provides the generic capabilities needed by any DCE RPC client.

client stub   Code within a DCE client program that is specific to a particular client/server interface. It is generated by the IDL compiler.

client/server computing   Computing using a network containing two types of processor: workstations or PCs, the clients, and a computer or computers acting as servers to the clients.

client/server model   A processing flow model in which the client makes requests for services and the server responds to requests from clients.

closely coupled multiprocessor   A computer with two or more processors, characterized by high-speed channels to shared memory and peripheral devices and executing a shared operating system to perform a shared pool of tasks.

communication protocols   Rules and message formats used to send and receive data across a network.

computer   Mainframe, minicomputer, workstation, server, supercomputer, PC, etc. A system in which the developer can modify the software.

concurrent execution   Execution of multiple threads or processes, overlapping in time. See also **simultaneous execution.**

condition variable   A facility of DCE Threads that allows threads to coordinate their processing flows. See also **mutex.**

conformant array   An array, used as an RPC parameter, the size of which is determined at runtime.

connectionless   Mode of communications in which each message is self-contained and not dependent on any other message, and which does not provide delivery guarantees. Also called a **datagram service.**

connection-oriented   Mode of communications in which a connection, or session, is established between two computers before messages are sent, thereby assuring delivery. Also called **virtual circuit service.**

constant declaration   Within a DCE interface definition, a declaration that associates names with constant values.

container object   An object that can contain other objects, for example, a file system directory.

context   State information, maintained by a server, that is associated with a particular client session.

context rundown   The server process of cleaning up a failed session.

context switching   The operating system action of saving information associated with one process and restoring that of another process.

conversation key   A temporary key established by the DCE Security Service for an exchange between two principals.

cooperative processing   Client-server computing in which the client is concerned with implementing a human interface.

Coordinated Universal Time   International time standard. (Replaced Greenwich Mean Time.)

courier   In the DCE Distributed Time Service, a server that requests time information from a global server on behalf of a clerk.

DARPA   See **ARPA.**

Data Encryption Standard   The U.S. Government standard encryption algorithm. It is a private-key encryption system.

database server   A server that maintains a database on a single node, providing access to clients on other nodes, typically via SQL requests.

datagram service   A network protocol service that moves data across the network on a best-effort basis. See **connectionless.**

DCE   See **Distributed Computing Environment.**

deadlock   A situation in which two or more threads (or processes) can make no progress because they are waiting for resources that have a circular dependency relationship.

deadly embrace   See **deadlock.**

decryption   Transformation of a message from ciphertext to cleartext.

de facto standard   An unofficial standard acknowledged by widespread usage.

de jure standard   A standard established by a standards organization.

delivery assurance   An attribute of a transport service that all messages will be delivered error-free and in order, with no duplication. A property of a virtual circuit service.

denial of services   A security threat in which legitimate users are denied the ability to make use of some resource.

DES   See **Data Encryption Standard.**

DFS   See **Distributed File Service.**

directory   A kind of entry in the DCE Directory Service. Directories are container objects that hold other directories, objects, and soft links.

directory object   An entry in the DCE Directory Service.

directory object class   In the DCE Directory Service, a set of directory objects that have the same attributes.

Directory Service   The DCE-distributed name service mechanism by which distributed applications associate information with names available throughout the network. It incorporates the **Cell Directory Service** (CDS) and **Global Directory Service** (GDS).

discriminated union   A data structure that can hold any one of several data types. The choice of type is determined by a selection variable.

Diskless Support Service   The DCE component supporting nodes that have no local disk.

distributed computation   An application in which a multithreaded client distributes pieces of work to multiple servers for simultaneous execution.

distributed computing   The use of a distributed system.

Distributed Computing Environment   The distributed computing toolset licensed by the Open Software Foundation (OSF).

distributed database   A database, portions of which reside on different nodes in a network, but which appears as a single logical entity.

Distributed File Service   The DCE component that provides the ability to access files on a file server as if they were on a local system disk.

distributed processing   The use of a distributed system.

distributed system   A combination of hardware, software, and network components in which the software components execute on two or more processors and communicate via a network.

Distributed Time Service   The DCE component that synchronizes clocks on network nodes.

DNS   See **Domain Name Service.**

Domain Name Service   A distributed directory service used on the Internet. DNS may be used as the DCE Global Directory Service as an alternative to an X.500-based directory service.

DSS   See **Diskless Support Services.**

DTS   See **Distributed Time Service.**

dynamic endpoint   In DCE, an endpoint assigned to a server when it starts executing.

dynamic storage   Memory space obtained and released by a program at any time, allocated from the memory pool called the heap. Also called **dynamically allocated storage.**

dynamically allocated storage   See **dynamic storage.**

encapsulation   In object-oriented terminology, the clear separation between the visible, external properties of an object and its internal state and implementation. Also called information hiding.

encryption   Transformation of a message from cleartext to ciphertext. It involves the use of an encryption algorithm and an encryption key.

encryption algorithm   An algorithm used to encrypt and decrypt messages.

endpoint mapper   A DCE software component (server) that maintains a list of the endpoints associated with servers currently active on a node.

Entry Point Vector   A table of pointers to DCE server operation (remote procedure) routines.

epoch   A timestamp used in the DCE Directory Service to mark replicas that have been updated as a consistent set. Used by a skulk to detect errors.

EPV   See **Entry Point Vector.**

Ethernet   A LAN specification developed by Digital Equipment Corporation, Intel Corporation, and Xerox Corporation. Later codified (with minor modifications) as the IEEE 802.3 standard.

explicit binding   In DCE, a binding method in which the client provides a binding handle with each remote procedure call. See also **automatic binding** and **implicit binding.**

extended entry type   A DCE access control list (ACL) entry type provided for future use.

fast mutex   In DCE, a type of nonrecursive mutex that operates quickly by omitting error checking. See also **nonrecursive mutex** and **recursive mutex.**

fixed array   An array, used as a DCE RPC parameter, the size of which is determined at compile time.

foreign cell   A different DCE cell from the one associated with the object protected by an access control list (ACL).

full pointer   A DCE interface definition language (IDL) datatype that supports the full semantics of a C pointer.

GDS   See **Global Directory Service.**

Global Directory Service   The DCE Directory Service component that locates other cells.

global recursive mutex   A DCE mutex conventionally used to protect code that is not thread-safe.

global server   A server in the DCE Distributed Time Service that provides time information to servers outside its local LAN.

group   An entry in the DCE Security Service authorization database that is used to associate a set of principals for the purpose of access control.

group address   See **multicast address.**

group entry   A DCE name service entry containing server binding entries that are to be selected in unspecified order. See also **profile entry.**

handle   An opaque piece of data used to refer to something.

idempotent attribute   An attribute in a DCE operation declaration that signifies that a call may be retried without ill effects.

IEEE   Institute of Electrical and Electronic Engineers. A professional organization that defines network standards.

IDL   See **Interface Definition Language.**

immediate propagation   A DCE replication technique in which changes are disseminated as soon as they occur. See also **skulk.**

impersonation   A security threat in which a user misrepresents his or her identity.

implicit binding   A DCE binding method in which the client provides a binding handle as a global variable. See also **automatic binding** and **explicit binding.**

import declaration   A declaration that imports DCE interface definition constant and typedef declarations from a named file, to allow different interfaces to share data structure definitions.

inaccuracy component   A portion of a DCE time value that expresses the potential inaccuracy associated with the value.

inheritance   In object-oriented terminology, the ability of subclasses to be defined as variations or extensions of superclasses.

initial container object ACL   A DCE access control list (ACL) associated with a container object. It provides default values for the ACL associated with a container object created in that container.

initial object creation ACL   An access control list (ACL) associated with a container object. It provides default values for the ACL associated with noncontainer objects created in that container.

interface   In DCE, a set of remote procedures and their parameters. In data communications protocols, the boundary between adjacent protocol layers.

interface declaration   In DCE, a declaration that declares the name and certain other attributes of an interface.

interface definition   In DCE, a set of declarations that defines all the attributes of an interface.

Interface Definition Language   The DCE language used to declare the properties of an interface.

International Organization for Standardization   The international organization responsible for a variety of international standards including the Open Systems Interconnect (OSI) standard.

internet   A network comprised of both LANs and wide-area links running protocols capable of transmitting data end-to-end.

Internet   The largest internet, an international collection of networks connecting public and private organizations, which evolved from the ARPANET.

ISO   See **International Organization for Standardization.**

jacket routine   A routine that allows multithreaded programs to call system routines that are not thread-safe, by automatically calling the global recursive mutex.

job   See **process.**

junction   A technique used by the DCE Directory Service to allow a namespace maintained by a server to appear as a subtree of a cell namespace.

Kerberos   An authentication and key distribution protocol invented at MIT. Named for a three-headed dog that guards the entrance to Hades in Greek mythology.

key   A short piece of data used in conjunction with an encryption algorithm to encrypt or decrypt a message.

LAN   See **local-area network.**

LAN Manager   The file server developed by Microsoft Corporation.

late binding   In object-oriented terminology, the association of caller and callee at run-time rather than at compile or link time.

links   Communications paths between computers in a network.

local-area network   A network connecting nodes in a limited geographic area, usually a single building. It is characterized by multiple access, bandwidth of 1 mbps or more, and usually is owned by a single organization.

login context   The security keys and tickets granted to a user as part of the DCE login process.

loosely coupled multiprocessor   A group of computers running independent operating systems, connected by a high-bandwidth communications path.

MAN   See **metropolitan-area network.**

marshaling   The process of converting the arguments of a DCE RPC from the form used within a program to the form used to transmit the data over a network. See also **unmarshaling.**

mask entry   One of two basic DCE access control list (ACL) entry types, used to limit permissions allowed an authorization class.

master replica   The authoritative copy of a directory in the DCE Directory Service.

master/slave multiprocessor   See **asymmetrical multiprocessor.**

maybe attribute   A DCE operation declaration attribute indicating that a call should be made on a best-effort basis only.

messaging model   A distributed processing model in which programs retrieve requests for work from queues and optionally send requests to queues.

metropolitan-area network   A network covering a geographical area intermediate in size between a LAN and WAN, 50–100 miles.

monolithic system   A nondistributed system.

multicast address   An address that refers to two or more nodes as the destination of multicast messages.

multicast message   A message sent to more than one node, usually on a LAN.

multiprocessing system   A computer that has two or more processors.

multiprogramming   See **multitasking.**

multitasking   The operating system technique that allows more than one process to be active concurrently.

mutex   A facility of DCE Threads allowing threads to coordinate their access to data. See also **condition variable.**

Name Service Interface   DCE RPC runtime routines that allow clients and servers to make use of the Directory Service to store and retrieve binding information.

NDR   See **Network Data Representation.**

NetBIOS Network Basic Input/Output System. A session-layer interface for PC networks, developed by IBM and Microsoft Corporation.

NetWare The Novell, Inc. file server.

Network Data Representation Data transmission format used by DCE RPC.

network diameter The distance between the two nodes in a network that are farthest apart.

Network File System A protocol for remote file access developed by Sun Microsystems, Inc.

network geography The physical location of network nodes.

network partition An error condition in which one or more communications links have failed.

network topology The pattern of connections between the nodes and links within a network.

NFS See **Network File System.**

node A computer in a network.

nonpreemptive scheduling A scheduling discipline in which processes (or threads) continue to execute until they explicitly give up the processor.

nonrecursive mutex A DCE mutex that can be locked only once, such as a fast mutex, but which tests for various error conditions.

NSI See **Name Service Interface.**

object ACL An access control list (ACL) protecting an object.

object binding model Binding by a DCE client to a uniquely identified server or particular resource controlled by a server.

objects In DCE, one of the kinds of entries maintained by the DCE Directory Service. They are the named entities created by an application program. In object-oriented terminology, software constructs consisting of data (attributes) and procedures (methods).

open array An array, used as a DCE RPC parameter, in which the size of the array and the quantity of data to be transmitted are determined at runtime.

Open Software Foundation A consortium established to further the development of software for open systems computing.

Open Systems Interconnection A set of standards for data communications using network protocols based on the seven-layer OSI reference model.

operation declaration The declaration in a DCE interface definition that declares a remote procedure and its attributes and parameters.

organization One of the entries in the DCE Security Service authorization database, used to associate a set of principals for purposes of administration. Usually, it corresponds to a real organization such as a company.

OSF See **Open Software Foundation.**

OSI See **Open Systems Interconnection.**

PAC See **privilege attribute certificate.**

parameter declaration The declaration in a DCE interface definition that declares a parameter to a DCE operation (remote procedure).

peer-to-peer The relationship of software in a distributed system model in which software can act as a client or server at different times.

period of time A value representing a duration or frequency of events.

permissions Elements of a DCE access control list (ACL) entry that represent the actions a given class of principals are allowed to perform.

pickled data A feature to be included in a future version of DCE to allow data to be converted to network data representation (NDR) format for use by applications, e.g., to be stored on disk.

polymorphism In object-oriented terminology, the ability to invoke a generic operation defined for a variety of objects, which may be implemented differently for different object types.

POSIX A set of standards intended to provide portable interfaces to operating systems services. Also known as IEEE 1003.

preemptive scheduling A scheduling discipline in which an executing process (or thread) may be interrupted at any time to allow other processes (or threads) to execute.

principal A party to an interaction secured by the DCE Security Service.

principal's project list In the DCE Security Service, a list of the groups a principal belongs to.

private object An object created by the DCE XDS or XOM interfaces that cannot be directly manipulated by an application program.

privilege attribute certificate A DCE principal's authorization attributes as certified by the Security Service.

privilege attribute entry One of two basic DCE ACL entry types, specifying a principal, group, or other authorization class that has a certain set of permissions in regard to an object protected by the ACL. See also **mask entry.**

privilege service A DCE Security Service service that issues privilege attribute certificates (PACs).

privilege-ticket-granting ticket In the DCE Security Service, an encrypted message containing a principal's authorization privileges, or privilege attribute certificate (PAC).

procedure Routine, subroutine, function.

process Instance of a program active on a computer, having its own address space and other resources.

profile entry A DCE name service entry containing server binding entries which are to be selected in priority order. See also **group entry.**

program counter The processor state mechanism that records the instruction currently being executed.

propagating the exception When errors are dealt with as exceptions, the DCE mechanism for finding an exception-handling routine.

protocol stack The collective name for layers of communication protocols.

protocol suite A set of related communication protocols.

PTGT See **privilege-ticket-granting ticket.**

Pthreads The threads interface-specified by POSIX 1003.4a, draft 4, on which DCE Threads is based.

public key encryption An encryption scheme in which one key is used to encrypt a message and another to decrypt it. Also called an asymmetrical key encryption.

public objects DCE XDS or XOM interface objects that can be directly manipulated by an application.

race condition In DCE, an error condition in which the behavior of concurrently executing processes or threads differs from when they execute sequentially.

read/write lock A lock mechanism similar to a mutex. It has three states: unlocked, read-locked, write-locked.

ready-to-run In DCE, one state of an active thread, meaning it is eligible to use the processor.

realm The term for a cell in the context of DCE security, a holdover from Kerberos specifications.

receiver makes it right The DCE term for format conversion of data at a client or server.

recursive mutex A DCE mutex that can be locked repeatedly and must be unlocked the same number of times as it was locked.

reference pointer A DCE interface definition language (IDL) datatype that is more efficient to use than a reference pointer, but that does not support the full semantics of a C pointer.

registry The DCE Security Service authorization database.

relative time A format in the DCE distributed time service (DTS) representing the difference between two absolute times.

remote procedure call A procedure call executed remotely at another node of a network.

replica A physical instance of a directory in the DCE Directory Service, containing the items making up the namespace. Replicas include a master replica and read-only replicas.

response A performance metric that reflects the time required for an interaction to occur.

RPC See **remote procedure call.**

running One state of an active thread, meaning it is executing instructions.

scheduling The action of an operating system selecting a process (or thread) to execute.

scheduling policy The algorithm control that determines scheduling of one thread relative to others.

scheduling priority A value that controls the treatment of a particular thread under a scheduling policy.

secret key encryption   An encryption algorithm in which the same key is used to encrypt and decrypt a message.

Security Service   The DCE component that provides mechanisms ensuring that distributed services are available only to authorized parties.

semaphore   See **mutex.**

server   A program that responds to requests from a client.

server binding model   In DCE, the type of binding that allows clients to bind to any of a group of servers that are interchangeable.

server control   The portion of a DCE server that interacts with the DCE RPC environment.

server endpoint   The communications address within a node used by a given server with a given protocol.

server entry   A DCE name service entry that corresponds to a server.

server operations   The portion of a DCE server that constitutes a remote procedure.

server runtime   The DCE-provided portion of the server that performs generic actions.

server stub   The portion of a server that performs actions specific to a given interface, e.g., marshaling and unmarshaling. It is generated automatically by the interface definition language (IDL) compiler.

simultaneous execution   The execution of threads or processes on different processors at the same time, as in a multiprocessor or network. See also **concurrent execution.**

skulk   A DCE replication technique in which changes are accumulated and propagated in a batch. See also **immediate propagation.**

soft links   A kind of entry maintained by the DCE Directory Service that points to other entries in the namespace, allowing creation of synonyms and aliases.

spoofing   See **impersonation.**

static storage   Memory present for the duration of a program's execution, at a fixed location in the program address space.

string binding   A technique for performing binding without using the DCE Directory Service.

subroutine   Routine, procedure, function.

symmetrical multiprocessor   A multiprocessor in which all the processors can perform the same tasks.

task   See **process.**

TCP/IP (Transmission Control Protocol/Internet Protocol)   Widely used network protocols developed for use on the Internet. TCP is a transport protocol providing reliable transmission of data. IP is a network protocol providing connectionless datagram service.

TDF (time differential factor)   A factor added to the UTC international standard time to determine local time.

TGT   See **ticket-granting ticket.**

theft of services A security threat in which an unauthorized user obtains access to a service.

thread An instance of an executing program that has its own program counter but shares its address space with other threads in the same process.

thread barrier A control structure in which a number of threads pause until they are all released.

thread-safe Code that will function correctly when executed by multiple concurrent threads.

Threads The DCE implementation of POSIX Pthreads.

threat A computer security term for a potential security breach.

throughput A performance metric reflecting the quantity of work some system can perform in a unit of time.

ticket An encrypted message that a DCE principal passes on but cannot read.

ticket-granting ticket A ticket used by principals to ask the DCE Security Service for access to application services.

time provider A special-purpose server in a DCE cell which receives time information from an external time source.

timesharing See **multitasking.**

timeslicing See **preemptive scheduling.**

timestamp A value representing a particular UTC international standard time.

type In object-oriented terminology, a set of objects with the same attributes.

typedef declaration In a DCE interface definition, a declaration used to create a data type and give it a name.

unicast message A message sent to a single node in a network.

Universal Unique Identifier A bit string generated by DCE in a way that ensures it will never be duplicated.

UNIX name The name of a principal's local account in the DCE Security Service registry.

unmarshaling The process of converting the arguments of an RPC from the form used to transmit the data over a network to the form used within a program. See also **marshaling.**

UTC See **Coordinated Universal Time.**

UUID See **Universal Unique Identifier.**

varying array An array, used as an RPC parameter, in which the size of the array is determined at compile time but the quantity of data to be transmitted is determined at runtime.

virtual circuit A logical path set up to ensure reliable communication between two network devices.

virtual circuit service A communications transport service that provides delivery assurance.

waiting   The state of a thread that is waiting for DCE mutexes, condition variables, or I/O operations to complete.

WAN   See **wide-area network.**

well-known endpoint   In DCE, the protocol endpoint that has been designated for some particular purpose throughout the network.

wide-area network   A network that includes wide-area links, usually crossing public rights-of-way and of unlimited geographic scope.

XDS   See **X/Open Directory Service.**

XOM   See **X/Open Object Management.**

X/Open Directory Service   An API defined by the X/Open Company, Ltd. for access to directory services.

X/Open Object Management   An API defined by the X/Open Company, Ltd. for manipulating generalized objects. It is intended for use in conjunction with other X/Open APIs, such as XDS.

X Windows   The distributed, network-transparent, device-independent, multitasking windowing and graphics protocol developed at MIT.

Recommended Reading

Bernstein, Philip, Hadzilacos Vassos, and Nathan Goodman. *Concurrency Control and Recovery in Database Systems,* Addison-Wesley Publishing Company, 1987.

Bloomer, John. *Power Programming with RPC,* O'Reilly & Associates, Inc., 1991.

Ceri, Stefano and Giuseppe Pelagatti. *Distributed Databases,* McGraw-Hill, Inc., 1984.

Cypser, R. J. *Communications Architecture for Distributed Systems,* Addison-Wesley Publishing Company, 1978.

Davies, D. W., D. L. A. Barber, W. L. Price, and C. M. Solomonides. *Computer Networks and Their Protocols,* John Wiley & Sons Ltd., 1979.

Ellis, Robert L. *Designing Data Networks,* Prentice-Hall, Inc., 1986.

Filman, Robert and Daniel Friedman. *Coordinated Computing,* McGraw-Hill, Inc., 1984.

Gray, Jim and Andreas Reuter. *Transaction Processing: Concepts and Techniques,* Morgan Kaufmann Publishers, Inc., 1993.

Martin, James. *Computer Networks and Distributed Processing: Software, Techniques, and Architecture,* Prentice-Hall, Inc., 1981.

Martin, James with Kathleen Kavanagh Chapman. *SNA: IBM's Networking Solution,* James Martin and The ARBEN Group, Inc., 1987.

McNamara, John. *Technical Aspects of Data Communications,* Digital Press, 1978.

Open Software Foundation, *OSF DCE Application Development Guide,* Prentice-Hall, Inc., 1993.

Open Software Foundation, *OSF DCE Application Development Reference,* Prentice-Hall, Inc., 1993.

Padlipsky, M. A. *The Elements of Networking Style,* Prentice-Hall, Inc., 1985.

Popek, Gerald and Bruce Walker, Eds. *The LOCUS Distributed System Architecture,* The MIT Press, 1985.

Rosenberry, Ward, David Kenney, and Kerry Fisher. *Understanding DCE,* O'Reilly & Associates, Inc. 1992.

Shirley, John. *Guide to Writing DCE Applications,* O'Reilly & Associates, Inc., 1992.

Tanenbaum, Andrew S. *Computer Networks,* Prentice-Hall, Inc., 1981.

Index

ABOUT THE AUTHOR

Harold W. Lockhart, Jr., a distributed systems design and development expert, has nearly 20 years' experience in networking, software development, and engineering management at large corporations—including Bell Atlantic, Siemens, Westinghouse, Merck, Citicorp, Raytheon, Reuters, and Grumman. He is a graduate of Wesleyan University and resides in Newton, Massachusetts.

ABOUT THE SERIES

The J. Ranade Workstation Series is McGraw-Hill's primary vehicle for providing workstation professionals with timely concepts, solutions, and applications. Jay Ranade is also Series Editor in Chief of the J. Ranade IBM and DEC Series, and Series Advisor to the McGraw-Hill Series on Computer Communications.

Jay Ranade, Series Editor in Chief and best-selling computer author, is a Senior Systems Architect and Assistant Vice-President at Merrill Lynch.

DISK WARRANTY

This software is protected by boh United States copyright law and international copyright treaty provision. You must treat this software just like a book, except that you may copy it into a computer to be used and you may make archival copies of the software for the sole purpose of backing up our software and protecting your investment from loss.

By saying, "just like a book," McGraw-Hill means, for example, that this software may be used by any number of people and may be freely moved from one computer location to another, so long as there is no possiblity of its being used at one location or on one computer while it is being used at another. Just as a book cannot be read by two different people in two different places at the same time, neither can the software be used by two different people in two different places at the same time (unless, of course, McGraw-Hill's copyright is being violated).

LIMITED WARRANTY

McGraw-Hill warrants the physical diskette(s) enclosed herein to be free of defects in materials and workmanship for a period of sixty days from the purchase date. If McGraw-Hill receives written notification within the warranty period of defects in materials and workmanship, and such notification is determined by McGraw-Hill to be correct, McGraw-Hill will replace the defective diskette(s). Send requests to:

Customer Service
TAB/McGraw-Hill
13311 Monterey Avenue
Blue Ridge Summit, PA 17294-0850

The entire and exclusive liablility and remedy for breach of this Limited Warranty shall be limited to replacement of defective diskette(s) and shall not include or extend to any claim for or right to cover any other damages, including but not limited to, loss of profit, data, or use of the software, or special, incidental, or consequential damages or other similar claims, even if McGraw-Hill's liability for any damages to you or any other person ever exceed the lower of suggested list price or actual price paid for the license to use the software, regardless of any form of the claim.

McGRAW-HILL, INC. SPECIFICALLY DISCLAIMS ALL OTHER WARRANTIES, EXPRESS OR IMPLIED, INCLUDING BUT NOT LIMITED TO, ANY IMPLIED WARRANTY OF MERCHANTABLILTY OR FITNESS FOR A PARTICULAR PURPOSE. Specifically, McGraw-Hill makes no representation or warranty that the software is fit for any particular purpose and any implied warranty of merchantability is limited to the sixty-day duration of the Limited Warranty covering the physical diskette(s) only (and not the software) and is otherwise expressly and specifically disclaimed.

This limited warranty gives you specific legal rights; you may have others which may vary from state to state. Some states do not allow the exclusion of incidental or consequential damages, or the limitation on how long an implied warranty lasts, so some of the above may not apply to you.